The Letters of Margaret of Anjou

THE
LETTERS
OF
MARGARET
OF ANJOU

EDITED BY HELEN MAURER
AND B. M. CRON

THE BOYDELL PRESS

First published 2019
The Boydell Press, Woodbridge
Paperback edition 2021

ISBN 978 1 78327 424 6 hardback
ISBN 978 1 78327 682 0 paperback

The Boydell Press is an imprint of Boydell & Brewer Ltd
PO Box 9, Woodbridge, Suffolk IP12 3DF, UK
and of Boydell & Brewer Inc.
668 Mt Hope Avenue, Rochester, NY 14620–2731, USA
website: www.boydellandbrewer.com

A catalogue record for this book is available
from the British Library

The publisher has no responsibility for the continued existence or accuracy of URLs for
external or third-party internet websites referred to in this book, and does not guarantee that
any content on such websites is, or will remain, accurate or appropriate

This publication is printed on acid-free paper

Typeset by BBR Design, Sheffield

In memory of my Dad, Wayland Chester,
who told me to keep pedalling,
and of Rose Maurer,
who provided a magnifier and an example

And in memory of my beloved husband,
Jim Cron, editor extraordinaire

CONTENTS

FIGURES

PREFACE AND
ACKNOWLEDGMENTS

I first encountered Margaret of Anjou's letters while studying her exercise of power. From the start they fascinated me. Even when I had published a book in which they played a significant part, they stuck in my head. Soon after, I received an email from Boni Cron, who had likewise been going after the accreted 'wisdom' surrounding Margaret. We began an electronic correspondence and were soon discussing Margaret's letters. When Boni asked if I had any further projects planned, I suggested that the collection published by Cecil Monro in 1863 badly needed re-editing. And wouldn't it be great if *all* of Margaret's letters could appear together, in one place? Boni was intrigued. We talked about joining forces and decided to give it a try. So, there we were, two somewhat sideways-of-the-mainstream historians who had never edited anything or collaborated with anyone else before, and there were Margaret's letters.

We dove in. I had a general organizational picture in mind, but we agreed to figure out the rest of it as we went along. We also agreed that we were doing it for fun, no pressure. But as the pages added up, we knew that we were both committed. It turned out to be a long journey. That we were able to finish the project despite the interruptions and setbacks that our lives presented, moreover, that we did it in a state of reasonable agreement, seemed to us an achievement in itself. The book's completion also offers testimony to the power of technology, for we shared our research, our drafts, and our revisions entirely online.

Along the way, we have incurred debts to persons who have provided us with assistance, encouragement, and good advice. Since we did not always follow it, they should in no way be blamed for our shortcomings. In alphabetical order, we would like to thank Caroline Barron, Lisa Benz-St John, Glynnis Cropp, Jim Given, Miki Goral, Andrew Gough, Alison Hanham, Samantha Harper, Ann Kettle, Delphine Mercuzet, Sharon Michalove, Belinda Peters, Compton Reeves, John Sisson, Dunstan Speight, and Vanessa Wilkie. A special thank you to my husband Ed, who supported this effort in countless ways and never once suggested that pursuing the letters of a long-dead queen was anything but the most normal and obvious thing to do.

And, finally, I am grateful beyond all measure to Boni for having chosen to join me in this venture. Together, we were more than the sum of our parts, and without her, it wouldn't have been half the fun.

Helen Maurer, 2018

ABBREVIATIONS

Beaucourt	G. du Fresne de Beaucourt, *Histoire de Charles VII*, 6 vols (Paris, 1881–91)
'Benet's Chronicle'	G.L. and M.A. Harriss, eds, 'John Benet's Chronicle for the Years 1400 to 1462', *Camden Miscellany* 24 (1972), pp. 151–233
BL	British Library
BNF	Bibliothèque nationale de France
CCR	*Calendar of the Close Rolls*
CFR	*Calendar of the Fine Rolls*
CLRO	Corporation of London Record Office
CPL	*Calendar of Entries in the Papal Registers … Papal Letters*, VIII, X–XII, ed. W.H. Bliss and J.A. Twemlow (1909–33)
CPR	*Calendar of the Patent Rolls*
CSP, Milan	*Calendar of State Papers … in … Milan*, I, ed. A.B. Hinds (1912)
EETS	Early English Text Society
EHR	*English Historical Review*
Emden	A.B. Emden, *A Biographical Register of the University of Oxford to A.D. 1500*, 3 vols (Oxford, 1957–59)
Fasti	J. Le Neve, *Fasti Ecclesiae Anglicanae, 1300–1541*, 12 vols, ed. J.M. Horn, *et al.* (1962–67)
Flenley	R. Flenley, ed., *Six Town Chronicles of England* (Oxford, 1911)
Foedera	T. Rymer, ed., *Fœdera, conventiones, literæ, et … acta publica, inter reges Angliæ …*, X, XI, XII (1704–35)

Gairdner, *PL*	J. Gairdner, ed., *The Paston Letters*, 6 vols (1904)
GEC	G.E. Cokayne, *The Complete Peerage* ..., 12 vols in 13, ed. V. Gibbs, *et al.* (1910–59)
'Gregory's Chronicle'	J. Gairdner, ed., *Historical Collections of a Citizen of London in the Fifteenth Century*, Camden Society, new ser. 17 (1876)
Griffiths	R.A. Griffiths, *The Reign of King Henry VI: The Exercise of Royal Authority, 1422–1461* (1981)
Maurer	H.E. Maurer, *Margaret of Anjou: Queenship and Power in Late Medieval England* (Woodbridge, 2003)
Monro	C. Monro, ed., *Letters of Queen Margaret of Anjou and Bishop Bekington and Others*, Camden Society, o.s. 86 (1863)
Myers, 'Household'	A.R. Myers, ed., 'The Household of Queen Margaret of Anjou, 1452–3', in *Crown, Household and Parliament*, pp. 135–209
Myers, 'Jewels'	A.R. Myers, ed., 'The Jewels of Queen Margaret of Anjou', in *Crown, Household and Parliament*, pp. 211–29
ODNB	*Oxford Dictionary of National Biography* (2001–04)
PPC	N.H. Nicolas, ed., *Proceedings and Ordinances of the Privy Council of England*, VI, *22 Henry VI 1443 to 39 Henry VI 1461* (1837)
PROME	*The Parliament Rolls of Medieval England, 1275–1504*, ed. C. Given-Wilson, *et al.* (Leicester, 2005)
Reg. Whethamstede	H.T. Riley, ed., *Registrum Abbatiae Johannis Whethamstede*, 2 vols, Rolls Series (1872–73)
Reilhac	A.A.M.J. Reilhac, *Jean de Reilhac, secrétaire ... des rois Charles VII, Louis XI et Charles VIII* (Paris, 1886)
RP	*Rotuli Parliamentorum*, V, *1439–1468* (1832)
Scofield	C.L. Scofield, *The Life and Reign of Edward IV*, 2 vols (1923)
Stevenson	J. Stevenson, ed., *Letters and Papers Illustrative of the Wars of the English in France during the Reign of Henry VI*, 2 vols in 3, Rolls Series (1861–64)
Vale's Book	M.L. Kekewich, *et al.*, eds, *The Politics of Fifteenth-Century England: John Vale's Book* (Stroud, 1995)

VCH   Victoria History of the Counties of England
Wedgwood   J.C. Wedgwood, *History of Parliament: Biographies of
                             the Members of the Commons House, 1439–1509* (1938)

The place of publication is London unless otherwise noted.

INTRODUCTION

Margaret of Anjou has had a bad press. As queen of the last Lancastrian king, Henry VI, she was on the losing side in the first phase of the Wars of the Roses, the struggle between the Houses of Lancaster and York, and so became the scapegoat for a civil war. For later English (male) historians her guilt was a natural deduction: she was female, she was French, and she was forceful. The tradition was born that her interference in English affairs and her political favorites created faction and fractured the bonds of English society, which weakened the rule of law until, inevitably, civil war resulted.

Margaret's life falls into three parts. She was married to Henry VI at the age of fifteen to seal a truce between England and France that was supposed to lead to a perpetual peace, but which lasted a bare five years. From her arrival in England in 1445 until 1453 Margaret played little part in national affairs. She performed the duties traditionally expected of a queen consort but failed in her primary duty to produce a son.

The second phase of Margaret's life began in 1453 with two major events: her long-awaited pregnancy and Henry VI's collapse into a prolonged state of mental and physical incapacity. Their only child, Prince Edward of Lancaster, was born in October of that year. After Henry's recovery, and the duke of York's attempt to take over the government in 1455, Margaret devoted herself in the ensuing years until civil war broke out in 1459 to rebuilding the Lancastrian affinity, to maintaining King Henry's authority, and to safeguarding Prince Edward's inheritance. She feared that York might disinherit her son, as indeed he eventually did.

Margaret emerged as the leader of a 'Lancastrian party' only after the battle of Northampton in 1460, where most of Henry VI's loyal magnates were killed and Henry became the earl of Warwick's prisoner. Margaret's success in winning the second battle of St Albans and recovering the person of the king was short-lived. Her adherents were finally defeated at the bloody battle of Towton in 1461, and the duke of York's son assumed the throne as King Edward IV.

Margaret spent the next ten years in exile, first in Scotland and then in France, waiting for an opportunity to reclaim the throne for her husband. It came in 1470 when the earl of Warwick fell out with Edward IV, changed sides and launched a Lancastrian 'readeption'. Margaret and Prince Edward landed in England on the very day that King Edward defeated Warwick at the battle of Barnet in 1471. The Lancastrian army was defeated again at Tewkesbury; Prince Edward was killed, and Margaret became King Edward's prisoner. Margaret remained in England until 1475 when King Edward ransomed her to King Louis XI of France. Largely forgotten, she died in France in 1482 at the age of fifty-two.

Our study of Margaret's letters focuses on both the normalcy of her activities as queen and the uniqueness of her political experience. Accordingly, we divide the letters into two main parts, further subdivided into chapters. Each part is handled differently.

Part I, 'Great and Good Queen', consists mostly of the letters found in BL, Add. MS 46,846, which Cecil Monro edited in 1863. It is a memorandum book containing royal and other letters – only some of them by Margaret of Anjou – and various other items. Once owned by John Edwards, receiver of Chirkland in 1498, it was in the possession of the Puleston family of Flintshire when Monro saw it. Margaret's letters are all copies, in a fifteenth-century hand. A.J. Otway-Ruthven suggested that George Ashby, Margaret's clerk of the signet, compiled them, but there is no evidence of this.[1] We have transcribed all of Margaret's letters in Add. MS. 46,846, including seven Monro missed. This section is arranged topically so that we can discuss the letters by the activities they represent and compare those of similar type. Readers will notice that some letters overlap our chosen divisions. That was inevitable, given that each letter had to go somewhere within the system that suited us best.

Since we separated the letters in this section from Margaret's 'political' letters, it is reasonable to ask: just how apolitical are they? Monro characterized some of them as unwonted meddling into matters that were none of Margaret's concern. Almost a decade later, her biographer Mary Ann Hookham (1872) countered by applauding the queen's matchmaking and charity as evidence of her interest in the affective and the personal, as opposed to the political.[2] Towards the end of the Victorian era, the influential historian J.H. Ramsay (1892) expanded on Monro's complaint:

> The letters do not give a favourable impression of her dealings with her husband's subjects ... the majority contain requests for favours involving greater or less

---

1   A.J. Otway-Ruthven, *The King's Secretary and the Signet Office in the XV Century* (Cambridge, 1939), pp. 119–20. For Ashby, see pp. 140–3.
2   M.A. Hookham, *The Life and Times of Margaret of Anjou*, 2 vols (1872), I, pp. 380–7.

interference with private rights ... Most objectionable [are those] in which she seeks to interfere with pending litigation ... for or against favoured parties, by the simple process of ordering their opponents to abandon their 'unconscientious' suits.[3]

A year later, T.F. Tout enshrined this view of Margaret's activities in the original *DNB*, describing her as 'unscrupulous in pushing her friends' interests and ... constantly interfering with the course of private justice', and then concluded that her letters 'are of no great value'.[4] Following Tout, J.J. Bagley (1948) declared that there was 'not a single letter of political importance' among them.[5]

These judgements miss the point. More recent assessments of these letters see them as examples of the patronage practiced by all high-ranking persons and expected of good lord- or ladyship.[6] To the extent that Margaret's activities affected their beneficiaries' status or altered perceptions of the queen's own power, they might be considered to have political ramifications. But since not all of the letters in Part I involve patronage, we describe them differently. The eight chapters of this section broadly express concerns that Margaret or any great lady could have had, both personal and public. Indeed, they often show her acting as good lady to the benefit of her servants and other supplicants, and thus to her own credit according to contemporary understanding (while allowing that such favor, though sought after, might also be resented by others). But they also show her acting in her personal interest in business matters, in her enjoyment of sport, and in accordance with her faith.

The letters in Part II, 'Political Queen', are overtly political. They are particular to the circumstances of Margaret's life; no other queen of England could have written them. These letters come from various sources, published and unpublished. Some are by Margaret; others were written to her, and we have included excerpts from letters *about* her that have occasioned interest or controversy. Because the letters in this section follow a narrative arc, it was convenient to organize them chronologically into four chapters.[7] The first deals with Margaret's correspondence with Charles VII of France in the 1440s; the second, with the increasing domestic tensions of the 1450s; the third, with Henry VI's deposition and its immediate aftermath; and the fourth, with Margaret's years of French exile and her final attempt to prevail.

3   J.H. Ramsay, *Lancaster and York*, 2 vols (Oxford, 1892), II, p. 141.
4   *Dictionary of National Biography*, v. 36 (1893), pp. 142, 148.
5   J.J. Bagley, *Margaret of Anjou, Queen of England* (1948), p. 56.
6   Griffiths, p. 258; C. Dunn, 'Margaret of Anjou, Consort of Henry VI', in *Crown, Government and People in the Fifteenth Century*, ed. R.E. Archer (New York, 1995), pp. 117ff.
7   Two letters cannot be dated with certainty, and it made sense to alter the order in a few other cases. These discrepancies are noted in the text.

Our source for each letter appears in its attribution. In the case of letters originally edited by Monro, we have also included a reference to his work as a matter of interest. Many of our letters are undated or only partially dated. Dates in both parts are provided as they appear in the letters. Those in square brackets are based on existing evidence, often external to the letter, and our own best judgment. The more speculative ones have an added question mark. Square brackets inside a letter's text always indicate our insertions. When we used text transcribed by others, their insertions are indicated by parentheses. In our transcriptions we have retained the spelling of letters in Middle English, except for replacing the now-obsolete thorn with 'th' and modernizing the use of 'u/v' and 'i/j'.

Part I

GREAT AND GOOD QUEEN

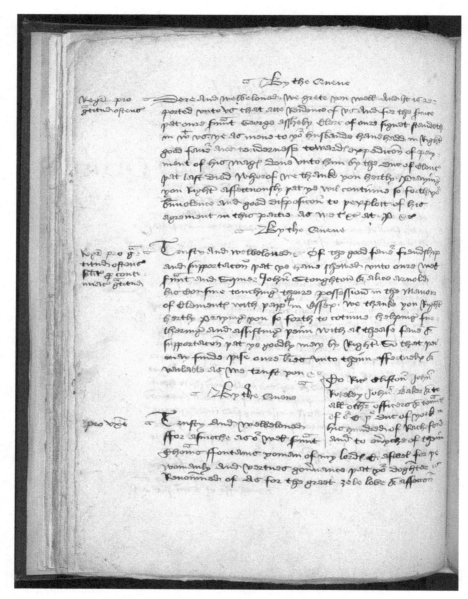

Figure 1 Letters by Queen Margaret to Lady Emmeline Fiennes [76], to the duke of York's officers and tenants in the hundred of Rocheford [59], and the beginning of a letter to William Gastrike [4]. A typical page from BL, Add. MS 46,846.

One

MATCHMAKER

Margaret of Anjou was a committed matchmaker, as Mary Ann Hookham once noted. When she praised the queen for her interest in promoting 'the course of true love', she spoke to the romantic sensibilities of Victorian England.[1] Margaret would have viewed her matchmaking activities a little differently. In her time, marriage was a practical arrangement that created connections, wealth acquisition, and advancement for the individuals and families involved.[2] In the political realm, marriage could serve dynastic purposes, and Margaret favored using it for peacemaking at the highest level.[3] After all, her own marriage was supposed to set the seal on peace negotiations between France and England. Although affective relationships did occur, a 'good marriage' was one that yielded practical benefits in the form of increased wealth, power, or influence. Matchmaking was therefore a serious business. When Margaret promoted advantageous marriages, she performed an act of good ladyship – unless, of course, someone objected to the match! From her perspective, such marriages strengthened existing bonds of loyalty and service or created new ones.

Wardships were a form of patronage, and a lucrative one. When a tenant in chief died, leaving an underage child as heir, control of his or her lands reverted to the crown during the child's minority. The king could grant the child's wardship, for a substantial fee, to someone who may or may not have been the child's relative, and who was required to keep the lands intact until the heir came of

---

1   Hookham, *Life and Times*, I, p. 382.
2   As, indeed, it still did in Hookham's time – though one might not guess it from reading her remarks.
3   The marriage of Margaret's cousin Marie, illegitimate daughter of her uncle Charles, count of Maine, to the earl of Devon's heir forged ties with the Courtenays, while detaching the earl from the duke of York (see Maurer, pp. 136–7, for this and other examples of her political matchmaking).

age, but who in the meantime had the right to collect their income. The king also granted wardships in payment of a crown debt owed to the recipient, since marriages could be both bought and sold. A wardship allowed the holder to arrange the marriage of the heir: in effect, to sell it for whatever the market would bear. This was particularly important when the ward was an heiress, whose lands would be controlled by her husband as in the case of Isabel Ingoldesthorpe, whose wardship Margaret held.[4]

In a patriarchal society the social and economic benefits of marriage tended to be calculated from a masculine point of view. For a man, marriage – the act of *becoming* married – would ideally 'enhance his standing in the public world of other men'.[5] It was helpful to marry a woman who brought wealth in the form of property to the marriage. But there were other, less tangible factors that could affect male standing and, hence, have some bearing on the desirability of the prospective bride. Chief among these was the woman's reputation, which amounted to a public assessment of her behavior and whether or not she conducted herself in such a way as to bring admiration or scorn to her spouse. Testimonials in Margaret's letters to a woman's 'virtuous governance' or 'demeaning' are formulaic, but these necessary phrases are firmly based upon social values.

The following excerpt from one of the Paston letters illustrates some of the points raised here:

[1] Margaret Paston to John Paston, 20 April 1453 (excerpted)
(Gairdner, II, pp. 284–5)

> As for tydyngs, the Quene come in to this town on Tewysday last past after none, and abode here tyll itt was Thursday, iij after none; and she sent after my cos(in) Elysabeth Clere by Sharynborn to come to her; and she durst not dysabey her commandment, and come to her. And when she come in the Quenys presens, the Quene made ryght meche of her, and desyrid here to have an hosbond, the which ye shall know of here after. But as for that, he is never nerrer than he was befor. The Quene was right well pleasid with her answer, and reportyht of her in the best wyse, and seyth, be her trowth, she sey no jantylwoman syn she come into Norffolk that she lykit better than she doth her.

In the spring of 1453, the queen traveled to East Anglia to visit the shrine of Our Lady of Walsingham to give thanks for her pregnancy and probably to pray for

---

4   For Isabel's wardship, see below, pp. 95–6.
5   A. Dronzek, 'Gender Roles and the Marriage Market in Fifteenth Century England', in *Love, Marriage and Family Ties in the Later Middle Ages*, ed. I. Davis *et al.* (Turnhout, 2003), p. 76.

a safe delivery. The encounter described by Margaret Paston occurred during several days the queen spent at Norwich.

Elizabeth Clere was a close friend of the Pastons.[6] She was the heiress of Thomas Uvedale of Tacolneston, Norfolk, and his wife Margaret Rees, herself an heiress. Married to Robert Clere of Ormesby, Norfolk, in 1434, she bore him three sons and a daughter before his death in 1446; thus, at the time of the queen's visit she had been widowed for roughly seven years. A taxation list for 1451 reckoned her annual net income from lands at £45, placing her among its wealthier persons and, therefore, an attractive marital prospect.[7] Margaret would have heard of her from Edmund Clere, one of her household esquires, who was Elizabeth's brother-in-law.[8] The 'Sharynborn' who conveyed the queen's summons was Thomas Sharneborne, another of her household esquires.[9] Despite Elizabeth's favorable – and politic – response to Margaret in the matter of marriage, she kept her own counsel and remained a widow until her death in 1493. Her husband had made her his sole executor, with custody of all his lands for life. Available evidence indicates that she was an active, capable, no-nonsense sort of woman, with practical business acumen.[10] It may well be that Elizabeth preferred the freedom of action provided by a well-to-do widowhood to the strictures of a new marriage, even at the queen's request. One wonders, also, which of her qualities so impressed Margaret: whether it was an amiably pleasant manner or an underlying – but unabashed – forthrightness.

The five letters that follow attest to Margaret's interest in arranging marriages, either for her servants or for others at their behest. The first letter involves an heiress sought for a second marriage, and the second, a daughter who appears to have been an heiress. The status of the women in the next two letters is less certain, though the second of them had already made up her own mind in favor of her suitor, so it may have been a love match, after all. The last letter shows the queen's exercise of good ladyship and charity towards a poor couple in need.

6   For Elizabeth, see C. Richmond, 'Elizabeth Clere', in *Medieval Women*, ed. J. Wogan-Browne *et al.* (Turnhout, 2000), pp. 251–73. His suggestion of a proposed spouse seems doubtful.

7   R. Virgoe, 'A Norfolk Taxation List of 1451', in *East Anglian Society and the Political Community of Late Medieval England*, ed. C. Barron *et al.* (Norwich, 1997), p. 71.

8   For Edmund Clere of Ormesby, see below, p. 45, n. 16, and p. 204, n. 41.

9   See below, pp. 65–7, for Sharneborne.

10   Richmond, 'Elizabeth Clere', pp. 253–71, for her activities, and thus her character.

[2] Queen to Dame Jane Carew re Thomas Burneby [1447–50]
(BL, Add. MS 46,846, fols 50–50v, Monro, pp. 96–8)

By the Quene
Right dere and welbeloved, we grete you well. And for asmoch as oure trusty and welbeloved squier Thomas Burneby, sewer for our mouth, aswel for the greet zele, love and affeccion that he hath unto your personne as for the womanly and vertuouse governance that ye be renowned of, desireth with all his hert to do yow worship by wey of mariage bifore all creatures lyvyng, as he saith; we, desiryng th'encres, furtherance and preferring of oure said squier for his manyfold merites and desertes, as for the good service that he hath don unto my lord and us and yet therin dayly continueth, praye you right affectuously that, at reverence of us, ye will have our said squier towardes his said mariage especialy recommended, inclynyng you to his honest desire at this tyme, the rather by contemplacion of this oure praier, wherin we trust verreily ye shul mow pourvey right well for your self, to your greet worship and hertsease, and cause us to have yow both in suche tendernesse and faver of our good grace that by reason ye shul holde you right well content and pleased. And how ye thinke to be disposed to our pleasure in this partie, ye will acertein us by the bringer of thise. As our singler trust is in yow. Yeven, etc., at Eltham, the etc.
    To Dame Jane Carew

Jane Carew was the only daughter of Sir Hugh Courtenay by his second wife Philippa Arcedekne, an heiress.[11] She married Sir Nicholas Carew in 1424 or 1425; by the time of his death on 3 May 1447, she had borne him five sons. Although she was probably in her later thirties when Margaret approached her, the seventeen manors in her disposal as her mother's heir would have made her an attractive item on the marriage market. Jane eventually married Sir Robert de Vere (license dated 5 October 1450), the younger brother of John, 12th earl of Oxford.[12] Sir Robert, who was born in 1410 and was thus of similar age to Jane, had served in France in the later 1440s. During the 1450s, he appears on all commissions for Devonshire and was an MP for that county in 1455–56.[13] This second marriage produced one son. Sir Robert's role in the events surrounding Henry VI's deposition is unknown, but he was reported killed in Cornwall in early 1461.[14] The twice-widowed Jane divided the estates of her inheritance more or less equally among all her younger sons, including the one by de Vere, with

11   Sir Hugh was the younger brother of Edward, earl of Devon, who d. 1419. His grandson succeeded to the earldom in 1485.
12   The earl and his eldest son were executed by Edward IV in 1462 for allegedly plotting against him.
13   Wedgwood, p. 905.
14   Gairdner, *PL*, III, p. 269, letter dated 18 April.

the properties entailed to each individually. According to family tradition, she did this after a quarrel with her eldest son, whom she then disinherited.[15] Another explanation seems more likely. The eldest son, Thomas, had inherited his father's patrimony and had, in any case, died sometime before October 1461, leaving an underage son.[16] It may be that with the eldest line taken care of Jane felt herself free to provide for her younger children. She was still living in June 1464 but had died by September 1465.[17]

Thomas Burneby, for whom Margaret unsuccessfully promoted a marriage with Jane Carew, was a king's sergeant in 1443.[18] He apparently entered Margaret's service as one of her esquires soon after she arrived in England and quickly established himself in her favor. Burneby received a gold armlet as the queen's New Year's gift in 1445–46, and again in 1448–49. He received a purse and a gold ring in 1451–52, and a silver gilt wine flagon in 1452–53.[19] In that same year Margaret's sole surviving household account records a payment to Thomas of £10 15s 7d for 345 days of service, the second highest payment to one of her esquires.[20] Cardinal Beaufort's bequest to him in 1447 of £20 and a cup of silver gilt provides further testimony to his usefulness and perhaps engaging personality; he was one of very few individuals to receive a personal bequest.[21] Burneby became sheriff of Merioneth, North Wales, in October 1447, together with Edmund Hampden, who was also in Margaret's service. The office was granted to him again in 1453, this time with Thomas Park.[22] Burneby was exempted from the 1450 Act of Resumption as an officer of the household.[23] In 1461, his name appears in a list of men who were with the queen in Scotland following the Lancastrians' defeat at Towton.[24] He was not attainted, but at that point he drops out of sight. The origin of Thomas Burneby's family is unclear. Monro believed it to have been Devon, but in 1445 another Thomas Burneby, gentleman, of Westminster, Middlesex, is mentioned in the patent rolls; he could have been the father of the household Thomas.[25]

15   R. Carew, *The Survey of Cornwall*, ed. J. Chynoweth *et al.* (Exeter, 2004), fols 102–3.
16   *CPR, 1461–67*, pp. 65, 75.
17   Monro, pp. 96–7, note e; *CPR, 1461–67*, p. 461.
18   *CPR, 1441–46*, p. 221.
19   E 101/409/14; E 101/410/2 and 8; Myers, 'Jewels', p. 225.
20   Myers, 'Household', p. 184.
21   The translation of Beaufort's will in N.H. Nicolas, ed., *Testamenta Vetusta*, I (1826), p. 97, mistakenly identifies Burneby as a page; the original Latin refers to him as *scutifer* or esquire (J. Nichols, ed., *A Collection of all the Wills ... of the Kings and Queens of England* [1780; repr. Union, NJ, 1999], p. 341).
22   *CPR, 1446–52*, p. 107; *1452–61*, p. 77.
23   *PROME*, XII, p. 129.
24   Gairdner, *PL*, III, p. 307.
25   *CPR, 1441–46*, p. 424.

[3] Queen to R. Kent re Thomas Shelford [1445–46]
(BL, Add. MS 46,846, fols 50v–51; Monro, pp. 89–90)

By the Quene

Welbeloved, we grete, etc., and late yow wite that our welbeloved servant Thomas
Shelford, whoom for his vertues and the agreable service that he hath don unto us
herbefore, and in especial now late in the company of our cousin of Suff[olk], we
have taken into oure chambre there to serve us abowte our personne, hath reported
unto us that for the good and vertuous demening that he hath herd of a gentilwoman beyng in your governance, which was doghter to oon Hall of Larkfeld, he
desireth full hertly to do hir worship by wey of mariage, as he saith. Wherfor we
desire and praye you hertly that, setting apart all instances or labors that have or
shalbe made unto yow for eny other personne what so ever he be, ye wol by all
honest and leafull menes be welwilled unto the said mariage, entreting the said
gentilwoman unto the same, trustyng to Goddes mercye that it shalbe both for
hir worship and availle in tyme to come. And if ye wol doo your tendre diligence
to perfourme this oure desire, ye shal therin deserve of us right good and especial
thanke and cause us to shewe unto you therfore the more especial faver of oure
good grace in tyme to come. Yeven, etc.

To R. Kent

R. Kent may have been Robert Kent, to whom Henry VI granted the reversion
of the manor of Langley, Kent, in 1444, together with Master Thomas Kent. In
1447, the king made the same grant to Thomas and his wife, this time omitting
Robert.[26] Robert probably held the wardship of the 'gentilwoman' whom Thomas
Shelford wished to marry, and as there was competition for the lady's hand, she
may have been an heiress. The queen's letter was intended to enhance Shelford's
chances of becoming the chosen suitor. He was a king's sergeant and groom of
the chamber by May 1447;[27] he may have been in Suffolk's service before being
taken into the queen's household and subsequently transferred to the king's. The
letter would then date to late 1445 or, more likely, to 1446.

[4] Queen to William Gastrike re Thomas Fountains [1447 or later]
(BL, Add. MS 46,846, fols 49v–50; Monro, pp. 152–4)

By the Quene

Trusty and welbeloved. For asmoche as our wel[beloved] servant Thomas
Fontains, yoman of my lordes [crown], aswel for the womanly and vertues
governance that your doghter is renowned of as for the greet zele, love and affeccion
that he hathe unto hir personne before all creature lyvyng, desireth with all his hert

---

26   *CPR, 1441–46*, p. 244; *1446–52*, p. 74.
27   Ibid., p. 53.

to do hir worship by wey of mariage, as he seith. Wherupon my said lord hath tenderly wreten unto you for his recommendacion in this bihalf, whiche we suppose, vereily, that ye have clerely conceived and well emprinted in your remembrance. We, desiryng also th'encres, wele and furtherance of my said lordes servant and oures, to th'accomplissement of my said lordes entencion in his honest desire at this tyme, aswel for his many and greet vertues and good condicions and also for the good and tr[e]we service that he hathe doon unto my said lord and us and yet therin dayly continueth, pray right effectuously that, at reverence of us, sith your doghter is in youre reule and governance as reason is, ye will yeve your good assent, benevolence and frenship t'enduce and t'excite your seid doghter t'accepte my said lordes servant and oures to hir husband, to the good conclusion and tendre exploit of the seid mariage, as our full trust is in you. In which thing ye shull mowe doo us right greet plesance and cause us to have you and yours in suche thinges ye shul mowe have for to doo towards us in tyme comyng in such tendre remembrance of oure good grace that by reason ye shul holde you well content and pleased, by Goddes myght, which have you in his blessed keping. At oure manoir of P. the etc.

To William Gastrike

Direct evidence regarding the persons named in this letter is scanty. Thomas Fountains, a king's sergeant, was granted the office of bailiff of Tewkesbury in June 1446.[28] A William Gastrik of Goushill, Lincolnshire, gentleman, was pardoned 14 April 1440 for failing to appear regarding a £14 debt.[29] In 1446, a William Gaskrike of Killinghome and others were commissioned to collect taxes in the parts of Lindsey, Lincolnshire.[30] The name is odd and appears to have left few traces; it seems likely that these references are both to the same man. Monro believed that William Gastrike of the letter (which he mistakenly transcribed as 'Gastrick') was a William Gascarick or Gaskryk, 'lord of Middle Soyle in the town of Killingholm', whose wife descended from a member of the Fountains family and whose only daughter, Elizabeth, was his sole heir. According to Monro, the royal appeals were unsuccessful, and Elizabeth eventually married Henry Booth, son of Thomas Booth of Barton and a nephew of William Booth, archbishop of York and Margaret's first chancellor. We find this doubtful, at least in its particulars. The only sources for such a Gastrike/Booth marriage (indeed, for the existence of *this* Henry Booth) appear to be pedigrees compiled in the seventeenth century, based upon information collected during the heralds'

28   *CPR, 1441–46*, p. 436.
29   *CPR, 1436–41*, p. 327.
30   *CFR, 1445–52*, p. 39.

visitations of 1562–64 and later, which the compilers expanded and embroidered back into the Middle Ages.[31]

Allowing for a certain amount of genealogical slippage and confusion, there was, in fact, a Henry Booth, son of a Thomas of Barton (who d. 1368.), who was the *uncle* of Archbishop Booth rather than the nephew. This Henry did marry a lady named Elizabeth (of unknown surname), who died in 1409. Henry himself died in 1446, by which time he must have been nearly eighty.[32] Clearly, this Elizabeth cannot have been the daughter referred to in Margaret's letter.

Whatever the name of Gastrike's daughter and whoever she eventually married, she was apparently reluctant to accept Thomas Fountains. The queen's letter follows up a request already made by King Henry, and she urges Gastrike not only to give his consent but to talk his daughter into agreeing to the marriage. This letter dates to the second half of 1447 or later since it is written from 'our manoir of P', which would be the manor of Pleasaunce at Greenwich. It became a royal residence following the death of Humphrey, duke of Gloucester, and the first recorded visit to it by the king and queen was in July 1447.[33]

[5] Queen to Nicholas Strange of Iseldon re T. Bugdon, 3 May
(BL, Add. MS 46,846, fol. 47; Monro, p. 125)

By the Quene

W[elbeloved]. For asmoche as we have understande by certein oure servants right negh attending about oure personne how albeit that T. Bugdon hath nowe late made a lawfull contracte with Katerine your doghter and hertly desireth to do hir worship by wey of mariage, aswel for his deute and lawful contract as for the great zele, love and affeccion that he hath unto hir personne bifore al creatures levyng, as it is said; yet ye of wilfulnesse and by sinistre excitacion, not havyng regarde unto the said contract, wol not applie you ne condescende unto the said mariage, ne yeve therto your benevolence ne assent, but rather induce your said doghter to the contrarye, ayeinst God, the chirche and al trouth, as unto us is reported, to oure greet merveil. We therfore desire and praye yow, and also on Godes bihalf exhorte and require you, if it so be that thanne ye incline you to th'accomplissement of the mariage without seking eny f[o]rmal delay or empechement otherwise thanne right lawe and good conscience asken and requiren in this partie, demenyng herin in such wyse [*sic*] goodly wise that the said T. may, atte reverence of us, be unto you

---

31   Monro, cited College of Arms, Vincent's MS 150, p. 220. Augustine Vincent served at the college from 1619 until his death in 1626.

32   J.S. Roskell, L. Clark and C. Rawcliffe, *The House of Commons, 1386–1421*, 4 vols (Stroud, 1993), II, p. 291. He was the younger brother of John Booth of Barton.

33   B.P. Wolffe, *Henry VI* (1981), p. 366.

especially recommended and fare the better by contemplacion of this oure prayer. As we trust yow, etc. Yeven, etc. at P, the iii day of May.

To Nich[olas] Straunge of Iseldon

We are not able to date this letter or to identify Nicholas Strange, his daughter Katherine or T. Bugdon. It is worth noting that Margaret learned of this situation through her servants, who wished to render a favor to Bugdon through the queen's intervention, for which they would then be credited. In a largely face-to-face society, this was a normal and accepted way to achieve goals and advance interests: in short, to make things happen. Margaret's jewel account for 1448–49 contains a record of a cash gift of 6s 8d to a Ralph Strange.[34] One might wonder – as a highly romantic speculation – whether he was a relative of the Stranges of Iseldon who took pity on the couple's plight and appealed to Margaret on their behalf. The 'lawfull contracte' referred to was likely to have been a verbal commitment made by the couple to each other, either a promise to marry in the future or a statement in the present tense to the effect that they accounted themselves married. The latter was considered binding, even when consummation had not yet taken place. While this may argue that the relationship was based upon affection, most marriage arrangements had more to do with property and status, and these considerations may have prompted Bugdon's supporters to speak up in his behalf. 'P', where the letter was written, would have been Pleshey, Margaret's dower castle in Essex.[35]

[6] Queen to the Archbishop of York, the Earl of Dorset and Richard Waller re W. Fruter and Agnes Knoghton, 18 M [May 1447–48 or March 1448?]
(BL, Add. MS 46,846, fols 48–48v; Monro, pp. 101–2)

By the Quene

Moost worshipfull fader in God, oure right, etc.; right trusty and right welbeloved cousin, and trusty and welbeloved, we grete you well. And for asmoche as my lordes servant and oures Piers Preston, yomanne of the crowne, hath leten us wite that oon W. Fruter and Agnes Knoghton, poure creatures and of vertuous conversacion, pourposyng to leve under the lawe of God in th'ordre of wedlok, have made togedre a lawfull contract likly by thaire discrescions to be of sad [serious] and commendable reule if they were put forth and releved by some aulmes at this tyme; wheruppon my said lordes servant and oures right humbly hath besoght us that it wolde please us to have theym towardes you in seyng unto theym of aulmes of the goodes of our beal uncle [good-uncle] the cardinal, on whos soule God have

34 E 101/410/2.
35 Margaret used 'P' indiscriminately for both Pleshey and Pleasaunce. Reference to her manor of P is Pleasaunce. Where no manor is indicated, P refers to her dower land at Pleshey Castle.

mercye, especialy recommended. We, atte instance and humble supplicacion of oure said servant, and in especial the meritorie in relevement of the said pore creatures of so vertues pourpos and laudable entencion, as it is reherced, desire and hertly praye you that ye wil, atte reverence of us and for the merit of oure said uncle[s] soule, have theym in such tendernesse and faver in departing with theim of the said aulmesse that they may perceive thise oure lettres unto theym vailable. And that thei fare the better by contemplacion of this oure prayer, as our full trust is in yow. In which thing, etc. At W. the xviii day of M.

To th'archbisshop of York, Cardynal; th'erle of Dorset, and Ric[hard] Waller, Executores of our Oncle late Card[inal] of England.

Margaret took an interest in promoting marriage even if no property was involved. Acts of charity were, of course, incumbent on her as queen and good lady. Cardinal Henry Beaufort, bishop of Winchester, died on 11 April 1447. He was the richest man in England and left the bulk of his fortune to various religious foundations. The residue of his property was left to his executors to dispense as charity at their discretion, 'such as relieving poor religious houses, marrying poor maidens [and] succouring the poor and needy'.[36] The letter is addressed to three of his executors: Cardinal John Kemp, archbishop of York; Edmund Beaufort, earl (marquess) of Dorset, the cardinal's nephew; and Richard Waller, master of Cardinal Beaufort's household. The different forms of address used in the letter, tailored to each individual's identity and status, should be noted.

Although the letter may date to May 1447, a month after Cardinal Beaufort's death, his will was not proved until the following September. Even allowing that its provisions were known, the executors were unlikely to make any but very urgent handouts before that time. A date of May 1448 presents other difficulties. Edmund Beaufort was created duke of Somerset on 31 March of that year and left for Rouen shortly thereafter. In that case, his inclusion may have been a formality, and the style of address used was his title at the time of his uncle's death. A third possibility is that the 'M' for the month atypically stands for March and that the letter was written in 1448 before Somerset's promotion and departure. King Henry was at Windsor on each of the possible dates, and Margaret was probably with him whenever the letter was written.[37] Peter Preston was a yeoman of the chamber and had been keeper of the houses (i.e. bailiff) of Kings Langley Manor, Hertfordshire.[38]

36   Nicolas, *Testamenta Vetusta*, I, pp. 251–2.
37   Wolffe, *Henry VI*, pp. 365, 366–7.
38   *CPR, 1441–46*, p. 60. In 1452–53 he collected £4 17s 9d of Margaret's income from Hertford (Myers, 'Household', p. 158).

Two

HOLY ORDERS

Good ladyship dictated that Margaret should try to obtain benefices for her clerics whenever possible. But there was also a practical side to this: once the cleric held a benefice, he was assumed to have an adequate income, making it unnecessary to continue paying him wages as a household servant.[1] A pair of examples demonstrates how this worked. Nicholas Caraunt, secretary of the queen's council, was in full orders and beneficed; therefore, he received no salary although he was remunerated for his writing materials.[2] George Ashby, Margaret's clerk of the signet, who was only in minor orders and thus ineligible for a cure of souls position, received a wage.[3]

The first letter, to Master Gilbert Kymer, provides a fairly generic example of Margaret's search for such positions. Her assurance of the high quality of her clerks is ramped up in the next two letters to a formulaic insistence that her candidates are worthy for their 'vertues, merites, and clerkly governance, as for [their] famows and clene lyvyng'. Such endorsements were to be expected. In the later Middle Ages, when popular criticism of clerical competence and morality was high, they may also have been necessary. In this regard, Margaret's use of the words 'fame' and 'famous' deserves note. The medieval understanding of fame, or *fama* in the Latin from which it derived, involved public reputation; moreover, reputation that was talked about.[4] When she used these words, Margaret implied

---

1   R.F. Green, *Poets and Princepleasers* (Toronto, 1980), p. 27, citing the *Liber Niger*, p. 111. See *CPL, 1447–55*, pp. 95–6, 177–8; *1455–64*, pp. 154–5, 558, 562, for Margaret's petitions on behalf of persons not discussed below.

2   Myers, 'Household', p. 198.

3   Ibid., pp. 185–6. Myers (p. 91, n. 2) was mistaken in assuming Ashby to have been more important than Caraunt because he was salaried. See below, pp. 32–4, for Caraunt; p. 140ff, for Ashby.

4   T. Fenster and D.L. Smail, *Fama* (2003), pp. 3–4.

that the value judgment was not merely her private assessment, but a matter of public knowledge and public expression. We have seen this phenomenon in the queen's letters promoting marriage, and we will see it again and again in other situations: reputation was a public matter, to be publicly known and proclaimed.

Although most of Margaret's clerical recommendations naturally involved men, her attentions were not limited to male clergy. Three letters in this chapter concern the election of prioresses. In the case of Wix Priory, Margaret was asked for license to elect as she held the advowson of the priory. This she was willing to grant, apparently without intruding her own wishes upon their selection.

The last group of letters involves situations that were not so straightforward. Two letters take the side of Master Richard Chester in a dispute over an office claimed to be his 'of right'. In this, they bear some similarities to a series of letters in which the queen intervened to protect persons from various intrusions and harassments, dealt with below.[5] Margaret's letter regarding the deanery of Wells followed a disputed election that had been resolved, but which left some unfinished and unpleasant business in its aftermath. This and the last two letters become more noticeably political in the machinations involved in each case. They also show Henry VI's vacillation in political and administrative affairs. The last letter, involving Master John Hals, may show lurking tensions between the Neville family and the crown.

[7] **Queen to Master Gilbert Kymer, Chancellor of Oxford and Dean of Wimborne Minster [1447–53]**
(BL, Add. MS 46,846, fols 56v–57; Monro, pp. 135–6)

By the Quene
Right trusty and welbeloved, etc. Lating you witt that we have certein right good and notable clerkes of greet fame and vertues disposicion attending in our service as yet by us unpromoted and destitute of benefices. We, havyng knowelech that there is like in shorte tyme to voide a prebende in the ministre of Wyborne longyng unto your yefte and collocacion as patron therof, as it is said, desire and hertly praye you that ye wil graunte us the nexte prebende that first shall voide there for to avaunce therewith oon of our said clerkes. Wherinne trusteth verreily ye shul not mowe oonly pourvei right well for the wele and worship of your said prebende to Godes pleasance, but also cause us to have you in tendre remembrance of our good grace therefore in tyme comyng. And how ye thinke to please us in this mater ye will acerteine us by our well[beloved] the bringer of thise, etc.

To Maister Gilbert Kymer, chan[cellor]

5   Chapter 5, 'Protector and Peacemaker'.

Gilbert Kymer had a longstanding association with Oxford University, where he was principal of Hart Hall as early as 1411.[6] He received his MA by 1412 and a doctorate in medicine *c.* 1423. He was twice chancellor of Oxford, from December 1431 to March 1434, and from February 1447 until his resignation in May 1453. He was dean of Wimborne Minster, Dorset, from November 1423 and dean of Salisbury Cathedral from June 1449 until his death on 16 May 1463. This letter would have been written during his second term as chancellor, and most likely towards its beginning, when Margaret's queenship was still relatively new and her need to find provision for her clerics more pressing.

Kymer's career as a distinguished physician is intriguing. Having accompanied Henry V to France as a doctor, he was soon serving Humphrey, duke of Gloucester, to whom he dedicated his treatise *Dietarium de sanitatis custodia* in 1424, and whose physician he had become by 1433. It is likely that he had Gloucester's backing when, in 1423, he led an ultimately unsuccessful effort to establish a licensing system for physicians.[7] He may have been instrumental in obtaining and encouraging Gloucester's generous patronage of Oxford, particularly in his extensive gifts to its library.[8] On 11 January 1454 or 1455, he was granted a papal indult, good for ten years, to rent or let the proceeds of his benefices to others while he was residing in any one of them, in Oxford or in any other university where he was studying, in the papal court, or if he was occupied 'in the service of king Henry or queen Margaret'.[9] The first three qualifications are standard; the last is more interesting in its suggestion that Kymer could have been serving either the king or queen as physician around this time. Considering how long it would have taken messages to travel to Rome and back, the likelier patient is Henry, whose catastrophic illness lasted from August 1453 to the end of 1454. Kymer is not named, however, in the list of physicians and surgeons appointed by the council in March 1454 to attend the king.[10] Does this suggest, if he was attending Henry during this time, that it was Margaret who sent for him? He was indeed summoned by privy seal on 5 June 1455 to be at Windsor on the twelfth to treat the king for his 'sicknesse and infirmitees'.[11] This summons

---

6 For his career, see Emden, II, pp. 1068–9; C.H. Talbot and E.A. Hammond, *The Medical Practitioners in Medieval England: A Biographical Register* (1965), pp. 60–3.

7 J. Catto, 'Masters, Patrons and the Careers of Graduates in the Fifteenth Century', in *Concepts and Patterns of Service in the Later Middle Ages*, eds A. Curry and E. Matthew (Woodbridge, 2000), p. 61.

8 Emden, II, p. 984.

9 *CPL, 1447–55*, p. 159. The date is incomplete.

10 *PPC*, VI, pp. 166–7; *CPR, 1452–61*, p. 147. Surgeons were hands-on practitioners; a physician was looked to for medical advice.

11 *Foedera*, XI, p. 366.

has provided fodder for historical speculation that Henry suffered a second bout of mental illness. On balance, this seems unlikely.[12] Although, the king had been wounded in the neck by an arrow during the battle of St Albans (22 May), the June date seems a little late to have involved this injury, just as Kymer's position as a physician makes it doubtful that he would have treated it.[13] We are left with no definite answer regarding Kymer's business with the king. Henry was suffering the aftermath of the shock of his defeat at St Albans, and Kymer's advice as a distinguished physician may have been sought on what today we would call psychological grounds. Henry needed reassurance about his health, mental and physical.

[8] Queen to the Abbot and Convent of Peterborough re Henry Stonham
(BL, Add. MS 46,846, fols 64v–65; Monro, pp. 138–9)

By the Quene

Trusty, etc. And for asmoche as we be enformed that the paroissh chirch of Cotyngham is voide or like withinne shorte tyme to voide, wherof ye be patrons, as it is said; we therfore, havyng consideracion aswell to the vertues, merites and clerkly governance as for the famows and clene lyvyng that our welbeloved Sir Henry Stonham is renomed of, desire and hertely praye you that, atte reverence of us and contemplacion of this our especiall writyng, ye woll have hym unto the said chirch whensoever it shall nexte voide before all other especially recommended. Wherinne we truste verreilly ye shull mowe pourvey right notable for the wele and worship of your said benefice to Goddes plesaunce. And doubteth not but of us ye shull mowe [de]serve in accomplissement of our entencion in this partie good and especiall thanke. Yeven, etc., at Wind[sor] the firste daye of Marche.

To th'abbot & covent of Petirborgh

Cottingham, in Northamptonshire, belonged to the Benedictine abbey of Peterborough. Sir Henry Stonham of the letter seems likely to have been the Henry Stoneham, clerk, who along with David Selly and John Randolf, esquires, and John Bristowe, another clerk, received a gift of the goods and chattels of John Bedyngham, verger of St Stephen's chapel, Westminster, in March 1458.[14] He may have been related to Robert Stonham of Rattlesden, Huntingdonshire,

---

12 J.R. Lander, 'Henry VI and the Duke of York's Second Protectorate', in idem, *Crown and Nobility 1450–1509* (1976), pp. 77–9, traces the 'legend' of Henry's relapse, concluding it is unsubstantiated. Cf. Griffiths, pp. 717–18 and n. 14.

13 Three surgeons were paid in mid-July for attending Henry (Lander, 'Henry VI', p. 78, n. 34, citing E 403/801 m. 7. Since payments for services were almost always in arrears, they may have treated Henry's arrow wound in May.

14 *CCR, 1454–61*, p. 283.

who served as MP and sheriff and died in 1455.[15] There is no record of him having received the requested benefice.

The abbot of Peterborough, Richard Ashton (elected 1438, resigned 27 June 1471),[16] had a checkered career. In visitations of 1442 and 1446–47, he was charged with 'favouritism, maladministration, and immorality' and forced to live apart from the abbey for a time at Oxney, except for necessary business visits, though it seems that he was later reinstated.[17] He received a general pardon from Edward IV on 4 September 1461, and some six months later he and the abbey were granted 'the goods of felons, fugitives and outlaws' within all their hundreds in Northamptonshire and elsewhere and the right of gaol delivery of Peterborough.[18] In September 1463, the abbot and convent were granted custody of all its temporalities during voidance, in return for a payment of £40 for each occurrence.[19] Richard Ashton received a second general pardon several months after his resignation, on 20 November 1471.[20] While one should not read too much into the two pardons, and although the intervening grants appear to attest to a good relationship between the abbot and the king, their dates, taken together, seem a little close to Edward IV's accession and final victory over the Lancastrians to be entirely coincidental. One is left with questions regarding the abbot's sympathies.

[9] **Quene to the Bishop of Exeter re Master N., 28 May [*c.* 1447?]**
(BL, Add. MS 46,846, fols 65v–66; Monro, p. 138)

By the Quene
Reverend fader in God, etc. And for asmoche as we desire th'encres, furtherance and promocion of our welbeloved clerc M[aister] N., aswell for his vertues, merites and clerkly governance as for his famows and clene livyng with the goodly dispoosicion that he is renomed of, praye you right hertly that, at reverence of us, ye will have our said clerc to the nexte benefice accordyng to his degree that first shall voide in your yeft and disposicion especially recommendet. Wherinne we truste verreily ye shull mowe pourvey right notably for the wele and worship of your said benefice to Goddes pleasance. And doubteth not but of us ye shull mow deserve in accomplissement of our entencion in this partie good and especial thanke unto our right greate and singuler pleasance. Yeven, etc., at W. the xxviij day of M.
To the Bisshop of Exc[estre]

---

15 Wedgwood, p. 814. Henry could not have been Robert's son, as the latter left an only daughter.
16 On 16 July the prior and convent of Peterborough received license to elect an abbot to replace Ashton (*CPR, 1467–76*, p. 266).
17 Emden, I, p. 58.
18 *CPR, 1461–67*, pp. 43, 191; the grant was dated 20 March 1462.
19 Ibid., p. 275.
20 *CPR, 1467–77*, p. 292, in which he is styled 'monk, late abbot'.

Given the fact that neither 'Master N.' nor the bishop of Exeter is specifically named in this letter, any effort to identify them must ultimately be speculative. It is possible that Margaret's clerk was the 'Master Nevyle' who appears in the queen's first jewel account for 1445–46 at the head of a list of sixteen fairly high-ranking servants who each received from her a gold armlet. He appears again – this time alone – in the account for 1446–47 as 'Master Thomas Nevyll', at which time he received a brooch worth 33s 4d.[21] If this identification is accepted and the letter is presumed to have been written around this time, the bishop of Exeter would have been Edmund Lacy, who was elected to the see in 1420 and served until his death in September 1455.

Efforts to determine what became of this Thomas Neville have been unsuccessful. He is unlikely to have been the man who became rector of Brancepeth, Durham, from 1456 until his death in 1498. The latter was born in *c.* 1433, and age alone would seem to disqualify him from having been in Margaret's service in the mid-1440s.[22]

[10] **Quene to the Archbishop of Canterbury, Chancellor of England, re John Wygram [1446–49]**
(BL, Add. MS 46,846, fol. 67; Monro, pp. 156–7)

By the Quene
Right Reverend Fader, etc., we grete you well. Latyng you witt that we be enformed that our welbeloved clerk M[aster] John Wygram, a prest of my lordes chapell, brought you my lordes offryng on the twelfday, for the which as we understond there is a lawdable custume that the brynger of the offryng shall have the first benefice that shall voide withinne th'extent. Wherfore we praye you to call it unto your remembrance and have herin our said clerc for our sake the more especialy recommended. As we truste you and our lord, etc.
To th'archebisshop of Cant[erbury], Chaunceller of Englond

John Wygram attended Merton College, where he became a fellow in *c.* 1423. He was rector of Devizes, Wiltshire, from 1423; canon of Wells and prebendary of Combe from 1449; canon and prebendary of St George's chapel, Windsor, and canon of Lincoln and prebendary of *Decem Librarum*, both from 1457. He continued to hold all of these positions throughout his life. Apparently, they were insufficient, for in 1458, Wygram received a papal dispensation to hold an additional incompatible benefice. In 1459 he became rector of Templecombe, Somerset, a position he vacated in 1463 in exchange for the rectorship of

21   E 101/409/14 and 17.
22   Emden, II, pp. 1351–2.

Batcombe in the same county, which he held – along with all his other posts – until his death in October 1468.[23]

Monro observed that the identification of the archbishop and chancellor to whom the letter was addressed – and, by extension, the date of the letter – was problematic. Three men held both positions concurrently during Margaret's queenship. The first of these, John Stafford, was archbishop of Canterbury from 1443 to 1452 (the year of his death) and chancellor to 1450. John Kemp, then archbishop of York and a cardinal since 1439, succeeded Stafford as chancellor in January 1450. Following Stafford's death, Kemp became archbishop of Canterbury in July 1452. He held both posts until his death in March 1454. Kemp was succeeded as archbishop of Canterbury by Thomas Bourgchier, who only became chancellor in March 1455 and was replaced in October 1456 by William Waynflete, bishop of Winchester.[24] The letter, therefore, can have been written no later than 1456. But which man was the recipient? Archbishop Kemp was also a cardinal, and it seems likely that Margaret would have addressed him by this title, as she did in her letter to him as one of Cardinal Beaufort's executors.[25] If, as the letter implies, Margaret had only recently learned of the custom, it indicates an early date, and Stafford would be the obvious choice.

[11] Queen to the Abbot and Convent of Ramsey re David Robert
(BL, Add. MS 46,846, fols 67–67v; Monro, p. 129)

> By the Quene
> Trusty and welbeloved in God, we, etc. And for asmoche as Maister Ric[hard] Here, parson of Barton in the Cley of the diocese of Lincoln, is in will to resigne his said benefice to th'entent that our welbeloved Sir D[avi]d Robert shuld have the said benefice of your yefte; we desire therfore and praye you that, the said resignacion so don, ye will at reverence of us have the said Sir D[avi]d to the said chirch especially recommended and graunte hym therof your lettres of presentacion under your covent seall in deu forme. And the rather by contemplacion of this our prayer, as we trust, etc. In which thing, etc.
> To th'abbot and covent of Ramsey

The advowson to the church of St Nicholas in Barton-in-the-Clay belonged to the Benedictine abbey of Ramsey, Huntingdonshire, from the earliest times. The church was valued at £26 9s 6d in 1535, suggesting that it would have provided

---

23 Emden, III, p. 2108.
24 After Kemp's death, Richard Neville, earl of Salisbury, served as chancellor during the duke of York's first protectorate.
25 See above, p. 16.

a tidy income in the mid-fifteenth century.[26] The abbot of Ramsey was John Stowe, who was elected in 1436 and resigned in 1468.[27] We have found no traces of either Richard Here or David Robert and cannot determine what became of this request. A William Danyell was rector of Barton-in-the-Clay at the time of his death on 13 October 1464.[28]

In the next letter Margaret writes on behalf of a woman whom she proposed as a prioress. The subject of her letter appears to have led an interesting life. There is a story lurking here, of which only the faintest traces still remain.

[12] Queen to the Sub-prioress of Nuneaton and the Master and Brethren of Nuneaton re Maude Everingham [1447–48]
(BL, Add. MS 46,846, fol. 53v; Monro, pp. 163–4)

By the Quene
Dere and welbeloved in God, we grete yowe well. And we suppose verreily that it is clerely in your remembrance how that we have now late writen unto you for the recommendacion of our right welbeloved Dame Mawde Everyngham to be accepted and elited for your priouresse there what tyme ye shall nexte be destitute of a priouresse. And it is nowe soo that we understand that your priouresse is passed to Goddes mercy, wherupon my most doubted lord writeth unto yow at this tyme right especialy for the recommendacion of the said Dame Mawde unto th'eleccion of your priouresse there. Wherfore we desire and praye you eftesones that, in accomplissement of my lordes request and oures in this partie, ye will have the said Dame Mawde in your nexte eleccion right tenderly recommended and chese hir to be your priouresse and governer by consideracion of hir many vertues, religiouse governance and good fame that she is renomed of. And the rather by contemplacion of this oure prayer, as oure full truste is in yow. In which thing ye shul, etc. Yeven, etc.

To the Suppriouresse of None Eton
To the Maister & Brethern of, etc.

Nuneaton Priory was founded in the mid-twelfth century as an alien priory under the abbey of Fontevrault. In 1459 it numbered around forty nuns, a drop by more than half from the eighty-nine residents it had in 1328. Maude (or Matilda) Everingham first appears as prioress in 1448; her position received papal confirmation on 6 December of that year.[29] The previous prioress, Elizabeth Walcote,

26   VCH: *Bedfordshire*, II, p. 312.
27   VCH: *Huntingdonshire*, I, p. 384.
28   A. Gibbons, *Early Lincoln Wills* (Lincoln, 1888), p. 182.
29   *CPL, 1447–55*, p. 40. Our account of Nuneaton and Maude Everingham is taken from VCH: *Warwickshire*, II, pp. 68–9, except as noted.

died in 1446 or soon after,[30] suggesting that Margaret's letter was written in 1447–48. Since time could elapse between Maud's nomination and confirmation, she may have served as acting prioress before her position became official.

During the 1450s the priory experienced difficulties. In 1451, in response to a complaint that the house had become impoverished and that its tenants had been 'oppressed by the taking of their goods' at an annual fair, the priory was granted the right to acquire lands in mortmain to the value of 20 marks, in return for a payment of 27 marks, while goods brought to the fair were exempted from purveyance.[31] Margaret's accounts show that she was owed 36s in queen's gold on this transaction.[32] (She was unlikely to receive this money unless payment served as a 'sweetener' in requesting some specific favor from her.) In December 1459 the prioress and convent obtained the parish church of Nuneaton, with its lands, rents and services, from the priory of Jesus of Bethlehem at Sheen, Surrey, along with the latter's claim to a portion of the tithes from the church of Roteby, Leicestershire, in return for an annual rent of £24 from Nuneaton's overall income.[33] This transaction seems dicey. Whether it was actually a good deal for the priory of Nuneaton would depend on the value of the parish church (added to that of lands they already held) and their ability to make good on the claim to Roteby's tithes.

Maude's troubles became more personal – and political – under Edward IV. On 20 September 1462 the king took the priory and its possessions into his hands 'on account of the bad and wasteful governance of Matilda, the prioress'. He then gave their custody to the abbots of Leicester and Merevale, the prior of Coventry and others, who were to apply all issues to the priory's relief and investigate 'all excesses and alienations committed'.[34] In 1465, Maude and Sir Simon Byllyngay, 'broder of the same place', were removed by the abbot of Merevale and the prior of Coventry on the grounds of misrule and wasting goods.[35] Maude's successor was Elizabeth Barton. In January 1471, during Henry VI's readeption, Maude appeared as prioress again, apparently having ousted Elizabeth, and was again charged with wasting.[36] Whatever the immediate outcome, Elizabeth Barton had

30 Elizabeth had held office since 1412, and this is the last year that she appears as prioress.
31 *CPR, 1452–61*, p. 500. It would not have been unreasonable to expect the investment to pay itself off.
32 Myers, 'Household', p. 176.
33 *CPR, 1452–61*, p. 532.
34 *CPR, 1461–67*, p. 199.
35 In this same year, Maude had presented Simon to the vicarage of Claybrooke.
36 Simon was charged with Maude. He had been presented in August 1468 to the parish church of Chilton in the diocese of Bath and Wells, a position he exchanged in March 1469 for a chaplaincy in the chantry of St Leonard, Hungerford Farleigh, in the same diocese (*CPR, 1467–77*, pp. 96, 151).

reacquired the office by February 1483 and continued to hold it into 1485.[37] The redoubtable Maude was not to be beaten, however: she reappeared as prioress under Henry VII from 1486 to 1499, in which year she probably died.[38] The length of her off-and-on tenure poses a question: since she was likely to have been quite young when she first became prioress – unless she lived to great age – had she professed from vocation or had she been pressured to do so to keep the family property intact?

While it is possible that Maude was simply a bad administrator, the likelihood that some of her difficulties stemmed from politics is strengthened if we assume that she was related to Thomas and Henry Everingham, a pair of Midlands gentlemen with strong Lancastrian connections.[39] Thomas Everingham of Newhall, Leicestershire, had a distinguished career in France, was twice MP for Leicestershire in 1449 and 1453–54, and served on various commissions during the 1450s. He was a feoffee of John, duke of Somerset, and a client of John, Viscount Beaumont, who obtained the stewardship of Bagworth for him from John, Lord Lovell.[40] On 21 December 1459, Thomas was named to a commission of array to resist York's rebellion. Then on 10 May 1460 he received a life grant of the stewardship of Cottingham, Yorkshire, 'in the king's gift by the rebellion of Richard, duke of York, and Richard, earl of Salisbury', both for his earlier service to Henry V overseas and for his much more recent service against the rebels.[41] He was specifically excluded from Edward IV's offer of pardon on 6 March 1461 and was subsequently attainted for having fought at Towton, where he may have died.[42]

Henry Everingham's political career is sketchier, though no less enigmatic. He was one of the king's squires by 1447, a life annuitant of the earl of Warwick 1450–60, and served as MP for Warwickshire in the parliament of 1459 that attainted the Yorkists.[43] He appears to have been knighted by the Lancastrians sometime after May 1460 during the turbulence surrounding Henry VI's

37   *CPR, 1476–85*, p. 334.
38   Her successor was Christine Topcliff.
39   Wedgwood, pp. 307–8, suggests that they were either brothers or father and son. Griffiths, p. 370, n. 65, believed them to be brothers, and C. Carpenter, *Locality and Polity* (Cambridge, 1992), p. 461, n. 69, suggested a connection between Thomas and Maude. Only one marriage of Thomas is known: to Margaret Bugge after 1445. He held the Newhall estates in her right (E. Acheson, *A Gentry Community* [Cambridge, 1992], pp. 228, 241). Unless there was an earlier marriage that left no record, he could not have fathered either Henry or Maude.
40   *CPR, 1441–46*, p. 349; Gairdner, *PL*, III, p. 143. Suggestions that Thomas was related to Beaumont appear to be mistaken.
41   *CPR, 1452–61*, pp. 560, 580.
42   *CCR, 1461–68*, p. 55; *PROME*, XIII, p. 44.
43   Carpenter, *Locality and Polity*, p. 697.

deposition. A letter in the name of Prince Edward of Lancaster, requiring the city of Coventry to render assistance and obedience to Sir Edmund Mountfort, Sir Henry Everyngham and William Elton, squire, 'and fayleth not so to do as ye wolle answere to my lord [Henry VI] & to us at your perille', indicates that he was a knight by early 1461. Although the letter is undated, the copy of a grateful letter on the verso from the newly crowned Edward IV suggests that it was written somewhat earlier.[44] On 14 September 1468, Henry Everingham received a pardon.[45] He appears to have died by the early 1470s.[46]

[13] The Convent of Wix to Queen Margaret, 28 October 1450
(BL, Add. MS 46,846, fol. 59v)

Serenissime et Illustrissime Domine, nostre Domine Margarete Regine Anglie et Francie et Domine Hibernie, filie Regis Cicilie et Jerusalema. Vestre humiles et devote que oratrices Agnes Welling presidens et conventus prioratus de Wykes Londoniensis diocesis vestri patronatus, devota suffragia beatorum precumque effusiones ad vestrem [*sic*] prosperitatem votive semper augmentent.

Dolenti animo amoreque harum litterarum nostrarum tenore reserimus [*sic*] et denunciamus quod prioratus noster predictus per mortem Domine Katerine Wellynge priorisse solacio destitutus existit. Unde devotis animis et precum instantia humiliter supplicamus ne idem prioratus noster qui de patronato vestro existere denoscitur propter ipsius vacacionem diutinam incomodam quod absit deploraret aliam nobis et dicto prioratui nostro eligendi in priorissam licenciam concedere vestram dignetur celsitudo quam felicibus successibus semper preservet qui solus omnium conditor est summus deus. Date in domo nostra capitularis xxviij^{vo} die mensis Octobris anno domini millesimo ccccl.

Most serene and illustrious lady, the Lady Margaret, Queen of England and of France and Lady of Ireland, daughter of the king of Sicily and Jerusalem. [From] your humble and faithful bedeswomen, Agnes Welling, who is presiding, and the convent of the priory of Wix in the diocese of London in your advowson; may the devout intercessions of the blessed and effusions of prayers for your prosperity ever increase according to [our] vow.

---

44 M.D. Harris, ed. *The Coventry Leet Book*, EETS, o.s. 134, 135, 138, 146 in one vol. (1907–13), pp. 313–14. Adjacent entries refer to men who collected money from the city for 'the Erle of Marche … after losyng of the feld at seynt Albons'. The second battle of St Albans was fought in February 1461. Prince Edward was then seven years old. This letter disproves suggestions that Henry was either knighted at Queen Elizabeth Woodville's coronation (Wedgwood, p. 307) or during Henry VI's readeption (Carpenter, *Locality and Polity*, p. 86, n. 174).

45 Wedgwood, p. 307.

46 On 7 February 1472 he was named as a former feoffee of one John Purefey (*CCR, 1468–76*, p. 256). It is not clear whether he was living or dead at this time.

With grieving heart and love, by the content of these our letters, we reveal and announce that our aforesaid priory, by the death of Lady Katherine Welling, is left without the comfort of a prioress. Wherefor with faithful hearts and the urgency of prayers we humbly beseech that our same priory, which is known to be in your advowson, may not complain of a long, inconvenient vacancy [of the office] – which God forbid – and that Your Highness deign to grant your license to us and our said priory to elect another as prioress. Whom God the highest, who alone is the creator of all things, always preserve with favorable outcomes. Given in our chapter house the 28th day of the month of October in the year of our Lord 1450.

[14] Queen to her Chancellor on behalf of the Convent of Wix, 5 November [1450]
(BL, Add. MS 46,846, fols 59v–60)

Per Reginam
Reverende in Christo pater nobis sincere dilecte. Cum prioratus de Wykes Londoniensis diocesis nostri patronatus per mortem Domine Katerine Wellynge ultime priorisse ibidem sit monasterii solacio priorisse destitutus. Supplicaverunt que proinde nobis humiliter et devote Agnes Wellyngs presidens et conventus eiusdem loci ut eis aliam in ipsorum et dicto prioratu priorissam eligendi licenciam concedere dignaremur, sicuti per litteras suas patentes sigillatas quas vobis presentibus mittimus interclusas plenius poterit apperere. Nos igitur earum supplicacionem in ea parte favoraliter inclinate licenciam ipsam duximus concedendam. Et ideo vobis mandamus quod sub magno sigillo nostro in custodia vestra existente super hoc nostras litteras patentes fieri faciatis. Et hee littere etc. date etc. v° die Novembris anno etc.

Reverend father in Christ, by us sincerely beloved. Whereas the priory of Wix in the diocese of London, of our advowson, was left destitute of the comfort of a prioress of the monastery by the death of Lady Katherine Welling, the last prioress in that place, Agnes Welling, who is presiding, and the convent of the same place have therefore beseeched us humbly and faithfully that we see fit to grant them license to elect another prioress in their said priory, as by their letters patent under seal that we send you enclosed with the present [letters] will more fully appear. We therefore, [being] favorably inclined to their supplication in that regard, have thought that the license should be granted. And, therefore, we command you that, under our great seal that is in your custody, you cause our letters patent to be made in this regard. And these letters, etc., given the 5th day of November, in the year, etc.

The priory of Wix in Essex was a Benedictine house founded in the reign of Henry I by the Mascherell family.[47] Further grants accrued to the priory over

---

47   VCH: *Essex*, II, pp. 123–5, for Wix Priory.

the years, and by 1438, when Henry VI confirmed all its grants and privileges, the priory held lands in Essex and in Suffolk.[48] The advowson of the priory belonged to the manor of Wix, which formed part of Queen Margaret's dower lands. Katherine Welling became prioress in 1419 and appears to have been followed by Katherine Peper, presumably the prioress elected in 1450 or 1451.[49] She was still alive in 1464, but by 1465 she had been succeeded by Agnes Welling.

Margaret's instruction was to William Booth, her chancellor at the time. Her letters patent to elect would have been issued by him under her great seal.[50] The election of a prioress for Wix would have had to be confirmed by the queen and by the bishop of London, Thomas Kemp, in whose diocese Wix lay. He was the nephew of the chancellor of England, Cardinal John Kemp.

[15] Queen to Master W[illiam] S[crope] re Richard Chester
(BL, Add. MS 46,846, fol. 41; Monro, pp. 120–1)

> By the Quene
> Trusty, etc. For asmoch as we be enformed that ayeinst all law, trouth and good conscience ye occupie the hospital of Gretham, longyng of right unto my lordes clerc and oure M[aister] R.C; we wol and exhorte yow that if it so be, that thanne ye doo make due restitucion of the seid hospital with his goodes unto our seid clerc, or elles to certiffie, etc., etc., etc.
> To M[aister] W.S.

[16] Queen to the Bishop of Durham re Richard Chester [1450–51?]
(BL, Add. MS 46,846, fol. 42v; Monro, p. 121)

> By the Quene
> Worshipfull fader, etc. And we suppose verreily that [it] is clerely in your remembrance how that now late we wrote unto yow for the recommendacion of my lordes clerke and oures Maister Ric[hard] Chestre unto the restitucion of th'ospital of Gretham and his goodes, longyng unto hym there of right, as it is said. Wherin as yet ye have not accomplissed oure entencion, to oure greet merveil. Wherfore we praye yow eftesones that ye suffre oure said clerk to rejoyse [re-enjoy] his said hospital with the seid goodes, as right, law and good conscience requiren, or elles to certifie us the cause in writing whie ye wil not, nor oght not, so to do of right.

---

48 Among its more interesting privileges was the right to keep two greyhounds and four braches to course hares in the forest of Essex.

49 Katherine Peper is first noted in 1457, following Katherine Welling, who last appears in 1439.

50 Queens of England had their own great and privy seals to transact the business of their councils (T.F. Tout, *Chapters in the Administrative History of Medieval England*, V [Manchester, 1930], pp. 286–9).

As ye desire to stande in the favor of oure good grace in tyme commynge. Yeven
at W. the etc.

    To the Bisshop of Duresme

The hospital of SS Mary and Cuthbert, Greatham, was founded in 1272 by the
bishop of Durham to house 'poor men' born on the bishop's manors. Presumably,
these would have been men who, by reason of age or infirmity, stood in need
of – or sought out – room and board.[51] In 1447, the hospital was valued at up to
£100 a year: a tidy sum, assuming of course that its actual worth was not considerably less.[52]

    Richard Chester first appears as a fellow of Merton College, Oxford, in 1415.[53]
It is clear that he was favored by Henry VI. In 1441, he obtained a papal indulgence
for Henry's foundation of Eton, and was subsequently linked to Eton and King's
College by collecting books for them.[54] Henry rewarded '[his] chaplain' in 1442
with a grant of 12d a day for ten years, 'for good service to the king at the Roman
curia and about the king's person'.[55] Chester was made an administrator of the
effects of Humphrey, duke of Gloucester, in 1447, and a councilor of Ireland in
1448. In connection with the latter appointment, when Henry learned in January
1449 that Chester had been unable to collect his annual fee of £20, he granted
him the same amount for life from the customs of Dublin and Drogheda. Four
days later, on 29 January, the king granted Chester two tuns of Gascon wine
annually for life 'for his labours, expenditure, and imprisonment in his journey
to the Roman Curia for the good of Eton College and in consideration of his
age'.[56] This grant has the look of a valedictory, summing up what Henry perceived
to have been the height of Chester's service to him, and he does not appear as a
royal beneficiary thereafter.

    Chester's ecclesiastical career was no less impressive. By the later 1440s he had
acquired – and kept – various benefices including vicar of St Mary, Lancashire
(1431), rector of St Mary Woolchurch, London (1442), canon of St Patrick's,
Dublin (1444), and canon of Hereford by 1447. At some point between 1441 and
1447, he became the master of Greatham Hospital, having been collated to the

51   VCH: *Durham*, II, pp. 121. Some inmates were attended by servants and received better food
     than others, which suggests that they were not all impoverished in our sense of the word.
52   *CPL, 1447–55*, p. 338.
53   Emden, I, pp. 407–8, for his career.
54   M.M. Harvey, *England, Rome and the Papacy, 1417–1464* (Manchester, 1993), pp. 118, 120. Andrew
     Holes and Richard Caunton were also involved in obtaining the indulgence, and it appears
     that none of them got on well together.
55   *CPR, 1441–46*, p. 132. Chester appears in other grants from the 1440s as king's clerk or chaplain
     or both (ibid., pp. 73, 314; *1446–52*, p. 209).
56   Ibid., pp. 45, 209.

position by Robert Neville, bishop of Durham, upon the resignation of John Lathom. In 1447, however, Chester apparently felt that his position as master had become insecure, for he petitioned the pope to have it confirmed. On 9 September 1447 a papal mandate instructed William Waynflete, bishop of Winchester, to look into the matter and to confirm Chester's collation if he found it lawful.[57] Although we do not know the outcome of Waynflete's inquiry, it is likely that he found in Chester's favor. Waynflete was the king's confessor, and Henry had probably recommended Chester for the position in the first place.[58] The last of Chester's clerical appointments came in March 1449, when he became a canon of St Paul's, London, and prebendary of Twyford, near London. He died sometime before 1464.[59]

The nature of the dispute between Richard Chester and William Scrope is difficult to untangle. As the papal mandate to Waynflete makes no mention of any dispossession, it would appear that Chester had not yet been ousted from his position at that time.[60] William Scrope became archdeacon of Durham in September 1448, presumably as the choice of Bishop Robert Neville.[61] George Neville, the bishop's nephew, had replaced him as archdeacon by April 1452.[62] In 1451 at the latest, Scrope was occupying the mastership at Greatham.[63] Can it be that the bishop took the hospital from Chester and gave it to Scrope as recompense for his own replacement? The grants to Chester in 1449 suggest that he was at court at that time; if this was the case, his absenteeism could have provided the excuse to replace him with Scrope. If this chain of speculation is correct, we may guess that Margaret's first letter to the bishop (referred to in her extant letter) was written soon after Chester was ousted and appealed to her to intervene, perhaps in 1449 or 1450. The extant letter would have been written somewhat later, perhaps in 1450 or 1451, when we know that Scrope was

---

57 *CPL, 1447–55*, p. 338; VCH: *Durham*, II, p. 122, shows Lathom occupying the office of master in April 1441, and William Scrope in 1451; Chester does not appear in this list.

58 Waynflete would become Henry's chancellor in 1456.

59 He was still vicar of St Mary, Lancashire, in 1455, but given the absence of references to him from the 1450s, one may wonder how long before 1464 his death occurred and whether his last years were spent in failing health.

60 Margaret's insistence in her letters that his possession was lawful *may* support the view that Waynflete had by that time found in Chester's favor, though it would be unwise to make too much of this, as she was hardly apt to have claimed anything less.

61 *Fasti*, VI, p. 113. Two prominent Yorkshire families named Scrope had family seats at Bolton and Masham. John, Lord Scrope of Bolton, was a retainer of Richard Neville, earl of Salisbury, the bishop's brother (M. Hicks, *Warwick the Kingmaker* [Oxford, 1998], pp. 91–2). We are unable to identify any connection of William Scrope to either family.

62 *CPL, 1447–55*, p. 118.

63 *Fasti*, VI, p. 113. He also was granted the wardenship of St Leonard's Hospital, York, sometime prior to January 1456, when he surrendered that post to George Neville (*CPR, 1452–61*, p. 277).

in possession. Her letter to Scrope himself could have been written at any point within this period.

The last three letters involve situations where more information is available and where politics are more directly implicated, involving as they do the activities of the king and queen, as well as the pope and various high-ranking lords.

[17] Queen to Thomas Forest, executor of John Forest, late Dean of Wells, re Nicholas Caraunt
(BL, Add. MS 46,846, fols 44v–45; Monro, pp. 93–4)

By the Quene
Trusty and welbeloved. We suppose verreily that it is wele knowen unto youre wisdam that oure right welbelovyd clerc and secretary M[aister] N. C., dean of Wellys, ought of law, right and good conscience to be recompensed for the reparacion of the said deanry with the goodes of the last recumbent there, to whome ye be executor as it is said. We, havyng consideracion unto the good service that oure said s[ecretary] doth unto us dayly and unto the right and dewte longyng unto hym in this matere, desire and praye yow hertely that, at reverence of us and the rather by contemplacion of this oure prayer, ye wil have oure said secretary towardes yow, in contenting him of his said reparacion, especially recommended, shewing him suche benevolence and favor that he may finde you so frendly disposed and tretable that by your good diligence oure seid secretary may have no cause in your defaulte to pourvey him of other remedie, as we trust yow. In which thing ye shul not mowe ownly deserve of us right especial thanke, but do us also right good and singuler pleasure, and cause us to have you therfor in right tendre remembrance of oure good grace in tyme comyng. Yeven, etc. at etc.
To Maister Thomas Forest, executor of John Forest.

This letter was written in the aftermath of a disputed election to the deanery of Wells Cathedral. In May 1442, Henry VI promised the appointment to his almoner, John de la Bere, as soon as the ailing incumbent, John Forest, should die, and de la Bere petitioned Pope Eugenius IV for confirmation.[64] Against all expectation, John Forest lived until March 1446. The right to elect a new dean lay with the canons of the cathedral chapter, and their unanimous choice fell on Nicholas Caraunt, the queen's secretary, a licentiate in civil law and a prebendary of Wells

64 *CPR, 1441–46*, pp. 442, 447, establish the date of Henry's early support; see *CPL, 1427–47*, pp. 312–14, for the papal reservation. Thomas Gascoigne accused de la Bere of bribing right and left at the papal court to ensure judgement in his favor (T. Gascoigne, *Loci e Libro Veritatum*, ed. J.E.T. Rogers [Oxford, 1881], pp. 35–6).

for a number of years.[65] He was also a local man whose older brother, William, had served as a royal official and was a member of parliament for Somerset.[66]

Thomas Bekynton, bishop of Bath and Wells, confirmed the election; Caraunt made his profession of obedience and was duly installed as dean. De la Bere then brought a suit in the papal court against the bishop, the canons of Wells and Nicholas Caraunt. Eugenius IV ordered the canons to evict Caraunt and install de la Bere, under pain of interdict and excommunication.[67] The canons, meanwhile, had defended their right to elect their preferred candidate in letters to the king, the pope and the archbishop of Canterbury's court. At this juncture, Margaret was asked to enact her traditional role as arbitrator, and both parties agreed to accept her verdict, although good ladyship dictated that she would find in Caraunt's favor. Pope Eugenius died in February 1447, enabling Margaret to address a petition to the new pope, Nicholas V, on behalf of her secretary. The canons submitted their position to him as well, and Nicholas confirmed Margaret's judgment.[68] De la Bere was compensated for his loss and rewarded for his compliance with the see of St David's in July 1447.[69]

John Forest had allowed the deanery and other manors belonging to it to fall into disrepair. Caraunt claimed that the costs of putting the buildings to rights should be borne by the late dean's estate, but the executor, Thomas Forest, proved recalcitrant. Margaret's letter to him makes it clear that she will not be pleased if her secretary is put to further expense to recover what is rightfully his, as too much time and money had already been wasted. But Thomas Forest was not easily intimidated. He had made his career in the service of Cardinal Beaufort, bishop of Winchester, and after Beaufort's death he remained as clerk of the diocese under Bishop William Waynflete.[70] Caraunt appealed to the archbishop of Canterbury's court, and Forest was ordered to pay £227 towards the cost of the repairs. Both parties appealed this decision to the pope, and the dispute was sufficiently important for Henry VI and Margaret to write to Nicholas V requesting that the case be heard by an ecclesiastical tribunal in England. Nicholas granted

---

65   Emden, I, p. 353. Caraunt received a rosary worth 33s 4d as the queen's New Year's gift in 1445–46 and a silver gilt paxbread worth 48s in 1446–47, when he is designated as her secretary (E 101/409, 14 and 17).

66   Roskell, Clark and Rawcliffe, *House of Commons*, II, pp. 480–2.

67   H.C. Maxwell-Lyte and M.C.B. Dawes, eds, *The Register of Thomas Bekynton*, II, Somerset Record Society 50 (1935), pp. xliv–xlvii, for the affair.

68   *CPL, 1447–55*, pp. 2–4, dated 31 July 1447. Margaret subsequently obtained papal permission for Caraunt to hold a further incompatible benefice for a term of ten years (ibid., pp. 43–4, dated 16 May 1448).

69   Emden, I, pp. 556–7.

70   Cardinal Beaufort left Thomas Forest £40 in a second codicil to his will, just before his death in April 1447 (Nicolas, *Testamenta Vetusta*, I, p. 254).

papal authority to three men from the diocese of Salisbury to hand down a final judgment.[71] The outcome is not known, but Caraunt was a prebendary of Salisbury, so the judgment may have gone in his favor. He remained dean of Wells until his death in 1467, and Margaret's secretary until 1458 and possibly longer.[72]

[18] Queen to the Abbess and Convent of Shaftesbury, re Michael Tregury, 2 March [1448]
(BL, Add. MS 46,846, fol. 52v; Monro, pp. 91–3)

By the Quene
Dere and welbeloved in God, we grete you well. And albeit that at oure reverence and prayer ye presented not long agoo our right welbeloved clerk and chapellein Maister Michel Tregury[73] unto the parsonage of Corfcastell, wherof we thanke you, yet nevertheles for many reasonable causes your presenting is not put in execucion, for sone [there]upon oure saide chapelein was by my lordes writing recommended unto the Bisshoprich of Leseux [Lisieux], and so oure said chappellein, eschewing principally the hurte of your title that was like [to] be gretly laboured by our cousin the Marquis of Dorset, and also his owne grete costes and expenses in defensse therof, hath laboured the parsonne of Corf for more ease to resigne frely the said chirch so that it is come to lapse. Wherfore we praye yowe hertly that ye wilbe unto our said chappellein benevolent and good lady as to souffre hym to come in by the bisshop by wey of lapse, sith it is unto your title no hurt nor prejudice at this tyme, and at nexte avoidance, which we trust shalbe in hast by the promocion of our said chappellein, ye may dispose it thanne in observing and keping your right. Wherinne we shall the rather for our said chapellein sake have you in tendre remembrance of our good grace. In which thing, etc. At Ples[hey] the ij day of March, etc.
To th'abbesse and covent of Shaftesbury

Edith Bonham was the prioress of St Edward's Abbey of Shaftesbury, Dorset, until she was elected abbess in November 1441. William Aiscough, bishop of Salisbury, in whose diocese Shaftesbury lay and to whom Margaret refers in her letter, confirmed her election to the king. Her fealty was taken by William Caraunt.[74]

It appears that Edith had agreed to bestow the rectorship of Corfe Castle, which was in the abbey's gift, on the queen's chaplain Michael Tregury at Margaret's request. The presentation had been held in abeyance because there

---

71 *CPL, 1447–55*, p. 116, dated 2 January 1453.
72 Ibid., XI, p. 184.
73 Tregury's name has been spelled many different ways. We have followed the form preferred by Emden and the *ODNB*. In the letter, it is spelled 'Tregr' with an extension mark.
74 *CPR, 1441–46*, pp. 27, 32. She died before March 1460, when the prioress and convent had license to elect her successor (*CPR, 1452–61*, p. 573).

was a possibility that Tregury would receive a higher preferment. The bishop of Lisieux died in July 1447, and Henry VI recommended Tregury as his successor. Lisieux was in English-held Normandy and subject to the king of England. Nevertheless, the canons of Lisieux unanimously elected the future chronicler Thomas Basin as their bishop, and his appointment was confirmed by Pope Nicholas V in October. Basin did homage to Henry VI but broke his oath in August 1449 when the war between England and France resumed. By his own account, Basin opened the gates of the city and handed it over to King Charles VII of France.[75]

Disputes over benefices could be costly to all concerned, and Tregury acted prudently, applying himself to persuading the incumbent at Corfe to 'resigne frely' so as not to complicate matters. The castle and lordship of Corfe had been granted to John Beaufort, the first earl of Somerset, by his half-brother Henry IV,[76] which gave the Beauforts, as lords of Corfe, a claim to present to the rectorship. In 1447 Corfe was held by John's son, Edmund Beaufort, marquess of Dorset, who apparently had a mind to exercise his right of presentment. On 2 March 1448, Margaret wrote to Edith from Pleshey to urge her to confirm the grant to Tregury. She made it clear that she recognized the abbey's rights over those of Beaufort and declared that the bishop of Salisbury was willing to ratify the appointment 'by way of lapse,' thus endorsing Edith's right to present. Furthermore, it was highly likely that Tregury would receive another promotion in the near future, in which case the abbess would once again have the benefice in her gift.

And this is precisely what happened, although not in the way Margaret anticipated. In August 1449, Richard Talbot, archbishop of Dublin, died. Richard, duke of York, had arrived in Dublin as the king's lieutenant in Ireland only a month earlier, and Talbot's death could not have come at a more opportune time. A feud between the Talbots and the earls of Ormond had smoldered on and off for twenty years, seriously disturbing the always fragile balance of Irish politics. York had brought Ormond with him as his deputy, and one of his first tasks was to quell the enmity between the archbishop and the earl. And with Richard Talbot dead, York named Michael Tregury as his successor.

Tregury had been elected a fellow of Exeter College, Oxford, in 1422; he became a senior proctor of the university in 1434.[77] In 1439, he was appointed a rector of the University of Caen, founded in Henry VI's name in 1431. He occupied this position for about a year, but his subsequent whereabouts are unknown. If

75   M. Spencer, *Thomas Basin (1412–1490): The History of Charles VII and Louis XI* (Nieuwkoop, 1997), pp. 20–4.
76   G.L. Harriss, *Cardinal Beaufort* (Oxford, 1988), p. 353.
77   Emden, III, p. 1894, for his career.

he remained in Normandy, he probably served in the administration of the duke of York, who was the king's lieutenant there from 1441 to 1445. Either Tregury accompanied the earl of Suffolk's entourage to Rouen to form part of Margaret's household as one of her chaplains, or he was already in Rouen and became attached to her household when she arrived there in 1445.[78] He received New Year's gifts from the queen in every year thereafter until he became archbishop, when Margaret gave him his episcopal ring.[79] He held several benefices after 1445, but was apparently never confirmed as rector of Corfe.[80]

York's license to elect was granted seven days after Talbot's death, too soon for it to have been at the direct request of Queen Margaret.[81] Why Tregury was York's choice for a position at the center of the Irish administration is a mystery, unless his abilities had come to the duke's notice in Normandy in the early 1440s. Or did York choose Tregury because he knew that it would please the queen? Tregury had a checkered career as archbishop in his relations with the papacy until his death in 1471, but he never, apparently, became embroiled in Irish politics. If he was indeed apolitical, this may have provided an additional reason for York's choice.

[19] **Queen to the Chapter of Exeter Cathedral re John Hals, 7 November [1458]**[82]
(From *English Historical Documents*, IV, ed. A.R. Myers, p. 280,
© 1969 Routledge, reproduced by permission of Taylor & Francis Books UK;
from Exeter Cathedral MS 3498/23)

Trusty and well-beloved, we greet you well. Keeping well our remembrance how that both my lord and we have now lately written unto you at various times our

78   He was paid £9 2s in the account for her household in transit (BL, Add. MS 23,938).
79   A rosary worth £1 10s 8d in 1445–46; a paxbread worth 18s 8d in 1446–47; a silver salt worth £2 0s 8d in 1448–49 (E 101/409/14 and 17; E 101/410/2). A second gift in 1448–49 is illegible, but a 'gold pontifical' is in the list of purchases, and Margaret may have presented it to him when his election as archbishop was confirmed.
80   Archdeacon of Barnstaple, June 1445; rector of Arksey, Yorkshire, June 1446 to June 1447; canon and prebendary of Crediton, Devon, June 1447; rector of Swafield, Norfolk, June 1447–April 1448; canon and prebendary of Exeter, no date given.
81   P.A. Johnson, *Duke Richard of York 1411–1460* (Oxford, 1988), p. 74 and n. 171. Tregury's election was confirmed by the crown on 23 September (*CPR, 1446–52*, p. 304), and the pope's approval came in October (*CPL, 1447–55*, p. 439).
82   This letter and a similar one from King Henry bear no year date, but have traditionally been ascribed to 1457, probably based on John Le Neve's original *Fasti* of 1716, p. 85. In the most recent edition of the *Fasti*, however, Joyce M. Horn established that Hals's predecessor, John Cobethorn, was dean and prebendary of Exeter until his death in 1458, 'probably during Michaelmas term', and that Hals became dean in that year (*Fasti*, IX, pp. 5 and 48). A papal dispensation at Margaret's petition for Hals to hold three incompatible benefices, dated

several letters of especial recommendation for our right well beloved clerk Master John Hals, our chancellor, to the deanery of the cathedral church of Exeter in your next election. Whereupon since our said writing we understand by various reports made to us that some persons of you, having no regard that my lord is your founder, whose request you own in duty to obey before all other, labour the contrary of my lord's said intention and ours, to our great marvel and displeasure if it be so. Wherefore we desire and heartily pray you forthwith that for reverence of us, leaving aside and apart all other labours and means you will, considering the hearty and immutable desire that we have to our said clerk's preservation at this time, be inclined and yield to the accomplishment of my lord's invariable intention and ours in this matter, giving my lord's highness and us no other cause than to have everyone of you according to your desert in such things as you may have to do towards us both, for your preservation and also otherwise in tender remembrance of our good grace for this time to come. Praying you further that unto our trusty and well beloved squire Edward Ellesmere, master of our jewels, fully instructed of our intention, you will give full faith and credence in such things touching the foregoing as he shall declare unto you on our behalf. As we trust you in this thing you may deserve of us especial and singular thanks to our great pleasure on this account in time to come. Given under our signet at Westminster the 7th day of November.

(Signed) Marguerite

John Hals joined Margaret's household as one of her chaplains not long after she arrived in England, but he was less fortunate than Tregury and Caraunt in achieving early ecclesiastical promotion.[83] His first opportunity came when Edmund Lacy, bishop of Exeter, died in September 1455. Lacy's death was not unexpected; he was probably in his mid-eighties.[84] There is some indication that Margaret was rallying support for the promotion of Hals to the see of Exeter as early as 1453. She gave rings to the duke of Somerset and the earl of Wiltshire (both men of considerable influence in the West Country), probably as tokens to authenticate them as her emissaries in whatever negotiations seemed

25 September 1457, cannot be used as evidence that a particular one was envisioned (*CPL, 1455–64*, pp. 153–4). A date of 1458 places the letters in a more likely political context, as we argue below.

83 Hals is ranked with the dean of the Chapel Royal and the king's almoner in Margaret's New Years' gift lists. He received a rosary worth 30s 8d in 1445–46, a parcel-gilt paxbread worth 15s 4d in 1446–47, a silver salt of uncertain, but undoubtedly greater value in 1448–49, a rosary worth 30s in 1451–52, and a silver-gilt paxbread worth 43s 9d in 1452–53 (E 101/409/14 and 17; E 101/410/2 and 8; Myers, 'Jewels', p. 223).

84 *ODNB*, XXXII, p. 179. In 1447 he appointed a suffragan to oversee the diocese because of his frailty.

appropriate with members of the cathedral chapter.[85] It is likely that King Henry recommended Hals as Lacy's successor during the latter's lifetime, which was not unusual. Be that as it may, when Bishop Lacy died in 1455 the canons elected John Hals 'in answer to royal letters', and Pope Calixtus III confirmed his appointment.[86]

Unfortunately for Hals, there was a stumbling block. During King Henry's mental breakdown Thomas Bourgchier, bishop of Ely, had been promoted to the archbishopric of Canterbury following the death of John Kemp. The powerful Neville clan headed by the earl of Salisbury, who was chancellor in 1454, hoped to have George Neville, Salisbury's youngest son, replace Bourgchier as bishop of Ely. Instead, the choice fell on William Gray. To placate the Nevilles, the council promised that the next vacant bishopric would be awarded to George.[87] In May 1455, Salisbury and the Neville clan supported the duke of York's rebellion, defeating the king's forces at the battle of St Albans, where they took Henry VI into polite custody. Parliament was summoned in July to justify and legalize York's actions. King Henry was unable or unwilling to attend its second session in the autumn, and the commons requested that York become protector for a second time.

The second protectorate came into being just as Hals was about to be installed as bishop of Exeter, and the Nevilles, on whose support York depended, demanded that the promise to George Neville be honored. The crown was forced to revise its position. Two letters to the pope in Henry VI's name and also signed by the council requested that the bishopric be given to Neville.[88] Calixtus III was not pleased. He had provided Hals at Henry VI's specific request, and Hals was by far the more suitable candidate: he was Devon-born, a fellow of Oriel College, Oxford, with a good reputation as a scholar; he had been a prebendary of Exeter Cathedral since 1438 and was well thought of at court.[89] George Neville, then 'in or about his twenty-fourth year', was undoubtedly precocious, but he was still too young to be consecrated as a bishop. More pressure was brought to bear; perhaps

---

85   Myers, 'Jewels', pp. 223, 227. Myers assumed that Margaret was trying to obtain the archdeaconry of Norwich for Hals. This seems unlikely. Hals had been appointed archdeacon of Norfolk in 1448 by Walter Lyhert, bishop of Norwich, who was also the queen's confessor. Lyhert could easily appoint Hals to Norwich and probably did so, as he appears in that capacity in February 1456 (*Fasti*, IV, p. 27). There is no reason why Somerset or Wiltshire would have concerned themselves with an archdeaconry in East Anglia, but their influence would have been valuable in any bid for the bishopric of Exeter.

86   Harvey, *England, Rome and the Papacy*, p. 189; *CPL, 1455–64*, p. 30.

87   *PPC*, VI, p. 168.

88   *Foedera*, XI, pp. 367–8, dated 6 November 1455; *PPC*, VI, pp. 265–7, dated 4 December 1455. Henry claimed to have 'forgotten' the promise regarding George Neville. This was nonsense: as he was ill and *non compos mentis* at the time it was made, he probably never knew about it!

89   Emden, II, pp. 856–7, for his biography.

even Margaret added her own petition to the pope at this time.[90] If she did, it was because York and the Nevilles were in control, and discretion was the better part of valor. John Hals very prudently declined the appointment, and the pope compromised. In substituting Neville for Hals, he stipulated that George was to be the bishop-elect, as he could not be consecrated until he was at least twenty-seven.[91] Neville, who by then was chancellor of Oxford, was content to draw the temporalities of his see without actually residing there – he remained in Oxford.[92]

With the installment of new government officers that followed the end of the second protectorate, Lawrence Booth became keeper of the privy seal in September 1456, while Hals replaced him as Margaret's chancellor. And when John Cobethorn, dean of Exeter, died in 1458, Margaret was determined that this time John Hals would get his just reward. Both she and the king wrote to the cathedral chapter recommending him to the canons.[93] But Hals was not now automatically acceptable as dean. It may be that George Neville, who was about to be consecrated, did not want the man he had supplanted installed as dean of his cathedral.[94] Whatever the cause, both the king's and queen's letters make it clear that this was not their first request, and Margaret's is the more strongly written: she will not take no for an answer.[95] Edward Ellesmere, the bearer of both letters, had been keeper of the queen's jewels since 1451 and was one of her most trusted servants. He had obviously been briefed to argue the case in detail, not just to make the queen's wish known. The royal will prevailed, and John Hals was installed as dean of Exeter.

As an interesting sideline to all of this, in the scramble to make George Neville acceptable as bishop, he had been given two hasty preferments, one of them as warden of the rich Hospital of St Leonard, York, in January 1456. Hals was awarded the wardenship of St Leonard's in 1458, perhaps in part as a compensation for the lost bishopric.[96]

---

90 Calixtus wrote to both Henry and Margaret individually after he finally gave in (Corpus Christi, Cambridge, MS 170, pp. 235–6). This suggests that the queen had also weighed in on the matter.

91 *CPL, 1455–64*, pp. 30–1, dated 4–5 February 1456. The letters to Henry and Margaret, undated, were probably written at this time, as the entry makes note of a separate letter having been sent to the king. See also *CPR, 1462–61*, p. 281, dated 21 March 1456; *Foedera*, XI, p. 376.

92 He had become chancellor of Oxford in 1453 in succession to Gilbert Kymer, who also appears in Margaret's correspondence (Emden, II, p. 1347; above, pp. 19–20, for Kymer).

93 Henry's letter, dated 31 October, is published in *EHD*, IV, p. 281 (from Exeter Cathedral MS. 3498/22).

94 He was consecrated 25 November 1458 (Emden, II, p. 1347).

95 Maurer, pp. 64–5.

96 *CPR, 1452–61*, pp. 277, 470. In order to grant the wardenship to George Neville in 1456, the clerk to whom Henry VI had previously given it had to be dispossessed. George presumably

Hals had to wait only a short time for his next promotion, until Reginald Boulers, bishop of Coventry and Lichfield, died in 1459.[97] As Bishop of Coventry and Lichfield, Hals was instrumental in easing out the aging and infirm John de la Bere, bishop of St David's, and in installing in his place John Morton, 'a canon of Salisbury, a doctor of laws, chancellor of Edward prince of Wales, eldest son of king Henry, and acceptable to the said king and to queen Margaret'.[98]

Hals remained a loyal Lancastrian.[99] He was in the north with the Lancastrian lords supporting Margaret's attempts to regain control of the country in 1460 after the battle of Northampton in which Henry VI had been captured. The king was held in London while the earl of Warwick ruled in his name. Hals was one of two bishops who signed the pledge made by the Lancastrian lords to uphold the treaty of Lincluden between Queen Margaret and Mary of Guelders, Queen of Scots, in which a marriage between Edward, Prince of Wales, and a Scottish princess was mooted in exchange for Scottish aid for the Lancastrian cause.[100]

When Warwick changed his allegiance in 1470 and restored Henry VI to the throne, Hals became keeper of the privy seal, serving the short-lived government until the final defeat of the Lancastrians at Tewkesbury in May 1471. With all hope gone, Hals made his peace with the Yorkist regime and was pardoned by Edward IV. He outlasted the Yorkist dynasty and died in 1490.

recovered it after Edward IV became king in 1461 as Emden notes that he was 'still' warden in 1465.

97   *CPR, 1452–61*, p. 598; *Foedera* XI, p. 436.

98   *CPL, 1455–64*, p. 556, dated 12 September 1459.

99   According to a story told in J. Chandler, ed., *John Leland's Itinerary* (Stroud, 1993), p. 396, Hals arranged for Margaret to stay at Eccleshall Castle, one of his seats as bishop of Coventry–Lichfield, after the battle of Blore Heath in September 1459.

100   BNF, MS Fr. 20488, fol. 23. See also M. Hicks, 'A Minute of the Lancastrian Council at York, 20 January 1461', *Northern History* 35 (1999), pp. 214–21.

Three

POSITION WANTED

Margaret also exercised good ladyship by intervening on behalf of people who were seeking secular positions. Most of them had no detectable personal connection to the queen.[1] Instead, they were recommended to her by persons within the royal establishment, usually identified only by vague and general allusion (e.g., 'certain [of] our servants right nigh attending about our person' in the first letter). In the last two letters she followed up on appointments made by King Henry. In these, as in her letters recommending her clerics or praising the virtues of marriageable women desired by would-be suitors, Margaret often took pains to assert the candidates' abilities and suitability for the position in question as if they were known quantities.

We still speak of an 'old boy's network', often with deprecation. In Margaret's day, networking was the accepted way to obtain career advancement. The jobseeker would approach a friend or relative who was in a position to assist.[2] That person tended to have higher status or better connections than the petitioner. The appeal might then be passed to yet another party, deemed to be in an even better position to influence the outcome. If successful, the result was a credit to whoever helped to speed it on its way; it affirmed that person's status and importance. When Margaret's intervention or influence encroached upon established rights of provision or election, they were heartily resented. Many of her efforts to dispense patronage involved walking a tightrope between well-perceived benefaction and ill-perceived interference. The letters concerning Alexander Manning are a case in point.

---

1   The exception is 'Master J.C.' of the last letter, identified as the queen's 'late (i.e. recent) clerk and familiar servant'.
2   Or the reverse might occur, with someone adopting a mentoring position.

[20] Queen to the Mayor, Bailiffs and Commons of Coventry re T[homas] Bate, 6 March [1446 preferred, but no later than 1448]
(BL, Add. MS 46,846, fol. 47v; Monro, pp. 139–40)

By the Quene

Trusty and welbeloved, we grete you wel. And for asmoch as we be enformed that the recordership of the cite of Coventre is like within shorte tyme to be voide, unto your disposicion and yefte; we, desiring th'encres, firtherance and preferring of oure wel[beloved] T. Bate, aswel for his suffisiant of cunnyng [knowledge] and habilite therto as in especial for the humble instance and prayer of certein [of] oure servants right negh attending aboute oure personne, pray yow right hertly that, atte reverence of us sith it is oure first request of you after our coronacion, ye wil have the seid T. unto the said occupacion of recorder, when it shall nexte voide, bifore al other especialy recommended, as our ful trust is in you. In which thing ye shul not mowe oonly to do us greit pleasure, and deserve of us especial thanke, but also cause us to have you in remembrance of oure good grace therfore in tyme comyng. And of your good disposicion to our pleasure in this matere ye will acerteine us by the bringer of thise. Yeven at P. the vi day of Marche.

To the Mair, Baillifs, and good Communes of the city of Coventre.

Although this letter bears only a partial date, Margaret's observation that this was her first request to the city since her coronation – and that she called attention to this fact – tempts us to date it as early as 1446. Although the text contains many stock phrases, she seems particularly concerned to express her future gratitude, as well as to find out quickly in what spirit her request was received. These things too may evoke some sense of the young woman, to whom queenship was still new.

Thomas Bate was by this time well-established as a JP in Warwickshire.[3] He had also been an MP for the county in 1442 and would serve again in 1449. Through marriage he acquired links to the Stafford family and was a feed councilor to the duke of Buckingham from 1444 to 1455.[4] He may have been the same Thomas Bate who either lived or had property on Much Park Street in Coventry and who contributed 6s 8d towards a loan of £100 to the king in 1444, possibly to help bring Margaret to England.[5]

The office of recorder had been held by William Donyngton from 1430, and he continued in it well into 1448.[6] During the Michaelmas leet of 1448, however,

3 *CPR, 1441–46*, p. 480. He had served continuously since November 1441.
4 Wedgwood, p. 50; I. Rowney, 'Government and Patronage in the Fifteenth Century: Staffordshire, 1439–59', *Midland History* 8 (1983), p. 51; Carpenter, *Locality and Polity*, p. 699.
5 Harris, *Coventry Leet Book*, p. 212. Compared to other contributions, this sum falls into the upper middle range, but suggests no particular reason for the queen's favor.
6 Ibid., pp. 134, 157, 204, 218, 226, 228, 232.

it was determined that when Donyngton either resigned or died, he should be followed in office by Thomas Litelton. In January 1449, Donyngton still appears as recorder, but it was noted that 'at the Easter view of frankpledge last past Thomas Litelton was chosen recorder and a justice of the peace' in Donyngton's name.[7] Finally, during the Easter leet of 1449, the recorder was granted £10 for life, and it was decided that William Donyngton should thereafter 'be of counsel to the city' as he had been before serving as recorder.[8] Litelton then held the office into 1455. Apparently, he died during that year, for at the Michaelmas leet Henry Boteler was elected recorder.[9]

Margaret's request seems to have been ignored. Thomas Bate never held office as recorder, but his career did not suffer. Indeed, it took off: he continued to serve as a JP for Warwick and on numerous commissions in the county throughout the rest of the 1440s and well into the 1450s.[10] He died in the summer of 1459.[11]

[21] Queen to Mayor and Corporation of Southampton re Robert Bedale
(BL, Add. MS 46,846, fol. 54; Monro, p. 113)

By the Quene

Trusty and welbeloved. For asmuch as our welbeloved Robert Bedale, [who] desireth to do you service in th'office of waterbailif, is sergeant of Southamton, to the which, as we be enformed, he is right hable and sufficiant aswell in his trouth and discrecion as in other cunnyng; we, at instance and supplicacion of certein our servantes attendinge right negh aboute oure personne, desire and pray you therfore that, at reverence of us, ye will have the said Robert to the said occupacion especially recommended and admitte hym thereto bifore all other, as we truste you. In which thing, etc. At Wyndsor, the etc.

To the Mair and his brethern of Southamton

The water bailiff was an officer charged with the enforcement of shipping regulations, who had some involvement in the search and the collection of customs.[12]

---

7   Ibid., pp. 234, 235. These notices may be what gave Rowney the impression that Margaret had written to the city in 1448. A date of 1448 assumes that the need to replace Donyngton had come about suddenly. The reference to Margaret's coronation makes an earlier date more likely.
8   Ibid., pp. 335–6.
9   Ibid., pp. 266, 270, 276, 278, 280, 283.
10 *CPR, 1446–52*, pp. 139, 270, 299, 412, 596; *CPR, 1452–61*, pp. 44, 58, 343, 680.
11 Wedgwood, p. 50, will dated 24 June 1459; *CPR, 1452–61*, p. 508, referred to as deceased on 8 July of that year.
12 The *OED* offers examples of this usage from the mid-1400s. C. Barron, *London in the Later Middle Ages* (Oxford, 2004), pp. 191–2: the water bailiff was responsible for ensuring that nets and weirs on a river did not hinder the passage of young fish and for removing those that were illegal.

From the context, the position was in the gift of the City of Southampton and presumably paid by them, as opposed to the searchers, who were royal appointments made by the treasurer. In her letter Margaret claims that Robert Bedale's performance in his current position as sergeant of Southampton demonstrates his fitness for the position.[13] In fact, Bedale already had experience in the port, for in 1443 he was appointed surveyor of the search for Southampton during pleasure, along with John Hunter. We do not know the date – or outcome – of the queen's letter, but on 24 July 1455, Bedale and Robert Dukett were appointed controllers of the search in the port of Southampton.[14] The date of Robert Bedale's second known appointment raises some questions. This would have been soon after the first battle of St Albans. Viscount Bourgchier had become treasurer, replacing the earl of Wiltshire who had fought with the king's forces. If, as seems likely, Margaret's letter to Southampton was written before 1455, did she also play some part in recommending him for the position of controller? Or was Bedale simply a good man at what he did, as competent and knowledgeable as claimed? Whatever the case, he seems to have avoided political entanglements. In November 1461, under Edward IV, he was appointed controller of the scrutiny in the port of Southampton.[15]

[22] Queen to the Bishop of Norwich re T.S. [in or after 1448?]
(BL, Add. MS 46,846, fol. 57; Monro, pp. 119–20)

By the Quene
Reverend fader, etc. And for asmoche as our squier, Edmond Clere, desireth to have his cousin T.S. to become sergeant of Norwich by the grant of the mair, aldermen and commonalte of the cite of Norwich; we, havyng consideracion that thei wol be gretly reuled and demened by you in this partie, as it is said, pray you right hertly that, in accomplissement of our said squier['s] entencion in this mater, ye will have the said T. towardes your good lordship especialy recommended, and do such diligence by all goodly meenes that the said citezenis wol, at your request in contemplacion of our lettres at this tyme, admitte the seid T. unto th'occupacion aboveseid. As our singuler, etc. Yeven, etc.
To the Bisshop of Norwiche

This letter is unusual in its specific identification of the person who had appealed to Margaret for assistance rather than the more frequent – and vague – attribution

---

13   The sergeant of a town was a civil servant charged with carrying out the orders of its governing body. He might also be asked to arrest offenders or to summon persons to appear before the mayor and council.
14   *CPR, 1441–46*, p. 222; *1452–61*, p. 245.
15   *CPR, 1461–67*, p. 20.

of the appeal to unnamed servants. This does not, unfortunately, help us to identify T.S., who could have been any sort of distant relation of Edmund Clere.[16] The most we can offer is that his given name was likely to have been Thomas.[17]

The bishop of Norwich to whom Margaret wrote was Walter Lyhert, who had been provided by the pope in January 1446.[18] Lyhert had accompanied the duke of Suffolk to Rouen in 1444, being paid £15 18s 6d for his service, and he probably became Margaret's confessor at that time or shortly after when her household was established in England.[19] She gave him a rosary of chalcedony worth £8 at New Year 1446, her first as queen.[20] In July 1447, Henry named Lyhert to head an embassy to continue the peace negotiations with Charles VII before going on to attend an ecclesiastical conference in Lyons. He was away from England for some time, perhaps a year.[21] This letter would have been written in or after 1448 when he became active in Norfolk.[22]

It appears that Margaret had written to the city fathers of Norwich to recommend T.S. for what amounted to a civil service position. Nevertheless, she considered Lyhert's influence to be such that a word from him would carry more effective weight. This letter illustrates the chains of mediatory appeal: T.S. to Clere, Clere to Margaret, and Margaret to Lyhert – before the matter was laid before those who could actually decide it: the mayor and corporation of Norwich.

---

16   Two men named Edmund Clere were active during the mid-fifteenth century. They have been badly conflated by Wedgwood, p. 189. Only one was a king's esquire in the 1440s and 1450s: Edmund Clere of Ormesby. See below, p. 204, n. 41.

17   Although he might have been Thomas Sharnebourne, who had strong affiliations in Norfolk and was escheator and later sheriff of the county, as a member of Margaret's household he would scarcely have needed Clere to bring him to the queen's attention. But perhaps Lyhert knew Clere, making his recommendation 'useful' to the networking process.

18   Emden, II, p. 1188. He was enthroned in April.

19   BL, Add. MS 23,938. The January 1446 grant to Lyhert of the temporalities of the bishopric of Norwich refers to him as 'king's clerk' (*CPR, 1441–46*, p. 428), but this does not necessarily mean that he could not have been the queen's confessor as well.

20   E 101/409/14. Margaret also gave him a pair of gilded phials at New Year 1447 (E 101/409/17).

21   Wolffe, *Henry VI*, p. 194. Henry wrote to Charles on 28 July, and the embassy obtained an extension of the truce on 15 October. Lyhert had returned to England by 8 May 1448, when he was appointed JP for Norfolk and named to a commission of oyer and terminer on 13 September (*CPR, 1446–52*, pp. 236, 592).

22   Ample evidence exists in the Paston letters of Bishop Lyhert's active engagement in matters involving his diocese and local Norwich politics until his death in 1472.

[23] Queen to John Gedney, Citizen and Alderman of the City of London, re
Walter Briggs [1447?]
(BL, Add. MS 46,846, fols 57v–58; Monro, pp. 158–9)

By the Quene
Trusty, etc. And for asmoche as Waultier Brigger[23] hertly desireth to do you and
the citee service in th'occupacion of under sherreve in the countie of Midd[lesex],
wherto he is right able and suffisant aswell in his trouth, discrecion and cunnyng
as in other pollice [policy], sadnesse and good governance, as it is said; we, havyng
consideracion unto the premisses with his merites and desertes, and in especial
at instans and supplicacion of certein oure servantes attending right negh aboute
oure persone, to whoom the seid W. is cousine as we understande, desire and
pray you hertly that, as [*sic*, at] reverence of us, ye will have the seid W. unto the
seid occupacion, as fer as in you is, right tenderly recommended, and do therin
such diligence t'excite and sture all such personnes, citezeins of the seid cite of
London, that by you and the commonalte there shulbe elit shireves for this nexte
yere commyng t'accepte and admitte hym, for oure sake, to the seid occupacion
of undersher[eve] in the countie abovesaid; havyng th'expedicion of this matter so
tenderly to hert that we may verreily knowe the continuance of the benevolence
and good disposicion that ye have be of towardes us and oure request hirbefore, to
th'accomplissement of our entencion in this mater, wherof we thanke you. And that
he may finde thise oure lettres unto hym effectuelx and vailable, as our singuler trust
is in you. In which thing ye shull not oonly do us right greet pleasure and deserve
of us especial thanke, but cause us also to have you in tendre remembrance of our
goode grace, therfore, in tyme comyng. Yeven, etc.
To John Gedney, citezein and alderman of the cite of L[ondon]

By the fifteenth century, the office of sheriff had come to be regarded as a kind
of training post for younger men who might in due course become mayor of
London. Their duties, owed to both city and crown, were wide-ranging, involving
the maintenance of law and order on behalf of both parties and the payment of
the city's annual farm to the exchequer. Complicating matters, the two sheriffs
of London served as sheriffs for the county of Middlesex as well. Because of the
difficulties inherent in administering both city and county, the sheriffs appointed
two undersheriffs for London and one for Middlesex. If the office of sheriff
constituted a stepping stone, that of undersheriff was a starting point.[24]

John Gedney was a prominent draper of London, who served twice as its

23   In the manuscript, his surname is spelled 'Brigger' with an ending 'r'. We have found no
     approximations of this name in the patent rolls. We have, however, found various references
     to persons named Brig(g)e(s), with 'u' or 'y' sometimes providing a variant for 'i', and one of
     them is a Walter. It may be that some form of this surname was intended.
24   Barron, *London*, pp. 159, 162, 357.

mayor over a lengthy career. He was sheriff in 1417–18.[25] Ten years later, in 1427–28, he held the mayoralty for the first time.[26] Over the years he appears regularly in the records in connection with property transactions, loans to the crown and as a complainant in cases of debt.[27] During the 1440s he again became more active in city government and served a second term as mayor in 1447–48.[28] Gedney appears to have died soon after it expired; he was present for his successor's installation in October 1448, but does not appear in the civic records thereafter.[29] On 22 February 1449, the escheator for Middlesex was ordered to take the fealty of Joan Gedney and other feoffees for property held by John Gedney 'now deceased'.[30]

Although this letter could have been written in any year prior to John Gedney's second term as mayor, it most likely dates to shortly before the shrieval election of September 1447. The sheriffs were chosen, one by direct election and the other by mayoral appointment, before the next mayor's election, but at this point in his life Gedney could not have been considered a 'dark horse' candidate. His availability for office would have been known and, since many were reluctant to take on its stresses, his election could have been a foregone conclusion. In any event, he was a man of considerable influence among his colleagues, whose word would be presumed to carry weight. We do not know if Margaret succeeded in obtaining Briggs's appointment, though it seems unlikely.[31] Indeed, we have had little success in tracking him down, having found only one reference to a Walter Brigge who claimed a debt of 40 marks was owed him. As the pardon for the debtor's failure to appear was issued in London, he may have been our man.[32]

The next three letters all involve the case of Alexander Manning, who sought to regain the post of keeper of Newgate prison, from which he had been summarily dismissed. They show us a situation in which Margaret's tenacity ran head-on against the determined independence of the London city government.

25 Ibid., p. 338; *CPR, 1416–22*, p. 124.
26 Barron, *London*, p. 340. As part of his mayoral duties he also served as escheator for the city (ibid., p. 153; *CPR, 1422–29*, pp. 477, 526).
27 *CPR, 1416–22*, pp. 151, 234–5; *1422–29*, pp. 28, 150, 318–19, 386, 483; *1429–36*, p. 441; *1436–41*, pp. 11, 333, 394, 459, 464, 520; *1441–46*, p. 19.
28 Barron, *London*, p. 342; *CPR, 1446–52*, pp. 114, 161, 178, 211.
29 R.R. Sharpe, *Calendar of Letter-Books ... of the City of London: Letter Book K (1911)*, p. 327.
30 *CCR, 1447–54*, pp. 89–90. In 1451, Joan received a grant from the customs in the port of London in repayment of £200 loaned in defense of the realm (*CPR, 1446–52*, p. 452). In 1452, it was noted that John Gedney had died without an heir (*CPR, 1452–61*, p. 28).
31 Barron, *London*, pp. 357–8, for the undersheriffs of London. Briggs does not appear.
32 *CPR, 1441–46*, p. 301. This was in 1444.

[24] **Queen to the Sheriffs of London re Alexander Manning, 24 [October 1450]**
(BL, Add. MS 46,846, fols 46v–47; Monro, pp. 161–2)

By the Quene

Trusty and welbeloved. We suppose verreily that it is clerely in your remembrance howe that now late, for certein consideracions and greete instance, we wrote unto you for the recommendacion of Alexandre Mannyng unto th'office of keper of Newgate, longyng unto your disposicion as it is said, wherin as yet oure said writing hath take noon effecte ne expedicion, unto oure great merveil. Wherfore we desire and praye eftesones, right affectuously, that, at reverence of us, ye wil accepte and restore the said Mannyng ayeine unto the said office, with suche tendernesse and faver that he may perceive thise oure lettres unto him advailable, to th'accomplissement of our entencion in this partie. In which thinge ye shul, etc. Yeven, etc. at P., etc. the xxiiij day, etc.

To the Shirefs of the Cite of London

[25] **Queen to the Sheriffs that next shall be of the City of London re Alexander Manning [September 1451]**
(BL, Add. MS 46,846, fol. 54; Monro, pp. 162–3)

By the Quene

Trusty and welbeloved, we grete you well. And for asmoche as our welbeloved Alisaundre Mannyng desireth to do yow service in th'office of keping of Newgate, to the which, as we understand, he is right hable and suffisant, both in his trouth and discrecion and also in his governance, like as for the tyme that he occupied it hirbifore he was founden of good bering and of sad disposicion, as it is said. We, atte instans and supplicacion of certein oure servantes right negh attending about our personne, desire and hertly pray you that, atte reverence of us, ye will have him towardes you especialy recommended and at Michel masse nexte commyng t'admitte him to the said office, as we truste you. In which thinge, etc. At W. the, etc.

To the Shirefs that nexte shalbe of the cite of London

[26] **Queen to the Mayor of the City of London re Alexander Manning [September 1451]**
(BL, Add. MS 46,846, fols 54–54v; Monro, p. 163)

By the Quene

Trusty and welbeloved, we grete, etc. And for asmuch as our welbeloved A. Mannyng desireth to do service in th'office (*ut supra usque* recommended), exciting and stering the shirefs that shalbe for the nexte yere to admitte him to the said office at Michelmasse nexte commyng, after th'entencion of oure writyng unto theym in that bihalf, as we truste yow. In whiche thing, etc. *Ut supra, etc.*

To the Mair of the cite of London

The year 1450 was difficult for the mayor and sheriffs of London. When parliament resumed at Westminster in January, it was already in a state of upheaval over the loss of Normandy the previous autumn. Soldiers who were supposed to have gone to France as reinforcements were now pillaging the countryside, even as refugees had begun to trickle back across the Channel. By the end of the month, the duke of Suffolk, whom public opinion held responsible for the loss, had been arrested, placed in the Tower and charged with treason. A nightly watch was set in the city, while the people went 'in doute and feer' of the violence that might result from the lords coming to attend the parliament armed to the teeth.[33]

A rebellion raised by Jack Cade began in June at Blackheath, south of the city. The rebels occupied Southwark and crossed the bridge into London itself. For several days, they looted and murdered before being expelled on the morning of 6 July after a night-long battle on the bridge.[34] The end of the rebellion brought no respite to London, for the summer saw a fresh influx of disaffected soldiers returning from Normandy, some with their families and all their belongings. The mayor, aldermen and sheriffs were constantly on their guard, riding about the city with armed officers to keep the peace.[35] The situation remained tense into autumn. On 27 September 1450, Richard, duke of York, entered London with a large body of retainers, on his way to Westminster to see the king.[36] His arrival stirred up fresh agitation and considerable curiosity. It also coincided with the annual change of the city authorities, for on Michaelmas Eve, 28 September, the sheriffs traditionally handed over the keys of the city prisons to the mayor, to be passed on to the newly elected sheriffs. The requirements of this ancient ceremony distracted their attention from their peacekeeping duties, and a riot erupted in Newgate.

The prison at Newgate had recently been rebuilt thanks to the generous bequest of London's most famous mayor, Richard Whittington. It housed men (and women) accused of serious crimes. Hardened criminals were locked in airless basement cells, but less serious offenders, troublemakers whom the city officials preferred to keep under lock and key and men incarcerated for political reasons (especially those who could afford to pay), had more agreeable accommodation. They were lodged in the turret over the gate and allowed to take the air on the flat roof of the prison. Cells opening off the great hall were equipped with comforts

33 Flenley, 'Bale's Chronicle', pp. 125–8.
34 Griffiths, pp. 610–65.
35 Flenley, 'Bale's Chronicle', pp. 134–5.
36 'Benet's Chronicle', p. 202: 'On the Feast of Sts. Cosmos and Damien'.

such as chimneys and privies and housed less dangerous men.[37] On 28 September, the keeper of Newgate, Alexander Manning, was unwise enough to allow some of his charges up onto the roof. Possibly he succumbed to a combination of bribery and curiosity, hoping to catch a glimpse of the duke of York or his men. Whatever the reason, Manning released too many prisoners, and they got out of hand, breaking down doors and doing considerable damage. They stormed up onto the roof and bombarded passersby with stones and other missiles. Newgate was a busy thoroughfare, and a number of innocent citizens were injured.

The mayor and sheriffs arrived post-haste, but it took four hours of concerted effort to bring the prison under control.[38] The sheriffs, who were responsible for the prisoners' safekeeping, faced hefty fines if anyone escaped. And for Mayor Thomas Chalton, who was almost at the end of his demanding tenure, a riot at Newgate was the last straw. On 7 October, Chalton and the aldermen censured Alexander Manning for 'his negligent custody of the prisoners'. He was dismissed from his post and imprisoned in his own gaol.[39] Manning probably appealed to his kinsman, Thomas Manning (one of King Henry's chaplains, who went on to become the king's secretary), and Thomas appealed to Queen Margaret to get the decision reversed.[40] The post of keeper of Newgate was in the gift of the incoming sheriffs, John Middleton and William Deere. Margaret wrote, asking them to reconsider Alexander Manning's case. Understandably, in the light of the recent censure, the sheriffs took no action, and Margaret wrote to them again expressing surprise at their lack of response. This is the first of her extant letters regarding Manning.[41] It bears only a number for the day when it was written, which we believe to have been 24 October 1450.

Manning's case was reviewed by the newly elected mayor, Nicholas Wyfold, but the timing was unfortunate. During the torchlight procession through the city

37　M. Bassett, 'Newgate Prison in the Middle Ages', *Speculum* 18 (1943), pp. 233–46. She mistakenly attributes the riot that resulted in Manning's ouster to the time of Cade's Rebellion (p. 241).

38　Flenley, 'Bale's Chronicle', p. 135; 'Benet's Chronicle', pp. 202–3. The latter claims that Manning deliberately released the prisoners because he knew he was to be dismissed. This is a gloss. The strongly 'Yorkist' chronicler would not suggest that York's arrival triggered a riot. Johnson, *Duke Richard*, p. 84, n. 35, confuses John Gargrave, keeper of the King's Bench, with Alexander Manning, keeper of Newgate.

39　CLRO Journal 5, f. 48.

40　Otway-Ruthven, *King's Secretary*, pp. 155, 174–5. Thomas was Henry's secretary from 1455 to 1460. J. Blacman, *Henry the Sixth*, ed. M.R. James (Cambridge, 1919), pp. 21, 43, 49, named Thomas as one of his informants. It is interesting, in light of Margaret's description of Alexander Manning, that Abbot Whethamstede described Thomas as 'vir solidus, sobrius et sensatus' (*Reg. Whethamstede*, I, p. 317). Thomas was among the persons who were captured with Henry VI in 1465. Although he was pardoned, he died in poverty in 1469.

41　Its content indicates that it is a follow-up to a previous letter, now lost.

on 29 October following his inauguration at Westminster, Wyfold was accosted by a company of armed soldiers who disrupted his progress. He ordered them to disband, and when they refused, he commanded the city officers to disarm them and imprison the rowdiest.[42] Only a week after this distressing incident, Manning was brought up before Wyfold and the common council on 5 November, and his negligence and 'many [other] failings', although not specified, were reviewed. It was decreed that he should not be reinstated as keeper, nor could he be reconsidered for the post in future.[43] It is possible that this review was a result of Margaret's letters; in any case, her request was rejected (or ignored) and a new keeper was appointed.[44]

Margaret tried again a year later. She may have hoped that, by this time, the mayor would be better disposed and her continuing interest in the matter would have the necessary influence. Sometime before the installation of new sheriffs, though possibly not long before, Margaret wrote to Mayor Wyfold urging him to instruct the incoming sheriffs to favor Manning, and at the same time wrote a letter to the sheriffs-elect, extolling Manning's good qualities and asking them to reinstate him. Nothing more is known of the fate of Alexander Manning, except that he was not reinstated. Nor is it known if the mayor or sheriffs replied to the queen's letters. Margaret was acting in her role as 'good lady', but neither the mayor nor the incoming sheriffs appreciated her importunity in a matter that was within the City's jurisdiction.

[27] Queen to the Abbot and Convent of Byland re John Dacre
(BL, Add. MS 46,846, fol. 53; Monro, p. 165)

By the Quene

Trusty and welbeloved in God, we grete yow well. And for asmoch as oure trusty and welbeloved squyer John Dacres desireth the ferme of Belderdale, which he hath now of you, to have for x yere after his termes therof expired; we therfore desire and pray that, att reverence of us, ye wil have oure said squyer in accomplissement of his entencion in this partie especialy recommendet, shewing hym th'ease, faver and tendernesse that ye goodly may, and the rather by contemplacion of this our praier, so that he may fynde in effect thise oure lettres unto hym vailable. As we trust, etc. Yeven, etc. at Eltham, the, etc.

To th'abbot and Covent of Biland

---

42 Flenley, 'Bale's Chronicle', p. 135.
43 CLRO, Journal 5, f. 51.
44 Since the gaol could not remain without a keeper, someone had to be appointed, at least for the interim, which provides a further reason not to reverse the decision on Manning.

Byland Abbey was a Cistercian house in Yorkshire.[45] Belderdale was apparently
one of its properties,[46] and John Dacre sought to extend his position there as
farmer, i.e., the collector of its rents. Since Margaret held no dower lands in
Yorkshire and since, in any event, the position was in the abbey's gift, we are
unsure as to why this letter was written. The abbot at this time was William
Helperby.

The Dacres were a northern family with many branches; as a consequence,
identifying this John Dacre is next to impossible. Margaret had an Isabel Dacre
among her ladies, who may – or may not – have been related to this man.[47] If she
were related, she may have recommended John to the queen. He does not appear
in any of Margaret's extant jewel or household records, and therefore seems to
have had no specific connection of his own to her establishment. Her reference to
him as 'our trusty and well-beloved squire' need not be taken as the literal truth,
but as a formulaic term of courtesy. It would make sense, as would Margaret's
recommendation, if it started with someone in her household whom she sought
to favor by an act of intervention. Since she readily notes the wishes of 'certain of
[her] servants' in other letters, it is puzzling that she does not do so in this one.

[28] **Queen to John Joyse, Squire, Steward of Ashbourne, re Nicholas Cokker**
(BL, Add. MS 46,846, fol. 57v; Monro, pp. 159–60)

> By the Quene
> Trusty, etc. We desire and pray you, if eny another [other] lettres patentes be
> shewed unto you for th'office of baillif of Asshebourne, graunte unto Nich[olas]
> Cokker, ye will, at reverence of us, have him towardes you especially recommended,
> suffryng [him] t'occupie and enjoie the seid office after th'effecte and porport of
> our lettres patentes to hym granted, in that bihalf. As we truste you, for thus it
> pleaseth us, etc.
> To John Joyse, squier, Steward of Asshebourne

Monro believed that Ashbourne in Derbyshire was one of Margaret's manors
since it was part of the honor of Tutbury and, hence, among her dower lands. But
Margaret's dower comprised only a portion of the vast Tutbury honor, and it did
not include Ashbourne.[48] The duke of Buckingham was steward for the whole of
Tutbury, with numerous officials working under him. John Joyse, as steward of
Ashbourne, was one of these. Margaret had promised the vacant office of bailiff

45   For its history and the names of its abbots, see VCH: *Yorkshire*, III, pp. 131–4.
46   Monro could not identify it; nor can we.
47   Myers, 'Household', p. 182; Myers, 'Jewels', p. 224. She appears to have joined Margaret's
     household in 1448, as she first received a New Year's gift in 1449 (E 101/410/2).
48   R. Somerville, *History of the Duchy of Lancaster* (1953), p. 208, for Margaret's holdings in Tutbury.

to Nicholas Cokker by her letters patent, and she wrote to ensure that Joyse was aware of this and that he would not accept another candidate nominated by anyone else. Competition for duchy offices was strong, and local influence might be brought to bear on Buckingham in favor of someone other than Cokker. Had Ashbourne been Margaret's manor, she would have appointed him outright.

Apart from the obvious information contained in this letter, that John Joyce was the steward of Ashbourne and Nicholas Cokker was to be its bailiff, we have found no other traces of these men.

[29] Queen to M[aster] T[homas Kent], the Deputy of the Keeper of the Privy Seal, re W., 3 May
(BL, Add. MS 46,846, fols 46–46v; Monro, p. 128)

By the Quene
Right trusty, etc. And for as moch as we be enformed that my most doubted lord hath nowe late granted unto W. th'office of secundarye of the pipis in th'escheqer, after the continue and pourport of his lettres of suffisant warant to yowe directed in this partie; we, therfor, desire and pray that in accomplissement of my said lordes grant in this partie ye wil, at reverence of us, have the seid W. towardes you especialy recommended, shewing hym in the sealing [of] his lettres of prive seal th'exploit and good expedicion with al the faver and tendernesse that ye goodly may, and the rather by contemplacion of this oure prayer, so that the seid W. may fare the better and perceive in effect thise oure lettres unto hym fructuouses and vailable, as we trust yow. In which ye shul mowe deserve of us right especial thanke, unto oure greet plesaunce, in tyme commyng. At our m[anor] of P. the iii day of M[ay].
To M.T., depute unto the worshipfull, etc. Keper of the Prive Seal

We wonder: how on earth did Margaret expect the deputy keeper to know who 'W' was? Presumably because she wrote immediately after Henry had issued his letters patent?[49] This is the first of two letters in this section where she recommended someone in a follow-up to Henry's appointment.[50]

The clerk of the pipes was the man responsible for recording the annual accounts of sheriffs and other royal officials in the pipe rolls kept by the exchequer. His secondary was a subordinate officer of lower rank, much as the deputy keeper of the privy seal was a subordinate and sometime stand-in for the keeper. We believe the deputy keeper can be identified as 'Master Thomas' Kent, who was

49 The copyist may have chosen to abbreviate the name, but there is no particular reason to believe that he did so.
50 Maurer, pp. 62–6, for letters in which Margaret either followed up actions taken by Henry (which she may have instigated) or otherwise associated herself with the king's actions and authority.

appointed clerk of the council and secondary in the office of the privy seal in 1444.[51] He seems to have held both these offices into 1458, when the office of clerk of the council was regranted to him and Richard Langport in survivorship 'from Easter last ... in lieu of a grant thereof and of the office of secondary in the office of the privy seal to Thomas ... surrendered so far as concerns the former office.'[52]

When Margaret arrived in England, the clerk of the pipes was Robert Cawode, who had held the office since 1431, apparently having worked his way up through the ranks in the exchequer since the days of Henry IV. He received a reward for his long service in February 1447 with a grant to him and his wife in survivorship of 'a tun of good red Gascon wine ... between Martinmas and Easter'. In December of that year, Cawode was reconfirmed in the office, with the precautionary measure being taken of granting it to Richard Forde 'from next voidance'.[53] Indeed, Forde had succeeded him by October 1449.[54] Had he also moved up as Cawode had? Is there any likelihood that he had been secondary under Cawode and that his succession could provide a hint as to when that office fell vacant?

Another approach to the problem may be through Kent. He was acting privy seal, though his title remained deputy, for three weeks in January 1450, from Adam Moleyns's murder until the appointment of Andrew Holes on the 31st, and again, from 5 April to 12 May 1452, when Thomas Lisieux became privy seal. If the keeper was the one who enrolled the king's letters patent, these dates may suggest when Margaret could have written her letter. On the other hand, if it was the *deputy's* regular job to see to their enrollment, they are no help at all. As there is no record in the patent rolls as published of anyone who could be 'W', we are left to wonder who he was and why the queen was particularly concerned about his advancement.

[30] Queen to the Lord Chancellor re Master J.C., 30 May [1448–53?]
(BL, Add. MS 46, 846, fols 64–64v; Monro, pp. 131–2)

By the Quene
Right reverend fader in God, etc. Desiryng and praying you hertly that albeit that we suppose verreilly that ye be good and speciall lorde unto our welbeloved Maister J.C., late clerke and familiar servant of oures, ye will nevertheles, the rather atte reverence of us and for our sake, have hym towardes the faver of your good lordship especially recommended, shewyng hym th'exploit and expedicion of his

51   *CPR, 1441–46*, pp. 235, 277. The first appointment was made 'during good behavior', which must have proved satisfactory, for the second was for life.
52   *CPR, 1452–61*, p. 425.
53   *CPR, 1446–52*, pp. 31, 127.
54   *CCR, 1447–54*, p. 167. By January 1459, Forde had become a remembrancer of the exchequer (*CPR, 1452–61*, p. 480).

pursuit towardes yow for th'office of protonotarie of the chauncellrie that my lord hath granted hym, as in my lordes lettres of warant it appereth more at large, so that he may fynde in effecte th'accomplissement of my lordes entencion and oures in this behalf, as we truste yow. In which thyng ye shull mowe do unto us right grete plesaunce. Yeven under, etc. atte Wyndesor the xxx day of M[ay].

To the Chaunc[ellor] of Englond

The prothonotary was the chief clerk or registrar in the courts of chancery, of the common pleas and of King's Bench. He was also a doctor of law, with the title of 'Master'. At the time of Margaret's arrival in England, the prothonotary in chancery was John Stokes, who may have held the office for some time as he had a long career in the government. In 1423, described as 'clerk of the late king [Henry V]', he was regranted the office of notary of the chancery, 'which he held under the said late king'. A commission of that same year describes him as a doctor of laws.[55] Stokes certainly was prothonotary from before 22 August 1444, when the king granted the office to his clerk, Master John Derby, doctor of laws, to take effect upon Stokes's death. The wording strikes us as curious: while noting that 'John Stokys still survives', it insists that:

if [he] surrender his letters to any other intent than that he alone for life or with John Derby shall hold the office *or if any other grant hereof be made, whereof letters under the great seal have not yet passed,* John Derby shall hold the office as above, saving always the estate of John Stokys therin.[56]

Is it possible that Henry had granted (or promised to grant) this office to someone else? He sometimes double-granted offices, which led to squabbles and confusion. If this were the case, the enrollment of the grant to Derby would have ensured that no one else could claim it if anything happened to Stokes. Although Margaret could have had nothing to do with this specific situation, it may help to make sense of her letter. Whatever one thinks of this grant, Stokes continued very much alive and active as prothonotary into January 1448.[57] Then he disappears from the records.[58] He apparently died within the next few years, for Master John

---

55   *CPR, 1422–29*, pp. 65, 78.
56   *CPR 1441–46*, p. 285, our italics.
57   *CPR, 1446–52*, p. 142, which names Stokes, as prothonotary, and others to a commission of oyer and terminer in a maritime case. From the 1420s through the 1440s, there are many references to Stokes in the patent rolls in cases involving maritime affairs.
58   Later references to a John Stokes of Oxfordshire appear to involve a different man, a member of the country gentry (e.g., *CPR, 1452–61*, pp. 648, 675; *1461–67* contains numerous references to him). A single reference to a Master John Stokes, clerk, from 1461 is also likely to be someone else (ibid., p. 6).

Derby was prothonotary by February 1454 or 1455.[59] He continued in this office into September 1460.[60]

Margaret's claim that Henry had issued a warrant granting the office of prothonotary to 'Master J.C.', together with the grant to Derby in 1444 and his eventual receipt of the office, provide strong evidence of a double grant. Although the queen's letter could have been written before Stokes's death, it seems more likely to have been written after he died, by which time Henry may have forgotten that he had already granted the office in reversion to Derby. Since the chancellor Margaret addressed was a churchman, he was either John Stafford or his successor John Kemp. Kemp was followed by Richard Neville, earl of Salisbury, who held the office briefly until March 1455. By that time, certainly, Derby was ensconced in office. Margaret may have been unaware when she made her request that the office had already been settled in 1444. In due course Derby became prothonotary according to plan.

So who was 'Master J.C.'? Margaret's letter indicates that he was her own 'late clerk and familiar servant', suggesting that he had enjoyed at least a passing association with her household. At a guess, he may have been John Croke, who is described along with William Essex as the queen's attorneys in the exchequer in her sole surviving household account from 1452–53.[61] Croke and Essex were also clerks in the exchequer for the duchy of Lancaster from 1445–51.[62] This background could have placed him in a good position from which to move to prothonotary.

---

59   *CCR, 1454–61*, pp. 49–50. The document is dated '13 February 1454, 33 Henry VI'. If the regnal year is correct, the year should be 1455. References to Derby solely as 'clerk' or as 'doctor of laws' both before and after this entry do not help to determine exactly when he succeeded Stokes (*CPR, 1446–52*, pp. 434, 537; *1452–61*, pp. 53, 246, 346, 439, 443).

60   *CCR, 1454–61*, p. 205; *CPR, 1452–61*, p. 625.

61   Myers, 'Household', p. 194. Their payment was for the past three years (making them members of her household during that time). Assuming that J.C. was John Croke – a big assumption – Margaret's indication in her letter that he was no longer her servant suggests that she wrote it in 1453.

62   Somerville, *Duchy of Lancaster*, p. 458. Croke also appears as 'one of the clerks of the exchequer' in 1439 (*CPR, 1436–41*, p. 306).

Four

BUSINESS INTERESTS

Along with Margaret's commitment to good ladyship, as seen in her promotion of marriages or advancing the interests of her servants and petitioners, she transacted what may be simply considered good business. Her dower of duchy of Lancaster lands worth £2,000 made her a great magnate with extensive estates to manage. Some of her letters show her as a businesswoman, responsible for transactions as a landholder, as mistress of a large household or as someone who occasionally engaged in overseas trade. If necessary, she also followed up on the king's orders where her concerns or responsibilities coincided with his.

The letters in this chapter fall into two categories, beginning with what might be called 'regular business letters'. In the first Margaret ordered the sale of some beech trees to pay for needed repairs to two of her manors. Next come two letters from the king and queen relating to oaks from her property, to be given as a gift by King Henry. An order for what appears to be Christmas livery for one of Margaret's servants is followed by the provision of a buck to someone else.

The second category consists of Margaret's 'formal letters'. These official letters all begin with the formula 'Margaret, by the grace of God queen of England and of France and Lady of Ireland' and are addressed to officials of various kinds. The first provides formal notice of a grant of land; the second provides an annuity to one of her servants. Several letters address the requirements of persons traveling abroad on Margaret's business. Two more concern the services of a London cordwainer. The next letter grants immunity from purveyance, while the last formally establishes an award of damages.

[31] Queen to D[rew] B[arantyne], Steward of her Lordships of Great Haseley and Pyrton [1446–47]
(BL, Add. MS 46, 846, fol. 55; Monro, pp. 140–1)

By the Quene

Trusty and welbeloved. For asmoch as we be enformed that our manoir of Haseley and Periton neden of reparacion, we desire and praye you that such reparacion as shalbe necessarie in that partie ye will do make by the wodesale of our beches in our wode of Kelingrigge and Holmewode, as it apperteinet unto you by vertue of your office of oure steward there, so that, in your defaulte herof, we take no hurt ne prejudice in tyme commyng. As we trust yow, etc.

To D.B., Steward of oure lordship of Haseley and Periton

Great Haseley and Pyrton were among five manors in Oxfordshire that were granted in dower to Margaret in March 1446; their total value was set at £155 7s 9½d.[1] Pyrton had been part of Queen Katherine's dower. Upon her death in 1437 it reverted to the crown and was leased for seven years from 1438.[2] According to a survey dated to that year, all of its buildings were badly in need of repair, at an estimated cost of £17 6s 8d.[3] If the survey's date is indeed correct, it would appear that little had been done to rectify this situation before the property was granted to Margaret. This suggests that her letter dates from late 1446 or early 1447, by which time her officers would have been able to assess what needed to be done. Margaret was either an astute businesswoman, or she had excellent advice: there was no point in leaving a manor in ruins if it could be made to turn a profit by repairs. As she was constantly strapped for cash in her early years, the sale of the beech wood was intended to raise the money for the repairs. If the survey was made in 1438, the cost quoted may have been close to what she actually had to pay.

D.B. can be identified as Drew Barantyne, esquire, of Chalgrove and Haseley, Oxfordshire, who died in 1453.[4] Barantyne was notably active in Oxfordshire. In addition to being MP for the county in 1445–46, he served there on various commissions.[5] He was also the brother-in-law of Sir John Wenlock, who became

1   *RP*, V, p. 118b. The other three manors were Deddington, Kirklington and Ascot, in the 'South Parts' of the duchy of Lancaster. Margaret probably never collected the full amount on these properties. In 1452–53 the total receipts from the 'South Parts' only came to £174 16s 4½d (Myers, 'Household', p. 158).
2   *CPR, 1436–41*, p. 32; VCH: *Oxford*, VIII, p. 149.
3   Ibid., p. 160. Both 1421 and 1438 have been suggested as dates for the survey. Since the manor's pigeon house is known to have been a wreck in 1439, the later date may be preferred. For further information regarding the survey, see p. 149.
4   Wedgwood, p. 40.
5   *CPR, 1441–46*, p. 476; *1446–52*, pp. 139, 191, 297, 386, 413, 433, 585, 593; *1452–61*, p. 56.

Margaret's chamberlain in 1447,[6] both men having married the daughters and co-heiresses of Sir John Drayton. In 1449, Barantyne granted Wenlock and two others the wardship of his lands and marriage of his heirs in the event that he died during their minority.[7] The connection between Barantyne and Wenlock took an ominous turn in 1451, when the two allegedly raised a force of 3,000 men to oppose the widowed duchess of Suffolk and her feoffees (including Sir Thomas Tuddenham) in a property dispute that was to be settled at an assize of novel disseisin in September. They made death threats against both the feoffees and the assize judges.[8] Although their actions delayed the assize, they also got Barantyne and Wenlock into trouble. On 13 March 1452, Wenlock, Richard Drayton of Oxfordshire, and a Berkshire man were charged a recognizance of 500 marks, either to bring Barantyne to the chancery – where he was to do whatever the chancellor told him – or else to turn him in to Fleet prison by 9 May. A week later, on 20 March, Wenlock gave an additional recognizance of 2,000 marks to behave himself and keep the peace while the assize of novel disseisin went forward. Barantyne was charged a similar recognizance in a like amount on the 26th.[9] On 21 April 1452, 'at the instance of queen Margaret', Sir John Wenlock and Drew Barantyne received pardons for 'all trespasses ... misdeeds, and any consequent outlawries.'[10] Barantyne went back to serving on Oxford commissions (the last was of 23 September 1452) and died on 23 April 1453. Wenlock continued to serve as Margaret's chamberlain, at least into 1453.[11]

The next two letters involve the cutting of Margaret's oaks for someone else's use.

[32] **From King Henry to Queen Margaret re John Barham [1449]**
(BL, Add. MS 46,846, fol. 66v; Monro, p. 98)

By the Kyng
Right dere and right entierly bestbeloved wyf, we grete you hertly. And for asmoche as we, of our grace especiall, have granted unto John Barham x okes for tymbre, to be taken in your outwodes of Kenelworth, of our yefte; we therfore desire and praye you that ye woll see that the said John may have delyverance of

---

6   See below, p. 122, for the approximate date of Wenlock's appointment.
7   *CPR, 1446–52*, pp. 244–5. His expressed concern, that they should be responsible for 'sustaining the houses, closes and buildings' associated with his lands, may make him an even likelier overseer of the intended repairs of the queen's manors.
8   J.S. Roskell, *Parliament and Politics in Late Medieval England*, 3 vols (1981–83), II, pp. 246–7, for the incident and its aftermath.
9   *CCR, 1447–54*, pp. 338, 339.
10   *CPR, 1446–52*, p. 530.
11   Roskell, *Parliament and Politics*, II, p. 247; *Vale's Book*, p. 173.

the said okes, after th'entent of our said grante. And thise oure lettres shalbe unto you sufficiant warrant and full discharge of eny empechement of wast in this partie. Yeven, etc., the yere of oure reigne xxvij [1448–49].[12]

To oure right dere, etc., wyf the Quene

[33] Queen to the Bishop of Chester, her Chancellor [1449]
(BL, Add. MS 46,846, fol. 66v; Monro, p. 156)

By the Quene

Worshipful Fader in God, etc. For asmoch as my moost doubted lord, of his especiall grace, hath granted unto John Barham x okes for tymbre, to be taken in our outwodes of Kenelworth, of his yefte, wherappon my said lord hath desired and prayed us, by his lettres under his signet, that we woll see that the said okes be delyvered unto the said John after th'entent of his said grante, the which lettres he woll to be unto us sufficiant warrant and full discharge of eny empechement of waste on this partie; we therfor woll and charge you that under our greet seall beyng in your warde ye do a warrant directe unto the keper, etc., charging, etc., to delyver the etc.

To the Bisshop of Chestre our Chauncellor

Margaret's chancellor was William Booth, bishop of Coventry and Lichfield, at this time sometimes styled bishop of Chester. We have been unable to identify John Barham.[13]

The chain of command here should be noted. King Henry informed Margaret of his grant so that she could endorse it to her chancellor, who would then instruct the keeper of Kenilworth.[14] The king's grant of ten oak trees was a mark of royal favor: wood of any sort, but especially oak used for ship building as well as for housing, was particularly valuable. It could easily be turned into ready cash.

12   Henry VI's regnal year began on 1 September and ended on 31 August. We consider it more likely that these letters were written in spring or summer.
13   Apart from a similarity of name, we find no reason to believe that he was the John Banham, king's esquire and master cook, who is twice mentioned in the patent rolls (*CPR, 1441–46*, p. 343; *1446–52*, p. 510). Nor can we establish a link between this Banham and a John Banham who was a member of the Warwickshire gentry around this time (Carpenter, *Locality and Polity*, p. 647), which would at least put him in the proper neighborhood to be receiving oaks from Kenilworth.
14   Somerville, *Duchy of Lancaster*, pp. 560–1, does not name a 'keeper' for Kenilworth, but the constable and steward was Ralph Boteler, Lord Sudeley.

[34] Queen to her Wardrober re Lewis ap Meredith, 10 December 1448
(BL, Add. MS 46,846, fol. 34v; Monro, pp. 115–16)

By the Quene

Warderober. We wol and charge yow that unto oure welbeloved Squier Lewis ap Mered[ith] ye do delivere iij yeardes of fine russet cloth and ij yeardes dimidium of blake saten fugury,[15] to be taken of oure yeft. And this bill, signed with oure hand the x day of Decembre the yere of my lordes reigne xxvij, shalbe youre warrant.

Margaret had been married to King Henry by proxy on 25 May 1444 at Tours, and at some point during the next couple of months the king wrote to her. Lewis ap Meredith was marshall of Mantes at that time, and on 18 August, Henry ordered his treasurer to pay Lewis a reward of 50 marks for carrying the letter to 'notre treschier et tresame compaigne la reigne'.[16] Mantes lies on the Seine about halfway between Rouen and Paris. Lewis would have delivered the letter to Margaret in Anjou, where she remained until December, when she left Angers for Nancy in Lorraine.[17] In March 1445, the duke of York received Margaret at Pontoise, on the border of France and English Normandy, and they traveled down the Seine through Mantes to Rouen. It is likely that Lewis joined her entourage when it passed through Mantes, becoming an honorary member of her household on the journey to England, for which he was paid £18 0s 4d.[18]

In England he became an esquire of the household. In November 1446, for his service to the king and queen, he was given the keeping of all the lands in England and Wales that had been held by William Clement during his daughter Maud's minority, as well as her custody and marriage.[19] Unfortunately, as sometimes happened with Henry's grants, the keeping of some of Clement's property had already been granted to someone else. In April 1448, Lewis was granted £20 annually, to be paid by Gruffydd ap Nicholas, esquire, who had the keeping of the town of Caron and commote of Penarth during Maud's minority. Additionally, he was to have the keeping of all lands that should come into the king's hands thereafter during her minority.[20]

15   'Russet' could be either a coarse woolen cloth or a reddish-brown color. Since Margaret specifies that the cloth is to be 'fine', she may have had the color in mind. Of course, since it was given in the winter, it may also have been of wool. 'Dimidium' meant a half or a moiety; hence Lewis was to get about 2½ yards of the satin. The word 'fugury', variously spelled, appears to describe a particular kind of satin (*OED*). Monro suggested that it meant 'figured', which would at least make sense in context.
16   Stevenson, I, pp. 461–2.
17   Beaucourt, IV, p. 91.
18   BL, Add. MS 23,938.
19   *CPR, 1446–52*, p. 6.
20   Ibid., p. 150.

The name of Margaret's wardrober is uncertain. John Noreys was keeper of the queen's great wardrobe in 1452–53. He had been the treasurer of her chamber and keeper of her jewels from Michaelmas 1446 to Michaelmas 1452, when Edward Ellesmere replaced him in those posts. This was probably when Noreys became Margaret's wardrober.[21] Richard Wellden, whom Monro identified as keeper of the queen's wardrobe, in fact worked in *Henry's* great wardrobe under Robert Rolleston.[22] There is a gift to the clerk of the queen's wardrobe, who is not named, in Margaret's 1448–49 jewel account. He received a gold armlet, as did Lewis ap Meredith.[23] The queen's gift of cloth was probably intended to make up Lewis's Christmas livery.

[35] **Queen to her Parker of Pleshey re Robert Penall, 16 August 1456**
(BL, Add. MS 46,846, fol. 2v; Monro, p. 134)

By the Quene
Welbelovyd. We woll and charge yow that unto our welbelovyd servand Robert Penall, or unto the brynger of these in his name, ye do delyver a bucke to be taken within our forest or grete parke of Plashe of our yefte, any comaundment yeven to yow not withstondyng. And these our lettres shalbe unto yow therin sufficiant warant. Yeven under our signet, at Chestre, the xvj day of August, the yere of my lordes reign xxxiiij[to].

To oure welbelovyd the keper of our parke of Plashe or ellis to his deputee there

We have found no traces of Robert Penall and wonder whether 'well-beloved servant' was a courtesy rather than a strict identification of him as a member of Margaret's household. She was in Chester at the time, a long way from Pleshey, so was he a Cheshire man or an Essex man, or neither? A buck would have been a valuable gift, both as a source of meat and as a sign of the queen's esteem.

Margaret's condition, 'any commandment given to you notwithstanding', provokes a question. Did she anticipate opposition to her order? It may be that the queen, who in most circumstances was intent upon preserving the game in her parks,[24] simply intended the parker to know that she really wanted him to take the buck for Penall. The parker of Pleshey was probably John Merston, who

---

21   Myers, 'Household', p. 205, and notes 1 and 2. Noreys is not identified as keeper of the queen's wardrobe in the earlier jewel accounts, and it seems likely that he would have been accorded the title had he held the post. Robert Whittingham had become her wardrober by 1458 (*CPR, 1452–61*, p. 429).
22   *PROME*, XII, p. 118.
23   E 101/410/2.
24   See Chapter 8, 'The Queen's Disport'.

was constable of Pleshey Castle 'with keeping of the little park called Deer Park' from January 1437 for life.[25] His wife, Rose, was one of Margaret's attendants.[26]

[36] Queen re Sir John Montgomery, 22 November 1448
(BL, Add. MS 46,846, fol. 44v; Monro, p. 104)

Margareta, Dei gratia Regina Anglie et Francie, et Domina Hibernie, omnibus ad quos presentes litere pervenerint, salutem. Sciatis, nos vicesimo primo die Octobris ultimo preterito, apud Waltham Crosse, recepisse, de predilecto milite nostro Johanne Mongomery, fidelitatem, pro quadam parcella terre vocata Goldyngesfeld, infra dominium nostrum de Enfeld, quam de nobis tenet in capite, per servitutem supradictam. In cujus rei testimonium presentibus signetum nostrum fecimus apponere. Datum apud Eltham, mensis Novembris die vicesimo secundo, anno regni metuendissimi Domini me regis Henrici Sexti vicesimo septimo.

Margaret, by the grace of God Queen of England and France and lady of Ireland, to all to whom these present letters shall come: greeting. Know ye that on the 21st day of October last past we received the fealty of our dearly beloved knight John Montgomery at Waltham Cross for a certain parcel of land called Goldingsfield within our lordship of Enfeld, which he holds of us in chief by the service aforesaid. In testimony whereof we have caused our signet to be put to these present [letters]. Given at Eltham the 22nd day of November, in the twenty-seventh year of the reign of my most dread lord King Henry the Sixth [1448].

Sir John Montgomery was an up-and-coming Essex knight who made his way via service in France, magnate patronage and a judicious marriage. In December 1440 he was made bailiff and receiver of the scivinage of Calais and the 'Ilond de Colne'; in February 1446, the grant was extended to include his eldest son John, then king's serjeant, in survivorship.[27] In June 1439 he was one of the commissioners to take muster of troops arriving in Normandy, and sometime in 1442–43 he was granted the custom and toll of all carts bringing merchandise through the

---

25 Somerville, *Duchy of Lancaster*, p. 611. In 1439 the grant was enlarged to include John's brother Richard. John had been treasurer of the chamber and keeper of the king's jewels for Henry VI from 1424 until resigning the post to his brother in 1453, and was still alive in 1459 (*CPR, 1436–41*, p. 91; *1452–61*, pp. 293, 481).

26 Myers, 'Household', p. 183 and n. 2. Rose gave the queen a gift at New Year 1452 and 1453 (E 101/410/8; Myers, 'Jewels', p. 218).

27 *CPR, 1441–46*, pp. 238, 361, 398. Scivinage was a municipal tax on incoming goods; in this case it seems to have applied to the Pale of Calais. The grant also allowed Sir John and his son 'the profits and executions of commands in the courts within the ... scivinage' and further provided that if the 'revenues in time of war' did not cover their fees, they should 'have such a sum as they can levy therefrom' as remedy. This would seem to have created a potential recipe for bribery and extortion, unless the Montgomerys were a good deal more scrupulous than many of their contemporaries.

lordships of Marke and Oye by Calais.[28] Sir John's service to Richard, duke of York, was no doubt helpful to his career. In 1437–38 he became the duke's seneschal of Clare and of Thaxted. Reciprocally, and typically for that time, the service of men such as Montgomery would have provided York – and other magnates – with local influence.[29] Sir John was named as a justice of the peace for Hertford in 1443 and 1445, and for Essex in 1446 and 1448.[30] The visible mark of his 'arrival' among the elite came in 1439, however, when he was granted permission 'to fortify, crenellate and embattle' his manor at Faulkbourne.[31]

In the early 1420s, Sir John married Elizabeth, the widow of John Norbury and perhaps of William Heron, Lord Say, as well.[32] He probably met Margaret in Rouen in 1445; at New Year 1446 he received her gift of a gold belt.[33] Although it was Elizabeth who became one of Margaret's favorites, this letter is evidence of her interest in Sir John as well. Enfield in Middlesex was a part of Margaret's original dower. Sir John apparently died in early 1449, and his death may have been unexpected as it seems unlikely that the grant would have been made to a man known to be in rapidly failing health.

[37] **Queen to the Bailiffs, etc., of her Manor of Great Waltham re Thomas Sharneborne, 20 August 1449**
(BL, Add. MS 46,846, fols 12v–13; Monro, pp. 108–9)

A Close Letter

Margarete, by the grace of God Quene of Englond and of France and Ladye of Ireland, to our baillives, fermors or other occupiors of our manoir of Greet Waltham in the countie of Essex that now is or for the tyme shalbe: greting. For asmoche as we of our especial grace the ix day of October the xxvij yere of my lordes reigne [9 October 1448] have granted by oure lettres patentes unto our trusty and wellbeloved squier Thomas Sharborne xx^li of sterlinges, to be taken of our manoir of Greet Waltham in the countie of Essex every yere at the festes of Ester and Michelmasse by evyn porcions by th'andes of oure baillives, fermors and other ministres or occupiours of our said manoir, as in the said lettres patentes it appereth more pleinly; we wol and charge you that, the said lettres patentes by you seen, ye do thereupon after the cotinue [contents, *contenu*] and porport of the same lettres paie unto our said squier the said xx^li yerely att the times above prefixed, receivyng

28   *CPR, 1436–41*, p. 314.
29   Johnson, *Duke Richard*, pp. 20–1, 235.
30   *CPR, 1441–46*, pp. 470, 471; *1446–52*, p. 589.
31   Ibid., p. 320.
32   The date of their marriage is speculative. Their elder son, John, was born *c.* 1426, and the latest reference we have found to John Norbury is from 1414. See below, pp. 162–4, for Elizabeth, 'Lady Say'.
33   E 101/409/14. The belt was worth £2 4s 6d.

of oure said squier lettres of acquitances witnessing the payment which ye doo to hym. By the which lettres and thise presents we wol that ye have due allowance in your accompts. Yeven, etc., at our castell of Plasshe, the xx^th day of August the yere of, etc., xxvij [20 August 1449].

To our baillives, fermors or other occupiors of our manoir of Greet Waltham in the countie of Essex that now be or for the tyme shalbe.

Thomas Sharneborne of Shernborne, Norfolk, also appears in another of Margaret's letters and one from the Paston collection included in Chapter 1.[34] He became the queen's servant early on, probably in 1446, since he received a brooch worth 10s 8d at New Year 1447.[35] He married Jamon or Jamona, one of the queen's attendants who had accompanied her to England.[36] Margaret's grant of an annuity to Sharneborne, referred to in this letter, may well have been a wedding gift, suggesting that the marriage took place in October 1448. Twenty pounds was a tidy sum and would have been a tangible sign of her favor towards the couple. The marriage eventually produced three sons and a daughter, the latter named Margaret after the queen. In 1451–52, Queen Margaret gave Sharneborne a christening gift of £20 for her namesake.[37] In the following year, the only one for which there is an extant household record, he was paid £6 3s 1d for service as the queen's esquire.[38]

Sharneborne's career followed upon his connection with the queen's household. In November 1447 he became escheator of Norfolk and Suffolk and was an MP for Norfolk in 1449–50. In 1453 he was sheriff of Norfolk and Suffolk.[39] In June 1455 he became a customer of King's Lynn, and in March 1456 he and Henry

---

34 See pp. 8 and 92. In these other letters he appears either as the queen's messenger or as one of her informants. C. Richmond, *The Paston Family in the Fifteenth Century: Endings* (Manchester, 2000), p. 126–7, n. 156, offers a confusing account of his family background and argues that he took his grandmother's surname to establish his right to landed status.

35 E 101/409/17. In 1448–49 he was given a gold armlet, as was his wife (E 101/410/2).

36 In earlier accounts she appears only as 'Jamon', but in 1448–49 she is called 'Jamon Sharnborne'. She received letters of denization in March 1449 as 'Jamona de Sharneres, born in the duchy of Anjou' (*CPR, 1446–49*, pp. 212, 240). Monro (p. 107), following Spelman, *English Works*, II, p. 198, referred to her as 'Jamona Cherneys', which may be a corruption of 'Sharneres', and the latter a contraction of 'Sharneborne'. Spelman cannot be considered a reliable source: he gives July 1444 as the birth date of the couple's eldest son, only two months after Margaret's betrothal and nine months before her arrival in England with her ladies, and 1448 as the date of their daughter's death, several years before her actual christening and more than a decade before her mention in Sharneborne's will (see below and n. 47).

37 E 101/410/8. Oddly, Jamon is not named along with him. Thomas was given a gold armband in 1452–53, while Jamon received a wine flagon, as did the queen's other ladies (Myers, 'Jewels', pp. 225, 226).

38 Myers, 'Household', p. 184.

39 *CFR, 1445–52*, p. 83; Wedgwood, p. 764.

Bourgchier were granted custody of the lordship of Castle Rising for twenty years.[40]

Along the way Sharneborne made enemies. While escheator of Norfolk he ran afoul of Sir John Fastolf in connection with a property dispute. Fastolf had him ordered to appear before a commission of oyer and terminer in 1451 to face charges of 'divers trespasses, oppressions, extortions and other offences'. Sharneborne neglected to appear, subsequently claiming that 'he dared not ... through fear of death by the hands of ... his enemies.' In July of that year, on account of his 'good service to the king and queen', and perhaps thanks to Margaret's influence, he was pardoned of all penalties for his non-appearance.[41] By 1453, Sharneborne was at odds with John Mowbray, duke of Norfolk.[42] Norfolk had been engaged in a longstanding, and generally losing, rivalry with the duke of Suffolk over dominance in East Anglia. The latter's fall in 1450 allowed Norfolk greater opportunity to throw his own weight around. Together with the duke of York, he set about ousting Suffolk's men from positions of power and replacing them with their men. The failure of York's confrontation with the king in early 1452 created a setback and brought on a fresh round of local political contention. Sharneborne, in his capacity as sheriff of both Norfolk and Suffolk and representative of the royal court's interests, was seen by the duke of Norfolk as a threat. When elections for knights of the shire were called in February 1453, Sharneborne charged in his return that a party of fifty-seven named men, most of whom were servants and tenants of the duke, had so threatened his undersheriff, who had been put in charge of the Suffolk elections, that they could not properly be held. Sharneborne further alleged that these men, reinforced by 600 others in arms, improperly held their own election in which they chose their own knights for the shire.[43] Their return was, in fact, disqualified on technical grounds, and Sharneborne returned Sir Philip Wentworth, a courtier, and Gilbert Debenham instead. On 27 May 1454, more than a year after this incident took place, Norfolk retaliated by presenting a petition to the privy council charging that Sharneborne had lied in his report. The duke alleged that Sharneborne, 'ymagynyng and purposing to make knyghtes

---

40   *CPR, 1452–61*, p. 202; *CFR, 1452–61*, p. 152. Wedgwood suggests that the former post may have been 'a form of banishment' after the first battle of St Albans; however, the position of customs collector was generally considered desirable.

41   *CPR, 1446–52*, p. 454. For the property dispute, see P.S. Lewis, 'Sir John Fastolf's Lawsuit over Titchwell', *Historical Journal* 1 (1958), pp. 1–20; its effects on Sharneborne can be traced on pp. 7–8, 16–18. Fastolf did not obtain the property he sought until September 1453.

42   Virgoe, 'Three Suffolk Parliamentary Elections', in *East Anglian Society*, pp. 53–7, for a full account of the incident.

43   The 'tenor' of Sharneborne's return is contained in a letter by the king dated 9 July 1453, which only found its way into the plea roll of Hilary Term 1455 after Henry had recovered from his mental breakdown (ibid., pp. 59–62, for its text).

of the shire aftyr his owne intent and for his syngler covetyse and to hurt the
servants and tenants of the ... Duc', had tried to fix the election, while his own
men – some of whom had not even been present – were entirely innocent of any
wrongdoing. He asked that they be allowed to appear by attorney to clear their
names.[44] The timing of Norfolk's petition was opportunistic. The duke of York had
been named protector in March 1454, and in this newly favorable political climate
Norfolk evidently saw an opportunity to get back at Sharneborne, who had dared
to challenge his local power. Had he succeeded in making his charges stick,
Sharneborne would have been faced with a hefty fine, if not worse. But Norfolk
himself was by no means above election-tampering. When York returned from
Ireland in 1450, he had met up with Norfolk for the specific purpose of deciding
who they wanted returned for Norfolk and Suffolk in the parliament that was to
meet later that year.[45] As a coda to the 1453–54 affair, when Sharneborne's term
as sheriff ended in November, his replacement for Norfolk and Suffolk was John
Wingfield, who had been one of the knights chosen by Norfolk's men.[46]

In his will Thomas Sharneborne besought the queen 'to bee the principall
overseer of this my private testament ... and also to be good and gracious
ladie to Jamon my wife and to all myne children'. Since he died in early 1459,
Margaret's oversight would have been short-lived. According to Wedgwood,
Jamona Sharneborne received a pardon in February 1462 under Edward IV, and
was described as the executrix of her husband's will.[47]

[38] Queen to all Searchers, Custumers and Keepers of Ports re N.A., 20 March 1447
(BL, Add. MS 46,846, fol. 42v; Monro, pp. 136–7)

Margarete, by the grace of God Quene of Englond and of France and Lady of
Ireland, to all serchers, custumers, kepers of portes, and to all other my lordes officers
sendeth greting. And for asmoche as oure welbeloved servant N.A., chappelleyn
unto oure right entierly welbeloved moder the quene of Sicile purposeth to passe
over the see towardes oure said moder, we desire and praye yow that in his seid

---

44   *PPC*, VI, pp. 183–4. On balance, Virgoe gives greater credence to Sharneborne's version of the
     event. The knights returned for Norfolk, apparently without incident, were Sir Andrew Ogard,
     a knight carver of the queen's household who had formerly been one of York's retainers, and
     Sir Thomas Tuddenham, a member of the late duke of Suffolk's affinity, which automatically
     made him an enemy of Norfolk. Tuddenham had his own reputation for extortion.
45   Gairdner, *PL*, II, p. 184. Three of the four knights returned from the two shires were their
     nominees (Virgoe, 'Three Suffolk Elections', p. 54).
46   Griffiths, p. 728. For the Wingfields, see below, pp. 108ff.
47   Wedgwood, p. 764 and n. 9. Thomas Sharneborne's will was dated 31 January and proved 8 April
     1459. In addition to his wife, he left bequests to his sons John, Edward and Anthony, and to his
     daughter Margaret.

passage ye wilbe frendly, faverable and welwilled, with al th'ease and faver that ye
goodly maye, without eny empechement or interupcion to the contrary. As we truste
you. Yeven at P[leshey]. the xx day of Marche the yere of my lordes reign xxv [1447].

This letter of safe conduct was written at Pleshey, one of Margaret's dower castles.
It cannot be from Greenwich, known as Pleasaunce, as this was not granted to
Margaret until July 1447.

Margaret's mother, Isabelle, duchess of Lorraine, was styled 'queen of Sicily'
through her husband René, duke of Anjou's titular claim to be king of Sicily,
Naples and Jerusalem. We do not know how much correspondence passed
between Margaret and her parents, nor have we been able to identify N.A. In
1448 a Jehan des Dames was recorded at the court of Anjou as 'serviteur de la
royne d'Angleterre'.[48] He was probably a messenger from Margaret, but whether
to her father or mother – or to both – is unknown.[49]

Margaret sent René a gift in 1446, her first full year in England, probably
because French ambassadors were at court and about to return to France.[50] Her
letter to Chancellor Stafford on behalf of Baldwin Saheny, a merchant of the
Spinelli firm, indicates that she maintained some contact with her father, at least
in the early years.[51]

[39] Queen to the Officers of the King's Ports re Antony Hewet [1447]
(BL, Add. MS 46,846, fols 42v–43; Monro, p. 123)

Margarete, etc., *ut supra*, and to other officers of my lordes portes whom
apperteyneth: greting. Know ye that we have yeven in commandement unto Antony
Hewet of Rome [Rouen] for to bring unto us certein silver vessel[s], jewelx, ringes
and other thinges of pleasaunce for yeres yiftes and other disportes. Wherefore we
praye yow that, sith the said goodes bene oures and to oure use, ye will suffre the
said Antony to passe with the said goodes withoute takinge therefore eny custume,
and that without eny lating, empechement or disturbance in eny wise. As we truste
yow, and as ye thinke to do us pleasure. Yeven, etc.

Antony Hewet is a mystery to us. In Margaret's jewel accounts, the names of
goldsmiths from whom she purchased gifts are specified, and there is no Hewet
among them. In one year she rewarded three 'Lombards' with gifts of purses, but

48   F. Piponnier, *Costume et vie sociale: la cour d'Anjou XIV–XVe siècle* (Paris, 1970), p. 256.
49   Isabelle died on 28 February 1453, and Margaret dressed herself and her ladies in blue in
     mourning for her mother (A. Strickland, *Lives of the Queens of England*, II [1885], p. 207, citing
     Arundel MS 26, p. 30 [f. 29v]).
50   E 101/409/14.
51   See below, p. 117.

Hewet does not strike us as an Italian name. Although this letter describes him as 'of Rome', the name is not as transparent as we might think. According to the vagaries of medieval spelling, Rouen could also be written as 'Rome'.[52] We find this identification more likely. Silver vessels, rings and jewels were all typically given as New Year's gifts, commemorating – and in some sense imitating – the Wise Men's gifts to the baby Jesus. The question raised by this letter is how much foreign trading and buying did the queen do? Her interest here was in receiving Hewet's purchases unhindered – and free of customs duties.

Although this letter is undated, it directly follows the letter regarding Isabelle of Lorraine's chaplain in the manuscript and refers to it in the abbreviation of its addressees. It therefore seems probable that they were written around the same time.

[40] Queen re Safe Conduct granted to Guille[m] Alany, 1448–49
(BL, Add. MS 46,846, fols 44–44v; Monro, p. 147)

> Margaret, by the grace of God, etc., to all maner admiralles, capitains, lieutenant[s], custumers, serchers, kepers of portes, maiers, shirefs, baillefs, constables, and al other my lordes officers and trewe liege peuple: greting. And for asmoche as it hath liked my lordes highnesse of his especial grace to grante his lettres patentes of saufconduit unto Guille[m][53] Alany, maister of a shipp of Britaingne of portage of 1 [50] tonne clept the *Jenet*, to come into this reaume with certeine wyne of oures for oure use, we pray yow hertely that unto the seid Guille[m] and unto his mariners, after th'effecte and pourport of my said lordes lettres of saufconduit, ye wilbe welwilled, frendly and faverable, without suffring theim to be greved, interrupt or empechet to the contrarie, rather by contemplacion of this oure praier, as we trust yow and as ye thinke to do us pleasure. Yeven, etc., the yere of my lordes reigne xxvij [1448–49].

During the fifteenth century both the king and queen imported their own wine, as did England's great lords.[54] Most of the wine drunk in England was red from Gascony, which remained in English hands until 1453, and was transported in English ships that sailed to Bordeaux twice a year for that specific purpose. The danger of spoilage dictated the timing of the wine fleet. In the absence of bottling, wine began to deteriorate as soon as the barrel was opened, so most wine was

---

52 As in J.G. Nichols, ed., *Chronicle of the Grey Friars of London* (1852), p. 1, where the spelling is noted, and on subsequent pages.

53 Monro transcribed his given name as 'Guille', but there is an upward hook on the 'e' that may represent a truncated 'm'. The spelling of his name may help to determine his identity.

54 M.K. James, *Studies in the Medieval Wine Trade*, ed. E.M. Veale (Oxford, 1971), p. 178. By importing their own, they avoided paying the customs and subsidy charged to merchants who imported for resale.

drunk new. New wine from Gascony was shipped in late autumn, arriving in England towards the end of the year in time for Christmas. Wine that was left on the lees a little longer, and considered to be of higher quality, was shipped between April and June of the following year.[55] Throughout the first half of the fifteenth century, despite fluctuations of war and weather, the volume of wine imports remained relatively stable, with a high annual average of 12,000 tuns from 1444 to 1449 during the truce of Tours.[56] This happy situation came to an end in July 1449 when war broke out again between England and France. Imports for the following season dropped by a little more than half. The initial surrender of Bordeaux in 1451 and its final loss in 1453 brought an end to English dominance of the carrying trade with Gascony. Thereafter, the large English ships that had comprised the wine fleet were replaced by smaller ships of Brittany, and later by the Spaniards.[57]

Margaret's letter reinforces a safe conduct issued by Henry. It was *her* wine, and she seems to have added her voice as a specific precaution to ensure that it was safely delivered. Of Guille[m] Alany and his ship the *Jenet*, we have found no further obvious traces; however, there are several references to a William Aleyn or Alyn who appears to have been active in shipping, piracy – and possibly the wine trade – around this time. On 9 September 1445, he was relieved of 'certain uncustomed goods', unfortunately unspecified, from a ship he mastered called *le Cuthbert* in the port of Great Yarmouth. Interestingly, the forfeitures provided four yeomen and grooms of the pantry with payment for their expenses in 'crossing beyond the sea for the king's consort'. In May 1448, he and six others were charged with piracy and ordered arrested in the matter of a ship laden with goods in Flanders destined for London, which they commandeered and took to Fowey instead, where they apparently sold its contents for their own benefit.[58] The similarity between 'Guillem Alany' and 'William Aleyn' is intriguing; we may be seeing French and English versions of the same name. If so, his history suggests that this particular ship's master may have stood in unusual need of safe conduct.

---

55   P.W. Hammond, *Food and Feast in Medieval England* (Stroud, 1993), pp. 57–8. Bottling began in the sixteenth century. Since all wine would have been subject to similar conditions, it is reasonable to assume that shipping practices for other wines were similar, although only red wine was left on the lees.

56   M.G.A. Vale, *English Gascony, 1399–1453* (1970), p. 14.

57   James, *Studies in the Medieval Wine Trade*, pp. 84, 132–3.

58   *CPR, 1441–46*, p. 391; *1446–52*, p. 187. The line between legitimate shipping and piracy could be thin, the same men engaging in both. A William Aleyn turns up as a middleman in the wine trade of Southampton 'before 1456' (James, *Studies in the Medieval Wine Trade*, p. 186). The surname 'Alain' can also be found among Breton mariners doing business with England: an Yvon and a Pierre appear in 1468 and 1472–73 respectively (H. Touchard, *Le commerce maritime Breton a la fin du moyen age* [Paris, 1967], pp. 182, 176 n. 11).

Do these disparate pieces of information shed further light on when Margaret's letter was written? The timing seems tight for her to have written after 1 September 1448 in anticipation of an autumn shipping schedule. If Margaret preferred the more mature and 'better' vintage wines – at least for her own personal consumption – she could have written at any point in early 1449 and used a Breton ship simply because it was convenient. But the resumption of hostilities between England and France that summer would have changed the outlook. Although no one knew exactly how the wine trade would be affected, it was reasonable to expect difficulties and natural to worry. If Margaret was concerned about receiving her holiday shipment on time and in the quantity she wanted, she may have started organizing matters in August and turned to the intrepid Alany/Aleyn to handle the transport.

The next letter was not published by Monro, and we could see why. Our translation is relatively free – in some places more so than in others!

[41] Letters Patent by the Queen re Anthony Molaner, 9 August 1446
(BL, Add. MS 46,846, fols 43–43v)

Margareta, dei gracia Regina Anglie & Francie & Domina Hibernie, Universis & singulis regibus, principibus, ducibus, marchionibus, comitibus, nobilibus, baronibus, dominis, vicecomitibus, capitaneis, castellanis, constabulariis, gubernatoribus vicorum fortaliciorum & omnibus aliis amicis & benevolis nostris ac populis cuiuscumque status, gradus, dignitatis, preeminencie seu condicionis fuerint, ad quos presentes litteres pervenerint, Salutem. Cum dilectus serviens noster et famuliaris Antonius Molaner de Villania [*sic*] de Penerendo[59] pro certis negociis expediendi ad longinquas mundi partes habeat se transferre, universitatem nostram[60] multipliciter honorabilem & quemlibet vestrum per se attentius & efficatius quo possumus tenore presentium requirimus & rogamus quatenus eundem Antonium, cum ipsum per regna dominia & potestates vestra seu alicuius vestrum transire contigerit, nostre magestatis intuitu & harum litterarum nostrarum speciali interventu propensius recommendatum habentes eundem Antonium cum famuliaribus, equis, bonis, hernesiis & rebus suis quibuscumque recipiatis

---

59 Possibly Peñaranda de Bracamonte, south of Salamanca in Spain. *Villania* is a peculiar spelling that might better be understood as 'Villanova', a fairly commonplace name in southern France and Spain. The spelling of *Villania*, however, is very clear on the page. The second word begins with *p-* and ends in *-endo*, but what lies between is a guess. Perhaps the copyist was unsure of it but felt obligated to produce something that could pass as a word!

60 Occurring at the beginning of a line, this word is very faint. Possibly *in viam*, though that does not provide a good fit with what can be made of the spelling. It appears from this whole phrase (*universitatem ... per se*) that Margaret was casting as wide a net as possible by including both *her* people (*nostram*) and the subordinates of others whom Molaner might meet on his journeys (*vestrum*) in her appeal.

& inibi morari seu per eadem regna dominia & potestates cum sibi placuerit &
absque impedimento seu perturbacione quacumque redire permittatis Necnon
salvum & securum conductum et si necesse fuerit suis sumptibus habere faciatis
Non inferentes eis seu quomodolibet inferris permitentes in corporibus seu bonis
eorundem dampnum, impedimentum, violenciam, iniuriam, seu gravamen quam
pocius si egeant eis in eorum agenda ministrare dignere consilium, auxilium &
favorem ac scortam[61] salvamque & securum conductum per passus loca & dominia
vestra & cuiuslibet vestrum r[ati]o[n]alibus[62] sumptibus suis & expensis. Et si quid
eis in personis vel in rebus iniuriatum fuerit, quod vellemus id indilate reformare
curetis nostris precibus & amore. Nos siquidem subditis vestris & cuiuslibet vestrum,
cum ad regna seu dominia nostras aliquos ex ipsis declinare contigerit, favorem,
consimilem & maiorem si indiguerint grato animo impendere promittimus &
de facto veraciter impendemus. In cuius rei testimonem [*sic*] has litteras nostras
fieri fecimus patentes per unum annum durantes vel quandem nobis placuerit
duraturas. Datum sub signeto nostro apresente [*sic*] nostro magno sigillo apud
Westmonasterium mensis Augusti die nono Anno Regni metuendissimi domini
mei Regis Henricis sexto post conquestum vicesimo quarto.

Margaret, by the grace of God queen of England and France and Lady of
Ireland, to all and singly the kings, princes, dukes, marquesses, counts, nobles,
barons, lords, viscounts, captains, castellans, constables, governors of fortified places,
and all our other friends and well-wishers and people of whatever estate, rank,
dignity, pre-eminence or condition they may be, to whom these present letters
come: greeting. Whereas our beloved servant and household member Antony
Molaner of Villania has to travel to distant parts of the world to handle certain
business matters, we require and ask all most honorable [people] of ours and yours,
as attentively and effectively as we may according to the tenor of the present letters,
that when the same Antony happens to travel through your realms, territories
and jurisdictions, you receive the same Antony more readily, with his household,
horses, property, harnesses and goods he has conveyed, by the contemplation of
our authority and by the special mediation of these our letters. And when it pleases
him to remain there or in these realms, territories and jurisdictions, that he and
those accompanying him be permitted safe conduct to return without hindrance
or disturbance whatsoever. And if they need to obtain supplies for themselves, not
to inflict or allow to be inflicted on them any damage, hindrance, violence, injury
or grievance to their persons or goods. If they are in need, to deem it worthy of
providing them as much as possible with counsel, aid and favor in their business
matters, and also safe escort and secure conduct (or passage money) throughout

---

61   Some of the letters of this word are oddly formed. *Scorta* (or *scortum*) meant 'escort' during the
     Middle Ages (C.T. Martin, *The Record Interpreter* [1910], p. 315). In classical Latin, it meant
     'prostitute'.
62   The basic meaning of *ratio* was 'account', so it could mean a business matter or affair.

your lands and territories for their business-related supplies and provisions.[63] And if anything causes injury to them in their persons or affairs, we wish with our prayers and love that you see promptly to making amends. Accordingly, we freely promise to give favor, counsel and more to any of your subjects if they need it when any of them happen to visit any of our realms or territories, and in fact we [will] truly give it. In witness whereof we have caused these our letters patent to be made for the duration of one year, or for such term as pleases us. Given under our signet, our great seal being affixed[64] at Westminster, the 9th day of August in the 24th year of the reign of my dread lord Henry VI after the conquest.

This may best be described as a letter of credence, introducing Antony Molaner to whomever he may meet along his way and requesting that he be given all possible aid and assistance. While it specifically – and repetitively – asks for safe conduct, its appeal includes other kinds of help, as is made clear by Margaret's offer to reciprocate.

The large number of addressees who constitute its potential recipients seems noteworthy. Indeed, it appears that the queen was at pains to leave no one out. As a corollary, it also seems to have been directed to 'her people' (i.e., her husband's subjects) as well as to persons who were not subject to his jurisdiction. Patent letters were unsealed, so Molaner could have shown this to anyone he encountered during his travels.

The letter's date lends greater interest to these observations. At the beginning of August 1446, Margaret had been queen for little more than a year. She was sixteen years old. Despite the penchant for letters patent to wallow in often-repetitive detail, this one seems a bit excessive. In this formulaic letter is it possible to see traces of youthful enthusiasm in the exercise of power and position that were still relatively new? Margaret seems to leave nothing unconsidered in covering Molaner's possible needs, so it may also be that he was traveling in dangerous territory well outside any areas in which Henry's name could offer protection. This may also explain why the letter is in Latin.

Unfortunately, we know little about Molaner. He seems to have been a merchant engaged in trade, who would be traveling with a substantial party. In light of the wide range of persons to whom this was addressed, Margaret evidently hoped he would receive assistance – and avoid interference – from anyone he met

---

63 This is a difficult passage. *Auxilium* ('aid') frequently carried a monetary connotation, and *conductus* could mean 'passage money' or 'customary payment'. It is possible that the kind of assistance Margaret sought included aid in dealing with tolls or customs charges, or even help in obtaining the best deals.

64 The word *apresente* is perhaps a mistaken copy of *apensente*.

abroad or whom he encountered upon his return to England bearing whatever goods or information he had obtained for her during his travels.

[42] Queen to the King's Officers re John Lory, 22 June 1447[65]
(BL, Add. MS 46,846 fols 43v–44)

Margerete, by the grace of God Quene of Englond and of Fraunce and Ladye of Ireland, to all maners shireves, bayllifs, constables, and other my lordes officers and treue subgettes that thise oure present lettres shul come to: greting. Know ye that by good deliberacion and advis we have with holden Jenyn Lory of the citee of London, cordewainer, to do us service in his said crafte. And it is so that for such besynes [business] and neccessite that he must nedes have others, while in hasty deliverance therof it is expedient that he have greet helpe of wokmen [sic] of the same craft for the tyme. Wherfor we desire & praye yow, and also exhorte & require yow, that unto the seid J. in pourveying and taking up reasonably of such workmen for oure use, to serve us bifore any other in the said craft whanne the neccessite requireth, paying theym such wages and deutes as belongeth unto theym in this behalf, ye wilbe, at reverence of us, helping, furthering and supporting with all th'ease and faver that ye goodly may. And the rather by contemplacion of thiese oure request and prayer, as we trust, in which ye shul mow do us greet pleasaunce. In witnesse wherof to thise presente letres during oure pleasure we have do put oure signet. Yeven at Westminster the xxij day of Juyn the yere of my lordes reigne xxv.

[43] Queen to the Mayor and Sheriffs of London re John Lory, 11 November [1447]
(BL, Add. MS 46,846, fols 13–13v; Monro, p. 111)

By the Quene

Trusty, etc. We grete you well. Latyng you wite that John Lory, oure cordewaner, is so occupied in our service, other while in his craft and other while in comyng towardes us at such tymes as we shall have nede of his crafte and sende for hym, that he may not appere and attende in enquestes in the cite of London. Wherfore we praye you that duryng the tyme that he is in suche wise oure servant ye will not suffre hym to be empanelled, but therein sparing hym atte reverence of us, so that he be nomore vexed ne empeched in that bihalf. As we truste yowe. In which thing, etc. Yeven, etc., the iij day of November.

To the Mair and Shirefs of London

A cordwainer was a craftsman who worked with fine leather; he was primarily a shoemaker, though his work was not strictly limited to shoes. The term 'cordwain' is a corruption of Córdoba. The Moorish city had become famous for its superbly

---

65 This and the next letter concern the same person and subject and are discussed together.

tanned goatskin, its principal export, during the earlier Middle Ages. Although other areas would soon become suppliers of fine leather, the Spanish product retained its superior reputation and the name stuck.[66] Throughout the fifteenth century the London guild of cordwainers was frequently at loggerheads with the cobblers over the respective boundaries of their crafts. At that time the cobblers bought, repaired and resold *old* shoes; the issue was how much new leather could be added to the product and in what way before it became a *new* shoe – and infringed upon the cordwainers' monopoly of the right to work with new leather.[67]

It appears from these two letters that John Lory had been put in charge of a substantial project for Margaret that was both time-consuming and labor-intensive. Only one letter is fully dated, and we extrapolate from internal evidence that seems to put this letter at the beginning of the project that the second letter was written later in the same year. Lory was obviously a Londoner, and it appears from the second letter that he had already been 'vexed' by the mayor and sheriffs for having failed in his civic duties. On 9 April 1461, a John Lory named Sir John Wenlock, Thomas Brice, mercer, John Whitclyff, saddler, Robert Spayne, scrivener, and Richard Sherd and Andrew Scarlet, both cordwainers, as feoffees for all his goods and chattels. The enfeoffment was not enrolled until 15 January 1462 under Edward IV.[68] Enfeoffment was frequently used to set up a trust in order to avoid death duties, forfeiture and the like.[69] With this in mind, it may be that the circumstances of Henry VI's deposition had something to do with Lory's action. Sir John Wenlock had been Margaret's chamberlain until 1453, but by April 1461 he was the earl of Warwick's man. Lory could have met him while he was in Margaret's service, and Wenlock's name would have carried more weight, perhaps providing greater security for Lory's wealth, than those of his fellow Londoners.

The obvious difference between these two letters, apart from their headings, is that the first was written to men who were directly responsible to the king for their positions. Margaret needed their aid and cooperation to obtain the workmen needed to see her project through, and in this case, it made sense to use all of her titles and to frame her request as an order – a polite order, but an order nonetheless. The situation was different with the City of London. There, Margaret

---

66 C.H.W. Mander, *A Descriptive and Historical Account of the Guild of Cordwainers of the City of London* (1931), pp. 12–13.

67 Ibid., pp. 54–9.

68 *Cal. Plea Rolls, 1458–82*, p. 158. We are grateful to Caroline Barron for this reference, the only one we have found for John Lory outside of Margaret's letters.

69 Ibid., *1437–57*, pp. xxiv, xxvi.

had to ask more gently. When she pushed, she was apt to encounter substantial resistance, as occurred when she wrote in the case of Alexander Manning.[70]

[44] Queen to her Masters of Horses, Aveners,[71] Purveyors, etc., re the Convent of Stratford-at-Bowe, 17 August 1448
(BL, Add. MS 46,846, fol. 44)

Margerete, etc. To al the maisters of oure horses, oure avener[s], pourveors and other oure officers of oure stable and avenrie: greting. Know ye that for asmuche as we have granted unto th'abbesse and convent of the nonnrie of Stratford of the Bowe that they shulde be quiete and discharged of al maner taking and logging [lodging] there to oure use, we wol and charge yow that ye take no goodes of thaires ne logge in any of theire houses in the same towne. But suffre theim peisibly t'enjoye theire livelode to theire most availe and proufite withoute attempting interrupcion or empechement to the contrarie of this present grant and proteccion, at your peril, for thus it pleaseth us to be doon. Yeven etc. at Windesor the xvij day of August the yere of my lordes reigne xxvj.

The royal household frequently abused its right to purveyance – the taking of foodstuffs, animal feed and the animals themselves from the localities at need. Complaints against the practice were rife in parliament during the fifteenth century, though they were nothing new.[72] In this case, however, since no complaint is mentioned it appears that Margaret was protecting the convent from her own purveyors as a mark of her favor.

Stratford-at-Bowe was a Benedictine house located in Middlesex between London and Enfield that took its name from the bow-shaped bridge that had been built over the River Lee in the early twelfth century. Henry VI was there on 18 July 1447.[73] As he had come from Greenwich – which he had just granted to Margaret – it seems likely that she was with him, and she probably visited the convent on other occasions because of its proximity to her Middlesex properties. Thus, the queen may have granted Stratford immunity from her purveyors in return for its hospitality. The abbess to whom Margaret referred was probably Margaret Holbeche, who was elected to the office in 1436.[74]

Although we do not know whether he was among the persons addressed by

---

70 See above, pp. 48ff.
71 The avener was the chief stable officer, in charge of obtaining feed for horses.
72 J.R. Maddicott, 'The English Peasantry and the Demands of the Crown 1294–1341', *Past and Present*, Supplement I (1975), for purveyance in the early fourteenth century.
73 Wolffe, *Henry VI*, p. 366.
74 D.M. Smith, ed., *The Heads of Religious Houses: England and Wales*, III, *1377–1450* (Cambridge, 2008), p. 695. Her apparent successor was Katherine Washburne, who held the position in 1477.

this letter, an interesting story attaches to Jacques Blondell, one of Margaret's aveners. His name suggests that he was French and probably joined her household in Rouen because of the large number of horses that her reception demanded. If so, he followed her to England where he received gifts of a brooch from her in 1446–47 and a gold armlet in 1448–49.[75] He also had some connection to the duke of Suffolk, for in 1450 he requested leave to accompany Suffolk into exile.[76] If he was with Suffolk, he was probably among the duke's entourage that was put ashore at Dover after Suffolk was murdered. In any event, Blondell next appears in service to the widowed duchess of Suffolk as a farmer (of rents) for the manor of Cotton.[77] However he spent the next few years, in 1461 he allegedly proclaimed that 'he had noon othere soverain lord ne never wold have whiles he lyved, but king Henry and to him was sworn and to Queen Margaret'. His pronouncement notwithstanding, Blondell continued to serve the de la Poles, who had conveniently become Edward IV's supporters. Blondell soon followed them into the 'enemy camp', serving as Queen Elizabeth's avener in 1466–67 and becoming King Edward's cofferer in 1479. He must have had a long and interesting life: his will is dated 1492.[78]

[45] **Queen re William Newby of Leicester, 20 May 1449**
(Historical Manuscripts Commission: *Eighth Report*, Appendix, pp. 414–15)

Margarete by the Grace of God Quene of England and of Fraunce and Lady of Ireland, etc. Be it knawen to alle men to whom this present writyng shalle come that where as a certeyn comission of my fuldoutfull Lord was directed to certeyn persons to enquier as well of geving of lyvere as of other divers articles as in the seyd commission plainly appereth, by force of which commission before the commissioners of the seyd commission it was presented by William Newby and other of our tenauntes of Leicestre lawfully empanelled to enquire of the articles conteyned in the same commission, that certeyn persones in Leycestre had taken clothyng of diverse persones ayents the forme of the statute: that is to wete that some of hem had taken clothyng of the Viscount Beaumont and some of Sir Edward Grey, Lord Ferrers of Growby, and some of hem had taken clothyng of other divers persones, by cause of which presentment diverses persones, some of the houshold of the seyd Lord Ferrers and some of the clothyng of the said lord with other wele wilners

75   E 101/409/17 and E 101/410/2.
76   Virgoe, 'The Death of William de la Pole, Duke of Suffolk', in *East Anglian Society*, pp. 248 and 256, n. 15.
77   C. Richmond, *The Paston Family in the Fifteenth Century: The First Phase* (Cambridge, 2002), p. 236.
78   D.A.L. Morgan, 'The King's Affinity in the Polity of Yorkist England', *Transactions of the Royal Historical Society* 23 (1973), p. 14.

to the said lord as yet not to be knawen, by supportacioun and favour and for
pleasance to the said lord, as we ben enformed, by cause of the said presentement
betyn and sore woundetyn the said William Neuby and manesten to bete other
of our tenauntes of Lycestre in semblable maner, and sithyn that tyme diverses
persones longyng to the said Lord Ferrers at diverses tymes have manassed to
bete diverses tenauntes and inhabitauntes in our town of Leycestre. Also we ben
enformed that the said lord, his servantes and his wele willyng at divers tymes have
hunted and doun grete hurt and harme to our game in our lordshipe of Leycestre
as wele in our chaces as in our parkes there. We, consideryng the pease and the
wele of our tenauntes and of our chaces and parkes in our lordship of Leycestre
and the grete hurt and harme of the said William Newby our tenaunt, ordeyne,
deme and awarde that the said Lord Ferrers for hym and for those that betyn the
said William Neuby paye to the said William Newby a c. marcs of good money of
England: that is to wete xl. marcs the third day of Juyn next to come after the date
of this our present awarde, and xx *li.* the third day of Juyn then next following,
and xx *li.* the third day of Juyn then next suyng in amendement and satisfaccioun
for the betyng and woundyng of the said William Neuby. And that the said Lord
Ferrers be goode lorde to the said William Neuby and to all other tenauntes in our
lordship of Leycestre, and that the said lord shall not geve any clothyng or lyverey
to any persone dwellyng within our said lordship. Ne that the said lord mayntene
ne support any persone dwellyng within our said lordship in any forme agaynes
the rule of our towne of Leycestre or agaynes the rule of any other place of our said
lordship of Leycestre, and also that the said lord, his servantez and tenauntes, and all
other that be toward hym kepe the peas ayenst all the tenauntez and inhabitauntes
of our said lordship, and ayenst Thomas Farnham. And also we awarde that the sayd
lord delyver to Lowys Fitz Lowys an obligacioun by the which the said Lowys was
bounde unto the said lord in xx *li.* for to eschewe the bodely hurt which was likly to
have fallen to oon William Pecok, a tenaunt of us of our lordship of Stebbyng, by
the said lord or his servantz and for none other cause as we we [*sic* – be?] credebly
enformed. In witnesse of which thyng to this our present awarde we have made to
putte our sealls. Yeven the xx day of May the yere of the reigne of my most douted
lord kyng Henry the Sext xxvii.

Mutual obligations of service and lordship were integral to late medieval English
society; indeed, they were the glue that held it together. A person's identity was
determined by the services he performed for his superiors and by the protections
and benefits he received from them in return.[79] Such relationships also provided
the basic means of military recruitment: when the king needed to raise an army,
he turned to his lords, who in turn called up their retainers, the men who owed

79   For the importance of such relationships, see R. Horrox, *Fifteenth-Century Attitudes* (Cambridge, 1994), pp. 61–78.

them service. During the middle years of the fifteenth century, however, the granting of livery (i.e., clothing in the identifying colors of a particular lord) in return for service both fed off and contributed to the breakdown of law and the king's authority.[80]

The crown had long recognized that these mutually dependent relationships could lead to abuse, often in the form of private armies that carried out their masters' feuds and preyed upon the neighborhood. As a result, efforts had been made to regulate them. The most notable of these was the statute of 1399, which made it illegal for lords to grant livery of clothing to any but their household servants, officers and councilors.[81] As might be expected, the attempt to limit and regulate was never more than partially successful. In the mid-fifteenth century, when law by itself did not preserve order and some of the king's servants were perceived as predators, individuals resorted to various forms of extra-legal self-help to achieve their ends.

In early 1448 a series of commissions were appointed throughout the country to look into a wide range of lawless activities, including the granting of 'liveries of cloth, given and received contrary to Statute'.[82] William Newby and other tenants of the queen's honor of Leicester had been empaneled as a jury before the commission, and they had duly reported that Viscount Beaumont and Sir Edward Grey, Lord Ferrers of Groby, had been granting livery illegally. Beaumont was constable of England and one of Henry VI's confidantes; he had been steward of the honor of Leicester since 1437, and would become chief steward of the queen's lands by 1452. Margaret, as far as is known, did not reprimand Beaumont, but Ferrers was another matter. According to Margaret's complaint, men of his household along with others wearing his livery (i.e., illegally) proceeded to beat up William Newby and to threaten her other tenants, apparently with Ferrers's approval. Linked to these intimidation tactics, Ferrers and his men were also accused of poaching game in the queen's parks and chases; this was a stock indictment that was frequently added to other accusations of lawlessness. In any event, Margaret ordered Ferrers to pay Newby substantial recompense for his beating and, thereafter, to give no liveries to anyone within her lordship and to keep the peace with her tenants. Tacked on to this are the references to Thomas Farnham, appearing here as another victim of Grey's predations, and Lewis

---

80 See M. Hicks, *Bastard Feudalism* (1995), for a good overview of the practice of retaining in the later Middle Ages.

81 C. Given-Wilson, *The Royal Household and the King's Affinity* (1986), pp. 237–8.

82 *CPR, 1446–52*, pp. 139–40, for the commissions of 8 February. The first entry provides the list of wrongdoings to be investigated; the commission for Leicester is on p. 140.

FitzLewis, who seems to have been blackmailed for £20 to avoid any harm being done to William Pecok, said to be one of the queen's tenants of Stebbing, Essex.[83]

Margaret's description of William Newby as her tenant may perhaps give the impression of her willingness to come to the aid of the 'little guy' when he happened to be one of her own. In fact, Newby was a prominent Leicester burgess who was returned as one of the town's MPs in February 1449. Thus, he was its representative when the queen ordered the monetary settlement, giving her favor a political dimension that is otherwise not readily apparent from the letter itself. Her intervention apparently paid off. Four days later, 'two of Grey's followers ... bound themselves to Newby, probably in connection with the payment of the compensation'.[84]

Sir Edward Grey came by his title through his marriage to Elizabeth Ferrers, the granddaughter and heiress of William, Lord Ferrers, who died in 1445. He had served as a JP for Warwick from 1443 to 1446, but he was not actively involved in government. In April 1448, together with Thomas Farnham and three others, he received a commission of gaol delivery for Leicester, and in June, Ferrers and Farnham – along with Viscount Beaumont and others – were named justices of the peace for Leicester.[85] Although we cannot say whether Ferrers's enmity towards Farnham stemmed from this association, it is at least possible. Perhaps there was some rivalry – or a conflict of interest.[86] In 1449, and again in 1451 and 1453, Ferrers was involved in raising loans or in collecting the subsidy in Leicester and Warwick to support the war in France.[87] He died in 1457.

83   Fitz Lewis had been made steward of Havering-at-Bower, Essex, for life in 1442, following his father in that office. The grant was resumed in parliament in November 1449, but the stewardship was re-granted to him for life in April 1452, with all wages due from the date of the resumption (*CPR, 1441–46*, p. 131; *1446–52*, p. 542). Havering had been Margaret's land from 1447. For Stebbing, see the first letter in the next chapter.

84   One of these men, Henry Boteler, was also an MP at this time. S. Payling, 'Identifiable Motives for Election to Parliament in the Reign of Henry VI', in *The Fifteenth Century VI: Identity and Insurgency in the Late Middle Ages*, ed. L. Clark (Woodbridge, 2006), p. 99 and n. 46, sees Newby as an example of someone who sought election in order to advance his cause in a local dispute.

85   *CPR, 1441–46*, p. 480; *1446–52*, pp. 136, 590.

86   Farnham had already been a JP for Leicester in 1439, and again from 1442 to 1445 (*CPR, 1436–41*, p. 585; *1441–46*, p. 473). A brief biography is in Acheson, *Gentry Community*, p. 229.

87   *CPR, 1446–52*, pp. 298, 299, 412; *1452–61*, p. 53.

Five

PROTECTOR AND PEACEMAKER

One of the functions of any good lord or lady was to provide support and protection when their tenants or servants – or other persons with a claim on them – were threatened or harassed. Some disputes that Margaret dealt with involved actual threats to life and limb or more general 'vexation', alleged false charges of debt or trespass and complaints regarding purveyance. Another large group of complaints revolved around property matters and claims of wrongful disseisin. This occurred when someone was dispossessed of property, often by force. In her response to appeals for protection and aid, Margaret was doing no more and no less than what her contemporaries expected of persons in the upper strata – even when they took issue, usually on personal grounds, with the influence of someone on the outcome of a *particular* dispute.

The queen's response to these appeals took different forms. She might simply order the perpetrators to stop whatever it was that they were doing. Often, however, the matter was not so simple. When the offending party was attached to another lord, she would ask – or require – him to intervene on her appellant's behalf to resolve the matter. In other cases, she called upon some neutral person to be an arbiter. Her expectation that the outcome should favor her appellant is generally quite clear. Nevertheless, it should not be thought that Margaret simply set out to ride roughshod over other competing claims. In several instances, she was careful to indicate that complaints against her people should be brought before her council, or to acknowledge the possibility of legitimate grounds for contention. This chapter contains more letters than any other in this section. Their number provides testimony to the importance of these activities to Margaret as queen and good lady.

The first three letters involve general harassment and physical threats to

Margaret's people. Other specific forms of harassment follow: an accusation of trespass, two circumstances of alleged debt, a claim against purveyance, and another against the infringement of liberties. Next come the property disputes. Three letters require lords to put a stop to wrongful disseisins committed by their clients or servants. Two more request less specific 'help' in restoring property to its rightful owners. But lest we think that Margaret always stood on the side of the dispossessed, a further letter shows her encouraging the predators. In the next three letters Margaret plays the role of peacemaker: directly, in two cases involving property, a charge of assault and a long-running feud, and in the third, by calling on an arbiter to resolve a dispute. The last letter mysteriously refers to documents needed by one of her servants – assuredly to settle something!

[46] Queen to Sir Edward Grey, Lord Ferrers of Groby, re her Tenants of Stebbing
(BL, Add. MS 46,846, fols 48v–49; Monro, pp. 146–7)

> By the Quene
> Right trusty and welbeloved, we grete you well. And for asmoch as we be enformed that your baillif of Stebbyng wrongfully vexeth, troubleth and oppresseth oure tenantes of our lordship of Stebbing aswel in usurping and breking oure franchise there as in other grevous wise; we therfore desire and praye you, and also exhorte and require you, that ye do yeve in commandement unto your said bailiff for to cesse of his said vexacions and oppressing and put him in suche reule that oure said tenantes may leve in rest and peas, so that they have no cause to compleine ayeine unto us for lak of remedie in your defaulte, as ye thinke to stande in the faver of oure good grace and t'eschewe our displeasure, at your peril.
> Yeven *etc.* the *etc.*
> To the Lord Ferriers of Groby

This letter, like the one concerning William Newby in the previous chapter, also involves the actions of one of Lord Ferrers's men and Margaret's tenants of Stebbing. But unlike the Newby letter, which orders restitution after the offense, this one simply tells Ferrers to stop his man from harassing Margaret's tenants.

Stebbing in Essex, located about three miles northeast of Great Dunmow, one of Margaret's dower lands, was part of the Ferrers inheritance. Sir Edward Grey, through his marriage to the Ferrers heiress, became Lord Ferrers of Groby in right of his wife. Titles to a property did not necessarily involve the entirety of that property, as we might expect. One person could hold a portion of a manor, while someone else held the rest. Since this letter states that Ferrers had a bailiff at Stebbing and that Margaret had tenants there, it suggests that there was some sort of shared jurisdiction. The queen was not just claiming that Ferrers's bailiff was bothering her tenants, but that he was infringing on *her* rights. This may help to explain her last sentence, which threatens Ferrers with the consequences should he lose her favor.

Lord Ferrers's son, Sir John Grey, married Elizabeth Woodville. Sir John was killed fighting for Margaret and the Lancastrians at the second battle of St Albans in 1461. His widow went on to become Edward IV's wife and queen.

[47] Queen to Edmund Pyrcan, Squire, re William Southwood of Hertingfordbury, 1 March
(BL, Add. MS 46,846, fols 45–45v; Monro, p. 126)

By the Quene

Trusty and welbeloved. We late you wite that we be enformed that ye wrongefully vexe, trouble and manace to bette and sle [beat and slay] William Southwode, oure bailyff of oure lordeship of Hertingfordbury, so that he dar not, for drede of dethe, abide in oure saide lordship and attende upon oure service there as his dewte is, unto greet hindring and derogacion aswel of oure said bailiff as of oure right and deute there, as it is said. Wherof we merveil gretly. Wherfore we wol, exhorte and require yow that ye suffre oure said bailiff to leve at home in rest and peas, without vexing, diseasing or attempting any thing ayeinst our seid bailiff or the lest [least] of oure tenantes there, otherwise thanne right, trouth and good conscience asken and requiren. And in case ye finde yow agreved ayeinst any of oure seid tenantes there, yf ye wil compleyne yow to us or oure counceil, ye shul be remedied as the case justly requireth. And that ye fail not herof in no wise, as ye desire to stande in the faver of oure good grace and t'eschewe oure displeasure, at your peril. Yeven, etc. at oure manoir of Ples[aunce] the first day of Marche.

To Edmond Pyrcan, squier

[48] Queen to Sir John Forester, Knight, re her Tenants of Hertingfordbury
(BL, Add. MS 46,846, fols 45v–46; Monro, pp. 126–8)

By the Quene

Trusty and welbeloved. We late yow wite that this same day ther have be bifore us a greete multitude, both of men and women, oure tenantes of oure lordship of Hertingfordbury, compleynyng theim that ye have and yet be dayly about to distroie and undo theim for ever, in so ferthforth [far] that ye have do many of theim to be wrongfully endited nowe late of felonye bifore the crowner [coroner] by your owne famulier servantes and adherentes, not knowyng the trouth of the mater. And many of theym ye do kepe in prisonne, and the remenant of oure tenants dar not abide in theire houses for fer of deth and other injuries that ye dayly do theim, and al by color of a ferme that ye have there of oures that, as it is said, for your owne singuler lucre ye wrongfully engrose towardes you al oure tenantes lyvelode there, not ownly unto grete hindering and undowyng of oure said tenantes, but also unto grete derogacion and prejudice of us and of oure said lordship – wherof we merveil greetly – and, in especial, that ye that be jugge [judge] wold take so parceably the wrongfully [*sic*] destruccion of oure said tenantes. Wherfore we wol and expressly exhorte and require yow that ye leve your said labors and besinesse, in especial ayeinst us and oure said tenantes, until tyme that ye have communed and declared you in this mater bifore us; and that, the meene while, ye do suffre oure tenantes that be in prisonne to be mainprissed under sufficiant seurtie, and the remenant of oure tenantes, giltlesse, that be fled for fere of your destruccion may come home into oure said lordship. And if eny of oure tenantes have offended ayeinst the lawe, oure entent is that, the trouth knowen, he shalbe peynfully punysshed and chastised as the cas requireth. And howe ye thinke to be disposed herin ye wil acerteine us by the bringer of thise, wherto we shall truste, as ye desire to stande in the tendre and faverable remembrance of our grace therefor in tyme comyng. Yeven, etc. at Wynd[sor], the etc.

  To John Forestu [*sic*], Knyght

These two letters involve troubles and strife occurring in the queen's lordship of Hertingfordbury in Hertfordshire. Since they were written in different places and therefore at different times, it is unlikely that the situations they sought to remedy were related. Taken together, however, they suggest that Hertingfordbury was a difficult place. Certainly, the problems and threats alluded to were of a serious nature.

  Of the persons named in these letters, we have found no other traces of Edmund Pyrcan, Margaret's bailiff William Southwood, or Sir John Forester – and we see no reason to believe that the latter was the father of John Forster, esquire, who served as Queen Elizabeth Woodville's receiver general and as MP for Hertfordshire during the 1460s and 1470s.[1] We are left with the letters' allegations and, in the case of the second, an account of the action taken by the aggrieved party to remedy the situation.

  Although we do not know the original cause of strife between Pyrcan and Southwood, it seems to have had a personal dimension. As bailiff of Hertingfordbury, Southwood's position was that of an estate manager. If he went in fear of his life as described, it would have affected his ability to perform his normal duties, giving Margaret additional cause for concern beyond her obligation as good lady to protect one of her own. At the same time, her advice to Pyrcan to refer any legitimate complaints about her tenants to her and her

---

1   As suggested by Wedgwood, p. 345. For that John Forster, see A.R. Myers, 'The Household of Queen Elizabeth Woodville', in *Crown, Household and Parliament*, ed. C.H. Chough (1985), p. 260, who offers no thoughts on his ancestry.

council stakes out a claim to open-minded fairness in the dispensation of justice, while ensuring their protection.

Forester is identified as a farmer, i.e., a collector of rents from the tenants of Hertingfordbury. The farmer collected a fixed rent from the individual tenants pretty much as he saw fit before turning it over to the bailiff (who could have been William Southwood) or the sheriff, who handed it over to the queen's receiver for the area – in this case, William Nanseglos.[2] Margaret's tenants claimed that Forester was gouging them of more than they owed for his own aggrandizement and reported his use of harsh measures, including imprisonment, to force them to pay up. So distressed were they that, instead of waiting until the queen was in the neighborhood, they sent a delegation to appeal to her at Windsor, some distance away. As a matter of added interest, this delegation included women, perhaps in the belief that the queen would be more responsive to their plight.[3] Margaret's response seems appropriately firm, but fair. Although she would countenance the punishment of lawbreakers, all prisoners were to be released and anything that might be deemed harassment must cease until Forester had explained himself and his side of things to her, at which point she would be the judge. The queen, of course, had a double interest: she wanted to be able to collect the money due to her, but, at the same time, these were *her* tenants, and allowing rent gouging to go unchecked was a sure way to lose their loyalty.

[49] Queen to the Abbot of St Osyth re Humphrey Hayford, 3 February
(BL, Add. MS 46,846, fol. 46v; Monro, p. 124)

By the Quene

Trusty and welbeloved in God, we grete you wele. And for asmoch as we be enformed that ye wrongfully vexe, trouble and disease oure welbeloved servant and goldsmyth Humfrey Hayford by feined accions of trespas ayeinst al right and good conscience, as it is seid; we therfor desire and praye yowe, and also exhorte and require you, that, serching your conscience after God and trouth and calling unto your remembrance what dishonor it shulde sowne [reflect] unto you that bene a membre of chirche in doing the contrarye, [you] wil, atte reverence of us, demene you in suche wise that no thinge be attempted ayeinst oure said servant otherwise than feith, equite and good conscience requiren in this behalf, so that he have no

2   We cannot ascertain what amount would have been due for Hertingfordbury as it was granted to Margaret together with Pleshey, Hertford, and other manors, from which an annual total of £555 16s ¼d was expected. In 1452–53 these lands only returned £353 13s 5d (Myers, 'Household', p. 158).

3   See Maurer, p. 62, for female delegations.

cause to compleyne unto us for lacke of right in your defaulte, as we trust yow. Yeven, etc. at Windesor the iij day of Feverer.

To th'abbot of the monasterie of Saint Osy

St Osyth's Abbey was a house of Augustinian canons in Essex. Its abbot was John Deeping, who had been appointed in 1434 and was succeeded sometime after 1460 by William Kent.[4] The nature of Hayford's alleged transgression is unknown, but in 1455 one William Herward was pardoned for failing to appear 'to answer John, abbot of St Osyth, touching a trespass'.[5] Margaret's letter is a strongly worded appeal to Deeping's conscience as a man of the church, although she is careful to leave the door open to legitimate grievance. It may be that her appeal was successful – or else Hayford was more careful than Herward to appear to answer charges – for there is no record of this incident in the patent rolls.

Humphrey Hayford was a member of the goldsmith's company of London and was serving the City as warden in the 1440s. He eventually became mayor in 1477–78.[6] In his capacity as goldsmith, Hayford had extensive dealings with the queen. In 1446–47 he was given a ruby worth 40s and 5 pearls worth 100s with which to repair her crown.[7] Based on her extant jewel accounts, he appears to have been the only goldsmith to whom she gave a gift, a parcel gilt pyx worth 26s 8d in 1448–49. Interestingly, a parcel gilt pyx also appears in the list of jewels purchased *from* Hayford in that year; Margaret may have returned it to him as a personal gift, perhaps in recognition of his service.[8] Her 1452–53 account shows that she bought more from him than from the two other goldsmiths named and that she trusted him to restore and repair some items of household plate as well as some plate and jewels given to her by the king.[9]

Hayford's connection with the crown extended beyond his provision of jewels and repair services. At a date unknown, though likely to have been around 1450, Hayford and three other London merchants made a loan to the crown of £1,246 13s 4d to support an expedition to Gascony – which, in the event, never sailed.[10] On 13 February 1452 an effort was made to repay Hayford and his colleagues.[11] On 2 March, Hayford, named as a king's sergeant, received the

---

4   VCH: *Essex*, II, p. 162.
5   *CPR, 1452–61*, p. 187.
6   T.F. Reddaway, *The Early History of the Goldsmiths Company, 1327–1509* (1975), p. 296, outlines his career, though some of its references are unreliable.
7   E 101/409/17.
8   E 101/410/2.
9   Myers, 'Jewels', pp. 215–17.
10   *CPR, 1446–52*, p. 377.
11   Ibid., p. 573. The money was to be taken from the tenth granted by convocation in 1449, to come from the clergy of Canterbury.

offices of controller, changer and assayer of the mint in the Tower of London in recognition of 'his good service to the king and queen'.[12] It would appear that his loan was still outstanding.

After the accession of Edward IV, despite Hayford's efforts to remain on good terms with the new regime, his former Lancastrian connections got him into trouble. In June 1468, King Edward's agents apprehended a man identified as 'Cornelius' at Queenborough. He was found to be bearing letters written by Lancastrian loyalists in exile with Queen Margaret to persons in England.[13] Under torture, 'Cornelius' began babbling the names of persons whom he claimed were in treasonous communication with the queen. One of them was Humphrey Hayford, at that time the sheriff of London. There is no reason to believe that he was the intended recipient of any of the 'incriminating' letters. Had he been, he would have been arrested outright, with no need of 'Cornelius's' accusations.[14] But the charge is ridiculous on other grounds: Hayford was one of sixty-two rich Londoners who had just given a £10,000 bond at Edward IV's behest to representatives of Charles, duke of Burgundy, in support of his imminent marriage to Edward's sister Margaret of York.[15] He and the other accused were hauled off to prison. When they were brought to trial in July, Hayford and two others were acquitted of all charges, although they were still fined. In December, by the king's command, Hayford was deprived of his position as an alderman. He still might have considered himself lucky, however, for three others had been sentenced to death.[16] Another, Sir Thomas Cook, whose name came to be synonymous with the entire affair, was stripped of his goods and valuables by Edward's father-in-law and forced to pay a fine of £8,000 to the king and an additional sum of 'queen's gold' to the queen, although he had only been convicted of misprision of treason (i.e., failure to *report* the treasonable activity of others).[17] Despite his own setback, Hayford continued to thrive, becoming alderman again and eventually mayor. He died in 1480.

[50] **Queen to Thomas Bawlde, Squire, re John Browne of Walden, 23 May**
(BL, Add. MS 46,846, fol. 13v; Monro, p. 154)

> By the Quene
> Trusty and welbeloved. For asmoche as we be enformed that at th'excitation and stering of certeine personnes not welwilled unto John Browne, oon of our

---

12   Ibid., p. 529.
13   Scofield, I, pp. 454–5.
14   As happened to a Thomas Dalton.
15   Ibid., pp. 453–4.
16   One escaped execution by a last-minute pardon.
17   Ibid., pp. 459–61, for the 'Cook affair'.

tenantes of our lordship of Walden, ye sue ayeinst al trouth and good conscience our said tenant by an obligacion of a greet somme not deu, as it is said, putting hym wrongfully to greet trouble, vexacion and losse, likely to be his utter undoing for ever without summe pourveiance of remedie be the souner had unto hym in this mater. We, willyng that our said tenant may leve in rest and peax and in quiet from suche oppression and injurie, and to ministre indifferently to all parties justice as the cas requireth, desire, praye and exhorte you that ye will, at reverence of us, put th'examinacion of your said suit to us and to our counseil, where we shall by good deliberacion and advis see that ye shull have al that that rightfully belongeth unto you in that bihalf. And, the meene while, that ye will leve and surcesse of your suit by contemplacion of this our praier, demenyng you herin in such wise that we have noon other cause thanne to have you in faver of our good grace therfore in tyme commyng. And how ye thinke to please us in this mater ye wil acertein us by the brynger of thise, wherto we shall truste. Yeven, etc. at P[leshey] the xxiij day of May, etc.

To Thomas Bawlde, squier, etc.

People during the Middle Ages rarely used consistent spellings for their names, so tracing them can be difficult. In November 1453, one John Boldro of Hitchin, Hertfordshire, was pardoned for failing to appear 'to answer Margaret, late the wife of Thomas Boud, *alias* Bauld *alias* Bawld *alias* Baud [and others] touching a plea that he render £10'.[18] If this is the Thomas Bawlde of Margaret's letter, at least we know that he died in or before 1453. Some years earlier, a Thomas Baude – who may be the same man as the deceased – appears as a commissioner to raise a loan in Essex and Hertfordshire in June 1446.[19] More nebulously, a Thomas Baude was a member of Margaret's temporary household that brought her from Rouen to England in 1445.[20] The name, however one spells it, does not appear to have been common. The associations with Essex and Hertfordshire may indicate that at least two of these references are to the same person and that he was, in fact, 'our man'. Walden in Essex, now known as Saffron Walden, was part of Margaret's dower in the duchy of Lancaster.

In this letter, as in that to Edmund Pyrcan, above, the queen proposed to handle the dispute within her council, assuring Bawlde that he would be given a fair hearing and receive 'all that rightfully belongeth unto [him]'.

18   *CPR, 1452–61*, pp. 128–9.
19   *CPR, 1441–46*, p. 430.
20   BL, Add. MS 23,938.

[51] Queen to the Lord Chancellor, the Lord Archbishop of Canterbury, re John Goldston
(BL, Add. MS 46,846, fol. 59; Monro, pp. 149–50)

By the Quene

Right reverend, etc. And for asmoche as we be enformed that oon John Goldston, as borrowe [guarantor] for my lordes servante and oures Ric[hard] Rede, is arested in the c[ity] of London by an obligacion pretended to be due, where our said servant is redy to declare and prive that the seid obligacion is not dewe, ne of right and conscience ne peny ought to be paied as he saith; we, consideryng that this mater longeth unto the court of conscience, desire and hertly praye you that ye will call this mater bifor you and grante unto our said servant a *corpus cum causa* in this partie, shewing unto our said servant, at reverence of us, the faver, tendernesse and good lordship that ye goodly may, so that he may perceive by contemplacion of thise our lettres that he be defended from all such injuries and wronges purposed ayeinst hym, and he t'atteine by your help and supportacion unto all that that to hym rightfully apperteineth with brief expedicion in this bihalf. And in cas that ye may not, with your ease, attende unto the conclusion of this mater, that thanne ye will yeve in commandement unto the Clerk of the Rolles t'accomplisse our entencion abovesaid, without remitting this mater out of your handes if in eny wise it may goodly be doone, as our singuler trust is in your good faderhode. In which thinge, etc. At Eltham the, etc.

To th'archebisshop of Canterbury, Chauncellor of Englond

If this letter was written, as seems likely, towards the beginning of Margaret's queenship, the chancellor would have been John Stafford. The court of conscience fell under the jurisdiction of chancery and was used to settle small monetary claims as well as to supervise feoffees, ensuring that they did whatever they were supposed to do. When Margaret asked that Richard Rede be granted a *corpus cum causa*, she was requesting a writ of *habeas corpus*,[21] asking that he be brought before the court to determine whether or not there was lawful cause to imprison him – or to imprison Goldston in his place as surety – and if not, to let the prisoner go. The 'obligation' was evidently monetary, and Rede was insisting that he didn't owe a penny of it. Whatever the justice of his case, Margaret believed him and wanted the matter settled right away, hence her request that the clerk of the rolls be made to issue the writ if the chancellor were unable to handle it personally.

Richard Rede may have been the man who, along with John Hardwyk, underclerk of the kitchen, had been granted in survivorship the offices of chancellor of the greenwax and clerk of the common pleas in the exchequer of

21   The full legal term is *habeas corpus cum causa*.

Ireland in 1439.[22] Rede either died or otherwise became unable to serve, for in March 1446 the grant to him and Hardwyk was surrendered and then reissued to John Hardwyk, now a clerk of the kitchen, and Alexander Shelton, again in survivorship.[23] If Rede were dead, incapacitated, or outside of England, this may be the reason why John Goldston was imprisoned in his stead.[24] We note, however, that Margaret's letter accounts him much alive. Of the unfortunate Goldston we have found no traces, except for a single mention of a John Goldston of Asshewell, Hertfordshire, 'gentilman', who in November 1446 received pardon for failing to appear to answer a pair of London 'stokfisshmongers' regarding a debt of 115s.[25] Was this whole incident caused by a barrel of fish?

[52] Queen to the Corporation of London, re her Enfield Tenants
(BL, Add. MS 46,846, fols 53v–54; Monro, pp. 98–9)

By the Quene
Trusty and welbeloved, we grete you wele. Lating you wite that albeit that it hath pleased my lordes highnesse to take oure tenantes of Enfeld into his proteccion of any maner taking, as it appereth by his grant therof under his signet; yet, nevertheles, summe of your officers, havyng no rewarde [regard] therto, unadvisely toke fro day to day the horses of our said tenantes into [unto] greet contempte of my lordes proteccion and to oure displeasure. Wherfore we pray you that, at reverence of us, ye will yeve in commandement unto all your officers t'obeie my said lordes proteccion, suffring our said tenantes to leve in quiet and rest in that bihalf so that we have no cause to pourveil other remedie in your defaulte, as we trust you. In which thing ye shul mowe deserve of us right especial thanke therfore in tyme commyng. Yeven, etc. at Windesore, the, etc.
To the Maior and Aldermen of the Cite of London.
To the Shirefs of the Cite of London, and to either of theim.

This letter illustrates the difficulties that could arise when established rights conflicted with specially granted privileges. Enfield was located in the county of Middlesex, which lay within the jurisdiction of the sheriffs of London. When defense was required or in other times of crisis, the sheriffs had the right to take

22 *CPR, 1436–41*, p. 306, dated 24 August. A week later they received exemplification of a deed appointing John Blacton, their clerk, as their deputy in these offices (ibid., p. 357).
23 *CPR, 1441–46*, p. 419, dated 6 March.
24 Although there is no particular reason to believe that the bestowal of an office in Ireland meant that the holder actually went there – and most of them did not – Rede may have been an exception. There is an earlier notice of a Richard Rede, who in 1430 nominated two men as his attorneys in England for one year because he was then 'staying in Ireland' (*CPR, 1429–36*, p. 54).
25 *CPR, 1446–52*, p. 14.

horses within the county at need. It appears that Henry VI had issued a grant exempting the manor from all forms of purveyance ('any maner taking'), which would have included the taking of horses. If Henry's grant was a general exemption from all purveyance, it would have been directed to the royal purveyors rather than to the sheriffs and might not have affected the latter's rights.[26] Whatever the case, the sheriffs or their representatives had been taking horses from Enfield – wrongfully, in Margaret's view – and on more than one occasion. Horses were valuable. Replacing them would be expensive and could create hardship and even loss of earnings for Margaret's tenants.

Margaret's letter includes a fierce-sounding warning that if the recipients do not comply with her wishes and leave her tenants in peace, she may be forced to seek 'other remedie', but it is difficult to imagine what she might have had in mind. Unless Margaret expected a non-specific bluff to work, it is hard to imagine her making empty threats. The City of London and its officers were not answerable to the queen or her council. She might have passed the matter to King Henry and his council, expecting that he or they would take further action in her interest.

[53] Queen to the Steward and Coroner of the Marshalsea
(BL, Add. MS 46,846, fol. 57)

By the Quene

Trusty, etc. For asmoch as we be enformed that ye have do for to be empanelled certein of our tenantes of our town of Hertford for to passe in Marchasie ayeinst theire franchese and libertie and other wise thanne they have be accustumed for to do, we desire and praye you that, at reverence of us, ye wol not attempte that thinge that may be prejudice or derogacion of their seid franchese in contrarie of their custumes herbifor, but suffre theim t'enjoie thaire said fredams without empanellinge eny more in this bihalf, as we truste you. Yeven etc.

To the Steward and coroner of the Marchalsie

Like the letter to the mayor and sheriffs of London regarding John Lory, the cordwainer,[27] this letter sought to exempt certain persons from civic service. Margaret claims exemption for the free citizens of Hertford, who had been told to serve as jurors in the Marshalsea court. According to her letter, their exemption was a longstanding privilege to which they were accustomed.

---

26 Since the grant was made under the signet, there is no record of it in the patent rolls. Thus, we have no separate record of its extent, to whom it was addressed and whether or not it affected the sheriffs' activities.

27 See above, p. 74.

The Marshalsea court came under the jurisdiction of the steward of the household. The duke of Suffolk held this position until 1447, and his successor was Ralph Boteler, Lord Sudeley. The coroner would have been either Robert Fairford, who had served since 1422, or his son Alexander, who succeeded him in 1450.[28]

[54] Queen to the Duke of Exeter re Ralph Josselyn
(BL, Add. MS 46,846, fol. 66; Monro, pp. 106–8)

By the Quene

Right trusty and right entirely welbeloved Cousyn, we grete, etc. And for asmoch as our trusty and welbeloved squier Thomas Sharnborne hath do us to be enformed how, albeit that his cousin Rauf Josselyn, draper of London, was wrongfully disseised of the Manoir of Aspedon in Hertfordshire and theruppon an enquest late passed with hym, affermyng his trewe title and right as of verrey trouth and law they ought to do, as it is said; yet, nevertheles, th'adversaries of the said Rauf, seeing that they may not by right ne lawe opteine thaire entente ne wrongfull pourpos in this partie, have enfeffed you in the said manoir uppon hope and truste to be supported by you in thaire injurious entencion in that behalf. We, knowyng verreily your good and naturale disposicion towardes the faver and tendernesse of trouth and justice, desire and pray you that, the rather sith our said squier is by negh possibilite heritier to the same manoir, ye will, att reverence of us, be so good lord unto the said Josselyn that he may be suffred t'enjoie and possede his said right withoute eny interrupcion or medlyng by your supporte to the contrarie, soo that he may fynde in effecte thise our lettres unto hym vailable, as our full and singuler trust, etc. In which thing, etc. Yeven, etc.

To the Duc of Excestre

In this letter we again encounter the queen's esquire Thomas Sharneborne. On this occasion he appealed to Margaret on behalf of a man with whom he claimed kinship.[29] Ralph Josselyn first appears in the patent rolls in 1444, and again in 1446, as one of the executors of the will of another London draper.[30] In 1452 he was named in a group of eight men, some with court connections, who acquired the Essex manor of Erles in fee.[31] During the early 1450s, Josselyn, described as a citizen and draper of London, was a trustee of goods, chattels and property given into his keeping.[32] In September 1458 he was chosen by the mayor as one of the

---

28 Griffiths, p. 297.
29 For Sharneborne, see above, pp. 65ff. The word 'cousin' did not have the specific meaning that it has for English-speakers today. It could be applied to almost any relative more distant than a brother or sister, uncle or aunt.
30 *CPR, 1441–46*, pp. 215, 387.
31 *CPR, 1446–52*, p. 517.
32 *CCR, 1447–54*, pp. 255, 319, 497.

two sheriffs of London.[33] Around this same time he served in more politically charged capacities: in July 1458 he was named to a commission to investigate 'a conflict on the sea' – a euphemism for piracy – between the earl of Warwick and his retinue and ships of Lübeck 'under the king's friendship'. In 1459, as alderman and sheriff, he was given the task of arresting a German merchant.[34] Josselyn became mayor himself in 1464–65, and again in 1476–77.[35]

Josselyn purchased Aspenden Manor in 1451, probably around the time his fortunes began to rise.[36] The duke of Exeter would therefore have been Henry Holand, who obtained livery of his lands without proof of age in July 1450, soon after he turned twenty.[37] Thus Margaret's letter would have been written between 1451 and late 1458, with preference for the earlier years while Sharneborne was more active in the queen's service and before Josselyn had become prominent.

The letter is interesting for the situation it addresses. If Sharneborne can be believed, Josselyn's right to the manor had been affirmed by an inquest, at which point his opponents – who were probably Exeter's men – turned to the duke to keep Josselyn from asserting possession. Enfeoffment of property on a powerful lord for protection was fairly standard practice; as good lord, Exeter would be expected to uphold his servants' interests. What he was *not* supposed to do, however, was to uphold interests that were themselves unjust.[38] And that is where Margaret entered the picture. Sharneborne appealed to the queen partly because she was his own good lady (and he claimed to have a possible inheritance interest in the manor) and partly because some of her dower lands were in Hertfordshire, where she would have an interest in what went on. It may be doubted that Henry Holand had any 'good and natural disposition towards ... the tenderness of truth and justice'. He had a reputation as a hothead and a troublemaker; he seems to have enjoyed a fight for its own sake. Margaret's words provided a not-so-subtle reminder that he needed to get his priorities straight. Although we do not know what affect her letter had at the time, Josselyn was in full possession of Aspenden and able to settle the manor on his second wife prior to his death in 1478.[39]

---

33   Barron, *London*, p. 343; see also *CCR, 1454–61*, p. 394; *CPR, 1452–61*, pp. 459, 486, 487, 514.
34   Ibid., pp. 443, 516. *CCR, 1454–61*, p. 489, shows him as alderman of Cornhill ward.
35   Barron, *London*, pp. 344, 345.
36   VCH: *Hertfordshire*, IV, p. 19.
37   GEC, V, p. 212.
38   R. Horrox, 'Personalities and Politics', in *The Wars of the Roses*, ed. A.J. Pollard (1995), pp. 91–2, uses this specific case as an example of the conflicting interests engendered by personal relationships. Her conclusions differ from ours.
39   VCH: *Hertfordshire*, IV, p. 19.

[55] Queen to Sir Edmond Ingoldesthorpe, Knight, re Thomas and Isabel Gale
(BL, Add. MS 46,846, fol. 53; Monro, pp. 150–1)

By the Quene

Trusty and welbeloved, etc. And forasmoch as we be enformed that oon Henry Chevele, a servant of youres, injustly and ayeinst al right lawe and good conscience holdeth a certein place and lande in the towne of Asshedon within the counte of Essex apparteinyng of right unto oure welbeloved servant Thomas Gale and Isabell his wif by the decesse of Ric[hard] Wilwes, late brother unto the said Isabell, unto greet hindring, prejudice and derogacion of our said servant and his wyf, as it is said; we therfore desire and praye you that if hit so be, ye will thanne, att reverence of us, leying aside all parcialite, withoute eny comfort or supportacion yevyng unto the seid Henry, suffre oure said servant and his wyf peasably t'enjoie and occupie the seid place and land, and to have all that to hym [them] rightfully apparteineth in that bihalf, so that he [they] may finde your benevolence and trewe acquitail in suche wise disposed that they may atteine unto their right and have no cause to compleyne ayeine for lacke of justice. As we trust yow, etc. Yeven, etc. at Eltham the, etc.

To Sir Edmond Ingoldesthrop, kt

Sir Edmund Ingoldesthorpe first appears in the records in February 1448, when he was made a JP for Cambridgeshire and named to a commission there and in neighboring Huntingdon to look into evasions of customary fees and monies owed the king from wardships, marriages and other transactions.[40] The following November, having fulfilled these duties satisfactorily, he was exempted for life from serving on assizes, juries, inquisitions, or in a variety of public offices. Nevertheless – and typically – in September 1449 he was called upon to serve on a commission in Cambridge to raise loans to maintain the war in France, and a year later he appeared on a commission of oyer and terminer to investigate treasons committed by one Thomas Hylles in that county.[41] In 1453 he was back to raising money from Cambridge and Huntingdon to pursue the war; his activities followed English fortunes to the extent that the next year found him seeking money to defend Calais.[42] Rounding out his career, he served as a JP for Cambridgeshire in March and April 1455, and again in July 1456.[43]

Thomas Gale was deputy steward for the duchy of Lancaster lands in Essex, Hertfordshire and Middlesex in 1439, and he was confirmed in this position, at least in Essex, in 1450–51. He was also deputy receiver for these counties as

40   *CPR, 1446–52*, pp. 140, 587. The spelling of his name varies considerably in the records.
41   Ibid., pp. 201, 298, 431.
42   *CPR, 1452–61*, pp. 61, 148.
43   Ibid., p. 661.

well as for London and Surrey in 1438–39 and again in 1442–43.[44] Duchy lands, including extensive holdings in Essex and Hertfordshire, formed a portion of Margaret's dower. Assuming that Gale continued to hold his deputyships into the 1440s, they would have brought him into contact with the queen. In June 1448, Margaret appointed her own man, William Nanseglos, as receiver for the duchy in these counties.[45] Perhaps suggestive that Gale continued to serve under the queen's appointee, more certainly that he had her favor, he became deputy steward for her manor of Dunmow in Essex in 1449–50.[46] This would date Margaret's letter to after 1449. Further references to Thomas Gale are elusive; the latest one, associating him with Sawbridgeworth, Hertfordshire, is from January 1456.[47]

The offending Henry Chevele may have been the man who, together with Thomas Chevele, was among the feoffees in the manor of Dalham, Suffolk, in June 1455. A Henry Chevele is described as 'late [i.e., previous] escheator' in Huntingdon in December of the same year, and a year later a Henry Chevele of Chevele, gentleman, appears as a feoffee for a property in Cambridge.[48] The hundred of Cheveley lies in Cambridgeshire to the southeast of Newmarket; geographical proximity makes it likely that these references are all to the same man.[49] Ashdon is located about three miles northeast of Saffron Waldon, more or less on the boundary with Cambridge. It is possible that familial ties of the Gales and Chevele to the same general area lay behind the dispute, or at least put the latter in a good position to challenge property rights. Because Chevele was Ingoldesthorpe's servant, Margaret called upon the latter to bring his man to heel and to sort matters out, though she also clearly expected him to uphold the Gales' rights to the property. How this may have fit in with Sir Edmund's sense of good lordship towards Chevele we may only guess.

Ingoldesthorpe died within months of his last appointment, for in October 1456 the wardship and marriage of his daughter and sole heir were granted to Margaret.[50] Although it does not concern the matter of this letter, the story is of interest to any study of the queen. Isabel Ingoldesthorpe stood to inherit

---

44   Somerville, *Duchy of Lancaster*, pp. 605, 607.
45   Ibid., p. 608.
46   Ibid., p. 605.
47   Ibid., p. 607. For an earlier identification of Gale with Sawbridgeworth, see *CPR, 1436–41*, pp. 342–3. If Somerville is correct in stating that Gale was writing rentals for Saffron Walden and the Welsh sessions rolls in 1420–22, by 1450 or so he would have been getting on in years. Later references in the patent rolls to a Thomas Gale all involve someone consistently associated with Devon and Dartmouth, presumably a different man.
48   *CPR, 1452–61*, p. 244; *CCR, 1454–61*, pp. 90, 168.
49   VCH: *Cambridge and the Isle of Ely*, X, p. 28.
50   The grant was repeated in January 1457 (*CPR, 1452–61*, pp. 325, 359). The initial grant gives her name as Elizabeth; thereafter it appears as Isabel.

more than her father's properties. Her mother was sister and coheiress to John Tiptoft, earl of Worcester, who was childless after two marriages and who, at that point, had been a widower for five years. It was reasonable to suppose that in due course Isabel would inherit a portion of Worcester's estate.[51] Sir John Neville, the younger brother of the earl of Warwick, accordingly sought to marry her, and marry her he did on 25 April 1457. As the earl of Worcester himself was said to have 'brought about' the marriage, it could well have been arranged before Margaret obtained Isabel's wardship.[52] The girl was over the age of consent, but not yet of full age to inherit her father's property without the king's grant. To get that, Sir John had to buy Margaret out, to which end he agreed to pay her a total of £1,000 in ten £100 installments due each Whitsunday and Martinmas beginning in November 1458.[53] On 19 July 1459, by which time she would have received two payments, Sir John and Isabel received license to take possession of her lands, Margaret having surrendered the letters patent granting her Isabel's wardship and marriage, the latter being seventeen and Sir John 'having married [her] and satisfied the queen thereof'.[54] Viewed as a straight business transaction, with Sir John apparently upholding his end of the bargain, it was proper for Margaret to surrender the wardship, which she did. The matter acquires more interest if we take into account the confrontation between the crown and the duke of York and the Nevilles in the autumn of 1459. Despite a popular tradition of Margaret's overt hostility towards the Yorkists, the matter was clearly more complex.

[56] Queen to the Archbishop of Canterbury re John Reynold
(BL, Add. MS 46,846; fols 55v–56; Monro, pp. 99–100)

By the Quene
Right Reverend Fader, etc. And for asmoche as we understand by a supplicacion presented unto us by John Reignold, yoman of my lordes hall and oures, how that oon John Audeley, a squyer of youres, hath wrongfully put hym out of certein lyvelode apperteynyng unto our said servant of right, with many other dyvers

---

51 The earl eventually married for a third time in 1467 and had an only son, who died unmarried in his mid-teens. Worcester himself was executed in October 1470 during the Lancastrian readeption.

52 Gairdner, *PL*, III, p. 118.

53 *CCR, 1454–61*, pp. 300–1, for a series of recognizances dated May–June 1458, with various friends and relations as John's co-signers. The first of these was cancelled upon Margaret's acknowledgment, probably indicating that it had been paid in advance. John's parents had settled eight manors upon the couple in early 1458 (Hicks, *Warwick*, p. 131). He may have had to wait to begin payments to the queen until he had access to their income. The last payment would have been due in 1463.

54 *CPR, 1452–61*, p. 507.

vexacions and troubles, as in the said supplication closed within this ye may see more pleinly; we desire therfore and pray you hertly that, the said supplication by you diligently seen and deuly examined of the trouth, ye will, atte reverence of us, after god trouth and good conscience sett a good quiet and rest betwix theym in that bihalf, havyng our said servant after his honest desire in the seid supplicacion especialy recommended, shewing him therin th'ease, faver and tendernesse that ye goodly may, so that he may fynde your good lordship the better disposed to a good and final conclusion in this mater by contemplacion of this our praier. As our singuler trust is in yow. In which thing ye shul, etc.

To th'archebisshop of Cantebbury

John Reynold was a yeoman-usher of the king's hall in 1449 and until December 1451 when he was made one of the king's sergeants at arms, earning 12d a day from the issues of Bedford and Buckingham and 'a robe of the suit of other such sergeants' for Christmas.[55] Reynold was still a king's sergeant at arms in 1455, when he was ordered to arrest various men in Surrey on unspecified charges. The naming of a John Reynold, identified only as a member 'of the king's household', as a feoffee for a property in Surrey may suggest a connection with that county.[56]

The date of Reynold's promotion to sergeant suggests that the letter was written before the end of 1451, in which case the archbishop would have been John Stafford. John Audley, esquire, is impossible to identify with any degree of certainty as Audley was a very common name. A John de Audeley, 'gentilman', appears in 1448 in connection with a property in Surrey.[57] If a hypothetical link between Reynold and Surrey is accepted, this may have been our man – assuming that this Audley's status had risen a bit by the time Margaret wrote her letter. In any case, it appears that Reynold preferred to appeal to the queen to intercede with Stafford for him rather than to take his complaint directly to court. This may have been because his claim was inherently weak, or he was deterred by the expense of making it. Stafford, who, after all, was bound to be a 'good lord' to Audley, probably did not appreciate Margaret's intercession.

---

55 *CPR, 1446–52*, p. 503. A nearly identical entry (omitting only the Christmas outfit) appears for 12 December 1449 (ibid., p. 337), creating confusion regarding the date of his promotion. But an order to the sheriff of Bedford and Buckingham of May 1452, telling him to pay Reynold his wages and any arrears due from the previous December, confirms the 1451 date (*CCR, 1447–54*, p. 305).

56 Ibid., p. 348; *CPR, 1452–61*, pp. 256–7.

57 *CPR, 1446–52*, pp. 184–5. A John de Audeley, no status given, was named to two commissions in 1451 and 1452 (ibid., pp. 444 and 557), but whether he was the same as the previous gentleman is not known.

[57] Queen to the Archbishop of Canterbury re William Dorset
(BL, Add. MS 46,846, fol. 45v; Monro, p. 116)

By the Quene

Right worshipfull fader in God, etc. And for asmoch as oon William Dorset hath presented unto us a supplicacion compleynyng him of divers injuries and disheritances doon unto hym and his wif, as in the same supplicacion closed withinne thise ye may see more pleynly; we desire and pray yow that, the said supplicacion by yow seen, ye will pourvey therupon such remedie, as fes [*sic*, far] as in yow is, that the seid William may have al that to him rightfully belonge in that mater, havyng him towardes yow the more tenderly recommended, atte reverence of us and by contemplacion of this oure praier; as our singuler trust is in you. In which, etc.

To th'archbisshop of Cante[rbury]

The only reference we have found to a William Dorset is an undertaking by 'Katherine Dorset, widow, late the wife of William Dorset', dated 5 November 1451 and involving certain lands in Surrey that she held as her father's heir. These she granted by charter to her son William Apulton (apparently a son from a previous marriage) and his wife and their heirs, with reversion to herself and her heirs.[58] If this William Dorset was the person indicated in Margaret's letter, then he was dead by November 1451, and the archbishop would have been John Stafford.

Monro suggested that Margaret wrote this letter to the archbishop in his capacity as chancellor, but this is not necessarily the case. Three of her other letters were addressed to the chancellor specifically, even though he was also the archbishop, and all begin with the same or similar greeting.[59] Had Margaret wished to appeal to the archbishop as chancellor, she would have said so. The archbishop of Canterbury was a great landowner in his own right, so there was nothing odd in him being called upon to adjudicate in a land dispute. Alternatively, if the land claim came about through marriage, the archbishop may have been expected to act as a judge in his own ecclesiastical court, which had jurisdiction in matters involving religion.

[58] Queen to Sir John Steward re John Lovell
(BL, Add. MS 46,846, fols 54v–55; Monro, pp. 157–8)

By the Quene

Right trusty and well[beloved], we, etc. Desiring and praying you that in such things as John Lovell shall have for to doo towardes you touching his suit to the

---

58   *CCR, 1447–54*, p. 399.
59   See pp. 54, 89 and 149.

manoir of Hardington in Middelsex, wherof he hath just and lawfull title, as it is said, ye wil, atte reverence of us, have hym towardes you especially recommended. Considering that the recovre of his said right resteth greetly in your helpe and socour, as it is said, ye will by wey of charite and aulmesse to the pleasance of Almighty Jhesu do such diligence, as fer as ye may after god trouth and good conscience, that he may atteine by your good faver and supportacion unto his right and deute in that bihalf, as we trust you. Wherin ye shul mowe not oonly deserve of God right greet merite, but of us also right especiall thanke therfore in tyme commyng. Yeven, etc., at Wind[sor] the etc.

To Sir John Steward

Property disputes could become very complex. The manor of Hardington, or Harlington as it was later known, had a long association with the Lovell family. These were not the better-known Lovells of Titchmarsh and Minster Lovell who held a barony, but a gentry family who had some land in Middlesex and apparently came by Harlington through a marriage in the mid-1300s.[60] In 1415, Harlington and the adjacent manor of Dawley were subject to conveyances; as a result, Harlington ended up in the hands of a John Brown of Lincolnshire. Richard Brown, probably his son, was still in possession in 1428. After that, there is a gap to 1456, in which year 'John Lovell and his wife quitclaimed land in Harlington to Richard Brown and his wife'.[61] This John Lovell was almost certainly the resident 'of the parish of St Clement Danes without New Temple Bar, London, son and heir of Thomas Lovell of Middlesex, esquire', who on 14 February 1450 quitclaimed the manor of Dalley (Dawley) in Middlesex to a Robert Aubrey.[62] He is probably also the John Lovell of Margaret's letter. It is not clear whether the transaction of 1456 involved Harlington *manor* itself, or lands belonging to it. In any event, on 8 November 1459, Richard Brown 'of Hardyngton, Middlesex, gentilman' granted the manor and the advowson of the church to William Olyff of Surrey and his wife. The grant contains a curious proviso: '[I]f he [William] can recover the maner', he will guarantee Brown and his wife an annuity of 6 marks 4s for life.[63] From this it appears that Brown was not in physical possession of the manor at the time of the grant. Another gap

60 Our information comes from VCH: *Middlesex*, III, p. 262, except as noted. A large number of Lovells from different areas and different walks of life appear in the records. If they were all somehow related – an uncertain proposition – the connection was very distant by the fifteenth century.
61 This could have been the Richard Brown of 1428 or a son named Richard.
62 *CCR, 1447–54*, p. 181. In a pardon of November 1452, he is identified as 'John Lovell, gentilman' (*CPR, 1452–61*, p. 5).
63 *CCR, 1454–61*, pp. 423–4.

follows, until the mid-1470s when Thomas Lovell, probably John's grandson, is known to have held the advowson – and with it the manor – of Harlington.

So where does Margaret's letter fit? The 1456 transaction could represent free choice on Lovell's part, or it could have come about in the settlement of an already-existing conflict, but by 1459 possession of the manor was in dispute. It looks as if Brown granted it to Olyff in order to get the matter off his own hands in the hope that someone else would be able to take effective possession, which in turn would provide him with some income.

The only obvious '*Sir* John Steward' to whom Margaret could have written was the 'king's knight' whose service to the crown dates back to Henry V's reign.[64] During Henry VI's minority he was involved in the war in France as captain of the tower of Rysbank near Calais, and he also served on commissions to take musters.[65] In later years, his service to the crown focused on the county of Kent. There he served on commissions of oyer and terminer and of array, and was a JP for the county from 1442 through December 1447.[66] He also became constable and parker of Leeds Castle and received a grant of £30 p.a. from the issues of Rochester Castle, both in Kent.[67] Unfortunately, in light of what is definitely known about Hardington, Sir John was dead by 18 October 1449, when the offices of constable and parker of Leeds went to his designated successors.[68] If he was the addressee – and we have found no traces of another knight of the same name – this would provide a *terminus ad quem* for the queen's letter and also indicate that the dispute was ongoing before it surfaces in the official records. There is, however, a difficulty with this identification: there is no evidence linking Sir John Steward to Middlesex.[69]

There may be a second candidate in the person of John Steward, citizen and chandler of London, who was sheriff of London (and thus also of Middlesex) in 1456–57.[70] He was among the assignees for the goods and chattels of a number of his fellow Londoners from the late 1440s through the 1450s and was involved in the payment of a £2,000 recognizance along with – and likely on behalf of

64   *CPR, 1422–29*, p. 94, confirming a grant of £40 p.a., when he is identified as 'esquire'.
65   Ibid., p. 532; *CPR, 1429–36*, pp. 29, 489, 518, 607, 612; *CPR, 1436–41*, p. 539.
66   Ibid., p. 200; *CPR, 1441–46*, pp. 199–200, 472; *CPR, 1446–52*, p. 590.
67   *CPR, 1436–41*, pp. 33–4, 281 and 546; *CPR, 1441–46*, p. 137. In some of these grants he is identified specifically as 'king's knight' or 'knight of the body'.
68   *CCR, 1447–54*, p. 144.
69   While it may be slim grounds for argument, there is also no record of our John Lovell prior to the 1450s. During his father's lifetime, the elder Thomas would have been the one to lead a battle over property.
70   *CPR, 1452–61*, p. 325; Barron, *London*, p. 343.

– Sir John Bourgchier.[71] This Steward was a man of substance, with influence in Middlesex, particularly during his term as sheriff. But there is no record that he was ever knighted, certainly not during the period when Margaret could have written this letter. She may have used the 'Sir' as an honorific (or by mistake) when he was a sheriff. If this John Steward's connections make him seem the likelier recipient, then his title is wrong.

The queen's appeal to conscience and the decidedly religious cast she gives it points to a third possibility. It may suggest that Sir John Steward was a cleric.[72] We have found a single reference to a Master John Steward who was at Oxford University in 1448.[73] Since we have no other details of his life, it is impossible to know if he had any connection to John Lovell or was ever in a position to help him in a time of dire need. Although Margaret mentions Lovell's 'suit', the case may never have been brought before the courts. In the event that a private settlement was attempted, the influence of a respected priest – or perhaps pressure by the local sheriff – would indeed have been helpful.

[59] **Queen to the Duke of York's Officers and Tenants re John Stoughton and Alice Arnold [1448?]**
(BL, Add. MS 46,846, fol. 49v; Monro, pp. 145–6)

By the Quene
Trusty and welbeloved, etc. Of the good faver, frendship and supportacion that ye have shewed unto oure wel[beloved] servant and squier John Stoughton and Alice Arnold, his cousine, touching theire possession in the manoir of Clements with th'app[urtenances] in Essex we thanke you right hertly, praying you so forth to cotinue helping, furthering and assisting theim with al th'ease, faver and supportacion that ye goodly may by right, so that thei may finde thise oure lettres unto theim effectuelx and vailable. As we trust you, etc.

To Richard Clifton, John Rokeley, John Baker, and to all other officers and tenantes of our c[ousin] the Duc of York in his hundred of Racheford, and to everyche of theim

The saga of Clements manor goes back a number of years, more than would appear from this letter alone.[74] The manor, located in the parish of Hackwell in the

---

71   CCR, *1447–54*, pp. 20, 173, 270–1, 282–3, 425; CPR, *1454–61*, pp. 178, 263. A London draper, Alexander Haysant, is also named in the recognizance. The two guildsmen may have been the ones who actually put up the money.
72   'Sir' was often used to denote a priest.
73   Emden, III, p. 1776.
74   The story of Clements was first told by Johnson, *Duke Richard*, p. 72, and followed by Maurer, p. 84. We are now able to expand it.

hundred of Rocheford, Essex, had been in the possession of one Philip Clement, who enfeoffed it to various gentlemen on the condition that they convey it back to his wife for life, with the remainder to his daughter Agnes and her heirs. On 12 February 1441 the two surviving feoffees granted the reversion of the manor to eight new men, among whom were Henry Fylongley, esquire, and John Ingowe.[75] In due course, the latter married Agnes Clement, the heiress. The couple was said to have been in peaceful possession of the manor 'for three years and more' when, on 25 April 1448, John Bayhous, esquire, of Stratford Langthorn, Essex, and others forcibly entered the property and disseised the Ingowes. An inquest held on 11 May before William Tyrell, justice of the peace, found that Agnes Ingowe and her ancestors had held Clements for as far back as anyone could remember, whereas neither John Bayhous nor his ancestors had any claim to it. Moreover, the inquest reported that the marauding party had so threatened the Ingowes' tenant Thomas Lorkin that he despaired of his life and goods. Finally, it noted that Bayhous had enfeoffed Clements on the dukes of York and Somerset to maintain his claim ('pro mauntenencia habendi').[76]

The enfeoffment is surprising. While Bayhous probably intended to enfeoff the property on *somebody* who would then support his claim to it, we wonder if he actually had the time to do any such thing. It may be that in the heat of the moment he simply threw out the names of the most important men he could think of. Edmund, duke of Somerset, was in France and was expected to stay there, so why enfeoff him? The duke of York, at least, as lord of Rocheford, was a power in the area. In any event, the inquest found in favor of the Ingowes, and on 11 July the king ordered the justices of the peace to put them in full possession of the manor.[77]

Although Bayhous lost his case, the battle over Clements continued. Indeed, the next steps were taken before the king's orders were issued. The Ingowes, perhaps in anticipation of further trouble, enfeoffed the manor on William, duke of Suffolk, Sir James Ormond, Sir Thomas Tyrell, Robert Darcy the younger, Henry Fylongley and others.[78] Trouble arrived on 10 July when a new party

75 *CCR, 1435–41*, p. 490. One of the surviving original feoffees was a Robert Darcy, esquire. There were seven witnesses to this transaction, including William Tyrell, John Chetilbere, clerk, and John Baker. These names all reappear in the course of the story.
76 KB 9/259/48.
77 KB 9/260/88 rehearses the testimony at the inquest, with no mention of York, Somerset, or the unfortunate Lorkin. The only persons whose names appear are William Tyrell, who presided at the inquest, John Bayhous and his companions, who appear in the previous document, and the Ingowes, John and Agnes.
78 Ormond later became earl of Wiltshire. Darcy was probably the son of the man of the same name who was one of the surviving original feoffees in 1441, and Fylongley and Ingowe had been among the new feoffees at that time. Sir Thomas Tyrell was likely related to William

consisting of Alice Arnold, widow, formerly of Morton, Lincolnshire, John 'Stokton', esquire, formerly of Havering-atte-Bower, Essex, John Culle or Cole, a yeomen of Rumford, Essex, John Chetilbere, parson of the church of Rocheford, Essex, and John Wynter, parson of the church of Magna Sutton, Essex, and others attacked and took possession of Clements by force of arms. As Bayhous had done before, Alice Arnold and John Culle enfeoffed it on the dukes of York and Somerset. Again, as before, an inquest held before William Tyrell on 25 July found that the ancestors of Agnes Ingowe had held Clements for time out of mind and that Alice Arnold had no claim.[79]

The final act in the Clements affair for which we have direct evidence took place on 3 August. William Tyrell, the JP, stated that on that date, in his presence, a party of armed men led by one Roger Ree again attacked the manor and broke down a wall.[80] Although this document contains no reference to the duke of York, Ree was York's servant of long standing, becoming his usher of the chamber by 1451, and Ree's companions were York's tenants, mostly from Rayleigh in Essex.[81] Although Ree was not a named recipient of Margaret's letter, could his incursion have come about in response to her urging? The probable date for this letter is the summer of 1448, when the fight over Clements was ongoing.

John Stoughton, or Stokton as he appears in the inquest documents, served in the royal catery, charged with obtaining meat and fish for the household's consumption. He was a yeoman of the catery in 1436; by late 1444 he had advanced to sergeant and received other benefits: a life grant of the office of customer and collector of the 8d due to the king on each sack of wool or wool fells passing out of Calais and a life grant of the office of feodary of the honor of Richmond in Lincolnshire and Nottinghamshire. In 1443 he was appointed controller of the customs in the port of Boston.[82] Although the inquest noted his former ties

Tyrell, who had presided over the Bayhous case and had witnessed the 1441 transaction. It looks very much as though Suffolk and Ormond had been brought in to lend their influence and importance to a group of lesser men who already had connections of one sort or another to Clements and knew its history.

79 KB 9/260/91. Agnes is referred to here as 'sister and heir of William Clement, son and heir of Philip Clement'. Apparently, William had died before the elder Clement was at pains to protect his daughter's rights. See also KB 9/260/89, where Stokton appears as leader of the marauding band, and KB 9/260/90, where he is not mentioned at all and Culle is represented as the leader.

80 KB 9/260/88 *v.* Tyrell stated that John Ingowe had requested his presence at Clements, in connection with the enfeoffment of Suffolk, Ormond, and the others already named as feoffees in KB 9/260/91.

81 Johnson, *Duke Richard*, pp. 72, 237. Complicating matters, Robert Darcy (presumably the elder) had also been associated with York. That Darcy died in September 1448 (ibid., p. 230).

82 *CPR, 1436–41*, pp. 24, 123, 345; *CPR, 1441–46*, p. 149, 310.

to Havering, the patent rolls more frequently associate him with Haconby in Lincolnshire. Having obtained the manor in 1437, Stoughton enfeoffed it in 1443 on four other men, who granted it back to him and to Alice his wife.[83]

In September 1447, Stoughton was granted the large sum of £504 15s 8d from the customs and subsidies in the port of Boston to make up for tallies he had been unable to cash. The grant describes him as 'clerk, late serjeant of the catery'. In May 1449 he was pardoned of all 'offenses and liabilities incurred' while serving in the office of serjeant.[84] In 1451 he was supposed to go to Calais, where he was to be involved in its victualling, but he delayed his departure and was found to be 'tarrying' in Rayleigh, Essex, in February 1452, and in Middlesex in June, as reported by the sheriffs of those counties.[85] Although Stoughton seems to have made it to Calais by mid-July, his delays take on a more sinister tinge in the grant to his brother William, yeoman of the catery, of all his goods, which notes that around the time of his departure for Calais 'divers persons prosecuted John and outlawed him' so that his goods in Lincolnshire were seized.[86] The reference to Rayleigh is intriguing, as it provides a link to York's men who were involved with Ree in the Clements affair. If Margaret's letter was written about this time, and not in 1448 as suggested above, it shows Margaret seeking the cooperation of York's men, and perhaps by extension of the duke himself – all in a normally businesslike way, of course – at a time when York's relationship with the king had significantly deteriorated.

Stoughton's outlawry received a final, ironic twist in May 1454 during the duke of York's protectorate. On the thirteenth of that month, John Stoughton was pardoned of

> his outlawries in the husting of London and in Essex for not appearing [in the matter of a debt] and to satisfy the king of his ransoms for certain trespasses and contempts in entering with Alice Arnold of Morton by Brun, co. Lincoln, widow, a manor of James, earl of Wiltshire, Thomas Tyrell, knight, Henry Fylongley, esquire, Robert Darcy, esquire, and William Tyrell, esquire; he having surrendered to Flete prison and satisfied [the debt].[87]

---

83   *CPR, 1436–41*, p. 63; *CPR, 1441–46*, pp. 76, 196. This Alice should not be confused with Alice Arnold. 'Alice' was a common name, and the latter is described in all the documents as a widow.
84   *CPR, 1446–52*, pp. 104, 250. As the pardon does not refer to his current position, it is unclear whether he was still associated with the catery or not.
85   Ibid., pp. 512, 549–50. The first revocation of protection describes him as 'John Stoughton of the household, esquire, *alias* John Stokton late of Hacumby, co. Lincoln'. The second has him 'late of the household' and adds '*alias* late of Boston, co. Lincoln' to the description.
86   Ibid., p. 572, dated 15 July.
87   *CPR, 1452–61*, p. 150.

Here we have all of the persons who had been enfeoffed by the Ingowes in the summer of 1448, minus the duke of Suffolk, who was murdered in 1450, and with the addition of William Tyrell, who was likely added in a later enfeoffment. Was the manor alluded to in the pardon indeed Clements? It would seem so. Thus, it appears that further efforts to wrest it from the Ingowes also came to naught. Although we cannot be certain that this was the final act in what had been an ongoing drama, we may hope that, after all this time, the Ingowes were finally able to enjoy their manor in peace.

[60] Queen to the Abbess of Barking in Essex re Robert Osbern [1450]
(BL, Add. MS 46,846, fol. 41; Monro, p. 103)

> By the Quene
> Dere cousine and right welbeloved in God, we grete yowe wele. And for asmoche as oure welbeloved Robert Osbern, squier, and my lordes servant in th'office of his secretary, is inhabited nygh unto yow and is your tenant, as he seith, desiryng to do yowe service and pleasure and therto hath and soo purposeth to be disposed with all his hert, we praye youe cousyn affectuously that, considryng his will [and] sette purpose, ye wol, aswel therfore as at the reverence of us and this oure instance, be unto hym good and favorable ladye in his honest desires and resonable offers, and shew unto hym and unto his wif the tendre benevolence of your good ladyship in suche wise as they may fynde this oure writing unto thayme vailable, for oure sake and at oure contemplacion, as we therfore may have cause especialy to thanke yow. Yeven at, etc.
> To th'abbesse Berking

Katherine de la Pole, sister of William de la Pole, duke of Suffolk, was abbess of Barking in Essex from 1433 to 1473.[88] Henry VI's half-brothers, Edmund and Jasper Tudor, were placed in her care in July 1437 after the death of their mother Queen Katherine.[89] They remained in her custody until they were old enough for King Henry to summon them to court. As abbess, she received a grant of a tun of red Gascon wine annually from February 1445.[90]

Robert Osbern was a clerk of the signet in May 1440, when he was granted the alien priory of Allerton Mauleverer, Yorkshire, valued at £4 13s 4d annually,

88 Smith, ed., *Heads of Religious Houses*, p. 625.
89 *Foedera*, X, p. 828. Over the next two years, until the end of February 1439, the abbess received £50 for their upkeep. No further payments were made, and in November 1440 she petitioned for £53 12s to cover their costs up to 31 October 1440.
90 *CPR, 1441–46*, pp. 331, 336. Two grants were made the same day. The first was to Katherine for life; the second, to Katherine and to the prioress and convent 'and their successors for ever'. The second grant was replaced or renewed in November 1452 by a tun of red Gascon, to come from the king's wines in the port of London.

for life.[91] In May 1443, Osbern, William Gedney and William Crosby, all king's serjeants, received a grant in survivorship of £20 p.a.[92] We can be sure that this is 'our' Osbern, for in December 1444 he and Crosby were granted a tun of red wine each year at Christmas 'for their labour in the office of the king's secretary'.[93] Osbern's secretarial service was also rewarded in May 1444 with a grant of £10 annually from the issues of Lincolnshire made to him and Sir William Estfeld in survivorship.[94] His connections with Essex go back at least to June 1446 when, following the death of the duke of Warwick, Henry VI granted Osbern the office of steward and receiver of all the Beauchamp estates in Essex and Hertford.[95] In 1448, Osbern and Robert Rokke enfeoffed their lands in Barking 'and elsewhere in Essex', only stipulating that a rent of £13 6s 8d be paid to them.[96]

Margaret's letter was probably precipitated by a situation that arose in 1450.[97] On 26 February of that year, Katherine de la Pole entered a petition in chancery against Osbern, alleging that on Sunday, 8 February, when the churchwardens went to open the church gate, Osbern's servant wrested the key from them and gave it to his master, who refused to return it. The abbess then tried to have the lock changed, but Osbern assaulted her and knocked her to the ground. He, or presumably his men, then hit a workman (perhaps the locksmith?) over the head, and their demeanor became so menacing that the abbess and her people were afraid to go into the church after dark, so that the proper offices could not be sung.

Osbern counter-claimed that, as a tenant of the abbey, he held a forty-year lease on a tenement with houses and a garden, and therefore had a key to the gate leading into the parish churchyard, giving him access to his holding. Some years earlier the abbess had ordered that the lock be changed, and this had denied him the right of access for over a year. When his servant obtained a key for him, the abbess again had the locks changed. Osbern claimed that the disputed key was not for the gate of the abbey close, which was manned by a porter, but to the parish churchyard, which he was entitled to hold. He further alleged that servants

---

91   *CPR, 1436–41*, p. 404.
92   *CPR, 1441–46*, p. 186. Initially, it was to have come from the fee farm paid by the prior and convent of Coventry, but it was replaced a year later with £20 from the customs of Sandwich (ibid., pp. 280, 328).
93   Ibid., p. 314.
94   Ibid., pp. 252, 283. It appears that the grant to Osbern was rescinded in 1447 after Estfeld's death, when it was made instead to William Foljambe (see also *CPR, 1446–52*, p. 109).
95   *CPR, 1441–46*, p. 434. Osbern would have held this office until 1449, when the duke of Warwick's daughter and heir Anne Beauchamp died while still a minor. The Beauchamp estates passed to her aunt, another Anne Beauchamp, the wife of Richard Neville, who became earl of Warwick in her right.
96   *CCR, 1447–54*, p. 51.
97   *CPR, 1446–52*, pp. 320–1, for what follows and the commission to investigate opposing claims.

of the abbess had hunted over demesne lands in Barking granted to him by the king.[98] Finally, the abbess had complained of him to the king, the archbishop of York, the chancellor, the duke of Buckingham and other lords, and, as a result, he had been bound over in £300 to keep the peace; writs and warrants had been issued against him and his friends in an effort to make him abandon his property and even to leave the county.

Katherine's version is something of a gloss on the events, as it appears that she was trying to encroach on Osbern's rights. He was her tenant, and she may have wished to get rid of him. This was certainly his view of the case, but his recourse to violence did not help his cause. Osbern probably came off worse in this dispute and decided that he would be well-advised to make his peace with the abbess before she got him into any more trouble, hence his appeal to the queen to effect a reconciliation.

Margaret may subsequently have regretted her support for Osbern. His wife, mentioned in the letter, was Sybille Bowet, whom he married in about 1436 in the expectation that she would receive a substantial dowry. This did not eventuate, and in 1453 they sued in chancery to try to recover her rights in a manor called 'Great Hautbois', valued at £10 annually, which Sybille claimed was being withheld from her by her half-sister Lady Elizabeth [Isabel] Dacre. In this instance, too, Osbern did not hesitate to use violence.[99] In July 1453 the queen's attorney general, Robert Tanfield, attended to the queen's business in chancery, part of which included defending Isabel's interests ('pro quadam materia Domine de Dacres'). Isabel Dacre was one of Margaret's ladies.[100]

Osbern lost his grant of the priory of Allerton Mauleverer in the act of resumption of 1449–50, and Henry VI subsequently granted it to his foundation of King's College, Cambridge, for the term of Osbern's life. Osbern was still alive in November 1454 when he was named as a 'squire of attendance' in a list of ordinances drawn up for Henry's household.[101] In September 1458, the king re-granted the priory to King's College in mortmain, which suggests that Osbern died sometime in that year.[102]

---

98   The charge of poaching was a common accusation in disputes of this kind; it may or may not have been true.
99   Richmond, *Paston Family: First Phase*, pp. 219–20. He also slandered Isabel Dacre.
100 Myers, 'Household', p. 192. She first appears in the jewel account for 1448–49, when she received a gold armlet. In 1451–52, she received a silver gilt salt, and in 1452–53, a wine flagon (E 101/410/2 and 8; Myers, 'Jewels', p. 224).
101 *PPC*, VI, p. 224.
102 *CPR, 1452–61*, p. 466. Although the grant is dated 4 September 1458, its wording is confusing: 'Grant in mortmain ... of Allerton Mauleverer ... from 6 November 28 Henry VI [1449], for the life of Robert Osbern.'

[61] Queen to the Duke of Norfolk re Sir Robert Wingfield, 16 February [1453?]
(BL, Add. MS 46,846, fols 47v–48; Monro, p. 155–6)

By the Quene.

Right trusty and right entierly welbeloved cousyn, we grete yow wele. And for asmoch as our trusty and welbeloved knight Sir Robert Wyngfild and his sonnes have right humbly besoughte us that it wold like us to write unto you, desiryng you that, atte oure instance, ye wold admitte theim to come unto your presence, there ye to here theire declaracion upon certein matiers that ye fynde yow agreved and displeaased in as yet; we, havyng consideracion unto the good and acceptable service that oure said knyght and his sones have done unto us, aswel beyonde the see to theire greet charges, labores and costes as on this side – and yet oure said knyght therin dayly continueth – desire and praye you that, atte reverence of us, ye will have theym towards your good lordship after th'entent of theire humble request in this partie especialy recommended, and shew theim the more tendernesse and faver, by contemplacion of this our praier, so that they may fynde in effecte thise oure lettres unto theim vailable and fare the better to th'acomplissement of oure entencion in this partie, as we trust you. In which thing, *etc.* Yeven, *etc.*, at Eltham the xvi day of Ffr.

To the Duc of Norf[olk].

The long-running feud between John Mowbray, third duke of Norfolk, and his retainer and tenant Sir Robert Wingfield was of a particularly bitter and violent nature. Its origins dated back to the duke's father, who died in 1432. Robert Wingfield had been the elder Mowbray's ward and had married his half-sister.[103] Wingfield's principal manor of Letheringham lay only three miles from the ducal seat at Framlingham, and the elder Norfolk granted him the manor of Hoo, adjacent to Letheringham, for life.[104]

Wingfield was one of the young John Mowbray's most devoted adherents, and the new duke made him his chief steward in 1436.[105] Wingfield supported Norfolk in the latter's struggle to establish his authority in East Anglia over that of his rival, the earl of Suffolk. On more than one occasion, Wingfield's and Norfolk's henchmen engaged in violent clashes as well as litigation with Suffolk's clients, and in 1440, Wingfield was committed to the Tower, probably at Suffolk's behest. He spent nine months in prison for disorderly conduct and disturbing the king's peace, while the duke of Norfolk was required to furnish a bond of 10,000 marks

103 H. Castor, *The King, the Crown and the Duchy of Lancaster* (Oxford, 2000), p. 106.
104 R.L. Storey, *The End of the House of Lancaster* (1966), p. 226.
105 *CCR, 1441–46*, p. 213.

for his own future good behavior.[106] Within a short time, however, a falling out occurred. Norfolk may have resented the settlement of Hoo on Wingfield and wanted it back. Or Wingfield may have decided that he might do better as a client of Suffolk, and Norfolk retaliated for his defection by seizing Hoo, which he took by force in August 1443.[107] Wingfield brought charges, and the duke of Norfolk was bound over in the sum of £2,000 not to attack him. Wingfield was also granted 3,500 marks in compensation, and his tenure as steward of the Mowbray lands in Suffolk was confirmed. Norfolk was forced to grant Wingfield the manor of Weston in Hertfordshire in exchange for Hoo. Suffolk was on the panel that awarded these damages and compensation.[108]

In 1444, Suffolk included Wingfield and his sons in the entourage accompanying him to Rouen to welcome Margaret to England.[109] Over the next two years Wingfield, under Suffolk's (and possibly Margaret's) protection, continued to undermine Norfolk's authority, but in 1447 Wingfield and his son, another Robert, went too far.[110] If the allegations made against them (by Norfolk's supporters) are to be believed, the younger Robert threatened the duke's chaplain at Framlingham. Norfolk had him imprisoned, but – so it was claimed – within three hours of his arrest Wingfield's men raided the gaol and set Robert free. Norfolk then appealed to the king to prohibit young Robert from coming within seven miles of Framlingham. In defiance of the prohibition, Robert spent Christmas at Letheringham, from where he and his father raided Norfolk's lands, poached his deer and even broke into Framlingham Castle itself. Wingfield ended up before the King's Bench early in 1448, but he obtained a pardon and an acquittal.[111]

Sometime in the summer of 1448, Norfolk sent armed men to attack Letheringham. Although Wingfield probably exaggerated the damage they did, the attack was serious enough to earn Norfolk a short spell in the Tower while a commission of oyer and terminer was ordered to investigate.[112] No further action was taken against Norfolk, and Wingfield remained at court. He was named

---

106 Gairdner, *PL*, II, p. 47; *CCR, 1435–41*, pp. 395, 420, for Wingfield's imprisonment; p. 381, for Norfolk's bond.
107 Storey, *End of Lancaster*, pp. 226–7; J. Watts, *Henry VI and the Politics of Kingship* (Cambridge, 1996), p. 202; H. Castor, *King Crown and Duchy*, p. 113.
108 Ibid., pp. 113–14; *CCR, 1441–47*, pp. 196, 213, 215.
109 BL Add. MS 23,938.
110 *CPR, 1446–52*, p. 137, dated 18 December 1447, for a commission to look into their troublemaking in Suffolk. Some of the commission's members were the duke of Suffolk's men.
111 Castor, *King, Crown and Duchy*, pp. 114–15; *CPR, 1446–52*, p. 130, for the general pardon dated 14 February 1448.
112 Flenley, 'Bale's Chronicle', p. 123; *CPR, 1446–52*, p. 236, dated 1 September 1448. Wingfield claimed that Norfolk had brought cannon to the attack and had burned him out. The duke of Suffolk was one of the commissioners.

in the banishment petition presented by the parliament of 1450–51 (possibly at
Norfolk's instigation) as one of the 'eveil doers' about the king.[113]

On 5 June 1452, Norfolk attempted to recover the manor of Weston, which he
had been forced to grant to Wingfield in 1444. On 18 July, Wingfield petitioned
the council, rehearsing past grievances and demanding redress, claiming that
he had not received one penny of the compensation money awarded to him.[114]
Norfolk countered by claiming a debt of 800 marks, and Wingfield was again
summoned to the King's Bench to answer the claim.[115]

Wingfield sought Margaret's good ladyship as peacemaker, and she wrote to
Norfolk in an effort to end the feud. Her letter is dated 16 February, from Eltham.
There are two years when Margaret may have been at Eltham in February because
Henry VI was there: 1448 and 1453.[116] In 1448, Henry was at Eltham from 14 to
18 February, which coincides with the younger Robert's pardon. If Margaret's
efforts date to 1448, they were unavailing, and the duke of Norfolk ignored them.
In 1453, we can be reasonably certain that Margaret spent significant time with
Henry in January and February because their son was born in mid-October.
Henry was at Eltham at the end of January, but left on 7 February, though
Margaret may have stayed on. This year seems more promising. Wingfield may
have been ill and reluctant to continue the struggle. He made his will in October
1452, and no further disturbances or outrages are recorded.[117] He and his sons may
have decided that continuing conflict with Norfolk was not the way to enhance
the family's fortunes, hence their appeal to the queen. When Wingfield died in
1454, his son John became the steward for Norfolk's estates. He and his brother
Robert supported Norfolk in the ongoing property disputes between the duke
and Alice, duchess of Suffolk.[118]

113   *PROME*, XII, p. 185.
114   Castor, *King, Crown and Duchy*, p. 116, n. 192. His petition was considered on 20 July. Cf. Storey,
      End of Lancaster, pp. 226–7. The sequence of events only makes sense if the attack on Hoo took
      place in 1443, the attack on Letheringham in 1448 and the attack on Weston in 1452. Cf. Watts,
      Henry VI, p. 202, whose idiosyncratic interpretation casts Wingfield as 'the faithless knight' and
      concludes it was small wonder that Norfolk petitioned for license to go on pilgrimage. There
      is no evidence that he ever went, and his petition had nothing to do with Wingfield: 1450 was
      a Jubilee Year in which Christians pledged to undertake to visit Rome, whether they went or
      not. See below, p. 153, for Margaret's vow taken in that year.
115   KB 27/766.
116   Based on Henry's itinerary (Wolffe, *Henry VI*, pp. 366, 370).
117   Nicolas, *Testamenta Vetusta*, I, p. 275, where Wingfield's will is dated 6 October 1452, and probate
      recorded in November 1454. Confusing matters, there is an entry in the Fine Rolls for a writ
      of *diem clausit extremum* for Robert Wingfield, knight, of Norfolk and Suffolk, of 5 July 1452
      (*CFR, 1452–61*, p. 3). Available evidence suggests that he was very much alive in July of that
      year.
118   Castor, *King, Crown and Duchy*, p. 116 and n. 193.

[62] Queen to Henry, Lord Bourgchier, re Nicholas Browne and John Crowne
[late 1446?]
(BL, Add. MS 46,846, fols 40–40v; Monro, pp. 122–3)

By the Quene

Right trusty and welbeloved Cousyn, we greete yow well. And, sith it is soo that certein matiers hangyng in debate, travers and controversie bitwix oure tenantes of Walden and oon Nicholas Browne and John Crowne[119] be put in ordenance, award and arbitrement of yow and of your counseil; we, desirying a final conclusion therof to reste and quiete of oure said tenantes, praye yowe hertely that ye will, atte reverence of us, prefixe and set a day to mete with oure counseil and ther to dispose yowe t'abide and attende uppon the determinacion of all the grevaunces compromitted in maner above reherced, havyng oure seid tenantes towardes you in suche favor and tendernesse recommended, for oure sake, that they maye fynde in effecte that ye be unto theym good lorde to th'accomplissement of oure entencion in this mater, and the rather by contemplacion of this oure prayer, as oure full truste is in yow. In which, etc. at W. etc.

To the Lorde Bourgchier

In this intriguing letter we learn that Henry, Lord Bourgchier, had been asked to arbitrate in a dispute between the queen's Walden tenants and two otherwise unidentified men with the rhyming names of Browne and Crowne. Since there is no indication that these men were Bourgchier's tenants, he may have been enlisted because the dispute was in his local jurisdiction or because he was seen as a disinterested third party. In any event, Margaret's hope and intention was that he would not be too disinterested, but would settle matters in favor of her tenants as if he were their own good lord, and it was to this end that she asked him to meet with her council. Gentle persuasion, supported by documents and testimony, was likely what she had in mind. Anything stronger would have been overkill in this situation. As we do not know the particulars of the dispute, it is impossible for us to say which side was in the right, but Margaret's efforts to support her tenants' interests are in keeping with her good ladyship.

Bourgchier's mother was the daughter of Thomas of Woodstock, duke of Gloucester, the youngest son of Edward III. His older half-brother was Humphrey Stafford, duke of Buckingham. His wife was Isabel, the duke of York's sister. Thus, he was a man with important connections. King Henry created Henry Bourgchier as Viscount Bourgchier in December 1446 as compensation for his increasingly precarious hold on lands in France.[120] This may suggest that Margaret's

119 Monro transcribed this man's surname as 'Chowne'. The second letter is definitely an 'r'.
120 Griffiths, pp. 354–5, 372, nos 103, 110. Bourgchier was summoned to parliament by his new title on 14 December 1446.

letter was written before the end of that year. Rank and status were matters of supreme importance, and anything providing an upward nudge was unlikely to be ignored, particularly in direct address.[121] Arguing against this dating, Margaret only received her lands in March 1446, and it would have taken time to set up her council thereafter. For it to have the materials at hand to be actively involved in settling a land dispute seems very tight timing.

In 1455, after the first battle of St Albans, Henry Bourgchier was named treasurer at the behest of the victorious duke of York. It is fair to wonder where Bourgchier's own sympathies lay at that point. Although he had served under York in France and become a member of the duke's council, Bourgchier does not appear to have been a partisan of either side. His youngest brother, Thomas, had become archbishop of Canterbury at the beginning of York's first protectorate in 1454, following the death of John Kemp,[122] and he became chancellor in 1455 when Henry VI ended York's protectorate. Henry may have shared some of his brother's apparently broad acceptability.[123]

This changed in the autumn of 1456. The Bourgchier brothers were ousted from their political posts and replaced by men more clearly sympathetic to the king. In 1460 the Bourgchiers joined the earls of Warwick and March at Northampton, the archbishop, at least, as a member of the clergy whose ostensible purpose was to get the king to meet peaceably with the earls.[124] Following the Yorkist victory and Henry VI's subsequent deposition, Henry Bourgchier was created earl of Essex in June 1461 and served as treasurer for one year. He became treasurer again in 1471 and held the office until his death on 4 April 1483.

---

121   The title of viscount was relatively new to England – Viscount Beaumont was the only other – and was used somewhat interchangeably with 'lord'. A comparison with extant letters written to Beaumont indicates that 'viscount' was the preferred form in direct address (Gairdner, *PL*, II, pp. 78, 88, 118; III, pp. 121, 143), whereas 'lord' was generally used when he was referred to in the third person (ibid., II, pp. 150, 296; III, pp. 50, 87). Similar letters to Bourgchier are lacking, but there are third-person references to him as 'lord' (ibid., II, p. 325; III, pp. 31, 132, 299). For what it may be worth, one of Margaret's letters refers to 'Viscount' Beaumont (below, p. 129).

122   His elevation seems to have owed more to his own competence and his relationship to the duke of Buckingham than to any sense of favor towards the duke of York (Griffiths, pp. 727, 761–2, n. 64).

123   Although Griffiths, p. 748, considers that he 'may have been with York at St Albans', there seems to be no definitive evidence of his whereabouts or sympathies.

124   Sufficient evidence exists to suggest that few subscribed to any illusions regarding the likelihood of battle. The peace delegation was a part of the politically necessary window-dressing (Maurer, pp. 179–81).

[63] Queen to Sir John Bourgchier, Knight, re Thomas Hery [before 1453]
(BL, Add. MS 46,846, fols 58v–59; Monro, pp. 132–3)

By the Quene

Right trusty and welbeloved, we grete you well. Lating you wit that we wrote now late unto oon Thomas Downe, exciting hym to delyvere unto our welbeloved servant Thomas Hery, grome of our chamber, certein evidences longyng unto hym of right, which our request he is redy t'accomplisse and perfourme so that [if] ye will therto assente, as it is said. And it is so, as we be enformed, that at our instance and prayer by our lettres now late adressed unto you in this partie, ye be right well disposed and benevolent unto our said servant in this mater. Wherof we thanke you right hertly. And sith it is so that th'expedicion herof resteth oonly in your trew acquitail, we desire and hertly praye you that suche faver, tendernesse and frendship thatt ye have be gonne for our sake to shewe to our seid servant ye will continue forthe to the hasty conclusion thereof, in such wise that, without delaye for eny sinistre suggestion, he may have delyverance of his said evidences and fele in effecte brief exploit and accomplissement of our request, at reverence of us and by contemplacion of this our prayer, as our singuler trust is in you. In which thinge ye shull not oonly deserve of us right especial thanke, to our greet pleasure, but also cause us to have you, the rather, in tendre remembrance of our grace therfor in tyme comyng, etc.

To our knyght Sir John Bourgchier

Sir John Bourgchier was the youngest brother of Henry, Viscount Bourgchier.[125] Through his wife, the heiress Margery Berners, he became Lord Berners in 1453.[126] In the early 1440s, John served as a JP for Surrey, and he became active as a commissioner in the 1450s.[127] During that same decade he regularly served as a JP for both Surrey and Berkshire.[128] His politics were ecumenical. He fought for King Henry at the first battle of St Albans in 1455, but days later was made constable of Windsor Castle, together with William Neville, Lord Fauconberg, the earl of Salisbury's younger brother.[129] In November 1458 the constableship was re-granted to John Bourgchier alone.[130]

In 1460, Berners sat out the battle of Northampton, but joined the Yorkists

---

125 See previous letter.
126 C.A.J. Armstrong, 'Politics and the Battle of St. Albans, 1455', *Bulletin of the Institute of Historical Research* 33 (1960), p. 21, n. 6. The date of 1455 given in GEC is also refuted by earlier references to him in the Patent Rolls as Lord Berners. For John and his wife Margery, see *CPR, 1441–46*, pp. 81, 380.
127 Ibid., p. 479; *CPR, 1452–61*, pp. 58, 221, 305, 306, 307, 371, 403, 408, 437, 490, 557, 558, 604.
128 Ibid., pp. 660, 678.
129 Armstrong, 'Politics and St Albans', p. 21 and n. 1; the 'Stow Relation' in Gairdner, *PL*, III, p. 25; *CPR, 1452–61*, p. 243.
130 *CPR, 1452–61*, p. 470.

under Warwick at second St Albans in February 1461, where he was captured. The Lancastrians conveyed him north to York, along with his fellow prisoner John Neville, Lord Montagu.[131] The two were still there, unharmed, following the Yorkist victory at Towton, when they formed a sort of welcoming committee for Edward IV.[132] Lord Berners continued to serve the new dynasty, as he had the old, up to his death in May 1474.

The queen identifies Thomas Hery as a groom of her chamber. In September 1449, a Thomas Hervy, a yeoman of the crown, was a recipient of the goods, chattels and debts due to Richard Askham, a brewer of Southwark.[133] Having risen to king's serjeant, he served as a messenger, for in November 1452 he received a grant of 6d per day for life 'for his expenses ... in crossing to Normandy and other places without any reward in his office or otherwise'.[134] In 1457 a Thomas Hervy – who may or may not be the same person – was commissioned to hire workmen to build and repair the manor and park of Claringdon.[135] Since he was put in charge of the entire project, it was an assignment of considerable responsibility.

According to this letter Thomas Hery (or Hervy) was trying to gain possession of some legal documents, possibly having to do with property that he believed belonged to him. These documents were held by Thomas Downe, who was only waiting for Sir John Bourgchier's consent to hand them over. Downe has been difficult to trace. The most likely candidate is Thomas Downe, chaplain of the chapel within the household, who in November 1456 was granted a prebend in the college of Bridgenorth. In February 1460 he was presented to the parish church of Kyngeslane in the diocese of Hereford.[136] What his connection with Bourgchier may have been, and why the latter's permission was needed for Downe to relinquish the documents, is impossible to say.

---

131 For John Neville, see above, p. 96.
132 *Calendar of State Papers ... in the Archives ... of Venice*, ed. R. Brown (1864), p. 99–100.
133 *CCR, 1447–54*, p. 159. In October 1451 he – or a man of the same name – witnessed a similar gift of goods and chattels by a Norfolk man (ibid., p. 317).
134 *CPR, 1452–61*, p. 24.
135 Ibid., p. 399.
136 Ibid., pp. 326, 573. A Yorkshire chaplain named Thomas Doune appears in 1442 (*CPR, 1441–46*, p. 117).

Six

MONEY MATTERS

Throughout Henry VI's minority, military spending, supposedly covered by taxation but always in arrears, was the greatest expenditure of the regime.[1] The smaller expense of the royal household was largely covered by income from crown lands and Henry's personal estates, the duchies of Lancaster and Cornwall. When Henry VI reached his majority, household spending increased, as befitted an adult king, although from the first he was overgenerous in his grants to household men and court favorites. Henry's major interest was the endowment of his educational foundations – King's College, Cambridge and Eton – and he alienated valuable duchy of Lancaster lands to feoffees to support them. He also sought a bride.

Henry's marriage to Margaret was predicated upon the negotiation of a truce between England and France, in the hope that a temporary truce might lead to a 'lasting peace'. From a financial perspective, 'peace' carried the expectation of a diminution of military spending. As G.L. Harriss explains, the 'truce with France was the financial precondition of the king's marriage, the gratification of his desire to found colleges, and the enlargement of the royal household' – while avoiding bankruptcy.[2] Had all gone well, the plan might have worked.

When Margaret came to England as a virtually dowerless bride in 1445, Henry VI's finances were already in a parlous state. In early 1446 a further portion of the duchy of Lancaster was allocated to provide a large part of the new queen's dower. The effect of both alienations of duchy lands was a shortfall in Henry's income, making the royal household partially dependent on tax revenues from the exchequer. At the same time, military expenditure on the war in France continued into 1444 before being cut back, and a sudden upsurge in household spending

---

1   Our discussion here is based on the detailed analysis provided by G.L. Harriss, 'Marmaduke Lumley and the Exchequer Crisis of 1446–49', in *Aspects of Late Medieval Government and Society*, ed. J.G. Rowe (Toronto, 1986), pp. 143–50.

2   Ibid., p. 149.

was occasioned by the extraordinary expense of the king's marriage.[3] Thus, the year 1444–45 saw a great increase in the crown's financial commitment, at a time when tax revenues were falling. To try to meet the shortfall the government resorted to loans, by no means a new strategy but one that now proliferated. Creditors were issued with tallies (a form of IOU) to be cashed at the exchequer or 'assigned' to the customs revenues collected at a particular port.[4] Loans did not resolve the problem, but merely delayed the day of reckoning. By the end of 1445 there was a rush on the exchequer of military commanders seeking payment of arrears and an array of creditors competing to cash in their tallies. The result was disaster. Prevailing patterns of income and expenditure shifted, upsetting an already precarious balance and creating a financial crisis.

Margaret's dower lands made her an estate-owner comparable to the great magnates, and, naturally enough, she was interested in securing her income from all the sources available to her. Good ladyship dictated that she should also take an interest in the efforts of persons for whom she felt responsible – or who appealed to her – to obtain money they were owed. The first letter in this chapter involves a dispute between two individuals when Margaret was still a very new queen, and she exerted her influence to bring about a settlement. When the debtor was the government, the situation became more complicated. The second through fifth letters show some of the effects of the exchequer crisis upon Margaret herself, and on a servant in the royal household.

The next three letters relate to a wartime setting. One involves a ransom payment; another, the difficulty in obtaining promised restitution for land lost in France as a result of the efforts to reach a peace settlement. This initially meant the ceding of the county of Maine to the French. The handover was protracted until Charles VII lost patience, and the surrender was accomplished under military threat in 1448. A year later in July 1449, peace negotiations broke down and war resumed. The letters touch upon all these things.

The last three letters show Margaret again acting as a good lady to obtain assistance for someone in a financial matter and to resolve debts of long standing. In the final one, as in her letter to the duchess of Somerset elsewhere in this chapter,[5] we see female networking as she appeals to other women to influence their husbands on her behalf.

3   It cost almost £7,000 to bring Margaret to England (ibid., p. 148).
4   Some persons were allowed to keep the customs owed on wool they shipped to discharge debts owed by the crown. This diverted potential income from the crown and was particularly resented by the commons.
5   See below, p. 132.

[64] Queen to John Stafford, Chancellor, Archbishop of Canterbury, re Baldwin Saheny, 8 January [1446]
(SC 1/44/13)

By the Quene
Right worshipful fader in God, our right trusty and right welbeloved, we grete you wele. And for asmuche as the proctours of our servant Bawdewyn Saheny of Spynall, marchant, have doon us to be enformed that the accion and plee hanging bitwix the said Bawdewin and oon William Bowes of York, marchant, touching certeine money whiche hath be delaied on the part of the said William this viij yere or more, as it is said, is nowe broughte lawfully unto the point of sentence to be yeven in the courte of chauncellerie, we therfore pray you hertly, sith that ye havse be at al times for our sake unto the said Bawdewin good and especial lord in his rightes, ye wil now in his absence conclude your tendernisse and favour unto his proctours and in as goodly hast as ye may by lawe trouth and gode conscience to procede to juggement, shewing herein suche expedicion and benivolence as ye have doo hiderto as the cas hath required. Whereof we thanke you hertly. In whiche thing ye shul mowe not oonly doon us grete pleasance, but also unto our right entierly bestbeloved fader the king of Sicile in ministring th'expedicion of justice. Right worshipful fader in God, our right trusty welbelovid, our Lord have you in his blessed keping.
Yeven under our signet at my lordes castel of Windesore the viij day of Januer.

On 18 November 1445, a commission was issued to one of the king's sergeants at arms to arrest William Bowes, a merchant of York, and bring him to chancery to answer the charges laid against him by 'Baldwin Sahem, merchant of Spynnall'.[6] Margaret's letter would have been written soon after, on 8 January 1446, when she had been queen for less than a year. Baldwin was probably a Lorrainer, a merchant from the town of Épinal on the Moselle, and therefore a subject of Margaret's father René, as duke of Lorraine.[7] Her letter indicates that René had an interest in Saheny's case.

Saheny had already brought suit against Bowes *in absentia* through the use of proctors. Thomas Catesby, a mercer, acted as his attorney.[8] Although Margaret may have been informed of the particulars of the case by Catesby, it is even more likely that her father prompted her intervention. She and King Henry had received letters from Charles VII the previous autumn, to which they replied in December, and there is no reason to think that Margaret was not in contact with

6   *CPR, 1441–46*, p. 390. Baldwin's name appears as 'Saheny' in other documents regarding the case.
7   The Latin name for Épinal was *Spinalium*, and its natives were known as *spinaliens*.
8   *CCR, 1441–47*, pp. 444–5, for details of the case and the resulting settlement.

her father at the same time. A request from René would have ensured Margaret's mediation. Bowes had delayed paying the money claimed by Saheny for a number of years. Assuming that he was now available to answer charges, Margaret's letter served as a gentle reminder to the chancellor that it was time to move forward.

Chancellor Stafford appointed Thomas Cook, draper, and John Middelton, mercer, both of London, to settle the case by arbitration.[9] Since Saheny remained overseas, time was required for communications to pass back and forth before a settlement was reached in October. On the 27th, Saheny and Bowes each bound themselves in the amount of £1,000 sterling to obey and abide by the arbiters' decision. The settlement sealed two days later contained four provisions. First, Saheny was to withdraw all suits and fully discharge Bowes. Second, Saheny and Bowes were each to formally acquit each other of any charges or claims 'from the beginning of the world' to the present time. Third, Bowes was to pay Saheny £254 in installments of £100 at the next two Christmases, and the remainder at Midsummer 1448. And finally, that Bowes might recover half the £254 plus costs and damages (if permitted by law) from the executors of John of Bolton, late of York.

William Bowes seems to have been a man of some importance, which may explain how he was able to put off Saheny for so long. His father, William Bowes the elder, was 'one of the wealthiest and most influential York merchants of his day'.[10] In addition, he was escheator and mayor in York, and MP for York at various times. He died in 1439.[11] The younger William seems to have followed in his father's footsteps as MP for York in 1435 and mayor in 1443.[12]

Saheny's connection with the queen remains uncertain. Although she calls him her servant, this may represent courtesy more than personal contact, particularly if her intervention was prompted by her father. Since there appear to be no further appearances of Saheny and Bowes in the records, we assume that the case was settled.

[65] King [Henry VI] to the Chancellor of the Duchy of Lancaster [1447]
(BL, Add. MS 48031, fol. 69v)

Trusty and welbeloved. We wol and expresly charge you that, for certeiyne resonable causes moving us, innowise ye suffre passe undre the seal of our Duchie of Lancastre being in your warde any lettres prejudiciall t'any graunt that we have made to our

9 The dispute had evidently become difficult to sort out, having originated on the continent and by this time involving claims and counterclaims on both sides. Thomas Cook later became one of Margaret's collectors of customs (see below, p. 123).
10 Much of his business was at Calais. All information on the elder Bowes is from Roskell, Clark and Rawcliffe, *House of Commons*, pp. 318–19.
11 His will was proved on 6 August.
12 F. Drake, *Eboracum* (1736), pp. 357, 362. Information about the younger Bowes is scanty.

most dere and right entierly bestbeloved wyfe the quene, any commaundement by us yeven unto you un to the contrarye nat withstanding. And that ye fail not herof as ye wol eschewe our displeasir, at your perill. Yeven undre our signet, etc.

[66] Queen [Margaret] to the Chancellor of the Duchy of Lancaster [1447] (BL, Add. MS 48031, fol. 69v)

Trusty and welbeloved. We suppose that it is clearly in youre remembraunce how that it hathe pleased my lord of his especial grace for ta'graunte and t'assigne unto us a certeyne somme of moneye to be paid in the Duchie of Lancastre, wherfore we desire and praye you, and also exhorte and expresly charge you, that in no wise ye suffre passe undre the seal of the Duchie of Lncastre beyng in your warde any lettres prejudiciall to the saide graunte. Behaving you towards us in this partye in suche sad wise to your trewe acquitaill that we may finde that ye do us lawe [justice] and that we have no cause to be othre unto you thanne your good lady, at youre perill. Calling also unto youre remembraunce what actis of parliament have be made for us in this partye and what straite commaundements my lord hathe yeven you t'observe and accomplisshe our request in this behalve. Yeven undre oure signet, etc.

These two unsigned and undated letters deal with grants from the duchy of Lancaster to a queen. They are glossed in *Vale's Book* and tentatively ascribed to Edward IV and Elizabeth Woodville since they follow a letter from Edward IV in that collection.[13] But the documents Vale copied are not in strict chronological order, and we have found no source that either proves or disproves this ascription. *Vale's* editors also opine that the letters *could* be by Henry VI and Margaret of Anjou, and careful reading of their full texts supports this conclusion.

The king's letter is a warning and a reminder that duchy grants to the queen are to take precedence over all other grants from the duchy, *even if he should himself command otherwise*. Henry VI was notorious for making double grants; Edward IV was not. The injunction 'at your perill' indicates that he meant business: he intended his order to have immediate effect, with no exceptions. The queen's letter refers to a specific 'somme of moneye' to be paid to her from the duchy, but otherwise reinforces the king's instructions, with an added promise of good ladyship to sweeten a similar warning. Margaret often followed up Henry's orders with reminders of her own. It is less likely that Elizabeth Woodville had occasion to do so, since Edward IV kept a firm hand on financial matters.

So, what was the 'sum of money' to which the queen referred? It reads like a one-off grant of cash, rather than a component in her original dower.

Margaret's dower, granted by parliament in March 1446, was the traditional

---

13 *Vale's Book*, p. 173.

endowment to a queen of 10,000 marks, or £6,666 13s 4d a year. It comprised duchy of Lancaster estates to the value of £2,000 and an annuity from the duchy of £1,000. In addition, she was to receive cash grants of £1,008 15s 5d from the duchy of Cornwall, £1,000 from the customs of Southampton, and £1,657 17s 11d from the exchequer.[14] The parliament held at Bury St Edmunds in February 1447 acknowledged the difficulty of collecting the cash assignments, especially those drawn on the exchequer. They agreed that estates and fees reverting to the crown should be granted to Margaret in lieu, the total value not to exceed the assigned £3,666 13s 4d, and to be deducted from the amounts due from the cash grants.[15]

Humphrey, duke of Gloucester, the king's uncle and heir, died suddenly on 23 February while parliament was in session. On 24 February, in accordance with parliament's mandate, Henry VI endowed Margaret with some of the lands that reverted to the crown on Gloucester's death.[16] On 28 March, Henry also granted her Gloucester's annuity of 500 marks (£333 6s 4d) from the duchy of Lancaster, backdated to the previous Michaelmas.[17] We believe that this is the sum in question.

The plethora of grants issued by Henry VI at Bury St Edmunds immediately after Gloucester's death, which included a number of double grants of the same office to two people, caused administrative confusion, and the duchy officials were probably slow to implement the king's order. Grants from the duchy were paid biannually, from Michaelmas to Easter and Easter to Michaelmas. Easter fell on 9 April in 1447, but the backdated grant was not paid out, resulting in letters of admonition from the king and the queen.

Although we cannot prove that the 'somme of moneye' in the queen's letter was Gloucester's annuity, it is the most likely. Nothing in Elizabeth's Woodville's household account book matches the requirements as closely, although it has survived for one year only (1466–67).[18] On the other hand, Margaret's surviving account (1452–53) shows that she received the 500 mark annuity and that it was not in arrears.[19] The letters in question would have been addressed to the chancellor

---

14   *RP*, V, pp. 118–20.
15   *PROME*, XII, pp. 19–22; *CCR, 1447–54*, p. 13.
16   *Foedera*, XI, p. 155; *CPR, 1446–52*, p. 599. The 1447 grant to Margaret included the manor of Hampsted Marshall and the constableship of Gloucester Castle. She received neither one. The hundred of Tendrying in Essex does not appear in any subsequent confirmation of her grants, but may be part of the fee farm of Essex. The castle and lordship of Colchester and fee farm of the town were granted to Sir John Hampton on the same day as Henry VI granted them to Margaret. They were recovered in the resumption of 1451, but only granted to Margaret in 1453.
17   Somerville, *Duchy of Lancaster*, p. 208, citing DL 37/15/15.
18   Myers, 'Household'.
19   Myers, 'Household', p. 166.

of the duchy, and we suggest they date to 1447 when Walter Shirington held that office.[20] If our analysis is correct, the duchy officials took them very seriously.

[67] Queen to John Somerton, one of the Customers of Southampton [first half of 1448]
(BL, Add. MS 46,846, fol. 40v; Monro, pp. 111–12)

By the Quene

Trusty, etc. We desire and praye yowe, and also exhorte yow and require yow, that of suche money as is dewe unto us at Michelmasse terme last passed of oure douer [dower], assigned to be paied of the custumers of Suth[ampton] by your handes, ye will do your peyne and diligence that we may be contented and paied in al hast. And of the day of your payement ye will acerteine by writyng oure right welbeloved knyght Sir John Wenlok, oure chamberlayn, which knoweth in what wise the seid money must be emploied and bestowed in all possible hast; and that ye faile not herof as we truste and as ye thinke to stande in continuance of the favor of oure good grace and t'eschewe oure displeasure. Yeven, etc.

To John Somerton, oon of the custumers of Suth[ampton]

[68] Queen to Marmaduke Lumley, Bishop of Carlisle [first half of 1448]
(BL, Add. MS 46,846, fols 40v–41; Monro, pp. 112–13)

By the Quene

Reverend fader in God, etc., we grete, etc. Desiryng hertly and praying yow that ye doo write your lettres unto J. Somerton, oon of [the customers of] Suth[ampton], yevynge him stretely in commandement to paye and contente us of oure money dewe unto us at Michelmasse last passed of oure dower assigned to be paied of the customers of Suth[ampton], which we must paye in all possible hast for suche causes that lyen us right nigh to hert, havynge th'exploit herof in suche recommendacion and favour that we may cause to cun [give] yow therfor right especial thanke, as oure full trust, etc. At W. *ut supra*.[21]

To the Bisshop of Carliel, Tresorier of Englond

By the end of 1446, England was in the midst of the exchequer crisis that had been building since 1444 and had become critical over the course of the past year. Marmaduke Lumley, bishop of Carlisle, became treasurer in mid-December 1446, with a mandate to do something about it.[22] Lumley's overall goal was to provide for increased household expenses, occasioned in part by the king's

---

20 Somerville, *Duchy of Lancaster*, pp. 389–90.
21 The *ut supra* apparently refers to the letter that immediately precedes the one to Somerton in the manuscript, also written 'at W' and bearing no date. For that letter, see above, p. 111.
22 Harriss, 'Marmaduke Lumley', p. 152ff, for Lumley's actions.

marriage, while dealing with the claims of other creditors in a situation in which revenues had fallen. One of his first actions, taken at the end of the month, was to appoint new customs collectors, which effectively froze payments assigned on the customs. Since tallies for payment were issued in the customers' names, rather than to the ports themselves, the replacement of customers invalidated existing tallies until they could be reissued in the new collectors' names. In an effort to head off the inevitable claims of exemption and to forestall new claims, Lumley obtained a mandate from the king stating that there should be no assignments made upon the customs without the treasurer's specific approval, even if they came from Henry himself and included a clause of *non obstante*. Not surprisingly, given the king's predilection for making indiscriminate grants, the warrants for payment appeared just the same, but Lumley was apparently able to refuse or delay payment long enough to begin to make some headway towards his goals.

Of course, this made persons with a claim on money from the customs unhappy. Margaret was one of them. As part of her dower she had been granted £1,000 annually from the customs at Southampton, and in mid-January 1447, Lumley extended the freeze to include all such payments granted under the great or privy seals.[23] This affected Margaret directly by officially halting future payments to her from the customs. It appears from these letters that the queen's payment was in arrears and that she had outstanding obligations that needed to be met immediately.

John Somerton was a collector of customs in Southampton in September 1446. He was reappointed by Lumley, along with John Payn, on 31 December of that year. In July 1447, while Somerton remained a customer, Payn was replaced by Thomas Pound.[24] John Wenlock had entered Margaret's service as an usher of the chamber. He probably became Margaret's chamberlain in 1447, replacing Sir James Fiennes, her first chamberlain, after Fiennes became the king's chamberlain at the beginning of April.[25] With Margaret's payments frozen from the beginning of 1447 and the *dramatis personae* in place, a date during the first half of 1448 for these letters seems preferable.

It is clear that Margaret was having all sorts of difficulties in collecting the

23   See also *RP*, V, p. 120. Heritable annuities were excepted.
24   *CFR, 1445–52*, pp. 51–6.
25   *CPR, 1446–52*, p. 63, for a grant dated 18 June 1447 to James Fiennes, lord Saye, 'appointed king's
     chamberlain during pleasure … of 100 marks yearly from 1 April last from the great custom on
     wools and woolfells in the port of London so long as he stay in the office of chamberlain'. This
     suggests that Fiennes became the king's chamberlain on 1 April. He had been created Lord
     Saye and Sele at the Bury parliament in February 1447. Wenlock was still an usher in January
     1447, and the earliest reference to him as chamberlain is from April 1448 (Roskell, *Parliament
     and Politics*, II, p. 243).

money owed her on her dower by that summer. On 24 July, noting that she had been granted £1,657 17s 11d a year in cash from the exchequer (and implying that she had been unable to collect it), Henry gave Margaret the right to nominate one of the two customs collectors in Southampton, London and Kingston upon Hull, from whom she was to receive tallies good for the original grant.[26] This grant was designed to kill two birds with one stone: to provide a solution to her inability to collect directly from the exchequer, and to give her special leverage over the customs collectors themselves. In December 1448, Thomas Cook became one of the Southampton customers, and the man he replaced was John Somerton, making it likely that Cook was Margaret's choice since he had been instrumental in obtaining a monetary award for Baldwin Saheny.[27] While it is possible that Margaret wrote to Somerton after July 1448 while he still held office, if she had reason to be dissatisfied with his performance – and her letters argue that she did – it seems more likely that she would have waited to resolve the issue until he could be replaced by her own appointee.

By the end of 1447, Lumley had succeeded in obtaining further measures to shore up his authority and to resist efforts to claim exemption from the freeze. At the same time, pressure from creditors had increased while payments to the household still lagged behind. In this atmosphere, the situation at the ports has been characterized by G.L. Harriss as one of 'severe competition … [where] the successful extraction of money from the collectors depended less on strict mandates … than upon the personal influence which some creditors could apply on the collectors'.[28] And this was precisely what Margaret was trying to do. She was putting pressure on Somerton – beginning by 'exhorting and requiring' and ending with a thinly veiled threat about 'the continuance of [her] favor', with the notice that her chamberlain Wenlock would be expecting a prompt communication tucked in between. But she approached Lumley as well, albeit in a much gentler way, because he was ultimately the person whose acquiescence could deliver the desired result.

Although Margaret's efforts to obtain money from the customs of Southampton did meet with some success, over the longer term they proved an unsatisfactory source of revenue. In April 1449, she was still trying to get money from the collectors Pound and Cook, and her sole extant household account shows that

---

26   *CPR, 1446–52*, p. 172.
27   *CFR, 1445–52*, pp. 98–9. Somerton is described as 'late collector of customs' in a pardon dated February 1449, while in April both Pound and Cook appear as customers (*CPR, 1446–52*, pp. 213–14, 267). No one other than Somerton, Pound and Cook appears as a collector at Southampton between July 1447 and April 1449.
28   Harriss, 'Marmaduke Lumley', p. 160.

her payments from Southampton remained in arrears in 1452–53.[29] Cook was still a customer in that year and presumably still Margaret's nominee, but Somerton had been appointed again in September 1450.[30]

[69] Queen to Thomas Brown, Squire [*c.* April 1449]
(BL, Add. MS 46,846, fol. 13; Monro, p. 148)

> By the Quene
> Right trusty and welbeloved, we grete you well. Lating yow wite that we be credible enformed what diligence, faithfull labor and hertly love that ye have shewed us in our maters, and in especial now late in our assignement of the custumes of Southamton, for the which we thinke us greetly beholde unto yow and cun [give] you therfor right good and especial thanke, trusting fully that in suche thinges as ye shull mowe have for to do towardes us, we shall have you after your deserte in tendre remembrance of our grace therefore in tyme commyng. Yeven, etc. at Windesor the xth, etc.
> To T. Browne, squier, Under Tresourer of Engl[and].

Marmaduke Lumley named Thomas Brown as under-treasurer. Brown had already served for some years as a clerk of the exchequer and had been an MP for Dover, and later for Kent.[31] He was sent off to the Bury parliament in February 1447 'to make known … the state of the realm' and undoubtedly to impress upon all attendees the magnitude of the financial crisis facing the country and the need for drastic action. Perhaps in recognition of his new status and as reward for his efforts he was made steward of the lordships of Milton (Middleton) and Marden, Kent, formerly held by the duke of Gloucester but now granted to Margaret, and was leased the manor of Havering, Essex.[32] Over time he received other benefits. When Lumley resigned as treasurer in September 1449, it appears that Brown also stepped down.

Although this letter belongs to the same general circumstances as the letters to Somerton and Lumley, we do not see a direct link between them. This letter says nothing about *payment of money*, but refers instead to *assignment*, which was a different matter. Since this letter only mentions Southampton, it is unlikely to refer to the transaction of July 1448, when the portion of Margaret's dower

29 *CPR, 1446–52*, p. 267; Myers, 'Household', pp. 139–40, 166–7, 169–70. Lumley had by then resigned as treasurer – and had, in fact, died – so he cannot be blamed! Rather, parliament had assigned all customs revenues to the defense of Calais for two years.

30 *CFR, 1445–52*, pp. 191–2. Cook, who by this time was a member of the London common council, served a term as mayor in 1462–63 and was knighted in 1465 before running afoul of Edward IV in 1468, for which see above, p. 87. He died in 1478. See also pp. 226, 249, below.

31 Wedgwood, pp. 123–4.

32 *CPR, 1446–52*, pp. 84, 269, 282.

originally due from the exchequer (£1,657 17s 11d) was reassigned to the customs of Southampton, *London and Kingston upon Hull,* for which she was issued tallies.[33] On 10 April 1449, however, Margaret exchanged £3,657 17s 11d worth of uncashed tallies levied on Thomas Pound and Thomas Cook, customers of Southampton, for new tallies worth the same amount plus an additional 1,000 marks (£666 13s 4d) as recompense for payments she had made for the king.[34] This situation fits the language of the letter and – assuming that Brown handled all the paperwork involved in the reassignment, which would have been considerable – provides ample cause for the queen's gratitude.

Brown was knighted soon after he left the treasury; he continued to serve the government in Kent and elsewhere in various capacities. In 1459 he became sheriff in Kent and was mustering men against the anticipated Yorkist invasion in 1460. After the Yorkist earls entered the city of London at the beginning of July, he was among the Lancastrians who held the Tower. The defeat of the king's forces at Northampton on 10 July and his return to London on the 16th, effectively a captive, meant that the holdouts in the Tower had to capitulate. They surrendered on or around the 19th. Sir Thomas Brown and five others were tried, convicted of treason and subsequently beheaded on 29 July.[35]

[70] Queen to the Customers of the Port of Boston re John Wenham [after September 1448]
(BL, Add. MS 46,846, fol. 57v; Monro, pp. 141–2)

By the Quene
Trusty, etc. And for asmoche as it hath pleased unto my lordes highnesse to grante unto John Wenham x marcs in mariage with his wif duryng theire lyves, to be taken yerely in the porte of Boston by th'andes of the custumers there for the tyme beyng, as in theire lettres patentes therof unto theym made it appereth more pleinly; we, havyng consideracion unto the good service that our said servant hath don unto us and yet daily therin continueth, desire and pray you that, at reverence of us, ye will have hym in his payment of the said annuite after the continue [content] of my said lordes grant especialy recommended, and for your tyme to shew hym then th'ease and favor that ye goodly may, so that he may finde in effecte thise, etc., unto hym effectuelx and vailable. As we trust yown [*sic*]. In whiche thinge, etc.

To William Hauley, squier, and Ric[hard] P[er]pant, marchant, of the porte of Boston

33   Ibid., p. 172.
34   Ibid., p. 267. Myers, 'Household', pp. 166–7, 169.
35   W. Marx, ed., *An English Chronicle* (Woodbridge, 2003), pp. 89, 91; 'Benet's Chronicle', pp. 226–7; J. Gairdner, ed., *Three Fifteenth Century Chronicles*, Camden Society, new ser. 28 (1880), pp. 73–5.

John Wenham first appears as a king's sergeant in 1443, when he received a life-grant of 100s p.a. from the issues of Staffordshire in recognition of his 'good service to the king's mother and the king'.[36] He continued his service to the royal family, and perhaps specifically to Margaret, for he received a monetary gift from her in 1445–46 and a gold ring in 1448–49.[37] On 6 September 1448, in anticipation of his marriage as well as in recognition of his service 'to the king's mother, to queen Margaret and the king', he and Alice, daughter of William Vincent of Bekenesfeld, were granted an annuity of 10 marks in survivorship from the customs and subsidies of Boston, replacing his previous grant.[38] Boston, which lies on the Lincolnshire seacoast, had once been prominent in the wool trade, but over the course of the fifteenth century its importance declined. William Hawley and Richard Perpoynt became collectors of the customs for the port on 5 June 1447, and they were evidently still in office when this letter was written.[39] Unfortunately, Wenham did not long enjoy his marriage, for he was dead by November 1450.[40]

Margaret's letter would have been written after the grant of an annuity was made, probably towards the end of 1448. By this time, Treasurer Lumley's freeze on payments had eased a bit, but it would still have helped to have a powerful advocate. Margaret's letter appears suited to this purpose.

[71] Queen to the Earl of Northumberland re Matthew Gough, 8 March [1447]
(BL, Add. MS 46,846, fols 65–65v; Monro, pp. 109–10)

By the Quene.
Right trusty and right welbeloved Cousyn, we grete you well. Lattyng you witte that upon truste and seurte of your obligacion wherinne ye were bounden, as we be enformed, unto our welbeloved squier Mathew Gogh in ij^m [2,000] salutz for the finance of the lord Camoys, we were the rather inclined and benevolent to desyre our said squyer, by our lettres, to do all his peine and diligence for delyverance of the said lord, at whos instance and request our said squire toke upon hym to ley

36 *CPR, 1441–46*, p. 189. Queen Katherine had died in 1437.
37 E 101/404/14 and E 101/410/22. He seems to have been a yeoman of the household by the latter date, as gold rings were given to them in that year.
38 *CPR, 1446–52*, p. 226. This provided a gain of 33s over the previous annuity. Wenham does not seem to have received a special gift from the queen for his marriage; perhaps she thought that Henry's grant was sufficient.
39 *CFR, 1445–52*, pp. 52, 54, 56. The next customer of whom we have record was William Pychard, who was appointed in May 1452. Both he and Perpoynt were customers in April 1454 (ibid., pp. 232–4; *CPR, 1452–61*, p. 164).
40 On 30 November 1450 the office of porter of Somerton Castle, Lincolnshire, and the keeping of the warren there were granted for life to Richard Bircheley, king's sergeant and also a member of Margaret's household, with wages of 2d per day 'as [what] John Wenham deceased the last occupier had' (*CCR, 1447–54*, pp. 206–7).

his selee [seal] in this mater. And it is now soo that he hath acerteined us that the day prefixte of your payment is past and ronne, so that the charge lyth now upon hym and mustnedes be droven by justice t'answar therto hym self, and likly in your defaulte to be dishonured and rebuked for evere, the which we suppose ye will take right nigh to hert, in especiall sith he was brought in therto by your mene. Wherfore we desire and exhorte you, upon your worship, that in all goodly haste ye do content your said summe in savying ['in savyng' repeated] our said squier harmeles, so that we be no more called uppon in lake of your devoir and trew acquitall in this partie. Yeven, etc. at Wind[sor], the viij day of March.

To th'erl of North[umberland]

This letter shows Margaret involved in an incident that should more properly have been dealt with by King Henry as it concerned the release of an English prisoner of war. Roger, Lord Camoys was a soldier of fortune who assumed his father's title without license when his elder brother died with no male heir. He had been captured in an attack on a Breton town, probably La Guerche, in either 1438 or 1443.[41] Camoys owed his unnamed captor a ransom of 2,000 *saluts*,[42] which Henry Percy, earl of Northumberland undertook to pay because he was Camoys's half-brother.[43] Margaret was acquainted with the earl; she gave his wife a gold tablet worth £12 at New Year 1449.[44]

Matthew Gough and Roger Camoys may have been comrades in arms.[45] Gough was a professional soldier who had fought in France throughout Henry VI's reign.[46] The French respected his military prowess; their chroniclers called him 'Mathago'. Gough was also employed as a royal messenger, and in the summer of 1446, after delivering letters from Henry VI to King Charles in

41 An English attack on La Guerche occurred in each of these years. C.L. Kingsford, ed., *Chronicles of London* (Oxford, 1905), p. 145, dates Camoys's capture to 1438; Monro, to 1443. In October 1443, Camoys's wife Isabel received a grant because of his capture (*CPR, 1441–46*, p. 219).

42 About £300–400. The *salut* was a gold coin weighing 3.5 grams and worth between 3s 4d and 4s in the 1440s, not 25s as Monro claims. Its value was approximately the same as the French *écu*. It was issued by the Lancastrian administration in France and Normandy between 1423 and 1449 (M.G.A. Vale, *Charles VII* [Berkeley, CA, 1974], pp. 241–2).

43 GEC, II, pp. 507–8, 511–12. The earl's mother Elizabeth, widow of Henry 'Hotspur' Percy, married as her second husband Thomas, Lord Camoys. Their son Roger was born *c.* 1406.

44 E 101/410/2.

45 M.K. Jones, 'John Beaufort, Duke of Somerset and the French Expedition of 1443', in *Patronage, the Crown and the Provinces in Late Medieval England*, ed. R.A. Griffiths (Gloucester, 1981), pp. 93, 95. Gough was with Beaufort's expedition of 1443 that attacked La Guerche. We do not know where he served in 1438.

46 Stevenson, II, ii, pp. 385, 394; A.E. Marshall, 'The Role of English War Captains in England and Normandy, 1436–61', MA thesis, University of Wales (1974), p. 233. Gough fought at the battle of Cravant in 1423 and at Verneuil in 1424; he was captain of Bayeux from July 1440 until its final surrender in May 1450.

France, he went on to Brittany. The duke of Brittany's younger brother Gilles had been granted a pension by Henry VI in 1443 after Gilles swore fealty to him, and Gough was carrying an instalment of this pension on his journey.[47] This would have been when he arranged for Camoys's release.

Ransom was a fact of life while England and France were at war. It was common practice for a prisoner to be set free on promise of payment if he offered adequate securities. Failure to pay as promised was dishonorable under the laws of chivalry, and not only the defaulter, but his 'pledge' too, faced disgrace. The captor could label his enemy a 'false knight' and display the offender's arms in reverse or hanging upside down as a mark of contempt.[48] It appears that Margaret, relying on Northumberland's undertaking, issued Gough with letters of her own, endorsing his mission and possibly placing him under her protection, since she refers to him as 'our welbeloved squire'. Thus, when Northumberland defaulted, not only Gough but Margaret too felt dishonored. Her letter to Northumberland was probably written in 1447, since Gough visited Brittany in 1446 and Camoys's captor would have allowed some time thereafter for the ransom to be paid.

Meanwhile, Camoys returned to England, and in October 1446, Northumberland was again called upon to stand surety for him, this time in the very large sum of £2,000, to guarantee his appearance before the king's council when summoned (for unspecified reasons).[49] Presumably, Northumberland met this obligation, which may account for his delay in honoring his commitment to pay Camoys's ransom. He paid up eventually, for by the end of 1447, Camoys was back in Normandy, preparing to come to the defense of Le Mans.[50]

Ironically, Gough was appointed by Henry VI as a commissioner to arrange for the handing over of Le Mans and the county of Maine to the French under a treaty signed in London in July 1447.[51] But it was not until March 1448, after the threat of a resumption of hostilities, that the terms were implemented and

---

47 M. d'Escouchy, *Chronique de Mathieu d'Escouchy*, 3 vols, ed. G. du Fresne de Beaucourt (Paris, 1863–64), III, pp. 156–7. In July, Gough collected £116 13s 4d from the exchequer as part of Gilles's pension (L.E. James, 'The Career of William de la Pole, First Duke of Suffolk, 1437–50', B.Litt. thesis, University of Oxford [1979], p. 172, n. 1, citing E 403/762 m.11).

48 M. Keen, *Chivalry* (1984), p. 175. The French warrior La Hire displayed the arms of a 'pledge' for his defaulting prisoner reversed on his horse's tail.

49 *CCR, 1441–47*, p. 460. The mainprise is dated 18 October 1446. Watts, *Henry VI*, p. 238, n. 147, speculates that the summons was because Camoys had voiced criticisms of Edmund Beaufort, shortly to be appointed the king's lieutenant in France. This would add weight to the argument for 1438 as the date of Camoys's capture, when he served under Beaufort.

50 Escouchy, *Chronique*, III, p. 184.

51 Stevenson, II, ii, pp. 696–702.

Le Mans was surrendered.[52] Gough fought at the battle of Formigny in April 1450, where the English army was heavily defeated.[53] After the battle he fled to Bayeux, where he was captain, but in May he was forced to surrender the town after a sustained two-week bombardment; he returned to England shortly thereafter.[54] When Jack Cade's rebellion threatened London in June, Gough was second in command to Thomas, Lord Scales, who had been appointed to hold the Tower and defend the city. Gough took part in the battle of the Bridge against Cade's men and was killed in the course of the fighting.[55]

The earl of Shrewsbury was campaigning in Gascony in 1453. Camoys joined him with reinforcements and became seneschal of the duchy.[56] After Shrewsbury was killed at the battle of Castillon in July, Camoys withstood the siege of Bordeaux until October when he negotiated an honorable surrender. The English garrison was permitted to march out with the full honors of war and take ship for England.[57]

Camoys probably remained in France after the surrender, possibly in the service of King Charles VII, as Henry VI referred to him as 'oure rebel' in 1455 when he gave Camoys's valuable military accouterments, which had been forfeited to the crown 'by cause of his rebellion', to the earl of Salisbury.[58] An order was issued in May 1456 to assess what estates Camoys held in the county of Northampton, and since it does not say they were forfeit, he was probably dead.[59]

[72] Queen to the Duke of Somerset re Viscount Beaumont [1448]
(BL, Add. MS 46,846, fols 66v–67; Monro, pp. 118–19)

By the Quene
Right trusty and right entierly welbeloved Cousyn, we grete you full hertly and often tymes well. And for asmoch as my lord writeth his especiall lettres unto you, desiryng affectuously for certeyn consideracions comprised in the same [that] our cousyn the Viscont Beaumont to be recompensed and seen unto after his estate and after the quantite of the lyvelod that he hathe lefte in the counte of Manor [Maine], like as [in] the said lettres it more pleynly apperith. We, therfore, havyng respecte both unto my said lordes writyng and also unto the greet chierte [charity] that he

---

52 *Foedera*, XI, pp. 204–6. A declaration by the war captains in Le Mans, including Gough, denied that they had capitulated under pressure. See the next letter for resistance to the surrender of Le Mans.
53 Beaucourt, V, pp. 31–4.
54 Stevenson, II, ii, pp. 630–61.
55 Griffiths, p. 615.
56 Vale, *English Gascony*, p. 246.
57 Beaucourt, V, pp. 279, 283–5.
58 *PPC*, VI, pp. 251–2.
59 *CPR, 1452–61*, p. 303.

hath oure said cousyn in, pray you as hertly as we can that, aswell at the reverence of my lorde as at contemplacion of us and this our writyng, ye will ordeine and see unto the recompensacion of the same oure cousyn after my lordes desire and entent, and soo we may have cause to thanke you. Yeven, etc.

    To the Duc of Somer[set]

Edmund Beaufort, then earl of Somerset, was given a three-year appointment as lieutenant-general of France on Christmas Eve 1446. Beaufort had spent much of his life serving in France, and in March 1438 he had been appointed captain-general and governor of Maine. This was followed by a land grant of the entire county to him on 19 July 1442, but it included the important reservation that Maine could be restored to France as the price of a peace agreement.[60]

    A French embassy arrived in London in July 1447 to negotiate the ceding of Maine in return for an extension of the truce signed at Tours in 1444. But an agreement on paper can be difficult to implement in practice, and some of Beaufort's officers – and probably Beaufort himself – opposed the deal, which for them meant a loss of face as well as income derived from land and office. The matter was partially addressed when the French agreed to provide 'reasonable provision' to dispossessed landowners and the English council specifically undertook to compensate Beaufort. The surrender of Maine was to take place on 1 November 1447.[61] Nevertheless, obstruction by Beaufort's captains in Le Mans who were directly charged with the transfer continued, and the king sent an irate letter to Beaufort, who was still in England attending to his own interests, demanding that he put an end to the foot-dragging.[62] The upshot of this was that the November date passed without Maine changing hands, but on the 13th of the month the council set Beaufort's compensation at 10,000 *livres tournois* per year.[63] He was reappointed lieutenant-general at the end of the year, provided with 4,000 marks for general expenses, and on 31 March 1448 was raised to a dukedom to go with his new position.[64]

    By that time, however, Charles VII, who had grown tired of English stalling – and perhaps ineptitude as well – had surrounded Le Mans with an army and

60   M.K. Jones, 'Somerset, York and the Wars of the Roses', *EHR* 104 (1989), p. 292, notes the private power afforded by Somerset's 'almost vice-regal status' that allowed him to act without reference to the larger English war aims and effort.

61   Stevenson, II, ii, pp. 642–63; *Foedera*, XI, p. 175. No actual amounts were set.

62   Griffiths, pp. 500–2, for the English delaying tactics; Stevenson, II, ii, pp. 692–6, for Henry's letter. See also the previous letter for Mathew Gough, the captain of Le Mans at its surrender.

63   Jones, 'Somerset', p. 293 and n. 5. It was to come from the taxes on wine, cider and other beverages in Normandy. Jones calls it 'a very hard bargain' and also points out that Beaufort was able to collect it right up to the outbreak of war in 1449.

64   Ibid., pp. 293–4.

forced its unconditional surrender on 15 March 1448. Unsurprisingly, the resulting treaty (agreed to several days in advance of the inevitable surrender) reflected French terms: the handover of English-held Maine in return for a two-year extension of the truce. The interests of soon-to-be-dispossessed landowners were accommodated by Charles's agreement to forego the payments he had been receiving from the revenues of English-held Normandy since the truce of Tours in 1444, so that they might instead provide for reparations.[65] But before this money could find its way to those affected, further difficulties had to be overcome.

When Somerset arrived in Rouen in April 1448, he was faced with a cash crisis. The Norman estates had become increasingly unwilling to pay the expenses of a military occupation during peacetime; salaries of civil officials had been slashed, and payments to the garrisons were in arrears.[66] Beaufort did not have the personal financial resources of his predecessor, the duke of York, which might have helped to tide him over in a pinch.[67] To meet this challenge, Somerset attempted to root out corruption by ordering an audit of accounts and by replacing the local receivers with a more centralized tax collection system. The revenues that had been paid to Charles VII were now in Somerset's hands while, presumably, en route to other recipients. Much of this money was diverted to other needful causes, and, inevitably, diversion of this money to his own needs contributed to the belief that he was avaricious.[68]

One of the men owed reparations was John, Viscount Beaumont, who had served faithfully in the war and had been rewarded with lands, title and office, becoming England's first viscount in 1440 and constable of England in 1445. He had also been steward of the honor of Leicester since 1437, and in 1446 Leicester formed part of Margaret's dower lands. Beaumont became chief steward for all her lands in 1452.[69] When he found himself among the recently dispossessed who sought recompense for lands lost in Maine, he appealed to the king and queen. Margaret's mediation seems to have helped: Viscount Beaumont was the only

---

65 *Foedera*, XI, pp. 203–4.
66 Jones, 'Somerset', pp. 297–8.
67 York was not always able to collect his annual salary of £20,000, but Somerset's salary in the same amount was only *collectible* in wartime (Johnson, *Duke Richard*, p. 38; Stevenson, I, p. 479). The grant of 10,000 *livres tournois* compensation, while it seems a large amount, was most likely spent on maintaining the estate his position required.
68 Jones, 'Somerset', pp. 298–300. Somerset's alleged covetise would become a recurring theme in the duke of York's later campaign against him. Whether Beaufort was genuinely avaricious, or more so than the general run of magnates during the fifteenth century, is open to debate. Based on his recorded behavior, we can say that he was assiduous in looking after his own interests, but this was not unique to that – or any other – time.
69 Somerville, *Duchy of Lancaster*, p. 421; Myers, 'Household', p. 190.

man who is known to have obtained the compensation owed him for his losses.[70]
The queen's letter would have been written in 1448; when war broke out again in
1449 all such payments became impossible.

In later years Beaumont continued to serve the queen faithfully. When York's
protectorate was established in 1454, and Beaumont was asked to serve on York's
council, his response was provocative: he was the queen's man and would not
abandon this allegiance, reminding those present that it was in the council's rules
that 'every man shuld have full freedom to saye what he thowght in matters as of
counsales, without any displeasure, indignacyon or wrothe of any other person
for his sayinge.' To this, perhaps with second thoughts about his forwardness, he
appended the observation that, in any event, he lived too far away to attend all of
the council's meetings.[71] This last claim was nonsense as Beaumont had served on
Henry's council and, indeed, spent most of his time at court. In January 1457 he
became chief steward for young Prince Edward of Lancaster and was named to
the prince's newly established council.[72] He was killed on 10 July 1460, fighting
for the king at the battle of Northampton.

The next letter shows Margaret again applying gentle pressure, this time
through the mediation of the duchess of Somerset, to see that her husband paid
money that was owed.

[73] Queen to the Duchess of Somerset re Robert Edmund [1448–49]
(Bl, Add. MS 46,846, fol. 49; Monro, pp. 117–18)

By the Quene
Right dere and right entierly welbeloved Cousine, we grete you hertely well.
And for asmoche as it hath liked unto my lordes highnesse to graunte unto oure
wel[beloved] squier Robert Edmunde, the somme of iij^c iij^xx [360] frankes, as in my
said lordes lettres patentes it apperith more plainly, wherupon my lord writith at this
tyme unto oure cousyn your husband for the special recommendacion of oure said
squier in this bihalf; we desire and hertly pray yow that, atte reverence of us, ye wil by
your good and tendre mediacion shew herin such diligence to th'accomplissement
of my lordes entencion, that oure said squier may rejoisse [enjoy] my said lordes
graunt, and the rather by contemplacion of this oure prayer as oure full trust is in
yow. Wherein ye shull mowe deserve of us right especial thanke unto oure greet
plesaunce at this tyme. Yeven, etc. at Windesore, etc.
    To oure Cousine the Duchesse of Somerset

---

70   Jones, 'Somerset', p. 298, n. 5, citing BL, Add. MS 11,509, fols 21v–22. He received 3,000 *livres*
      tournois.
71   Maurer, p. 114; R.A. Griffiths, 'The King's Council and the First Protectorate of the Duke of
      York, 1453–54', in idem, *King and Country* (1991), p. 319; *PPC*, VI, p. 81.
72   *CPR, 1452–61*, p. 338.

This letter was written in 1448–49 during the duke of Somerset's lieutenancy in France since the requested payment in francs could only have been made while he was resident there.[73] On 19 April 1448, a Robert Edmond, esquire – surely this man – received payment of £26 17s for bringing news to England from Le Mans.[74] Although his mission could have taken place at any time after the city was surrounded by French troops in February, it seems most likely that Edmond's news had to do with its surrender and the accompanying treaty in mid-March.[75] At the time of Le Mans's surrender, Somerset was still in England; he sailed for France in April.[76] Thus, it appears that Edmond returned to Normandy after Somerset had become established there, bearing the king's letters patent awarding him this payment – for what past or future service we do not know.

Although Margaret refers to Robert Edmond as her squire, his connection with her is uncertain. There is a Margaret Edmond or Edmonds in the queen's jewel accounts. In 1445–46 she appears on her own as the recipient of an armlet with a sapphire worth 60s. In the following year she received a gilded cup worth £6 11s 4d as the only woman in a group of nine men that included the queen's highest-ranking male servants, her chancellor and her chamberlain.[77] These were very respectable gifts. In 1448–49, however, she only received an armlet worth 13s 7d – a considerable drop in status.[78] There is also a John Edmond who received a brooch worth 13s 5¾d in 1446–47. It is possible that these three Edmonds – Robert, Margaret and John – were related somehow, though we do not know what their relationship might have been.

The queen's letter to the duchess of Somerset in support of Edmond's grant raises a question regarding both women's roles in the matter. Monro was affronted that 'the mediation of the wife of the minister with her husband … should have been deemed requisite or fitting' to make a royal grant effective, but that view is a product of his own nineteenth-century sensibilities. In Margaret's time, women – and the queen especially – were expected to act as mediators, precisely the word that Monro uses. If her intervention in this case is reflective of anything, it is

---

73 Monro was mistaken in thinking that it was written after Somerset's return to England in 1450. Once Normandy was lost, payment in francs would have made no sense. The franc was a gold coin struck by Henry VI as king of France. It was valued at about 2.4 shillings sterling; hence, Edmond's 360 francs would have been worth roughly £43, a tidy sum.

74 Stevenson, II, ii, p. 576, note.

75 See above, pp. 130–1.

76 Jones, 'Somerset', p. 294.

77 E 101/409/14 and 17.

78 E 101/410/2, where she appears in a list of seventeen women who received the same gifts. The first twelve were definitely Margaret's ladies; Margaret Edmonds comes next, and the last four women were not members of the queen's household. Her status at that time is therefore uncertain.

more apt to be of a shrewd assessment of what it might take to get Somerset to pay up than it is of Henry's weakness as king. We do not know how this matter was resolved.

The duchess of Somerset was Eleanor Beauchamp, one of Richard Beauchamp, earl of Warwick's, three daughters by his first wife, Elizabeth Berkeley. Along with her sisters, Eleanor was coheiress to their mother's Berkeley and Lisle lands. Born in 1407, she had been married to Thomas, Lord Roos, with whom she had three children and who was killed in August 1430 while serving in France. Sometime before 1436 she married Edmund Beaufort.[79] She had eight more children with him. In 1451–52, Margaret gave Eleanor a gold cup worth £40 17s 6d. This was the most valuable gift on the queen's list for that year.[80] She also gave Eleanor's servants a gift of 66s 4d, indicating that the duchess had sent a gift to her.[81] These gifts undoubtedly reflect the duke of Somerset's new prominence at court as Henry's favorite and first minister. Margaret had already acknowledged this fact in appointing the duke to her council the previous November, a strategic move to harness his influence to her own concerns.[82] In 1452–53, Margaret gave the duchess a gold salt cellar decorated with rubies, pearls and yellow sapphires, valued at £28. She was the only person of ducal rank to receive a personal gift that year, and its value was exceeded only by the queen's gifts to the king and to Walsingham priory.[83]

The duke of Somerset was killed at the battle of St Albans in 1455. After King Henry resumed control of the government in 1456, he made provision for Eleanor and her eldest son, the king's namesake. On 8 March 1456 she was granted £200 p.a. for her son's sustenance. On 18 June she received livery by parcels of all the duke's possessions that had been designated as her dower, and on 12 August she

79 Their eldest son, Henry, named for his godfather the king, was born *c.* April 1436. Somewhat belatedly, on 7 March 1438, the couple received pardon for marrying without royal license and for any fine due as a result (*CPR, 1436–41*, p. 160).

80 E 101/410/8. No gift to the king is listed, although she surely gave him one. She gave two other cups, worth £35 8s 6d and £35 5s respectively, to the duke of York and to John, Lord Beauchamp of Powick, who was treasurer. Her gifts to Cardinal Kemp and the duchess of Bedford were worth substantially less.

81 Myers, 'Jewels', p. 218 note. This was typically the highest amount given to the servants of important persons in the years for which we have record. In 1451–52 the servants of the archbishop of Canterbury, Cardinal Kemp of York, the duke of York and the duchess of Bedford also received this amount.

82 Myers, 'Household', p. 196, for Somerset's grant of an annuity as reward for his 'good counsel and praiseworthy service' past and future. Myers is likely correct in adducing that he had become an 'outside' member of the queen's council (p. 151), but see Maurer, pp. 91–2, 93, for the relationship between queen and duke embodied in the grant.

83 Myers, 'Jewels', pp. 221–2. Maurer, p. 85 ff, for Margaret's gift giving as a form of political balancing.

received £111 2s 23d p.a. for life.[84] The duchess was a principal recipient of the loveday settlement of 1458. She was awarded 2,500 marks in recompense for Somerset's death, to be paid by the Yorkists in tallies.[85] Under Edward IV she eventually received a grant of £100 per year for life.[86] She died on 6 March 1467.

[74] Queen to the Duke of Somerset re Margaret Stanlowe
(BL Add. MS 46,846, fol. 54v; Monro, p. 115)

By the Quene

Right trusty and right entierly welbeloved Cousyn, we grete you well. Desiryng and prayng you that in suche thinges as oure dere and welb[eloved] servant, Marguerite Stanlowe, oon of oure gentilwoman, shall have for to do towardes you, ye will, atte reverence of us, have hir towardes you especially recommended: helping, furthering and supporting hir with all th'ease, faver and tendernesse that ye goodly may by right and trouth, demening hir in such wise that she may have cause to reporte unto us of your good disposicion towardes hir at this tyme, to th'accomplissement of our entencion in this partie. As we truste, etc.

To the Duc of Somers[et]

Margaret Stanlowe joined the queen's household in Rouen in 1445 and remained in her service thereafter.[87] Her annual wage was £10, and she received New Years' gifts in all five extant jewel accounts: a silver belt worth 6s 8d in 1445–46, a gold chain worth £6 4s 2½d in 1446–47, a silver cup worth £2 14s 8d in 1448–49, a silver salt worth £1 6s 3½d in 1451–52 and a wine flagon worth £2 1s 4d in 1452–53.[88] It appears that Margaret was the wife of John Stanlowe, who held the important position of treasurer of Normandy under both Richard Beauchamp, earl of Warwick, and Richard, duke of York, during their terms as the king's lieutenant in France.[89] John and a brother, Hugh, had begun their careers as soldiers in Normandy as early as 1421, serving as captains of garrisons (probably *in absentia* in John's case).[90]

84　*CPR, 1452–61*, pp. 277, 291, 293.
85　*CPR, 1452–61*, p. 424.
86　*CCR, 1461–68*, pp. 289–90; *CPR, 1461–67*, p. 472.
87　BL, Add. MS 23,938.
88　Myers, 'Household', p. 183; E 101/409/14 and 17; E 101/410/2 and 8; Myers, 'Jewels', p. 224.
89　Stevenson, II, p. 286; *CPR, 1436–41*, p. 314; *1441–46*, p. 422. He served during both of York's terms.
90　Marshall, 'English War Captains', p. 23, n. 3. John was captain of Eu in 1429–30, and of Verneuil in 1431, each time with Hugh as his lieutenant. Hugh got his own captaincy in 1435. There is an entry in *CPR, 1441–46*, p. 206, dated May 1442, for Hugh Stanlowe as treasurer. This may be a mistake for John, or perhaps Hugh was deputizing for his brother. A third brother, William, apparently never left England. He had a flourishing career as an escheator and a JP

When Somerset became the king's lieutenant of France in 1448, he replaced John Stanlowe as treasurer with one of his own men, Osbert Mundford.[91] John was still in Normandy in June 1448, when he was named as a commissioner in Rouen to adjust border disputes.[92] He then returned to England and entered the duke of York's service, becoming a member of the ducal council from 1448 to 1449. After that he disappears from all official records.[93]

It would have been a financial matter, involving money or property, for which the queen had occasion to solicit the good offices of the duke of Somerset on Margaret Stanlowe's behalf. It is impossible to tell from the vague wording of the letter what service he was expected to perform. It is unlikely to have had anything to do with a position in Somerset's household, as this would have been referred to his duchess, and in any event, we know that Margaret did not leave the queen's service.

It was probably in connection with John's term of office in Normandy that Margaret Stanlowe needed Somerset's assistance, but if this were so, one would normally have expected John to approach the duke. If, however, John died early in 1449, Margaret, as his widow, may have had a claim to money or property in Normandy and hoped that Somerset, who was in Rouen, would expedite her business. This would date the letter to 1449. But there is another intriguing possibility, offered by Griffiths: that the man named Stanlowe who was hanged at Maidstone in the aftermath of Cade's rebellion, either *as* a rebel or *by* the rebels, is to be identified with the John Stanlowe who was Margaret's husband.[94] If this speculation is valid, then Margaret might well have needed Somerset's intercession in order to lay claim to John's estate. This would date the letter to 1451, when Somerset had returned from Normandy and was in charge of the government at home.

Identifying women in the fifteenth century, even members of the royal household, is difficult unless they happened to be peeresses. Very little about Margaret Stanlowe is known for certain. A Jaynet/Jacquette Stanlowe serving in the queen's household in 1446–47 may have been Margaret's daughter.[95] If the identification of Margaret as John Stanlowe's wife is correct, she was certainly old enough to have a teenage child. Jacquette subsequently married Ralph Grey, the

in Lincolnshire, and was an official of the exchequer (*CPR, 1436–41*, pp. 195, 286, 523, 556, 585; *1441–46*, pp. 164, 473; *1446–52*, p. 591).
91 Griffiths, p. 509; Marshall, 'English War Captains', p. 145.
92 Beaucourt, IV, p. 310, n. 6.
93 Johnson, *Duke Richard*, pp. 17, 239.
94 Griffiths, p. 652, n. 26; Kingsford, *English Historical Literature*, p. 371: 'One Stanlow was drawne and hanged at Maydestone on the even of St John Baptiste.'
95 E 101/409/17.

son of Lady Elizabeth Grey, one of the queen's senior ladies in waiting, probably in 1452.[96] In that year Jacquette received a silver gilt salt valued at £8 2s 8d as a wedding gift from the queen.[97] Lady Grey had paid the hefty sum of 400 marks in 1443 for her son's wardship and marriage, so she would have arranged the match, possibly at Margaret's instigation.[98] After Edward IV became king in 1461, he did his best to woo Sir Ralph, as he had then become, into the Yorkist camp. Although he succeeded for a time, in the end Ralph returned to his earlier allegiance; he was executed in July 1464 as a traitor because he had held Bamburgh Castle for the Lancastrians and refused to surrender it when summoned.[99] Edward IV restored Ralph's Northumberland estates to Jacquette in 1465.[100] Margaret Stanlowe's fate is unknown.

[75] Queen to Sir John Dynham re John Asshe
(BL, Add. MS 46,846, fol. 27v; Monro, p. 144)

By the Quene

Trusty, etc. And for asmoche as we be enformed that ther is by yow dew unto our welbeloved John Assh the somme of £xiiij xiiijs [£14 14s] for divers vitailles taken unto your use, as it is said, we praye you, considering the necessite that he is in, [that] ye will, at reverence of us, have hym to the payment of his seid dewte [duty, i.e., debt] especially recommended, shewyng hym therin th'ease, faver and tendernesse that ye goodly maye to th'accomplissement of our entencion in this partie, so that he may fele in effecte thise our lettres, as we truste you. In which thing, etc. Yeven, etc.

To our knyght Sir John Denham

Sir John Denham, or Dynham as his name is more commonly spelled, was a Devonshire knight who served the crown on numerous commissions from the early 1430s and also was JP for the shire during the 1440s and 1450s.[101] His fellow

---

96 Ralph Grey came of age in 1449 (*CPR, 1446–52*, p. 220). This Elizabeth Grey, not to be confused with Elizabeth Grey, née Woodville, who later married Edward IV, was the widow of Sir Ralph Grey, who had been a JP for Northumberland (ibid., *1441–46*, pp. 258, 353, 376).

97 E 101/410/8. Myers's identification of the 'Jaquet' who is listed among the queen's chamberers in her jewel list of 1452–53 with Jaquet Stanlowe is unlikely (Myers, 'Jewels', p. 227). By then, she was Ralph Grey's wife and would have received a more valuable gift than three silver spoons. 'Jacquette Stanlowe' does not appear in the 1452–53 account. There is a Thomas Stanlowe listed for the first and only time among the queen's squires (ibid., p. 226). He may have been Margaret Stanlowe's son.

98 *CPR, 1441–46*, p. 258.

99 Scofield, I, pp. 337–8; Wedgwood, p. 398.

100 *CPR, 1461–67*, p. 388.

101 He first appears as a commissioner in 1432, and his last assignment was in December 1457, with many in between (*CPR, 1429–36*, p. 201; *1452–61*, p. 407). For his service as JP, ibid., *1441–46*,

commissioner was Sir William Bonville, who became Lord Bonville in 1449. Bonville's growing prominence in the region and the favor shown him at court had set him on a collision course with the headstrong Thomas Courtenay, earl of Devon.[102] In the autumn of 1451, Courtenay laid siege to Bonville in Taunton Castle. After several days the duke of York arrived and persuaded him to withdraw. All three – Bonville, Courtenay and York – were summoned to explain themselves to King Henry. Bonville obeyed, while the other two ignored the summons. In November, Bonville, Dynham and others were appointed to peace commissions for Devon and Cornwall, while Courtenay and his supporters, unsurprisingly, were dropped.[103] On 14 February 1452 a commission headed by Lord Bonville, along with Sir Philip Courtenay (a relative of the earl) and Sir John Dynham, was ordered to summon the king's lieges in Somerset, Dorset, Devon and Cornwall to punish and arrest rebels who had gathered 'to subvert the king's estate and the government of the realm'.[104] These 'rebels' were Courtenay's men, who were raised to support York in his encounter with the king at Dartford.

In 1454 during the duke of York's first protectorate Dynham continued to serve on commissions.[105] In the summer of 1455, Courtenay unilaterally embarked upon civil war against his rival Bonville.[106] His actions played into the Yorkists' hands and provided an immediate rationale for York's second appointment as protector. After considerable foot-dragging, York moved against his former ally, whom he arrested and imprisoned.[107] Courtenay never stood trial as the duke of York ordered his release on 9 February, before his protectorate ended.

Against this backdrop of political aggression and intrigue, Sir John Dynham remains a shadowy figure. A pair of surviving records may offer some insight into the sort of man he was. In July 1439 a commission in Devon was to make inquiry into a situation that had arisen following the death of Sir John's father.

p. 469; *1446–52*, p. 588, *1452–61*, p. 664. The last listing, of 16 June 1458, has to have been his son, for our Dynham was certifiably dead by then.

102 For the Courtenay–Bonville feud, see M. Cherry, 'The Struggle for Power in Mid-Fifteenth Century Devonshire', in *Patronage, the Crown and the Provinces*, ed. R.A. Griffiths (Gloucester, 1981), pp. 123–44; Storey, *End of Lancaster*, pp. 84–92, 165–75; Griffiths, pp. 574–7, 753, 755. Storey, p. 165, described Dynham as Bonville's friend.

103 *CPR, 1446–52*, pp. 587–8.

104 Ibid., p. 537.

105 Ibid., pp. 171, 178. One was of array; the other, to investigate a matter of piracy.

106 Storey, *End of Lancaster*, pp. 166–73, for what followed; Lander, 'Henry VI', pp. 84–9, for its role in the formation of York's protectorate.

107 On 5 December, the council sent a standard letter in the king's name to influential peers and knights in the area, including Bonville and Dynham, requiring them to assist York against the troublemakers (*PPC*, VI, pp. 267–71). York did not set out for the southwest until the middle of the month.

Sir John's sister Maud and her husband claimed that the elder Dynham had made a verbal promise of £500 for Maud's dowry and a further £100 worth of goods 'for her chamber'. They charged that Sir John had taken everything and refused to share any of it with Maud, denying that their father had ever 'declared any such will'.[108] A second incident occurred in August 1444, when the abbot of St Nectan in Hartland charged that Dynham had broken the close and taken a number of horses, cattle and sheep, to the value of £160, and had, in addition, 'cut down and consumed his corn and grass' and carried off other goods of value while threatening 'the life and limbs of the abbot and canons'.[109] We do not know how either matter was resolved. If there is any truth to these charges, it would appear that Sir John was a hard man, out for himself, who took what he wanted without much thought for the harm his actions caused.

John Asshe, whose plight at Dynham's hands prompted Margaret's letter, is probably the man who became a yeoman of the crown for life on 1 October 1449. On 6 September 1452 he received a further grant of 6d a day for life, including payment of arrears since his initial appointment.[110] But is this the same John Asshe who is described as deputy to the earl of Suffolk in his capacity as steward of the household in 1441?[111] If so, he was once a very important man indeed. His dismissal following Suffolk's attainder could explain a fall upon hard times. A position in the king's household during the 1440s would have provided a contact with Margaret, while the straitened circumstances of the man in her letter may account for the grant to him as yeoman of the crown. The queen probably wrote to Dynham in response to a petition from Asshe himself or from someone in her household who knew of his situation.

We do not know what finally became of Asshe, but Dynham died on 25 January 1458. His son, another John Dynham or Denham, threw in his lot with the Yorkists and helped the earls of Warwick, Salisbury and March to escape by ship to Calais after the debacle at Ludlow in 1459. Not surprisingly, he prospered under Edward IV.

---

108 *CPR, 1436–41*, p. 316.
109 *CPR, 1441–46*, p. 292. These were boilerplate accusations; nevertheless, they bear some similarity to the complaint made in Margaret's letter.
110 *CPR, 1452–61*, p. 19; *CCR, 1447–54*, p. 373.
111 *CPR, 1441–46*, p. 273. A number of entries in the patent rolls from the early 1430s on involve a John Asshe with distinct Middlesex connections (*CPR, 1429–36*, pp. 408, 620; *1436–41*, pp. 199, 586; *1441–46*, pp. 431, 474). Again, we cannot be sure that this is the same man.

[76] Queen to [Lady Emmeline Fiennes] re George Ashby [1447]
(BL, Add. MS 46,846, fol. 49v; Monro, p. 114)

> By the Quene
>
> Dere and welbeloved, we grete you well. And it is reported unto us that, atte reverence of us and for the service that oure servant George Assheby, clerc of oure signet, standeth in with us, ye, as mene to your husbande, have hadd [him] in right good faver and tendernesse towardes expedicion of payment of his wages deue unto him by the Duc of Glouc[ester] that last died, wherof we thanke you hertly, praying you right affectuously that ye wil continue so forth your benevolence and good disposicion to th'exploit of his agrement in this partie. As we, etc., at P. etc.
>
> [No addressee]

This letter provides a further instance of female networking, where the queen appealed to another woman to help accomplish her goals. Monro believed that its recipient was either the duchess of Suffolk or the duchess of Somerset, on grounds that their husbands were, successively, Henry's first minister. The greeting of this letter disproves his identification. Written at a time when status was constantly acknowledged in myriad ways, this letter's greeting seems far removed from the elaboration shown in Margaret's letter to the duchess of Somerset and much closer to the greetings in her letters to Jane Carew and the sub-prioress of Nuneaton.[112] Who, then, might the recipient have been? Since the letter involves payment of wages due from the deceased duke of Gloucester, the most likely candidate is Lady Emmeline Fiennes, the wife of Sir James Fiennes, Lord Saye, who was the highest ranking of Gloucester's executors.[113] At the time of Gloucester's death, Fiennes was Margaret's chamberlain. He received his title in February 1447 and became chamberlain of the king's household on 1 April.[114] Through her husband's service, Lady Fiennes had formed a connection with Margaret. In 1445–46 and 1446–47 she received New Year's gifts from the queen.[115] This letter was probably written in 1447, soon after the naming of Gloucester's executors. The debt was of long standing, and Margaret sought, through Lady Fiennes's influence, to have it settled promptly.

George Ashby, the man who was owed wages, was Margaret's clerk of

---

112   For the greetings to Margaret's other female recipients, see pp. 10, 24, 34, 105 and 132. A comparison with her letters to men demonstrates the same principle: the higher the status of the recipient, the more effusive and elaborate the greeting.

113   Fiennes was named executor on 24 March 1447, along with Sir Thomas Stanley, Master John Somerset and Master Richard Chester (*CPR, 1446–52*, p. 45). Stanley was comptroller of the household, and the latter two were clerics. For Chester's career, see above, pp. 30–1.

114   See above, p. 122 and n. 25.

115   A gold belt worth £2 4s 6d and a gold chain worth £7 10s (E 101/409/14 and 17).

the signet and the last of the Lancastrian poets, following in the footsteps of Lydgate and Hoccleve, though often regarded in later assessments as unable to fill their shoes.[116] The bare facts of his official career are sparse. He began serving Humphrey, duke of Gloucester, during the 1420s and, according to his own testimony, became Gloucester's clerk of the signet.[117] In 1437, when the office of king's secretary was re-established, Thomas Bekynton (who had been Gloucester's chancellor) was brought in to fill the post, and Ashby came with him as signet clerk. Soon after, he was rewarded with the constableship of Dinefwr Castle in South Wales and a grant for life of £10 yearly from the exchequer, the latter good until it could be replaced with an office of equal value.[118] In 1444, he traveled to France and joined Margaret's household in Rouen, at a wage of 1s 6d per day.[119] After Margaret's coronation, Ashby became her clerk of the signet, responsible for writing the queen's private letters. He held this office until the deposition of Henry VI in 1461, receiving an annual fee of £6 13s 4d.[120] In June 1446, Ashby became steward of Warwick Castle during the minority of the heiress, Anne Beauchamp, and in October the source of his grant of £10 p.a. was switched from the exchequer to the fee farm of the hundred of Framlond, Leicestershire.[121] In October 1452, King Henry requested a corrody for Ashby from the abbot and convent of Glastonbury, 'in consideration of his good and unpaid service with the queen on either side of the sea'.[122] As there is no evidence that he ever claimed his corrody, it seems best to regard the grant as insurance for the future. In 1459, Ashby was returned as MP for the borough of Warwick. His

116　His work, consisting of three poems, is published in M. Bateson, ed., *George Ashby's Poems*, EETS, e.s. 76 (1899).
117　Ibid., p. 3. For his life, unless otherwise noted, see Wedgwood, pp. 21–2; Otway-Ruthven, *King's Secretary*, pp. 139, 158; R.J. Meyer-Lee, 'Laureates and Beggars in Fifteenth Century English Poetry', *Speculum* 79 (2004), pp. 699–700, 710.
118　*CPR, 1436–41*, pp. 177, 550.
119　BL, Add. MS 23,938.
120　Myers, 'Household', pp. 185–6.
121　*CPR, 1441–46*, p. 433; *1446–52*, p. 20. Anne Beauchamp became the queen's ward in 1446; she died in 1449, and the earldom went to Richard Neville, her aunt's husband.
122　*CCR, 1447–54*, p. 451. We suspect that he and other members of Margaret's entourage were never paid the money they should have received for their service in Rouen. A corrody would have provided one means to redress the debt without costing the crown anything. Some years earlier, in 1437–38, the king had granted Ashby a corrody in the convent of St Bartholomew's in London. The prior contested it, arguing that his house had letters patent from Henry I – confirmed by Henry VI – freeing it from all grants by the crown upon its possessions, and that no corrody had ever been demanded of them until Ashby's came along. Henry withdrew his grant and confirmed the convent's exemption (*CPR, 1436–41*, p. 150).

election may have owed much to Margaret's influence in the earl of Warwick's absence, which had left a power vacuum following his flight to Calais.[123]

Ashby's fortunes – and perhaps his life's purpose – changed with Henry VI's deposition. Some months after the battle of Towton he was arrested and imprisoned in the Fleet, where he remained into 1463 when he wrote his first poem.[124] It seems likely that he was pardoned in that year or soon after, and that he made his way to France and joined Margaret's court in exile at Koeur, where he wrote two further works.[125] Ashby may have returned to England around the time of the readeption. By then an old man, he would have posed no threat to Edward IV. He died in Middlesex on 20 February 1475.[126]

Ashby's poems acquire more interest when considered not merely as 'poor attempts to emulate his [literary] forbears', but as sophisticated propaganda pieces.[127] His imprisonment provided the context for his first extant work, *A Prisoner's Reflections*. Although the poem belongs to a well-known genre, the consolation of the poet-prisoner, it breaks from it in its explicit identification of Ashby himself as the victim and in its focus on the details of his own experience, as well as in locating the source of his suffering in a specific political trauma, the Lancastrian deposition. His next work, the *Active Policy of a Prince*, an advice manual for Prince Edward of Lancaster, and its companion piece, the *Dicta & opiniones diversorum philosophorum* were probably written during the Lancastrian exile, c. 1468.[128] By then the prince would have been 'old enough to be a credible recipient of [such] advice'.[129] Besides providing the prince with instruction on how to rule well and avoid his father's mistakes, the *Active Policy* is directed towards a second, public audience in its repeated assertion that Prince Edward is both the rightful heir to the throne and worthy to rule. The question of his legitimacy had become an important feature of the Yorkists' propaganda after their attainder in 1459 when he was a small child, as part of their drive to supplant

123 Payling, 'Identifiable Motives', pp. 102–3.
124 In his poem, *A Prisoner's Reflections*, Ashby claims to have been held for 'a hoole yere and more' when he composed the work in 1463 (Bateson, *George Ashby's Poems*, pp. 2, 11).
125 See M.L. Kekewich, 'The Lancastrian Court in Exile', in *The Lancastrian Court*, ed. J. Stratford, Harlaxton Medieval Studies 13 (Donington, 2003), for Margaret's court.
126 Wedgwood, p. 22. He had by then acquired a property called Brakespeares, where he resided at the time of his death.
127 Meyer-Lee, 'Laureates and Beggars', p. 699; pp. 700–20 for the following discussion.
128 The *Dicta* serves as 'a bibliography … that lends authority' to Ashby's advice (ibid., p. 707).
129 Ibid., pp. 710–11. In view of Ashby's death in 1475, this date is also consistent with his claim to have written the *Active Policy* when he was nearly eighty (Bateson, *George Ashby's Poems*, p. 15). Wedgwood, p. 21, is dismissive, however: 'at that age one exaggerates'.

Henry VI.[130] By 1468, though not yet an adult, the prince was beginning to look like a viable alternative to Yorkist Edward IV. Henry VI had been captured and imprisoned in the Tower in 1465. If the *Prisoner's Reflections* was made public around the same time as the *Active Policy*, its description of Ashby's travails evokes the image of the imprisoned king and underlines the idea that the true dynastic order had been overturned and must be reinstated.

130 Maurer, pp. 45–8, traces the origins and uses of the rumor; see pp. 176–8 for its use by the Yorkists in 1460. Following Edward IV's assumption of the throne, his legitimacy (as opposed to Lancastrian 'illegitimacy') continued to be emphasized for several years, alongside the characterization of Margaret as a 'disorderly woman' (ibid., pp. 201, 203–4).

Seven

BELIEF AND
BENEVOLENCE

The evidence suggests that Margaret was conventionally pious. That is, she followed religious practices that were common among the nobility of her time, and, insofar as we can tell, her beliefs would have been those shared by her contemporaries.

The content of her days was dictated by religious practice. The daily routine at court began with matins and a mass for the Virgin. William Say, dean of the king's chapel, recorded that Margaret rarely missed attending.[1] Each day ended with evensong, followed by the Little Office of Our Lady, with prayers in between from a book of hours, and readings from such works as *The Life of our Lady* by John Lydgate.[2] As part of her regular observance, Margaret gave alms of 4d a day (a penny more than her yeomen received in wages), and on twenty-one 'special feast days' she made an offering of a gold coin.[3] Only two of these special days were secular: the anniversaries of the deaths of Henry V and Queen Katherine. These days marked her religious year, beginning with the Annunciation of the Virgin on 25 March, two days after Margaret's birthday, and ending with the Purification of the Virgin on 2 February.

Margaret's devotion to the Virgin was a common feature of late medieval piety.

1   W. Ullman, ed. *Liber Regie Capelle*, Henry Bradshaw Society 92 (1961), p. 7. Despite Henry's later reputation for extreme piety, the *Liber* observes that he was not as assiduous in attending the mass for the Virgin as was Margaret.
2   A copy of Lydgate's *Life* bears an inscription saying that it belonged to Queen Margaret. A. Doyle, 'English Books ... from Edward III to Henry VII', in *English Court Culture in the Later Middle Ages*, eds V.J. Scattergood and J.W. Sherborne (1983), p. 174, believes the queen to have been Margaret of Anjou, rather than Margaret of Scotland. The book is now Bodleian Library MS Hatton 73; the inscription is on fol. 121.
3   Myers, 'Household', p. 200.

Her prayer roll, in Latin, pictured a wheel with seven spokes, all inscribed with prayers to the Virgin. At its center, the Virgin is shown, wearing a crown, with the Christ Child on her right arm and a white flower in her left hand. Beneath the wheel two angels support Margaret's arms, while Margaret kneels at a *prie dieu* gazing up towards the Virgin.[4] In 1452 she commissioned a stained-glass window for a chapel at Westminster after fire had shattered its window and destroyed a jeweled statue of the Virgin as Our Lady of Pew (Pity) grieving over the body of Christ. The new window depicted King Henry and Margaret kneeling before the Virgin, with the queen's motto and the arms of the king, the queen, St George and St Edward.[5] In 1453, when Margaret knew that she was pregnant, she traveled in gratitude and hope to the shrine of Our Lady of Walsingham.[6]

Like her contemporaries, Margaret was concerned for the wellbeing of her soul in this life and its salvation after death. One of the ways in which contemporaries approached salvation was through the intercessory prayers of others. A great many entries in the patent rolls specify that prayers are to be said for the king and queen and, later, the prince. The majority of these occur in the context licenses issued to found chantries, where priests were endowed to say prayers for the souls of the founders and their kin. The inclusion of the royal family in these prayers came with the license, but represents a genuine belief in the efficacy of prayer in the pursuit of salvation.

Acts of charity were another means toward salvation, as well as integral to a queen's good ladyship. Four letters in this chapter concern suppliants to Margaret for charity and her appeals on their behalf. Another letter illustrates a common aspect of late medieval piety: the belief that divine intervention, often involving healing, could be obtained with holy water and through relics. Margaret believed as well that certain special obligations – fasting, pilgrimage and the like – also led to salvation and lessened the time that souls had to remain in purgatory after death. If she was unable to perform them for some reason, she needed to obtain absolution. This took the form of an indult – an indulgence – that generally required some other deed or activity to be substituted and frequently exacted a transfer of money to the Church. Three letters to Margaret from the Vatican are indults. One dates to early in her reign; the other two pertain to her life in exile.

---

4   Oxford, Jesus College MS 124.
5   Myers, 'Household', pp. 201–2. John Prudde was paid 39s for the work (Kingsford, *English Historical Literature*, p. 372).
6   See below, p. 197.

[77] Queen to the Master of St Giles in the Fields beside London re Robert Uphome
(BL, Add MS 46,846, fol. 56; Monro, p. 95)

By the Quene

Trusty, etc. And for asmoche as we be enformed that oon Robert Uphome of the age of xvii yere, late querester [chorister] unto the moost reverende fader in God our beal uncle the cardinal – whom God assoile – atte his college at Winchestre, is now by Goddes visitacion become lepour, we desire therfore and praye you, sith he hath noon other socour ne lyvelode to lyve upon but oonly of aulmesse of cristen peuple, as it is saide, that, at reverence of our blessed Creator and in contemplacion of this our prayer, ye will accepte and receive hym into your hospital of Seint Giles, unto such findinge and lyvelode as other personnes ther in suche cas be accustumed to have, as we trust you. In which thinge ye shul not oonly do right a [*sic*] meritorie dede to Goddes pleasure, but deserve also of us right especial thanke, etc.

To the Maister of Seint Giles in the feld besid the Cite of London

Medieval English attitudes towards leprosy, known today as Hansen's disease, were always complicated and frequently contradictory, pitting notions of sickness as punishment and the exclusion of the unclean, derived from the Old Testament, against Christian ideals of compassion and the belief that spiritual merit accrued to both the patient sufferer and his benefactors. During the fifteenth century, extreme examples of these disparate impulses appear in the Yorkist propaganda that depicted the first Lancastrian king, the usurping Henry IV, as a leper whose 'infection' subsequently contaminated his dynasty and the realm, and in the religious enthusiasm of Margery Kempe, who made a point of kissing female lepers for her love of Jesus.[7] More pragmatically, between about 1100 and 1250 a great many hospitals had been founded in England for the care of lepers. One of these was St Giles, in the fields of Holborn outside of London, founded by Queen Matilda (Maud), wife of Henry I, who endowed it with 60s annually from her customs of Queenhithe.[8] Over the years, it became one of the wealthier of the leprosaria. Located on one of the main roads leading to and from London, it probably received numerous offerings from travelers, along with donations and bequests from local individuals. Its location on the outskirts of the city where alms from passersby could be actively sought also illustrates the incomplete and porous nature of its patients' separation from normal society: they were not subject to incarceration. Indeed, it appears that the restrictions placed upon the residents

7   C. Rawcliffe, *Leprosy in Medieval England* (Woodbridge, 2006), pp. 44–5, 129, 321. Henry IV did not suffer from leprosy. Margery Kempe's expression of her devotion, though not unique, was by the fifteenth century distinctly bizarre.
8   VCH: *Middlesex*, I, p. 206. Income from Queenhithe formed part of Margaret's dower.

of the leprosaria, as at least quasi-religious institutions, had more to do with the preservation of morality than with the prevention of physical contact.[9] In return for abiding by the rules of the community, these residents were provided with food, shelter, clothing and spiritual sustenance.[10]

Margaret's letter was written after the death of Cardinal Beaufort in April 1447. Since there is no indication that Robert Uphome held any other position following his service as a chorister, it may not have been long after. If she wrote it in or after 1450, the master of St Giles would have been Sir William Sutton, who remained master to 1482.[11] Lepers from the royal household were habitually sent to St Giles through the 1450s, and its continuing use in this capacity is attested by its exemption from resumption in Edward IV's first parliament of November 1461.[12]

[78] Queen to Master Piers Stewekeley, Warden of the College of Maidstone, re Thomas Mowsherst [before 1450]
(BL, Add. MS 46,846, fol. 56v; Monro, pp. 151–2)

By the Quene
Trusty and welbeloved, we grete you well. And of the goode frendship, benevolence and tendernesse that ye have shewed unto our servant Thomas Mowsherst, and unto his fader and moder, we thanke you hertly, prayng you that in suche thinges as thei or eny of theym shall have for to do towardes you, ye wil, at reverence of us, in continuance of your good disposicion have him towardes you especialy recommended, helping, furthering and supporting theym as fer as ye goodly may by right, trouth and good conscience, the rather by contemplacion of this our prayer,

9 Rawcliffe, *Leprosy*, pp. 316–17. Her first chapter debunks the myth of the medieval leper as persecuted outcast.
10 Records from the late fourteenth century show that St Giles was producing most of its own food. Its gardens would have provided the residents with opportunities for light exercise and contemplation, regarded as integral parts of a healthful regimen (ibid., pp. 327–8).
11 VCH: *Middlesex*, I, p. 208. There is a lacuna in the list of masters from 1445 to 1450. Since 1299, except for a hiatus during the later fourteenth century, St Giles had been under the administration of the Burton Lazars – the Brethren of St Lazarus of Jerusalem – whose headquarters were in Burton, Leicestershire. The head of the order automatically became the master of St Giles.
12 *CPR, 1452–61*, p. 359; *PROME*, XIII, p. 322. In the late Middle Ages, the corporation of London became concerned that the crown was abusing its right of patronage by sending non-diseased persons to St Giles. An agreement was reached in 1354 that a specified number of lepers would always be housed there (Rawcliffe, *Leprosy*, pp. 296–7; Sharpe, *Cal. of Letter-Books: Letter Book G*, pp. 297–9). Nevertheless, the number of lepers – or of persons so diagnosed – declined, so that by the time of its dissolution in 1539, its inmates were all referred to as 'paupers' (VCH: *Middlesex*, I, p. 209).

so that they may fynde that they fare the better and finde thise oure lettres unto theyme fructuose and vailable. As we trust yow, etc. Yeven, etc.

To M. Piers Stewekeley, Warden of the College of Maydeston, and to R.G.

Thomas Mowsherst (also spelled Moshirst or Mouseherst) first appears as king's serjeant and groom of the queen's chamber in June 1446, when he became parker of Blakemore within the chase of Malvern, Worcestershire, during the minority of Anne Beauchamp.[13] It seems likely, therefore, that he had been assigned to Margaret from the king's household when she formed her first establishment, or soon after. He rose to the rank of yeoman by 1448–49, when he received a gold ring worth 2s 2½d from the queen as a New Year's gift.[14] In 1452–53, Mowsherst was paid 38s for 192 days of service to the queen. In that same year, Margaret gave him a gilded goblet worth £3 6s 9¼d as a wedding present, and he was also among the yeomen of her household who received a bow.[15] He may not have been the same man as the Thomas Mousehirst (no occupation given) who in 1447 claimed a debt of 40s against one Thomas Apurdevyle.[16]

The hospital of SS Peter and Paul had been founded in Maidstone, Kent, by the archbishop of Canterbury during the thirteenth century to maintain ten poor persons, though only five were recorded as living there in 1375. In 1395, when the parish church of Maidstone became a college, the hospital was incorporated into it. The hospital continued to house poor persons well into the sixteenth century, until its suppression in 1549. Peter (Piers) Stewekeley or Stackley was appointed master in 1444. His successor was Robert Smyth, appointed in 1450, who was likely to have been sub-warden under Stewekeley, and it is tempting to see 'R.G.', to whom this letter is also addressed, as the copyist's mistranscription of 'R.S.'[17] This would perhaps indicate a date closer to 1450 for Margaret's letter. In any case, it would have been written while Stewekeley was still the master or warden. At a guess, Mowsherst's parents were corrodians at Maidstone. Since Thomas Mowsherst was a member of the queen's household at the time, it may be doubted that he was personally needy. Rather, the request seems to have been made on his behalf, out of regard for him, although its true object was the welfare of his parents.

13   CPR, *1441–46*, p. 437.
14   E 101/410/2.
15   Myers, 'Household', p. 187; 'Jewels', pp. 227–8.
16   CPR, *1446–52*, p. 90. A Thomas Mouseherst, identified as a citizen and skinner of London, also claimed a debt against other persons in 1449 (ibid., p. 249).
17   VCH: *Kent*, II, p. 233. The presence of a sub-warden was noted in a visitation of 1511, and there was apt to have been one during the fifteenth century as well. Smyth died in 1458.

[79] **Queen to the Archbishop of Canterbury as Chancellor re Alice Marwarth, 26 May**
(BL, Add. MS 46,846, fol. 48v; Monro, p. 160)

By the Quene
Right worshipfull fader in God, etc. Lating you wite that [at] oure instance and request my most doubted lord hath now late granted unto a poure widowe, Alice Marwarth, certein pardon, as by a bill therof signed with my said lordes hand, which we send you sealed under oure signet by a servant of oures, ye may se more pleynly. Wherfor we desire and hertely pray yow that, att reverence of us, ye wil have the seid widowe in expedicion and deliverance of hir lettres patentes in this partie especialy recommended, with such tendernesse and faver that she, upon the socour and trust of oure moene [mediation] that she putteth in us, may perceive good and brief exploit to th'accomplissement of my lordes grant in this bihalf. As our ful trust is in you. In which, etc. Yeven, etc., at W. the xxvi of M.
To th'archebisshop of Cantelbury, Chauncellor

Here it appears that Henry VI had granted a pardon to Alice Marwarth at Margaret's request, but under his sign manual rather than the privy seal, making it more of a private grant. That the queen went to the trouble of sending Henry's bill along with her own letter by one of her servants instead of just giving them to Alice indicates that she wanted the matter quickly resolved. We have found no other traces of Alice Marwarth that might either identify her or help to elucidate the nature of her pardon. The archbishop was probably John Stafford. If it were John Kemp, he would also have been addressed as cardinal. A further, though less likely, possibility is Thomas Bourgchier, who became archbishop upon Kemp's death in 1454 and was briefly chancellor from 1455 to 1456. Since most of Margaret's letters in this manuscript collection date from the 1440s, Stafford seems the better choice.

[80] **Queen to the Prior and Convent of the Friars Minor**
(BL, Add. MS 46,846, fol. 56v)

By the Quene
Trusty, etc. in God. For asmoche as we understand that two freres, John Frogen and a litell noves [novice] destitute of theire abiding desiren to be under your religious governance and disposicion, we desire and pray you that, atte reverence of us, ye will have theym towardes you especialy recommended, shewing theym suche ease and faver to theire wele that they may finde thise our lettres unto theym affectuelx and vailable, as we trust you, etc.
To the prior and convent of frers meneurs

The Franciscans, also known as the Grey Friars or Friars Minor, arrived in England in 1224, setting up convents in Canterbury, London, Oxford and Northampton. With its emphasis on poverty and preaching, the order proved hugely popular and experienced rapid and widespread growth. By the fifteenth century there were some fifty-four houses of Conventual Franciscans in England, divided into seven custodies, and several more in Wales.[18] Some friars had permission to cross the territorial boundaries accorded each house and the custody to which it belonged and to function as real itinerant preachers. Friars also made regular appearances as preachers at the royal court, particularly during the religious seasons of Advent and Lent.[19] It was customary for friars engaged in preaching to travel in pairs, which may explain why the two were together. As the term 'novice' was also applied to more junior members of the professed community, this person may have already finished his year-long novitiate.[20]

It appears from Margaret's letter that Frogen and his companion had fallen on hard times. It is difficult to imagine how they could find themselves without support if they were locals or, indeed, if they were members of the English conventual community. So perhaps they had come from overseas; the name may suggest a Dutch or Germanic background. We also wonder why whoever brought their situation to Margaret's attention would have thought that she could do anything about it. In theory, at least, Margaret's letter could have been written to any of the English houses, although one of the larger establishments, such as the one in London, might be deemed more likely.

[81] Queen to the Prior of Christ Church, Canterbury, 30 April [1454]
(Inner Temple Library, Petyt MS 538.47, fol. 409x; courtesy of The Masters of the Bench of the Inner Temple)

By the Quene

Right trusty and welbeloved in God, we grete you wele. And for the grete zele, love and affeccion that ye have towards my lords helth and welefare as t'acerteine us of suche holy water and relik as ye have, we thanke you with al our hert. And to that entent that my lord may have sume of that blessed water, we sende therefore unto you at this time his amner [almoner], Maistre Henry Seyver, for to bringe it hider, after your mocion and benevolence in this partie. And our Lord have you in his keping. Yeven under our signet at Wyndesore, the xxx day of Avrill.

To our trusty and welbeloved in God the Priour of the Monasterie of Crist in Caunterbury

18 D. Knowles and R.N. Hadcock, *Medieval Religious Houses, England and Wales* (1971), pp. 33, 222–3.
19 M. Robson, *The Franciscans in the Middle Ages* (Woodbridge, 2006), p. 221, and n. 49, for a list of friars who preached at court during Lent from 1442 to 1452.
20 Ibid., pp. 174, 179.

Although this letter is not dated by year, it seems certain that it belongs to 1454, during Henry VI's illness when he resided at Windsor. In early 1454 he was catatonic, and the letter's association of holy water and relics with Henry's health and welfare corroborates the date. Saints' relics and the shrines that housed them had long been regarded as healing agents and sources of miraculous cures. The practice of pilgrimage in search of such cures was widespread. Given Henry's condition, it would have been impractical to cart him around the country in search of a cure. Instead, Margaret hoped to bring the cure to him.

The shrine of the martyred Thomas Becket at Canterbury was the most popular saint's shrine in England and among the most important of Western Europe. It claimed over 700 cures in the twelfth century, with another flurry of activity spurred by the translation of the saint's bones in 1220. The shrine generated its highest income in the fourteenth century, when pilgrims' offerings peaked again out of gratitude for having survived the Black Death or in the hope that they would yet be spared. The shrine had reported a miracle in 1445, and it was widely believed that holy water taken from the shrine had curative powers.[21] At the time of this letter, the prior was Thomas Goldston, who held the office from 1449 to 1468.[22] He may have remembered the miracle of 1445 and hoped that Becket's thaumaturgical power would work again in the case of King Henry.

Henry had abruptly fallen ill in August 1453 at Clarendon.[23] When it became apparent that his recovery was uncertain, he was moved to Windsor, where all the wisdom of fifteenth-century medicine could be brought to bear on his condition. In early 1454, a panel of three doctors and two surgeons was authorized to treat him with all manner of medicines and applications both internal and external, cuppings, bleedings and the like.[24] None of these measures helped, and they may have worsened Henry's condition as it was reported on one occasion that he required the support of two men to walk.[25] When medical knowledge proved ineffective, it made sense from Margaret's point of view to place her faith in St Thomas Becket's intervention.

Margaret's interest in a miracle cure was prompted by various factors, personal and political. She had borne a son and heir on 13 October 1453, not long after Henry fell ill. For as long as Henry remained alive but incapacitated, many years

21 R.A. Finucane, *Miracles and Pilgrims* (New York, 1995), pp. 123–4, 193.
22 *Fasti*, IV, p. 6.
23 Flenley, 'Bale's Chronicle', p. 140, reports that he 'sodenly was take and smyten with a fransy and his wit and reson withdrawen'.
24 Signed by the privy council on 15 March (*PPC*, VI, pp. 166–7) and issued by privy seal on 6 April (*Foedera*, XI, p. 347). Some of these treatments had likely been used on Henry before, but this gave the doctors official carte blanche to try anything.
25 *PROME*, XII, p. 259.

would have to elapse before the child could effectively wield authority. England had already experienced the uncertainties of a long minority with Henry himself, and in 1451, in the absence of a direct heir, one of the duke of York's councilors had petitioned in parliament to have him named heir presumptive.[26] Margaret would feel more secure about her son's eventual succession if her husband were back in control and on his throne. And that could only happen if Henry recovered.

Henry Sever, whom Margaret sent to fetch the holy water, had been Henry VI's chaplain since 1437.[27] A fellow of Merton College, he became the first provost of Henry's new Eton College in 1440, but left that position soon after becoming chancellor of Oxford University, where he served 1442–44. He was king's almoner by 1448 and still held the position in 1454. In July of that year, the privy council gave him seven horses with harness and a chariot, to which were added two cart horses, two sumpters and a hackney.[28] His name appears again in the ordinances for the regulation of the king's household of November 1454.[29] We do not know for how long Sever remained Henry's almoner. He apparently made his peace with Edward IV, for in September 1461 his estate in the chancellorship of St Paul's, London, and the deanery of Bridgenorth, Salop – positions he had held under Henry – was ratified.[30] He died on 6 July 1471 and was buried in the choir of Merton College chapel. In the years prior to his death, he gave the college a large number of books.

Although King Henry's illness lasted until the end of 1454, the length of time that passed before his recovery would not have dissuaded the king or his contemporaries from believing that the saint bore some share of the credit. Cures did not have to be instantaneous – and rarely were – for people to think that the intervention had been effective.[31] When Henry sent his customary annual offering to Canterbury at the end of December, he may have felt an added sense of gratefulness for his recovery.[32] As an ironic postscript, we note that after King Henry's death, he became the reputed source of several hundred miracles, including some cures, in the last decades of the fifteenth century. In an effort to have him officially canonized, a list was made of them to send off to the pope;

---

26 Johnson, *Duke Richard*, pp. 98–100.
27 Emden, III, pp. 1672–3.
28 *PPC*, VI, pp. 212–13. A number of horses and equipment belonging to Henry VI were assigned to various people at this time to save on his expenses.
29 Ibid., p. 232.
30 *CPR, 1461–67*, p. 41.
31 Finucane, *Miracles and Pilgrims*, pp. 75–6.
32 See below, pp. 203–4, for the letter describing Henry's recovery.

it is 'the last extensive collection' of such posthumous miracles from an English saint's shrine.[33]

While Margaret sought charitable aid for others in need as a requirement of her faith – as well as the healing of her husband through divine intervention – she did not overlook her own spiritual needs. At times she perceived herself to have fallen short of what she believed was required of her. In these cases, she appealed to the pope for absolution.[34]

[82] Pope Nicholas V to Queen Margaret, 5 October 1450
(*CPL, 1447–55*, p. 72)

To Margaret, queen of England. Indult, seeing that she is not able to visit Rome in person during the present year of Jubilee, that the confessor whom she and persons nominated by her shall choose may absolve her and them, after confession, from all sins, etc., even in cases reserved to the apostolic see, once only, and enjoin penance; and that he may grant to her and them, being penitent and having confessed, the plenary indulgence of the Jubilee for a fortnight's visits to four or more or less churches in those parts, as if they had visited Rome and the prescribed basilicas and churches there. He shall commute the labour of pilgrimage to Rome into other works of piety, and the queen and said persons shall give half of what they would have spent on pilgrimage to Rome to churches, etc., of those parts, and send the other half for the repair and fabric of the churches of Rome.

The year 1450 was a Jubilee Year during which people who could afford it were expected to make a special effort to go on pilgrimage to Rome and make substantial offerings to the churches there. The pilgrims' objective was a remission of their sins. The pope had the power to grant a plenary indulgence to lessen the time a soul spent in purgatory. Pilgrimage in general, whether to local shrines or to those further afield, both at home and abroad, was a common occurrence. Jerusalem in the Holy Land was the ultimate goal, but it required a long and dangerous journey, and few people attempted it. A pilgrimage to Rome was the next best thing. Besides obtaining spiritual benefit, many pilgrims also 'saw the sights', making pilgrimage an early form of tourism. Since most 'sights' had religious connections, this activity brought money to the Church. Pilgrimage could also be used to resolve tricky political situations. For example, William, earl of Douglas, who was *persona non grata* at the Scottish court of King James II,

---

33 Finucane, *Miracles and Pilgrims*, p. 195.
34 Margaret also corresponded with the papacy throughout her reign on matters of more earthly import, ranging from the provision to clerical office to dispute settlement. See above, pp. 33 and n. 68, 39 and n. 90; below, p. 203.

went with his brother to Rome in Jubilee Year.[35] John Talbot, earl of Shrewsbury, who had been left in French hands as a hostage after the fall of Rouen, undertook a pilgrimage to Rome as a condition of his release by Charles VII in 1450.[36] The French king wanted this most famous of English soldiers out of the way while he completed the reconquest of Normandy.

When someone was unable to perform the required act of pilgrimage in a Jubilee Year, exemption was available in the form of an indult. Such indulgences were a lucrative source of income for the papacy (and would later become a focus of complaint against the Church). In Margaret's case, she was never actually expected to go to Rome. Indeed, had she expressed any such intention it is doubtful that the English council or King Henry would have granted her the royal license, required of all would-be pilgrims before leaving the country. Had she gone on pilgrimage, however, she would have traveled with a sizeable entourage: her ladies, her chaplains, her household officials and a guard escort, some of whom would be included in an indult. All this would amount to a sizeable sum; though how much it would cost her to meet the indult's terms is difficult to estimate. Half the money was to be expended on visits to local shrines; the other half was to be sent to Rome. There is no record of which four shrines she chose to visit, or of when these visits were made. Presumably they occurred between 1451 and 1453, when she became pregnant and King Henry fell ill. The most probable destination would of course be the shrine of St Thomas Becket at Canterbury. Henry VI made numerous visits to Canterbury, where his grandfather, the first Lancastrian king, was buried. Margaret is known to have been there as a pilgrim on 17 September 1446, when she spent the day with Cardinal Henry Beaufort.[37] Another famous shrine was that of Our Lady of Walsingham in Norfolk, where Margaret made her pilgrimage of thanksgiving in 1453. This in itself would not have met the terms of her indult – unless she visited the shrine as a penitent on a separate occasion. But following her known visit, she traveled to Norwich, where the shrine of St William the Martyr was located.[38] Although there is no record that she made an offering to St William, she did persuade the rich merchant Robert Toppes to put up the money for a stained-glass window in the fashionable Church of St Peter Mancroft, which may have counted towards the

35   Griffiths, p. 411. They received a warm welcome to the English court on their return in early
     1451.
36   A.J. Pollard, *John Talbot and the War in France* (1983), p. 131.
37   W.G. Searle, *The Chronicle of John Stone … 1415–1471*, Cambridge Antiquarian Society 34 (1902),
     pp. 39–40, 42; Harriss, *Cardinal Beaufort*, p. 368.
38   The shrine to St William continued to attract attention up to the Dissolution (Finucane,
     Miracles and Pilgrims, pp. 120, 194).

indult requirement.[39] Margaret may also have visited the shrines of St William of Perth and St Paulinus at Rochester, two for the price of one. In the context of an indulgence permitting the queen to forego a pilgrimage to Rome, they would have made an oddly appropriate choice. William was on pilgrimage *to Rome* from Scotland when he was murdered near Rochester in 1201.[40] Paulinus was a missionary, sent by the pope *from Rome* to convert the then kingdom of Kent early in the seventh century. He became bishop of Rochester and died in 664. Henry VI visited Rochester on numerous occasions, and Margaret may have had dealings with John Lowe, its bishop at the time of Cade's Rebellion in the summer of 1450.[41]

[83] Pope Paul II to Queen Margaret, 30 September 1467
(*CPL, 1458–71*, p. 273)

To Margaret, queen of England. Indult that as long as she abides in places on this side the sea and beyond, in which olive oil cannot be found even at the dearest price, she may in Lent and on other days on which the eating of milk-meats is forbidden, eat butter and other milk meats along with those who shall eat at her table and three servitors who shall serve at the same table as her food tasters.

[84] Pope Paul II to Queen Margaret, 30 September 1467
(*CPL, 1458–71*, pp. 273–4)

To the same. Indult, at her petition (to the effect that, when living in England she, constrained by very many sufferings and tribulations, made divers and almost innumerable vows, impossible of fulfillment by her on account of her weak health, for example many fastings, the observance of which vows very often involves fasting four or five times a week and several pilgrimages to divers places unsafe for her, or rather inaccessible for her without manifest bodily peril, wherefore, as also because she is deprived of her moveable goods, she cannot conveniently fulfill, as is becoming and as she desires, the aforesaid and many other vows taken by her) to choose a fit secular or regular priest as her confessor who, after having heard her confession, may grant her absolution, once only, for her crimes, excesses and sins and perjuries and transgressions of any vows, and also from all sentences of excommunication, etc., even in cases reserved to the apostolic see, except offence against ecclesiastical liberty, violation of interdict imposed by the said see, crimes of heresy, any offence of disobedience or rebellion or conspiracy against the person or estate of the Roman pontiff or the apostolic see, etc., and, in general, in the cases

---

39   C. Rawcliffe, 'Women, Childbirth and Religion', in *Women and Religion in Medieval England*, ed. D. Wood (Oxford, 2003), p. 104.
40   He was canonized in 1256.
41   See below, pp. 193, 194.

contained in the usual bull of Holy Thursday, and in other cases not reserved to the said see absolution as often as opportune, enjoin salutary penance and commute into other works of piety all her vows, past and future, which she is or shall be unable conveniently to observe, except only the vow of Crusade, and moreover that the said confessor or other of her choice may grant to her, being penitent and having confessed, plenary remission of all her sins, once in life and once in the hour of death, *sic tamen quod idem confessor etc. ut in forma confessionalis.*

These two indults were issued on the same day, when Margaret had been living in exile with her small court at Chateau Koeur in her father's duchy of Bar since 1463. One is specific to Margaret and her situation; the other, although addressed to her in response to her petition, is more general. She was thirty-seven in 1467 and appears to have been in very poor health. The Church's dietary rules were strict. No meat of any kind could be eaten during Lent or on Wednesdays, Fridays and Saturdays, although fish was permitted. All animal products, such as butter and eggs, were similarly forbidden. Prolonged illness was an accepted reason for the more stringent rules to be relaxed, and milk-meats (i.e., dairy products) could be permitted. Olive oil may have been difficult to obtain in the north at certain times of the year, and was more expensive than locally produced butter. If the claim in the second indult was true, that Margaret had made vows to fast four or five times a week and had attempted to do so over a long period, she had been slowly starving herself. Add to that the almost constant anxiety of knowing that Henry VI was a prisoner in England and that she was wholly dependent on a small allowance from her father René and her ill health is no cause for wonder.

Margaret appears to have sought divine intervention throughout her years of adversity. As well as the physically punishing fasting, she had made vows to undertake pilgrimages that she had found impossible to fulfill. Since these vows were made in England, they probably refer to shrines in England that in 1467 were not only inaccessible to her, but also dangerous to attempt. Returning to England as a pilgrim was impossible; there was no one whom King Edward IV would prefer to lay his lands on more than Queen Margaret. Nevertheless, the vows had been made, and the Church took them very seriously. Margaret had sinned; she had imperiled her immortal soul, and she required absolution.

Pope Paul was prepared to grant it, on condition. The second indult was probably, at least in part, the standard formula issued by the Vatican bureaucracy to anyone seeking alternate means toward remission of sin. Margaret was to 'commute into other works of piety all her vows, past and future, which she is or shall be unable conveniently to observe'. (One wonders how many more vows the Holy See expected Margaret to make.) Works of piety was a euphemism for giving money to the Church, but Margaret had precious little to give. Even the obligatory offering of alms must have been a strain on her slender resources. The queen of England might require absolution for excesses, sins, perjuries (possibly) and transgressions, but she was hardly likely to have 'crimes' to confess, or to have come under sentence of excommunication. And even Margaret would not have vowed to go on crusade! Nevertheless, Margaret achieved her aim; the second indult is a plenary remission of all her sins, in life and in death, provided she was truly penitent.

Eight

THE QUEEN'S DISPORT

A number of Margaret's letters attest to her love of hunting. By the fifteenth century, the practice of hunting had become an elaborate ritual. No longer merely a source of food or sport, or even a means to acquire and maintain some of the skills required by warfare, it was a signifier of social status in and of itself. To be noble was to hunt.

In England, long before Margaret's time, the Norman and Angevin kings set aside vast areas of 'forest' (which, in fact, might not have comprised wooded land) in which the right to hunt large game was barred to all but themselves or those to whom they gave explicit permission. Over time, such permission was increasingly sought – usually for a hefty fee by those who could afford it – and private, territorially defined reserves were created, which proliferated by the fifteenth century. Such enclosed parks, themselves smaller-scale versions of the royal forests, were surrounded by a ditch and a complementary barricade such as a wall or hedge, and were mainly stocked with fallow deer. Parkers and keepers were employed to look after the game, to ensure that it thrived, and to protect it from illicit poaching by all outsiders.[1] Thus, from their beginning, parks constituted status symbols that set their owners apart and marked them as persons of power and privilege. In 1390 the Game Law completed the physical privatization of hunting, setting a base income requirement for the right to hunt at all and effectively ending any public right to hunt on the remaining free chase (i.e., land that was not afforested or emparked).[2] During this same period, hunting also became culturally privatized through the elaboration of terminology and ritual associated with it. The earliest English example of this codification is *The Master of Game* by Edward, second

1   S. Lasdun, *The English Park* (1991), chapter 2, for an overview of the medieval park.
2   The income requirement was set at 40s p.a. for laypersons and £10 for clergy.

duke of York, the grandson of Edward III.[3] By the mid-fifteenth century, this process had reached its apex, and as the parks' value for alternate uses such as livestock grazing or wood gathering diminished, making them more expensive to maintain, interest increasingly focused on their possession and on the park-based hunt as essential components of the noble lifestyle.[4]

It should surprise no one that the privatization of hunting was not accepted happily by all, but remained an ongoing source of social tension. Parks and their game became prime targets for rivals during feuds.[5] Meanwhile, the exclusions created by the 1390 law did not stop the practice of hunting for sustenance by persons of lesser status, but simply made it illegal and, accordingly, fostered resentment. This led to the emergence, in some instances, of hunting as a form of political protest.[6]

Seven letters in this section directly relate to Margaret's interest in hunting. Of these, the first three simply admonish the keepers or parker to preserve the game and make sure that it is plentiful pending her arrival. The next appears to have been written in response to a newly discovered poaching problem and is followed by two letters that demonstrate Margaret's efforts to foil a specific poacher. The last letter involves the training of dogs that would have been used for the hunt. We lead off, however, with a letter about an animal that was also important to hunting and was certainly a necessity to medieval people more generally: in it, Margaret seeks to acquire a particular horse.

[85] Queen to John Godwyn
(BL, Add. MS 46,846, fol. 56; Monro, p. 131)

By the Quene

Welbeloved. For as moche as we understand that there is a mare in that countrey that [is] right covenable [suitable] and according to our entent and purpos, wherof our secretory comuned with you in that bihalf; we wol and desire you that, ye

---

3   Edward, Second Duke of York, *The Master of Game*, ed. W.A. and F. Baillie-Grohman (1909). This little handbook, devoted to all matters associated with the hunt, was a translation of *Le Livre de Chasse* by Gaston Phoebus, count of Foix, to which Edward added material specific to its English practice.

4   S.A. Mileson, 'The Importance of Parks in Fifteenth Century Society', in *The Fifteenth Century V: Of Mice and Men: Image, Belief and Regulation in Late Medieval England*, ed. L. Clark (Woodbridge, 2005), pp. 19–37, for the park as a social institution.

5   I.M.W. Harvey, 'Poaching and Sedition in Fifteenth Century England', in *Lordship and Learning: Studies in Memory of Trevor Aston*, ed. R. Evans (Woodbridge, 2004), pp. 172–3. One of her examples is Sir Robert Wingfield's marauding, for whom, see above, p. 109. A charge of hunting-as-harassment was also made in the dispute between Robert Osbern and the abbess of Barking (above, pp. 106–7).

6   Harvey, 'Poaching', pp. 173–82.

aggreing with the owner of the said mare as reason wol, ye do sende or brynge hir
with hir colt unto us in all goodly haste, and that ye faile not, etc.

    To John Godwyn

Horses were integral to medieval life. In August 1444 in preparation for Margaret's
arrival in England, Henry sent to the abbot of Bury St Edmunds for horses of all
kinds to help with the transport of the new queen and her entourage.[7] Within
a year of her arrival Henry was again searching for horses when he ordered one
John Spryngwell to obtain coursers, palfreys, hackneys and sumpterhorses 'for
riding and other uses of the queen'.[8] The first three were horses to ride, with the
courser used for hunting; sumpterhorses were pack or light draft animals.[9]

    Riding horses were often classified by gait, with ambling horses the most
prized. The amble was a four-beat gait in which the legs moved laterally. Faster
than a walk, it was supremely comfortable for the rider (particularly as compared
with the two-beat trot in which the horse's legs move diagonally) and could be
maintained by the horse over distance.[10] While some individual horses and
certain breeds today have a natural propensity for the 'easy gaits', many do not,
and in the Middle Ages ambling horses were much sought-after. At Rouen,
shortly before her departure for England, Margaret was presented with a *haquenée*
bearing a saddle and accoutrements of gold as a gift from King Henry.[11] The
French term *haquenée* specifically referred to an ambling horse, particularly one
deemed suitable for a lady to ride. Despite some confusion of terminology applied
to medieval riding horses, we may be certain that Margaret's horse was of the
highest quality.[12]

    This letter indicates that Margaret had been looking for a particular kind of
horse, and that this mare had attracted her attention. Since she came with a colt,
it may be that the queen wanted her for breeding purposes, though it is also

---

7   Stevenson, II, ii, p. 467.

8   *Foedera*, XI, p. 125.

9   A. Hyland, *The Horse in the Middle Ages* (Stroud, 1999), p. 221; A. Ayton, *Knights and Warhorses:*
    Military Service and the English Aristocracy under Edward III (Woodbridge, 1999), pp. 31, 63.
    Besides hunting, coursers were frequently used in battle, being lighter, faster and less expensive
    than the heavy destrier.

10   Hyland, *Horse*, pp. 28–30, discusses gaits.

11   Escouchy, *Chronique*, I, p. 88.

12   The word 'hackney' in English, from which the French may have been derived, stood for a
    somewhat second-rate saddle horse, frequently one that was available for hire. In English, the
    preferred saddle horse for people of means was a palfrey; they were considered appropriate
    mounts for ladies, and some of them, at least, were amblers. The French *palefroi*, equally prized,
    was a riding horse used for travel, as opposed to a warhorse; gait either may have been assumed
    or was not the defining factor.

possible that she wanted her for riding. In either case, we may assume that the mare was somehow special and therefore desirable.

We have found no other records of John Godwyn.

[86] **Queen to J. B[ury], the Keeper of Sheen Park [before 1452]**
(BL, Add. MS 46,846, fol. 54v; Monro, p. 137)

> By the Quene
> Trusty and welbeloved. For asmoche as we suppose that in short tyme we shall come right negh unto my lordes manoir of Shene, we desire and praye you hertly that ye will kepe ayeinst our resorting thedre, for oure disporte and recreacion, two or iij of the grettest bukkes in my lordes parc there, saving alweyes my lordes owne commandement there in his presence. As we trust, etc.
>
> To my lordes squier and ours, J.B., keper of Sheen Parke, or his depute there

During the 1440s, the keeper of 'le Newe park' of Sheen was John Bury, then a yeoman usher of the hall.[13] In July 1447 he was granted 2d a day to repair the park, 'which is now in a ruinous state', and to provide 'a house for the king's deer there with hay and other food for winter'.[14] Margaret's letter was written prior to 1452 when Bury, by that time a serjeant at arms to the king, was replaced as keeper by Thomas Barton, yeoman of the crown.[15] The bucks that Margaret planned to hunt would have been fallow deer.[16]

The letter's most intriguing aspect may be its suggestion that Henry VI also enjoyed hunting. The idea that Henry was an otherworldly saint, who despised all manner of 'vain sports and pursuits' and 'would [never] take part in the killing of an innocent beast', derives from a posthumous encomium written by John Blacman.[17] As king, of course, Henry would have been expected to hunt and taught to hunt from childhood. The extensive renovation of the royal hunting lodge of Clipstone in Sherwood Forest from 1435 to 1446, presumably for his own use, and numerous references to hunting dogs in the patent rolls would seem to

13   *CPR, 1436–41*, p. 416. He was appointed to the post in May 1440.
14   *CPR, 1446–52*, p. 68; *CCR, 1447–54*, p. 2.
15   *CPR, 1446–52*, pp. 557–8. Bury may have been in failing health; on the same day, he and Barton were made keeper of the manor of Sheen in survivorship, an office he had held alone since 1437 (*CPR, 1436–41*, p. 128). No further references to him appear in the records.
16   The male fallow deer was called a buck; the female, a doe. The male red deer was a hart or stag; the female, a hind. *Master of Game*, pp. 23–40, devotes separate sections to the nature and habits of the hart and the buck.
17   Blacman, *Henry the Sixth*, pp. 27, 40, the latter observation made specifically in the context of hunting. R. Lovatt, 'A Collector of Apocryphal Anecdotes', in *Property and Politics: Essays in Later Medieval English History*, ed. A.J. Pollard (New York, 1984), discusses Blacman's purpose and credibility.

provide evidence of such interest, at least at one time.[18] We note, however, that
the last two references to Henry's hunting dogs date from October 1452 and
March 1460, with a huge gap in between: a gap encompassing Henry's illness
and its aftermath. It is necessary to distinguish Henry-before from Henry-after,
with his illness the watershed.[19] This letter may preserve a trace of one aspect
of the earlier Henry, who may have enjoyed his 'disport and recreation' as much
as Margaret did. There is a final reference to him hunting. In October 1460,
while Henry was in Yorkist custody, his captors took him to hunt at Eltham and
Greenwich before parliament gathered.[20] Under the circumstances, the visit was
probably intended to preserve an appearance of normalcy and to quiet potential
speculation regarding the Yorkists' plans.

[87] **Queen to the Keeper of Faulkbourne Park, 30 August 1449**
(BL, MS 46,846, fol. 58v; Monro, pp. 105–6)

By the Quene
Welbeloved. For asmoch as oure dere and welbeloved Dame Elizabeth, the
Lady Say, hath granted us to have our disporte in hir park of Falborne at what
tyme it shall please us to resorte thedre and in to this contrey, we wol and charge
you that the game there be faveured, cherisshed and kepte, without suffrying any
personne of what degre, estat or condicion that he be of to hunte there, or have
cours, shit [shooting] or other disporte in amentising [diminishing] the game
abovesaid, without an especial commandement of us or of the said Lady Say, and
that ye faill not herof in no wyse. Yeven, etc., at Plasshe the xxx day of August, the
yere, etc., xxvij.
To the Keper of Falborne Park, or to his depute there

The Lady Say of this letter was Elizabeth Boteler, sister of Ralph, Lord Sudeley,
who became a prominent man at the Lancastrian court and who died in 1473, at an
advanced age.[21] How Elizabeth came by her title is puzzling. Monro mistakenly
believed that she acquired it through her *second* marriage, to Sir William Heron
who had previously been married to another Elizabeth, daughter and eventual
heir of William, Lord Say. Heron held the title in her right and continued to

18   Griffiths, p. 250; *CPR, 1436–41*, pp. 298, 508; *1441–46*, pp. 53, 220, 321, 452; *1446–52*, pp. 115, 235,
     241, 276, 503, 521; *1452–61*, pp. 20, 87, 551.
19   A point made by Lovatt, 'Collector', pp. 183–4.
20   Gairdner, *PL*, III, p. 233.
21   GEC, XII, i, p. 421, note n. Their parents married on or before 18 July 1385, and their father died
     21 September 1398. Ralph served as chamberlain of the household, treasurer of England and
     steward of the household (ibid., pp. 419–21). He attended Edward IV's first parliament, but in
     February 1462 was exempted from all further service on the grounds of age and infirmity (*CPR,
     1461–67*, p. 72).

be styled Lord Say from her death in 1399 until his own death in 1404. We have found no conclusive evidence that Elizabeth Boteler ever married Sir William Heron, but if she did, it would have been between 1399 and 1404, when she would have been quite young, perhaps still a child.[22] Some years after Heron's death, in 1412, Elizabeth appears in the records as the wife of John Norbury, esquire, and mother of his two sons named Henry and John.[23] She was not styled 'Lady Say' at that time. After Norbury's death, Elizabeth married Sir John Montgomery, by whom she had two more sons: John, born *c.* 1426, and Thomas, born *c.* 1430.[24]

Margaret may have met Elizabeth and her husband in Rouen in 1445. Sir John Montgomery was then serving in the duke of York's retinue, and Elizabeth was godmother to York's son Edward (later Edward IV) in 1442.[25] From around this time we find references to her as 'Lady Say' in official records.[26] Lady Say appears in all but one of the queen's extant jewel accounts, suggesting that she became one of Margaret's favorites.[27] Sir John probably died in early 1449, certainly by July of that year.[28] At that point Faulkbourne in Essex, which had been one of his estates, became his widow's property. It lay a few miles east of Pleshey, making it convenient for Margaret to hunt there when she was in the neighborhood.

After Henry VI's deposition, Elizabeth's son John Montgomery was accused

22   The only source for this marriage, cited by both Monro and GEC, VI, p. 493, note e, is P. Morant, *History and Antiquities of the County of Essex* (1768), p. 116. GEC observes that Morant 'gives no authority' for it. Adding to the mystery, the *inquisition post mortem* for William Heron does not mention a surviving wife (GEC, VI, p. 493, note f). Nevertheless, the fact that later sources referred to her as 'Lady Say' suggests that she had some right to use this title, and the only way we can discover for her to have obtained such a right would have been via a marriage to Sir William Heron.
23   *CPR, 1408–13*, p. 404. Henry Norbury was the godson of Henry IV. Monro believed that a *Henry* Norbury was Elizabeth's *first* husband, but clearly this was not the case.
24   John Norbury last appears in the patent rolls in December 1413, when the king granted him an annual fee of £40 for life, and in January 1414 as a JP for Hertfordshire (*CPR, 1413–1416*, pp. 161,419). In July 1433, Elizabeth is described as wife of John Montgomery, knight, and 'previously the wife of John Norbury' (*CPR, 1429–36*, p. 296). See Wedgwood, pp. 604–5, for Elizabeth's sons by Montgomery.
25   Scofield, I, p. 1. For Sir John Montgomery, see above, pp. 63–4.
26   On 14 January 1445, 'the king's knight John Moungomery and Elizabeth, lady of Say, his wife', were granted a tun of Gascon wine annually at Christmas (*CPR, 1441–46*, p. 318). A similar grant to 'Elizabeth Say' alone was made on 18 March of the previous year (ibid., p. 257).
27   She received a gold belt in 1445–46, a gold chain in 1446–47, a silver gilt salt cellar in 1451–52, and a silver gilt wine flagon in 1452–53 (E 101/409/14 and 17; E 101/410/8; Myers, 'Jewels', p. 224). Myers's suggestion that the recipient was Lady Saye and Seyle is incorrect. The latter, named Emmeline, was the wife of Sir James Fiennes, created Lord Saye and Seale in 1447. Emmeline appears elsewhere in the jewel accounts. See also above, p. 140.
28   He is last mentioned as a JP for Essex on 8 December 1448, and a writ of *diem clausit extremum* is dated 5 July 1449 (*CPR, 1446–52*, p. 589; *CFR, 1445–52*, p. 97).

of complicity in the earl of Oxford's conspiracy and was arrested and beheaded on 23 February 1463.[29] By contrast, his younger brother Sir Thomas became a knight of the body and a favorite of Edward IV. He was with Edward in France in 1475, negotiated the terms of Margaret's ransom by Louis XI and handed her over to the French king in January 1476.[30] By that time Elizabeth, Lady Say, had died, in 1464.[31]

[88] Queen to the Parker of Ware [1448?]
(BL, Add. MS 46,846, fol. 55v; Monro, pp. 90–1)

By the Quene

Welbeloved. For asmoch as we knowe verreily that our cousin th'erl of Salesbury wolbe right well content and pleased that at our resorting unto our castell of Hertford we take our disporte and recreacion in his parke of Ware; we, embolding us therof, desire and pray you that the game there be spared, kepte and cherisshed for the same entent, without suffring eny other personne there to hunte or have shet, cource or other disporte in distroing or amentissment of the game above said, until [such] tyme [as] ye have other comandement from our said cousin to the contrarie in that bihalf. As we trust you, etc.

To the Parker of Ware

Hertford Castle was part of Margaret's dower lands, while the town of Ware belonged to Richard Neville, earl of Salisbury. It appears from the letter that Salisbury had invited the queen to hunt there. The earl's affiliation with a Yorkist faction from the mid-1450s makes the dating of this letter highly intriguing, but also problematic. Any effort to date it must take politics into account, and all results are speculative.

Monro believed that it could not have been written in or after 1455, since this was the year in which Salisbury and his son Richard, earl of Warwick, joined the duke of York to confront the king's army at the battle of St Albans. Contrarily – and much more recently – Michael Hicks has suggested that Margaret's visit to Ware took place in the immediate aftermath of that battle.[32] Hicks's timing works out, barely. The battle took place on 22 May 1455. On the following day the Yorkists, who had since reaffirmed their loyalty to Henry, ceremoniously escorted him back to London, where Margaret had taken refuge with her son

---

29 Scofield, I, pp. 231–3.
30 Ibid., II, pp. 149, 157–8; J. Calmette and G. Périnelle, *Louis XI et l'Angleterre, 1461–1483* (Paris, 1930), pp. 210–11; *CPR, 1467–77*, p. 571; *Foedera*, XII, pp. 21–2.
31 In June 1465, her grandson John Norbury (son of Sir Henry) inherited lands she had held (*CPR, 1461–67*, p. 459).
32 Hicks, *Warwick*, p. 121.

in the Tower.[33] Henry (and presumably his wife and child) remained in London into early June, but was at Windsor by the twelfth when Gilbert Kymer, his physician, was to attend him there.[34] Somewhat later in the month the royal family repaired – or were moved by the Yorkists – to the queen's castle of Hertford, though Henry was back at Westminster by 6 July. While Henry was at Hertford, York positioned himself at Ware, and Warwick, at Hunsdon a little farther east, presumably to keep an eye on the king.[35] Although the timing seems tight, it is possible that Salisbury extended his invitation to Margaret as soon as the move was planned and that she wrote to the parker before leaving Windsor. If this is what happened, his invitation would likely have been intended to reassure and even mollify the queen. While this may make a certain kind of sense, it also draws attention to the weak point of the argument. Although Margaret was fond of hunting, the eagerness – and apparent lightheartedness – of the letter ('we, embolding us therof') seems incongruent so soon after a military encounter in which the king's person had been threatened and their son's godfather, the duke of Somerset – and others – had been killed. Moreover, would she have gone to Ware while York, the author of these events, was in the neighborhood?

Two further dates may be considered. The first involves a visit of Henry to Hertford from 12 to 21 June 1451. As it was Margaret's castle, it seems likely that she would have accompanied him. She does not request that game also be kept for him, however, and her letter to the keeper of Sheen Park, above, indicates that he might also have been expected to hunt. The second possible date would be the autumn of 1448, when Henry went on progress to the north. Since Salisbury was warden of the West March, he would have accompanied the king. Margaret apparently stayed behind, for on 21 October, while the king's party was traveling from Lincoln to Grantham, she was at Waltham Cross taking Sir John Montgomery's fealty.[36] Salisbury may have invited the queen to amuse herself at Ware while Henry was away. This date would put her visit well before there was a Yorkist faction, at a time when Salisbury would appear to have been on excellent terms with the king and Margaret was perhaps more apt to have regarded his invitation with delight. Like the other suggested dates, however, it cannot be proven.

---

33 Watts, *Henry VI*, p. 317, n. 246.
34 Wolffe, *Henry VI*, p. 370; *Foedera*, XI, p. 366. The letter to Kymer was sent from Westminster on the 5th, so it appears that the summons could not have been considered urgent. See above, pp. 19–20, for Kymer.
35 Gairdner, *PL*, III, p. 32. Salisbury was more distant, at Rye on the Channel coast.
36 Above, p. 63, for the meeting with Sir John; Wolffe, *Henry VI*, p. 367, for Henry's whereabouts.

[89] Queen to the Keeper of Apchild Park, 28 August 1449
(BL, Add. MS 46,846, fols 58–58v; Monro, pp. 100–1)

By the Quene

Welbeloved. We wol and expressly charge you that, for certein consideracions moeving us, our game within our parc of Apechild wherof ye have the sauf garde and keping ye do with all diligence to be cheresshed, favored and kept, without suffrying eny personne of what degre, estat or condicion that he be of to hunte there or have course, shit or other disporte in amentising oure game above said, to th'entent that at what tyme it shall please us to resorte thedre, your trew acquital may be founden for the good keping and replenissing thereof, to th'accomplissement of our entencion in this partie. And that in no wise ye obeie ne serve eny other warrant but if hit be under our signet and signed with our owne hande. And if eny personne presume t'attempte to the contrarie of the premisses, ye do certifie us of their names; and that ye faill not herof, as ye will eschew our displeasure, at your perill and upon forfaiture of the kepying of our said park. Yeven, etc., at Plasshe, the xxviij day of Auguste, the yere, etc. xxvij.

To the Keper of our parke of Apechild or his depute there

Apchild Park (also written as Abchild, Apechild, Epechild and Abfield) was attached to the manor of Great Waltham, Essex, one of the queen's dower lands, a few miles from Pleshey. From this and her letter to the keeper of Faulkbourne written two days later, it appears that Margaret intended to hunt and wished to ensure that the game remained plentiful for her sport. However, her sternness here also suggests that she learned, while in the neighborhood, that there had been some poaching going on and wished to put a stop to it.

The keeper was probably John Penycok, yeoman of the (king's) robes, who held the office by 1438–39.[37] In addition to Apchild, he was also keeper of Byfleet in the duchy of Cornwall, Havering in Essex (also part of Margaret's dower lands), Shilbottle in Northumberland, and two bailiwicks in the park of Wedgnock in Warwickshire where he was also surveyor of the game, increasing the likelihood that he would have been represented by a deputy at any given time.[38] Penycok became an esquire of the body in March 1448 and prospered throughout the 1440s and 1450s as the recipient of various grants, offices and privileges.[39] He appears in all but one of Margaret's jewel accounts and in 1445–46 received the unusual gift

---

37   *CPR, 1436–41*, pp. 224–5, 242.
38   Ibid., pp. 58, 376, 560; *1441–46*, pp. 74, 332, 437. Wedgwood, p. 676, says he was confirmed in a life grant as keeper of the duke of Norfolk's park of Knappe, Sussex, in 1447 (*CPR, 1446–52*, p. 38), but we suspect that this grant was made to his son John.
39   Ibid., pp. 150, 163, for his new rank. See also *CPR, 1441–46*, pp. 254–5; *1446–52*, p. 211; *1452–61*, pp. 37, 103–4, 432, 484; *CCR, 1447–54*, pp. 416, 452; *1454–61*, p. 331.

of twelve silver spoons worth 35s 4d, perhaps supporting Wedgwood's belief that he took part in her coronation.[40] Wedgwood was mistaken, however, in thinking that Penycok managed to avoid any negative reference in contemporary verse: his name appears in a longer version of the satiric dirge for the murdered duke of Suffolk.[41] Politically, he remained a steadfast Lancastrian. Although he was pardoned by the Yorkist regime on 28 October 1460 after Henry VI's capture at Northampton, orders for his arrest as a rebel were issued on 10 April 1461, soon after Henry's deposition. Penycok was subsequently attainted of high treason and his lands forfeited.[42] His whereabouts thereafter are unknown, as is his date of death. His attainder was eventually reversed by Henry VII in 1485, and he is referred to as deceased in November 1486.[43]

[90] Queen to John Stanley, Squire, re [N.] Chatterley [1450–51]
(BL, Add. MS 46,846, fol. 55v; Monro, pp. 142–3)

By the Quene
Trusty and welbeloved. We late you wit that we write at this tyme unto Chaterley, charging hym that he come no more into eny of our places and parkes in that countrey, nether to hunte ne serve no warrant in any wise. Wherfore we praye yow that ye delyvere him your lettres in this partie, seing as fer as in yow is that he com into non of our places that ye have governance of under us in that countrey. As we trust, etc.
To John Stanley, squier

[91] Queen to N. Chatterley, Yeoman of the Crown [1450–51][44]
(BL, Add. MS 46,846, fol. 55v; Monro, p. 143)

By the Quene
We merveile gretly that ye durst presume upon you ayeinst our writing unto you in that matere for to come into our parke of Aggresley, there distroing our game, where we were disposed to have cherisshed you in your disport in our other places. Wherfore we expresly charge yow that from hennes foreward ye com into noon of our places and parkes, nether to hunte ne serve warrant, without your especial

---

40 E 101/409/14, E 101/410/2 and 8; Myers, 'Jewels', p. 225; Wedgwood, p. 676.
41 Ibid., p. 677; cf. Gairdner, *Three Chronicles*, p. 101.
42 *CPR, 1452–61*, p. 629; *1461–67*, pp. 28, 36, 91, 484; *1467–77*, pp. 24, 46; *PROME*, XIII, p. 44.
43 *RP*, VI, pp. 278–9; W. Campbell, ed., *Materials for a History of the Reign of Henry VII*, 2 vols (1873–77), I, p. 116; II, p. 58. Wedgwood, p. 677, believed that Penycok was dead by 1471, and that it was his son who was pardoned and got the attainder reversed. Although this seems a reasonable assumption, we have found no evidence to support it.
44 Monro transcribed Chatterley's initial as 'W'. In the manuscript it looks very much like the 'N' of Master N. (above, p. 21), while it lacks the loop found on the 'W' of 'Welbeloved' or 'We'.

comandement in that bihalf, at your peril. For this [*sic*, thus?] it pleasith us to be doon. Yeven, etc.

To N. Chaterley, yoman of the Croune

In a sport where access was determined by status and rank, infringement of the rules was regarded as a serious transgression by those whose status gave them access. Margaret's other letters display a keen, ongoing concern that game should be preserved for her own enjoyment.[45] In these two letters, she deals directly with poaching that has already been committed. Agardesley Park in the honor of Tutbury, Staffordshire, was part of Margaret's dower lands. From the second letter, it appears that the queen had previously permitted Chatterley to hunt elsewhere in her holdings, but that he had presumed too much when he resorted to Agardesley. She was not amused.

Although Chatterley is here identified as a yeoman of the crown, we have found no traces of an N. Chatterley – or of a W. Chatterley for that matter – in either the patent or the close rolls. There are, however, two references to a Thomas Chatterley of Derby who held that position.[46] This Chatterley was returned as an MP for Derby in 1447, but was also sued in the same county for close breaking in 1451.[47] The Chatterley mentioned by Monro, who got into trouble around the time of Dartford, is not provided with a first initial, although his identification as a yeoman of the crown may suggest that he was the same man of Derby.[48] Whether he had anything to do with the Chatterley of this letter remains uncertain.

More than one John Stanley was active at this time. The likeliest candidate to have received this letter may be Sir John (also known as Jenkyn) Stanley of Pipe, Elford and Clifton in Staffordshire, who was sheriff of the county in 1450–51.[49] In that capacity he would have been the logical person to take action against Chatterley.

45 In January 1451, Thomas Vernon, esquire, of Derbyshire, was pardoned for failure to appear to answer a charge of poaching in the queen's parks of Barton and Stokley in Needwode, where he had illicitly 'chased … and carried away deer … contrary to the statute' (*CPR, 1446–52*, p. 395). This would have been the statute of 1390, which formally established the restrictions on hunting.

46 Ibid., p. 34; *CCR, 1447–52*, p. 125.

47 Payling, 'Identifiable Motives', p. 101 and n. 53. The specific crime involved unauthorized entry into someone else's property, an act also associated with poaching. The surname Chatterley may have been common in the area, for a John Chaterley, souter, and others were fined for various 'trespasses and rescues' for which they had been impeached (*CPR, 1446–52*, p. 418).

48 Gairdner, *PL*, I, pp. 335–6. 'And soon after was Chatterley, yeman of the Crown, maymed, notwithstondying he was takyn at Derby with money making and ladde to London.' The scrappy account in which it appears was first published in *Archaeologia*, first ser., vol. 29 (1842), p. 326. Payling (see n. 47) accepts that this was Thomas Chatterley.

49 Wedgwood, p. 799.

[92] **Queen to Robert Hiberdon, 16 August**
(BL, Add. MS 46,846, fol. 55; Monro, p. 141)

By the Quene

Trusty and welbeloved. For asmoch as we be enformed that ye have the crafte and cunnyng to make blode hondes in the best wyse, we desire and praye you that ye will, att reverence of us, take suche diligence and peine upon you as for to make us two blode hondes to oure use, keping theym saufly and seurly under your drawing, reule and demenyng until tyme that we do send for theym. And that ye faile not herof, as ye desire to do us pleasure and to stand in the favore of our good grace therfore in tyme comyng. At Windesore, the xvi day of August.

To Robert Hiberdon

Dogs were important to hunting. Like horses in the Middle Ages and unlike dogs today, they tended to be classified by type rather than as strictly delineated breeds, predictably capable of transmitting a particular set of characteristics to all their offspring. One type, called a lymer, was a scenting hound kept on a leash and used to locate and then start the deer. Another type, such as the greyhound or the alaunt, hunted by sight and was used to pursue and bring down game.[50] The patent rolls contain many references to the king's dogs – buckhounds, cochers (setters), heirers (harriers), herthounds, greyhounds, running hounds and something called a strevell – all apparently used for hunting.[51] The 'bloodhounds' that Margaret wished to have trained would also have been intended for the hunt, perhaps to hunt the fallow buck.[52]

When Margaret died in poverty in 1482, she evidently still had some dogs. Shortly after her death, Louis XI wrote to Madame de Montsoreau: 'Madame, I am sending to you my equerry, Jean de Chasteaudreux, to bring me all the dogs you have had from the late queen of England. You know she has made me her heir, and that this is all I shall get; also it is what I love best. I pray you not to keep any back, for you would cause me a terribly great displeasure; but if you know of anyone who has any of them, tell Chasteaudreux.'[53] These were likely to

---

50 *Master of Game*, pp. 148–50, 166–8, 235–7, for the lymer, which was specifically used to hunt the hart, but not the buck (p. 38); pp. 113–15, 216–18, for the greyhound; pp. 116–18, 202–3, for the alaunt. The greyhound should not be confused with the modern racing animal. It had strong jaws and varied in size. The alaunt was a fierce animal that could be used with more dangerous game.

51 *CPR, 1436–41*, pp. 298, 508; *1441–46*, pp. 53, 220, 321, 452; *1446–52*, pp. 115, 235, 241, 276, 503, 521; *1452–61*, pp. 20, 87, 551.

52 The term 'blode hound' is also found in BL, MS Egerton 1995 (cited by R. Hands, ed., *English Hunting and Hawking in the Boke of St Albans* [1975], p. 149), where it appears along with the alaunt, but is referred to as a hound that 'for the bowe drawythe'.

53 Scofield, II, p. 159, translating *Lettres de Louis XI*, IX, p. 276.

have been hunting dogs, and they were probably well trained, given Margaret's known fondness for the hunt and the dogs' apparent value to Louis. It leaves us with questions: was Margaret still able to ride out to hunt in her last years; was her household able to support a modest hunting establishment, or had she kept her dogs for sentimental reasons?

We have found no trace of Robert Hiberdon in other records.

Part II

POLITICAL QUEEN

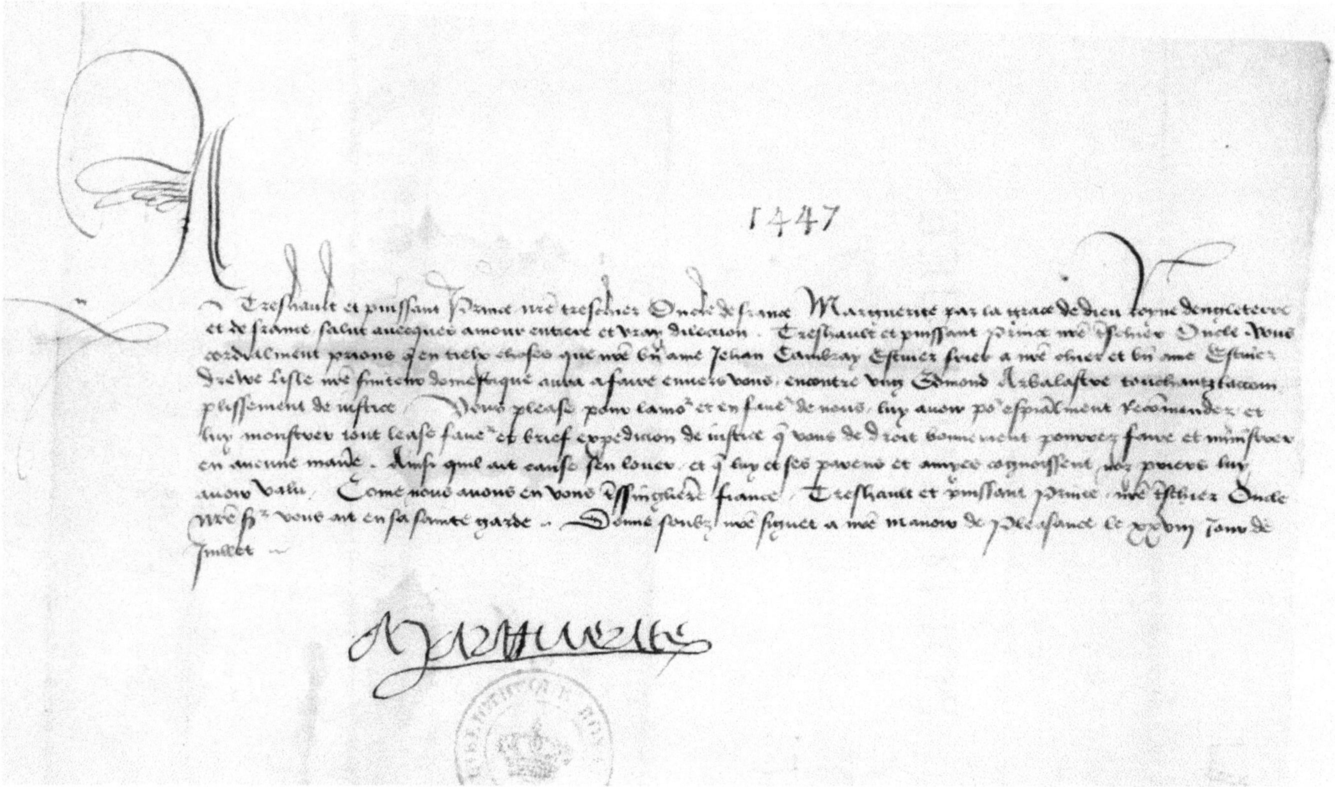
1447

Treshault et puissant Prince nre treschier Oncle de france Marguerite par la grace de dieu Royne dengleterre et de france salut avecques amour entiere et vray dilection. Treshault et puissant prince nre treschier Oncle nous cordialment prions que en telles choses que nre bien ame Jehan Cambray Escuier frere a nre chier et bien ame Escuier Andrew Lisle nre serviteur domestique aura affaire envers vous encontre ung Edmond Arbalastre touchant laccomplissement de justice. Vous plaise pour lamour et en faveur de nous luy avoir pour especialement recommande et luy monstrer toute la plus faveur et brief expedicion de justice que vous de droit bonnement pourrez faire et ministrer en aucune maniere. Ainsi quil ait cause sen louer et que luy et ses parens et amys cognoissent noz prieres luy avoir valu. Comme nous avons en vous singuliere fiance. Treshault et puissant prince nre treschier Oncle nre Sr vous ait en sa sainte garde. Donne soubz nre signet a nre manoir de Plesance le xxviij jour de Juillet

Margarete

Figure 2 Letter 97, by Queen Margaret to Charles VII of France, 28 July 1447. By this time she had given up playing the intermediary between kings. Instead, she wrote about a private matter – on the same day that Henry VI formally authorized the surrender of Maine to the king of France. From BNF, MS Fr. 4054, fol. 76.

Nine

EN FAMILLE

In the spring of 1445, when Margaret arrived in England as Henry VI's bride, the pageants welcoming her to London lauded their marriage as the means to a lasting peace, ending the off-and-on warfare that had plagued England and France for roughly one hundred years. They intimated that the longed-for peace would come about 'by mene of Margarete', i.e., specifically through her agency.[1] Unfortunately for the young queen, her gender denied her any recognized, concrete role in the negotiations that were supposed to lead to peace. Since no clear distinction was made between the expectations placed upon the marriage itself and Margaret's personal agency as a means of fulfilling them – an agency she realistically did not have – she was later blamed for the loss of English-held territory in France.

Another difficulty, affecting all the men involved in the discussions, was that England and France had different goals and different understandings of what a *satisfactory* peace would look like. As in all such transactions, each side demanded what it thought it could obtain, and conceded – at least on paper – what it thought it must, in the pursuit of a final settlement. Neither side was prepared to lose everything, but in the political and strategic gamesmanship that ensued France proved to be the better gamer. At the time of Margaret's marriage, however, the future remained uncertain. When she became England's queen, only a twenty-three-month truce had been agreed to, while peace talks continued.

Negotiations resumed in London in the summer of 1445. Although the truce was extended by seven months, the major issues of sovereignty over Normandy and Gascony and Henry VI's claim to the French crown were not resolved. The French floated a proposal that the kings of both realms should meet personally to discuss a final rapprochement. The English, including King Henry, responded

---

1   Maurer, pp. 20–1.

favorably, with the proviso that such a meeting must be a 'weighty affair', requiring
a truce of sufficient length for its accomplishment, as well as further discussion –
and perhaps some added sweetening – to make it seem worthwhile.[2] Charles VII
sent his envoys Guillaume Cousinot and Jean Havart to England in the autumn
of 1445 to begin further talks. They carried a procuration and an accreditation
from Margaret's father, René of Anjou, and authorized by Charles VII, offering
a lifetime alliance with the house of Anjou and a twenty-year truce, in return
for the cession of Maine.[3] Charles VII's personal letters to Henry VI and to
Margaret and the accompanying words of his ambassadors suggested that the
best step towards a lasting peace would be for Henry to accept René's proposal.[4]
This is the earliest written reference to Maine as part of a bargaining strategy.
But the possibility that it might become negotiable dated back to July 1442, when
Edmund Beaufort, the English captain-general and governor of Maine, was
granted land rights to the county. A clause inserted in his grant recognized that
it might be returned to France in the event of a peace agreement.[5] The notion
of ceding Maine would have pleased Margaret. Here was something that could
benefit her father, her uncles, her new husband and herself. If all went well, might
this not lead to genuine peace, which everyone endorsed?

A longstanding tradition existed of the queen as a mediator or intercessor
between the king and others. Based in part upon the Old Testament story of
Queen Esther and upon a common characterization of the Virgin Mary, her
specific capacity as an instrument of peacemaking between kingdoms had been
endorsed by Christine de Pisan. In her advice to the 'good and wise princess',
Christine wrote:

> If any neighboring or foreign prince wishes for any reason to make war against her
> husband, or if her husband wishes to make war on someone else, the good lady will
> consider this thing carefully ... She will ponder long and hard whether she can
> do something (always preserving the honor of her husband) to prevent this war
> ... and by good counsel she will do whatever she can do to find a way of peace.[6]

2   The French kept a journal of the discussions (Stevenson, I, pp. 87–148).
3   Published in A. Lecoy de la Marche, *Le roi René*, 2 vols (Paris, 1875), II, pp. 258–60.
4   Charles's letters are no longer extant, but their content is known from the responses of Henry
     and Margaret.
5   Jones, 'Somerset', p. 292. The land grant was for his lifetime only.
6   Christine de Pisan, *The Treasure of the City of Ladies*, trans. S. Lawson (New York, 1985), p. 50.
     For modern analyses of the medieval queen as intercessor, see L.L. Huneycutt, 'Intercession
     and the High Medieval Queen' and J.C. Parsons, 'Queen's Intercession in Thirteenth-Century
     England', in *Power of the Weak*, ed. J. Carpenter and S.-B. MacLean (1995), pp. 126–46, 147–77;
     P. Strohm, *Hochon's Arrow* (Princeton, NJ, 1992), pp. 102–4.

And so Margaret found, or was given, an informal role in the peace process, one that was an accepted part of the queen's duties. She could praise, placate and encourage, while being kept on the margins of any real decision-making. Margaret initially approached her new role with enthusiasm, though not without a certain necessary circumspection. It is likely that she had some advice in framing her responses to Charles VII. Had matters turned out well for the English, she would have been praised for her part in their success. But they did not go well, and Margaret would later be blamed for the whole sorry affair.[7]

Margaret's extant letters to Charles VII from the 1440s track her involvement in the negotiations over Maine from its hopeful beginning through growing disaffection, to a point where her correspondence did not speak of peace at all. A final letter from Charles to Margaret in 1449 brings this section to an end.

[93] **Queen Margaret to Charles VII of France, 17 December 1445**
(Stevenson, I, pp. 164–7, from BNF, MS Baluze 9037–7, No. 37)

A tres hault et puissant prince, notre tres chier oncle de France, Marguerite par la grace de Dieu royne de France et Dangleterre, salut, avec toute affection et amour cordiale.

Tres hault et puissant prince, notre tres chier oncle, par maistre Guillaume Cousinot, maistre des requestes de votre hotel, et Jehan Havart, escuier, votre varlet trenchant, avons receu voz gracieuses lettres, du contenu esquelles, pour ce que nous tenons que avez fresche memoire, ne vous en faisons a present long record. Mais en tant que appercevons la bonne amour et le vouloir entier que avez a monseigneur et a moy, le grant desir que avez de nous veoir, et aussi la fructeuse disposicion et liberale inclinacion que cognoissons estre en vous au regard de la paix et bonne concorde de entre vous deux, nous en louons notre Createur, et vous en mercions de bon cuer et si chierement que plus povons; car greigneur plaisir ne pourions en ce monde avoir que de veoir appointement de paix final entre lui et vous, tant pour la prouchainete de lignage en quoy attenez lun lautre, comme pour le relievement et repox du peuple Christien, qui tant longuement par guerre a este perturbe. Et en ce, au plaisir de notre Seigneur, tendrons de notre part la main,[8] et nous y employons effectuelment a notre povoir telement que par raison vous et tous autres en devrez estre contens.

Et quant au fait de la delivrance que desirez avoir de la conte du Maine, et autres choses contin ues en vos dictes lettres, nous entendons que mon dit seigneur en escript devers vous bien a plain; et neantmoins en ce ferons pour votre plaisir au mielx que faire pourrons, ainsi que tousjours avons fait, comme de ce pouviez estre acertenez par les dessus diz Cousinot et Havart, les quelz benignement vueilliez

7   Gascoigne, *Loci e Libro*, p. 221, writing around 1457.
8   This phrase, however translated, implies the use of one's influence towards a purpose.

oyr et adjouster foy a ce que de notre part par eulx vous sera expose pour ceste foiz; en nous faisant savoir souvent de voz nouvelles et de vestre bonne prosperite et sante, et nous y prendrons bien grant plaisir et en aurons singuliere consolacion.

Tres hault et puissant prince, nostre tres chier oncle, nous prions le doulz Jesu Christ quil vous teingne en sa benoiste garde.

Donne a Shene, le xvij jour de Decembre

       Marguerite[9]

To the most high and mighty prince, our very dear uncle of France; Marguerite by the grace of God queen of France and of England: greeting, with all affection and cordial love.[10]

Most high and mighty prince, our very dear uncle, we have received by master Guillaume Cousinot, the master of requests of your household, and Jehan Havart, esquire, your valet carver, your gracious letters, the contents of which we do not at present recapitulate because we know that you have a lively memory of them. But inasmuch as we perceive the good love and the sincere intention that you have towards my lord and myself, the great desire that you have to see us, and also the helpful [lit. 'fruitful'] disposition and generous inclination that we know you have in regard to peace and good concord between you two, we herein praise our Creator and thank you thereof with a good heart and as kindly as ever we may, for no greater pleasure can we have in this world than to see an arrangement for a final peace between him and you, as well for the closeness of lineage in which you stand to each other, as also for the relief and repose of Christian people who have been so long disturbed by war. And herein, to the pleasure of our Lord, we will upon our part lend a hand [Stevenson: 'stretch forth the hand'] and employ ourselves as effectively as we can, in such a way that you and all others will rightly be gratified therein.

And as to the deliverance that you desire to have of the county of Maine, and other matters contained in your said letters, we understand that my said lord has written to you at considerable length about this, and yet herein we will do for your pleasure the best that we can, as we have always done, as you may be assured by the abovesaid Cousinot and Havart, may it graciously please you to listen to them and to believe what they will relate to you on our behalf at that time, making us frequently acquainted with your news and of your good prosperity and health, and therein we will take very great pleasure and will have singular consolation.

Most high and mighty prince, our very dear uncle, we pray the sweet Jesus Christ that He preserve you in His blessed keeping.

Given at Sheen, the 17th day of December.

       Marguerite

---

9   The queen's autograph signature, as are all others in this chapter.

10 For this and the next letter, we have used Stevenson's transcriptions, but have altered the translations to improve readability and clarity. The transcriptions and translations of all others are ours, unless noted.

Charles VII was Margaret's uncle through his marriage to her father's sister. He was also Henry's uncle by blood, since *his* sister had been Henry's mother. Margaret knew Charles through personal contact – he had visited her grandmother's court at Angers where Margaret grew up – and, of course, by reputation, as king of France. She may have been fond of him: it was reported that she wept at their parting.[11] But her tears may equally have resulted from the magnitude and finality of the daunting step she was about to take: to make a new life in a new land with a man that she had never met.

Margaret was fifteen years old and still new to queenship. Although she knew what she wanted to accomplish, she probably had some help with her letter's composition, for it is more subtle than appears at first glance. It begins with an effusion of warm feelings, praise and thankfulness for Charles's good intentions (which she says she *knows* are sincere) and the assertion that a final peace is her own highest aspiration. This is all very good diplomacy. Then comes the offer that has given fits to countless latter-day historians: she will 'stretch forth the hand' and do whatever she can towards the goal of peace, which she trusts will please Charles ... *and all others*. Everyone. Both sides. In short, she sees herself as an intermediary, encouraging the good outcome – whatever it may be – that all desire.

Following this, she briefly refers to the specific matter of Maine, but adroitly sidesteps it by telling Charles that Henry has *already* written to him *at considerable length* on that subject. Nevertheless, she will do whatever she can, as she has always done, to please him, as his ambassadors will assure him upon their return. But since she has just said, effectively, that Maine is out of her hands, he should not expect too much of her. Her offer to please Charles is an expression that is found in other letters of this type.[12] It, too, is good diplomacy.

In point of fact, Henry's extant letter concerning Maine, written on 22 December, followed Margaret's by several days.[13] Like the queen's letter, it may reflect some advice in its composition. It is not the spineless capitulation that has sometimes been imagined.[14] Although Henry agreed to surrender Maine

---

11 Beaucourt, IV, pp. 93–4.
12 See, e.g., letters from Richard, duke of York, and Edmund Beaufort, duke of Somerset, to Charles VII regarding other matters (Stevenson, I, pp. 163, 231–2; discussed by Maurer, p. 37).
13 Stevenson, II, ii, pp. 639–41. A second letter from Henry VI of the same date dealt with the proposed meeting of the two kings, which had already been agreed to in principal (Escouchy, *Chronique*, III, pp. 151–3). Although the letters between Charles, Henry and Margaret are frequently described as a private correspondence, 'private' must be understood in relative terms. Watts, *Henry VI*, pp. 222–9, 232–4, has argued that most of the English lords would have recognized and agreed upon the need for concessions as part of a bargaining strategy, and we know that Maine had already come up hypothetically in this regard in 1442.
14 E.g., Wolffe, *Henry VI*, p. 185.

as Charles had requested to demonstrate his commitment to peace as well as his affection for Charles, 'whom [he] would desire to please ... *in every way which is honorable, possible, and lawful*', the stipulation is important; he was not merely a compliant puppet. There was a condition: Henry promised to cede Maine by the end of April next, *but only if* he had received letters patent authorizing René and his brother, the count of Maine, to make lifelong alliances and a twenty-year truce with England. Sandwiched between these two statements were two further reasons for agreeing to Maine's surrender, namely Henry's wish to please Margaret, 'who has requested [this]... many times', and his affection and familial bond towards René and his brother. These reasons are of secondary importance within the overall scheme of things, but there is something further going on here. A king had to appear strong and 'tough' in matters of this sort. A queen's intercession provided a king with both an opportunity and an excuse to make individual concessions without conceding his assumed strength as king.[15] The whole familial setting, of which Margaret's alleged pleading formed a part, invited Charles, the beloved uncle, to reciprocate further. It was a gamble, of course, but it might have paid off.

One further point about Margaret's letter deserves notice. In a formulaic introduction, Margaret styles herself queen of *France* and England, putting France first. This was the style that Henry used in his letters dealing with French or Norman affairs, which foregrounded his claim to the French crown.[16] When Margaret used it, she placed herself squarely in confrontation with her uncle. Whether done *pro forma* or not, this was an uncomfortable fact of which both would have been aware.

[94] Queen Margaret to Charles VII of France, 20 May 1446
(Stevenson, I, pp. 183–6, from BNF, MS Baluze 9037–7, No. 13)

A tres hault et puissant prince, notre tres chier oncle de France, Marguerite, par la grace de Dieu royne de France et Dangleterre, salut, avec entiere et parfaite dilection.

Tres hault et puissant prince, notre tres chier oncle, receu avons voz lettres donnees a Chinon, le xxiiij jour de Mars, et par icelles avons este acertenee de votre bon estat et prosperite, qui nous a este tres especiale et singuliere consolacion, et seroit a dez, se bien souvent vous plaisoit nous en faire savoir. Vous priant de vouloir entier que par les venans par de ca, si tres souvent que votre plaisir sera, nous en vueillez rendre certaine, et nous y prendrons grant plaisir et singulier esjoyssement.

15   Strohm, *Hochon's Arrow*, pp. 102–4.
16   Henry was still using it in his letters to Charles VII of 1449 (e.g., Escouchy, *Chronique*, III, pp. 212, 218).

Et pour ce que des notres oir savons vous estre desirant, monseigneur et nous estion a lescripture de cestes en tres bonne disposicion ne [*sic*, de] noz personnes, graces a notre Createur, qui par Son plaisir vous vueille tout temps le semblable octroier, ainsi que parfaictement le desirons, et que pour nous mesmes mielx souhadier le saurions.

Nous avons aussi bien sceu par vos dictes lettres le desir que avez de nous veoir a la convention prouchaine de mon dit seigneur et de vous, et que avez espoir que les matieres que en icelle se doivent traictier entre vous deux aiderons a notre pouvoir conduire et adrecier, et en ce desirez que vueillons tenir la main.

Si avons esperance, tres hault et puissant prince, notre tres chier oncle, que le plaisir de mon dit seigneur sera que avecques lui soions a la dicte convencion, et que en icelle, moiennant la grace du Saint Esperit, verrons effectuelement la fructueuse conclusion en la matiere de paix generale, que sur toutes choses mondaines de cordiale affection desirons estre conduicte en toute bonne perfection singulierement, pour entretenir et norrir union et vraye concorde entre vous deux, que estes si prouchaines en consanguinite, comme chacun scet; et de notre part nous y employerons et y tindrons la main en toute ce qui nous sera possible. Vous priant de cordial desir que en la bonne disposicion et inclinacion que savons vous avoir au bien dicelle paix, vueillez continuer et perseverer, et vous y conduire en toute desir de bonne concorde, comme nous esperons que ferez, ainsi que bon prince Catholique seult et doit faire.

Et tres hault et puissant prince, notre tres chier oncle, tous jours nous vueillez signifier toutes choses a vous aggreables, pour les acomplir a notre pouvoir joyeusement et de tres bon cuer; priant le Benoit Filz de Dieu quil vous ait et tiengne en sa tres especiale garde.

Donne a notre chastel de Wyndesore, le vingtisme jour de May.

Marguerite

To the most high and mighty prince, our very dear uncle of France; Marguerite, by the grace of God queen of France and of England: greeting, with sincere and perfect love.

Most high and mighty prince, our very dear uncle, we have received your letters dated at Chinon the 24th day of March, and by them we have been informed of your good health and prosperity, which to us has been a very special and singular consolation, and will be henceforth if it please you to let us know frequently thereof. Praying you with our full desire that it would please you to assure us very often of the same by those who come over here, and we will therein take great pleasure and singular enjoyment. And because we know that you wish to hear of our [health], at the time of writing these [letters] my lord and we were in very good bodily health, thanks to our Creator, who by His pleasure may always be willing to grant you the same, just as we fully desire of Him, and as we would best wish for ourselves.

We have also understood by your said letters the desire that you have to see us at the coming meeting of my said lord and you, and that you hope that we will help as much as we can to guide and put right the matters that shall be treated between you two, and in this you wish that we would be willing to lend a hand.

Indeed we hope, most high and mighty prince, our very dear uncle, that it will be my said lord's pleasure that we be with him at the said meeting, and that in it, by means of the grace of the Holy Spirit, we may effectively see a fruitful conclusion in the matter of a general peace, which, above all earthly things, we especially desire with heartfelt love to be brought to a very good completion in order to maintain and nourish union and true concord between you two who are so near in kindred, as everyone knows; and on our part we will employ ourselves and will lend a hand in all that shall be possible for us. Praying you with a sincere wish that you will be good enough to continue and persevere in the good disposition and inclination that we know you have towards this peace, and to conduct yourself therein with every desire of good concord as we hope you will do, as a good Catholic prince is accustomed and ought to do.

And, very high and mighty prince, our very dear uncle, always be good enough to let us know all things that are agreeable to you, so that we may accomplish them as best we can, joyfully and with a right good heart; praying the Blessed Son of God to have and preserve you in His most especial keeping.

Dated at our castle of Windsor, the twentieth day of May.

Marguerite

When Margaret wrote her second letter to Charles, the situation had grown murkier. The proposed date for Maine's cession had come and gone, and the county remained in English hands, although plans for a meeting between the kings later in the year continued to move forward.[17] Perhaps as a result, this letter began with lengthier and more effusive news and wishes relating to mutual health and wellbeing, before turning to Charles's expressed desire to see her at his meeting with Henry VI and his apparently explicit request that she lend him her support at that time. Margaret's response was circumspect. While she hoped to be present when the kings met, that decision was naturally up to her husband. And although she would do whatever she could in the cause of peace – a politic, but ultimately meaningless promise – the matter truly lay within the purview of the Holy Spirit.

The next sentence deserves special note. Considering the disparity of age, gender (which automatically implied authority) and experience, Margaret's hope that her uncle would continue to pursue peace and conduct himself 'as a good

17   Commissions sent out on 1 June to raise loans for Henry's journey to France provide evidence of his commitment to the meeting at that point (*CPR, 1441–46*, pp. 430–1). These efforts were still in train on 24 July; however, it appears that by then it was being suggested that the meeting might be postponed until the following March (*PPC*, VI, pp. 46–9, 51).

Catholic prince is accustomed and ought to do' is striking.[18] On the one hand, it seems to offer praise and encouragement, but, on the other, it may also have conveyed a warning. Charles's formal letters authorizing René to conclude an alliance and separate truce with England, the English condition for Maine's surrender, had not been forthcoming. In the face of Henry's failure to hand over Maine as agreed, was Margaret alluding here to Charles's failure to uphold his end of the bargain? The non-deliverance of these letters surfaced as an explicit issue somewhat later, in the autumn of 1447,[19] but it is the one obvious matter for which Margaret might have chided her uncle. Her standard offer of future, unspecified favor and her commendation of Charles to the Lord's good keeping abruptly conclude this letter.

It appears that Margaret had sensed the ground beginning to shift. The outcome of diplomatic negotiation, always uncertain, had become even less assured. If she had ever thought her role in peacemaking to be simple, perhaps she had acquired a greater sense of just how powerless she really was. By May 1446, Margaret perhaps felt that she had done all she could, and all that Charles or anyone else might reasonably expect of her, in the cause of peace. It was now out of her hands.

[95] **Queen Margaret to Charles VII of France, 10 December 1446**
(BNF, MS Fr. 4054, fol. 94)

A treshault et puissant prince, notre treschier oncle de France; Marguerite par la grace de dieu royne d'Angleterre et de France; salut, avecques amour entiere et vray dileccion.[20]

Treshault et puissant prince, notre treschier oncle, voz lettres de credence escriptes le xxvi jour de Septembre a nous presentees par maistre Guillaume Cousinot et Jehan Havart voz conseilliers avons tresvolentiers receues et icelle credence tant de la prosperite, sante et bon estat de votre tresnoble personne que autrement avons tresjoieusment come raison est oye et bien au long entendue. De la quele votre prosperite rendons graces devoutement a dieu notre benoit createur en lui priant que tousjours la veulle permaintenir et augmenter de bien en mieulx selon votre desir. Et come pour nous meismes le vouldrions souhaiter. Et vous prions tres affectueusement quil vous plaise souvent nous en faire savoir la certainete. Car

---

18   The wording is unique to this letter.
19   Stevenson, II, ii, pp. 671–83.
20   In this and in Margaret's two remaining letters, her title is reversed to 'queen of *England* and of France'. Typically, the secretary would have supplied the heading, and he would have used whatever was the accepted format. Perhaps he felt that this letter was entirely personal, unlike King Henry's letters, although it touched – briefly and obliquely – on the peace negotiations. In the letters that follow, the new order makes more sense.

ce nous sera singuliere consolacion d'en oir souvent en [?] tout bien. Et pour ce que par icelles voz lettres desirez semblement savoir de notre estat, nous vous signifions que a la faisance de ces lettres nous estions en bonne convalescence corporele sicome voz conseilliers dessusnomez porez sil vous plaist estre acerteine plusaplein, graces a Dieu le tout puissent que le semblable vous vueille ottroier.

En tant treshault et puissant prince, notre treschier oncle, que nous priez et exhortez a perseverament tenir la main par devers mon tresredoubte seigneur que de sa part il soit tousjours enclin au bien de la paix, vous plaise savoir pour verite que adez nous ysommes emploiee et emploirons du bon cuer si avant qu'il nous sera possible. Et savons certainement que mond tresredoubte seigneur y a tresbon et parfait vouloir.

Treshault et puissant prince, notre treschier oncle, vueillez nous souvent signifier sil est chose pardeca que puissions faire pour vous et tresvolentiers nous y emploierons au plaisir du benoit filz de Dieu qui vous ait en sa sainte garde et vous doint bonne vie et longue.

Donne soubz notre signet a Shene la disine jour de Decembre.

Marguerite

To the most high and mighty prince, our very dear uncle of France; Margaret, by the grace of God queen of England and of France: greeting, with sincere love and true affection.

Most high and mighty prince, our very dear uncle, with great pleasure we have received your letters of credence written the 26th day of September, presented to us by Master Guillaume Cousinot and Jean Havart, your councilors, and that report of the prosperity, health and wellbeing of your most noble person that we otherwise have heard [i.e. delivered orally] very joyfully, as is right, and we have discussed it at length. We devoutly give thanks to God our blessed Creator for your prosperity, praying Him that He will always maintain and increase it more and more according to your desire and as we would wish of Him for ourselves. And we beg you most affectionately that it please you to let us know often the exact state [of your health, etc.], as it will be to us a singular comfort to hear frequently that all is well. And because by these your letters you likewise wish to know of our welfare, we inform you that at the writing of letters we were in good bodily health (as [by] your above-named councilors you can be assured more fully, if it please you), thanks to God Almighty, may He see fit to grant you the same.

Most high and mighty prince, our very dear uncle, inasmuch as you ask and exhort us to continually extend the hand [i.e., influence, act as an intermediary] to my most dread lord, that on his part he may always be inclined to the good of the peace, may it please you to know that, in truth, we are busy therein all the time and will employ [ourselves] with a good heart insofar as we are able. And we certainly know that my most dread lord has therein a very good and perfect will.

Most high and mighty prince, our very dear uncle, will you frequently inform us if there is something here that we may do for you, and we will very happily employ

us therein, to the pleasure of the blessed Son of God, may He have you in His holy
keeping and give you good life and long.

> Given under our signet at Sheen, the tenth day of December.
>> Marguerite

The proposed meeting between the two kings for the autumn of 1446 did not
occur for various reasons: English doubts regarding the idea itself and its efficacy,
and of Henry's personal ability to stand up to his wily uncle; more pragmatically,
the lack of funds to send him to France in a manner worthy of a king and a general
unwillingness to dig deeper into pockets to finance such an expedition. Guillaume
Cousinot and Jean Havart arrived in England in December to express Charles's
annoyance at the delay and to issue his ultimatum: cede Maine or face war. They
also brought his personal letters to Margaret, as well as further news from him
delivered orally. Much of this was of a personal nature, having to do with his
health and wellbeing, along with appropriate expressions of concern about his
niece and nephew's health. These would have made a pleasant juxtaposition to
the harsher words that the ambassadors were having with their English counter-
parts, an assurance from Charles that, however sticky things became, *they* were
all still *family*. Naturally enough, Margaret responded in kind. Most of her letter
is taken up with affectionate, if formulaic, expressions of caring concern and the
sharing of familial news.

There was just one little thing to mar the friendly atmosphere, revealing the
tensions that ran beneath the surface. Charles was still asking Margaret to prod
Henry to be more cooperative, although he phrased it delicately as 'being inclined
towards peace'. Her response was peremptory. Yes, she was doing whatever she
could and would keep doing it. But her assertion that Henry's will towards
peace was already 'good and perfect' contradicted any suggestion that further
assistance from her might be needed. And she left it there. Nowhere did she
mention meetings, nor did she have anything to say about 'fruitful conclusions'.
Her imagined role as intercessor for the peace had come to nothing, and with
this letter it effectively ended. Her reaction to Charles's ultimatum might have
had something to do with this too.

[96] Queen Margaret to Charles VII of France, 20 December 1446
(BNF, MS Fr. 4054, fol. 79)

A treshault et puissant prince notre treschier oncle de France; Marguerite par
la grace de Dieu royne d'Angleterre et de France: salut, avecques amour entier et
vraye dileccion.

Treshault et puissant prince notre treschier oncle de France, nous summez
continuelment tresdesirante d'oir et savoir la certeinete de votre bon estat, sante et

prosperite donc vous prions cordialment que par les venans pardeca nous vueillez souvent faire savoir pour notre singuliere consolacion. Et pour ce que de l'estat de monseigneur et du notre savons certainement vous estre desirant, plaise vous savoir que nous estions a l'escripture de cestes en tresbonne disposicion et sante de noz personnes graces au doulz Jesu Crist qui le semblable par son plaisir vous vueille tout temps ottroier ainsi que de vouloir cordial le desirons et que pour nous mesmes mielx souhaidier le pourrions.

Treshault et puissant prince notre treschier oncle de France, nous avons presentement chargie le reverend pere en Dieu notre treschier et bon ame l'evesque de Chichestre et notre feal et bon ame le Sieur de Dudley, lesquelx vous prions avoir pour especialment recomendez, vous dire aucunes choses depar nous. Et vous prions de rechief que les vueillez ouyr et adiouster foy et creance [...]²¹ quilz vous dirant de notre part. Et par eulx nous signifier sil est chose par deca a vous agreable que faire puissions car de bon cuer nous y employerons. A l'aide de tout puissant Dieu qui par la saincte grace vous vueille avoir en sa benoite garde avec bonne vie et longue.

Donne soubz notre signet a Windesore le vintiesme jour de Decembre.

Marguerite

To the most high and mighty prince, our very dear uncle of France; Margaret, by the grace of God queen of England and of France: greeting, with sincere love and true affection.

Most high and mighty prince, our very dear uncle of France, we are continually most desirous of hearing and being informed of the true state of your wellbeing, health and prosperity; therefore, we heartily pray that by those persons coming here you will often make [it] known to us for our singular comfort. And because we surely know you to be desirous [to learn] of my lord's welfare and ours, may it please you to know that at the time of writing these letters we were in excellent disposition and bodily health, thanks to the sweet Jesus Christ, may He, by His pleasure, always be willing to grant you the same, as we of cordial will desire of Him and as we would the better wish of Him for ourselves.

Most high and mighty prince, our very dear uncle of France, we have at this time charged the reverend father in God, our very dear and well beloved bishop of Chichester, and our faithful and well beloved Lord Dudley, whom we ask you to have especially recommended, to tell you some things on our behalf. And we pray you moreover that you listen to them and give faith and credence [...] to what they will say to you on our part. And to signify to us by them if there is something here agreeable to you that we may be able to do, so that we may employ ourselves therein with good heart, with the help of Almighty God who by His holy grace may have you in His blessed keeping, with a good life and long.

Given under our signet at Windsor, the twentieth day of December.

Marguerite

21 A word cannot be made out here on our copy.

This letter, having nothing to say about the quest for peace, meetings or the still-unsettled issue of Maine, is essentially a letter of credence, asking Charles to listen to whatever Bishop Moleyns and Lord Dudley have to say to him on Margaret's behalf. Whether their intended news would have had anything at all to do with Maine or was to consist strictly of familial well-wishes and reports of health is impossible to say.

Both men were members of the inner circle at court. One of them proved to be a survivor; the other did not. Adam Moleyns's secular career had taken him rapidly upward from clerk of the council in 1438 to keeper of the privy seal by February 1444.[22] In that same month, he was commissioned to go to France with the earl of Suffolk's party to negotiate a truce and a marriage for Henry VI.[23] After Margaret's arrival in England, Moleyns joined the negotiating team that met with the French ambassadors in London during the summer of 1445.[24] He became bishop of Chichester on 3 December.[25] Moleyns continued to be involved in discussions with the French, and on 20 June 1446, in another flurry of diplomacy, he and John Sutton, Lord Dudley, were named ambassadors to France.[26] Lord Dudley's trajectory to prominence had taken place over a longer period. He had served in France under Henry V.[27] After a stint as lieutenant of Ireland in 1428–30, he was appointed lieutenant of the castle of Calais in 1437, and served in that capacity to 1442.[28] In October 1443 he received a life grant of £100 annually as a reward for these services.[29] When Moleyns and Dudley became ambassadors in 1446, instead of finalizing plans for the intended meeting of kings, they found themselves stuck with explaining why the meeting would have to be postponed. They were again named as ambassadors on 14 December.[30] This prompted Margaret's letter, her second in that month.

Moleyns and Dudley's embassy to France of early 1447 achieved a modest success, insofar as it resulted in an extension of the truce to January 1448, with the understanding that the two kings would meet before its expiration.[31] But matters were rapidly approaching a stalemate. Despite continued negotiations,

22 *CPR, 1436–41*, p. 203; *1441–46*, p. 284.
23 *Foedera*, XI, pp. 53, 58, 60.
24 Stevenson, I, p. 101; *CPR, 1441–46*, p. 359. Moleyns came late to the English team in August; its other members were appointed in July.
25 Ibid., pp. 375, 396.
26 Ibid., p. 456; *Foedera*, XI, pp. 138–9.
27 In 1420, at Melun, he was granted 6d per day as yeoman of the king's chamber (*CPR, 1416–22*, p. 317).
28 *CPR, 1422–29*, p. 475; *1429–36*, p. 48; *PPC*, V, p. 80.
29 *CPR, 1441–46*, p. 207.
30 *Foedera*, XI, pp. 152–3.
31 Ibid., pp. 153–5.

the meeting of kings did not occur, Maine was not surrendered, and no final peace was concluded. The most that could be agreed upon were miniscule extensions of the truce, accompanied by more promises that would not be kept. The surrender of Maine became a political hot potato in England, to the point that the duke of Suffolk felt obliged to swear in council that he had never acted unilaterally or contrary to crown interests. He demanded confirmation that action on Maine had been discussed by the council and that a decision had been reached collectively.[32] The ignominious denouement, which had the English scrambling to effect the cession in the face of a French military threat, cast a pall over everyone who had had anything to do with the negotiations, among them Moleyns, who was a principal in the eventual handover in March of 1448. In 1450 an army gathered on the south coast of England, preparing to embark for France. On 9 January, Moleyns was charged with delivering past due wages to soldiers already embittered by defeats in France and long delays in mustering. He was easy prey as a scapegoat for the government's failed policies. On his arrival in Portsmouth he was attacked and murdered by the mutinous soldiers.

Dudley was more fortunate, for although he was denounced as a traitor during Cade's Rebellion in 1450, he survived. He accompanied the king to St Albans in 1455 and was briefly imprisoned following the battle.[33] In January 1457 his career took an upswing when Margaret named him to Prince Edward's newly created council.[34] He continued as a loyal supporter of the government and in December 1459, as a reward for his services against the Yorkists, was granted £40 per year from their confiscated properties.[35] But Dudley was a trimmer; in 1460, after Henry's capture at the battle of Northampton, he reached an accommodation with the Yorkists. He was constable of the Tower under Edward IV when Henry VI died there on the night of 21 May 1471. Dudley, the survivor, continued to prosper, outliving two more kings before his own death on 30 September 1487, at the ripe old age of seventy-one.

[97] Queen Margaret to Charles VII of France, 28 July 1447
(BNF, MS Fr. 4054, fol. 76)

A treshault et puissant prince, notre treschier oncle de France; Marguerite, par la grace de dieu royne d'Engleterre et de France: salut, avecques amour entier et vray dileccion.

---

32   Ibid., pp. 172–4; *CPR, 1446–52*, p. 78. Suffolk's statement was endorsed by those present, who included the chancellor, the treasurer and the dukes of York and Buckingham.
33   Gairdner, *PL*, III, pp. 25, 33. He was reported at the time to have made accusations against 'many men'.
34   *CPR, 1452–61*, p. 359; *Foedera*, XI, p. 385.
35   *CPR, 1452–61*, p. 537.

Treshault et puissant prince, notre treschier oncle, vous cordialment prions que en tielx choses que notre bon ame Jehan Cambray, escuier, frier [frère] a notre chier et bon ame Escuier Drewe Lisle notre serviteur domestique aura afaire envers vous encontre ung Edmond Arbalastre touchantz l'accomplissement de justice. Vous please pour l'amour et en faveur de nous, luy avoir pour especialment recomendez et luy monstrer tout l'ease, faveur et brief expedicion de justice que vous de droit bonnement pourrez faire et ministrer en aucune maniere. Ainsi quil ait cause s'en louer et que luy et ses parens et amyes cognoissent noz priere luy avoir valu. Come nous avons en vous tres singuliere fiance.

Treshault et puissant prince, notre treschier oncle, Notre Seigneur vous ait en sa sainte garde.

Donne soubz notre signet a notre manoir de Pleasance le xxviij jour de Juillet.
Marguerite

To the most high and mighty prince, our very dear uncle of France; Margaret, by the grace of God queen of England and of France: greeting, with sincere love and true affection.

Most high and mighty prince, our very dear uncle, we heartily pray you that in those things that our well beloved John Cambray, esquire, comrade-in-arms [lit. 'brother'] to our dear and well beloved squire Drew Lisle, our household servant, will have to say to you on behalf of one Edmund Arbalaster touching the accomplishment of justice,[36] may it please you, for love and consideration of us, to have him especially recommended and to show him all the satisfaction, favor and speedy conclusion of justice that you of right may goodly do and administer in any way. So that he [Arbalaster] may have reason to be pleased and that he and his relatives and friends may know [that] our request is of value to him. As we have in you most singular trust.

Most high and mighty prince, our very dear uncle, Our Lord have you in His holy keeping.

Given under our signet at our manor of Pleasaunce, the 28th day of July.
Marguerite

On 28 July 1447, Henry VI signed letters patent in the presence of his council and the French ambassadors with whom they had negotiated, formally authorizing the surrender of the county of Maine to the king of France. Margaret's letter, written on the same day, makes no mention of any of this. Instead, she focused on an intercession on behalf of a particular individual.

The story behind this letter has to be teased out. Edmund Arblaster, esquire, of Staffordshire, went to France with the duke of York's expedition of 1441,

---

36 Although *encontre* most frequently meant 'against', it sometimes had the figurative meaning of 'on behalf of' (*The Anglo-Norman Dictionary*, AND² Online edition, http://www.anglo-norman. net/D/encontre [1]; accessed 16 February 2012).

where he apparently served initially as a man-at-arms under Henry Bourgchier, then count of Eu. He was promoted to captain to serve directly under York, the king's lieutenant in France, who had the general command.[37] Sometime after this, though probably before 1445 when York's lieutenancy ended, Arblaster was captured.

He was unable to pay his ransom, and William Neville, Lord Fauconberg, who was also serving in Normandy, stood surety for him. Fauconberg, of course, assumed that Arblaster would find a way to pay up once he had regained his freedom, but this did not happen. As a result, to avoid dishonor, Fauconberg eventually petitioned the council on 20 July 1454 that he be allowed to return Arblaster to 'one Blauncheford', who had been his captor. His request was granted.[38] We do not know what became of Arblaster after that; presumably he was shipped back to France.

The queen's letter, written in July 1447, establishes that Arblaster was still in France in that year and in need of help. The most likely explanation for his ongoing difficulties was that, although Fauconberg had stood surety for him, the unfortunate Arblaster had not yet been released. This was the matter in which justice was to be rendered.

Margaret's interest in Arblaster may have stemmed from a family connection. A Thomas Arblaster, 'the elder', appears in Henry VI's household list for 1454 as an esquire. More importantly, he was surveyor of Needwood Chase, which was part of Margaret's dower of Tutbury, as well as a client of the duke of Buckingham.[39] Margaret would have known, or known of, him. This Thomas, who was born in 1400, had served as an MP for Staffordshire from 1426 to 1440.[40] Since he is referred to as 'the elder', there must have been a younger Thomas, who would have been his son, though we have found no trace of him. It seems likely that Edmund was another, younger, son.[41] If so, the elder Thomas may have sought the queen's aid in obtaining Edmund's freedom. The problem with this suggestion is that Margaret does not mention Thomas Arblaster and his connection to her in her letter. Indeed, her impersonal reference to 'one Edmund Arbalaster' makes it seem that she did not know a whole lot about the man.

---

37   E 101/53/33 m. 3 and E 101/54/9 m. 2, from the AHRC-funded 'The Soldier in Later Medieval England Online Database', http://dev.www.medievalsoldier.org, accessed 23 March 2017. Both references are from 1441.
38   *PPC*, VI, pp. 208–9. For another case involving ransom, see above, pp. 127–8.
39   *PPC*, VI, p. 224; Somerville, *Duchy of Lancaster*, p. 546.
40   Wedgwood, p. 17.
41   A reference to an Edmund Arblaster from July 1440 involves a situation in which he was indebted to Henry VI and subsequently obtained the king's help in bailing himself out (*CCR, 1435–41*, p. 384).

Who, then, were John Cambray and Drew Lisle, and what were their roles in this affair? Five references identify John Cambray as a man-at-arms doing garrison duty under Sir John Montgomery or serving in his official retinue in France from October 1431 to November 1435.[42] Despite the lapse of time between these reports of him and Margaret's letter, it is likely that he is our man. He may have remained with Montgomery in one capacity or another beyond his recorded dates of active service. Montgomery continued to serve under York into 1445 and was present when Margaret arrived in Rouen. His wife became one of her favorites, and Sir John himself later received a grant of land from the queen.[43] This provides a possible link between Margaret and Cambray, and the assumption of the latter's continued presence in France may suggest a connection between him and Arblaster.

Drew Lisle's role is more elusive, though, unfortunately, it seems to be key to the whole affair. Margaret's letter identifies him as a servant in the royal household. This would have given him ready access to the queen as a petitioner. He was probably the son of Sir William Lisle who died in 1442, having settled his manor of Wilbraham Lisles in Cambridgeshire on his son Drew the year before.[44] There is no evidence that Drew was ever in France to explain why Margaret called Cambray his 'brother'. Nor is there any indication that they were half-brothers or stepbrothers. The only evidence of any connection between the two – and Arblaster – is this letter.

Based on these disparate bits of information, two scenarios seem possible. If Cambray remained in France and was aware of Arblaster's plight, he may have appealed to his *frère* Lisle, a member of the royal household, to see if he could enlist the queen's aid, while he presented the details of the case to Charles VII. Alternatively, if Lisle first learned of Arblaster's situation, either from Thomas the elder or from someone else at court who thought he might be able to help, he may have asked his *frère* Cambray to set the matter before Charles VII, while he appealed to Margaret for backup. In any case, it appears to have been Lisle who laid Arblaster's predicament before the queen. Otherwise, her reference to him in her letter makes little sense. Her stake in the outcome was the usual one in

42 BNF, MS Fr. 25770, nn. 633 and 735; MS Fr. 25772, nn. 918 and 1022; MS Clairambault 182, n. 21, from the AHRC-funded 'The Soldier in Later Medieval England Online Database', http://dev.www.medievalsoldier.org, accessed 23 March 2017.

43 See above, pp. 63ff and 162ff for Montgomery and his wife.

44 A.F. Wareham and A.P.M. Wright, 'Great Wilbraham: Manors and Other Estates', in *A History of the County of Cambridge and the Isle of Ely: Volume 10, Cheveley, Flendish, Staine and Staploe Hundreds (North-Eastern Cambridgeshire)* (2002), pp. 306–11. British History Online, http://www.british-history.ac.uk/vch/cambs/vol10/pp306-311, accessed 14 December 2011. See also *CFR, 1471–85*, p. 99. We have found no other person of that name.

matters of this sort: that the victim (Arblaster) and his friends and family (who had either sought her intervention or would later hear of it) would be pleased and satisfactorily impressed by the efficacy of her good ladyship.

[98] Charles VII of France to Queen Margaret, 3 June 1449
(Beaucourt, IV, p. 457, from *Chartes royales*, XV, n° 208)

A très haulte et puissante princesse nostre très chière niepce d'Angleterre, Charles, etc., salut et entiere dilection.

Très haulte et puissante princesse nostre très chière niepce, pour ce que pensons que estre acertenée de noz nouvelles en bien est chose que bien vous vient à plaisir, ainsi que de vous oir le semblable nous est singuliere resjoissance, se vostre plaisir estoit d'en savoir, à la rescription des presentes nous estions en bon estat et disposicion, graces au benoist filz de Dieu, qui le pareil tout temps vous vueille octroyer, ainsi que parfaitement le desirons et que pour nous mesmes mieulx le saurions souhaitier. Au seurplus, très haulte et puissante princesse nostre très chière niepce, nous envoyons presentement par devers très hault et puissant prince nostre beau nepveu, vostre espoux, nostre amé et feal varlet tranchant Jehan Havart, pour luy dire et remonstrer aucunes choses touchant l'estat et le demené des matieres de par deça, lequel Havart avons chargé vous aler faire la reverence et nous raporter au vray du bon estat, santé et prosperité de vostre très noble personne, que Dieu, par sa saincte grace, vueille tousjours conduire et entretenir de bien en mieulx. Si vous prions que, par icelui Havart, nous en vueillez faire savoir, ensemble s'il est chose a vous agreable que convenablement faire puissions, pour nous y employer de très bon cuer, au plaisir de Nostre Seigneur, lequel nous prions, très haulte et puissante princesse nostre très chière niepce, qu'il vous ait et tiegne en sa saincte et benoiste garde.

Donné a Raisilly, le iiie jour de juing.

To the most high and mighty princess, our very dear niece of England; Charles, etc.: greeting and sincere affection.

Most high and mighty princess, our very dear niece: Because we think that being well informed of our news is a thing that indeed gives you pleasure, just as hearing similar [news] of you is a singular enjoyment for us, may it please you to know that at the writing of these present letters we were in good health and disposition, thanks to the blessed Son of God, may He always be willing to grant you the same, as we completely desire of Him and as we would rather wish for ourselves.

In addition, most high and mighty princess, our very dear niece, we are presently sending to the most high and mighty prince, our good nephew your husband, our beloved and loyal valet carver Jean Havart, to tell and to show him some things concerning the state and the conduct of matters here; which Havart we have instructed to give [our] respects to you and to truly report to us the wellbeing, health and prosperity of your most noble person, whom God, by His holy grace, always be willing to guide and support more and more. And we ask you that you will make known to us at the same time by the said Havart if there is something pleasing to you that we may fittingly do, in order to employ us therein with a very good heart, to the pleasure of Our Lord, whom we pray, most high and mighty princess, our very dear niece, that He have and hold you in His holy and blessed keeping.

Given at Raisilly, the 3rd day of June.

This is the last letter that we have between Margaret and Charles VII for this period. Maine had finally been surrendered by the English in March 1448 in the face of a French mobilization. Further negotiations between the two realms proved unfruitful. In March 1449, François de Surienne, an Aragonese captain serving the English, made a surprise attack on the town of Fougères in Brittany.[45] Duke Francis of Brittany had sworn homage to Charles VII in 1446, and Charles claimed that the capture of Fougères constituted a deliberate breach of the truce. This was the state of affairs at the beginning of June, when Charles VII wrote to both Henry and Margaret.

Although Charles was at pains to inform Margaret that his envoy, Jean Havart, would speak of the situation to Henry (which, we may presume, would be made known to her as well), he spoke directly to her only of familial and personal matters: of health and good wishes and the ever-present polite offer to do something that might please her.[46] There is no hint that he wished for Margaret's aid or influence, and, in truth, by this time Charles did not need it. Matters would take their course.

On 31 July, Charles declared war on England, bringing an end to the truce that had existed since 1444 and had been the occasion for Margaret's marriage. The French effort to retake Normandy moved swiftly, and Rouen fell to Charles VII on 29 October.

45 M.H. Keen and M.J. Daniel, 'English Diplomacy and the Sack of Fougères in 1449', *History* 59:197 (October 1974), pp. 375–91.
46 In his letter to King Henry, Charles opined that Henry might believe something that was untrue. Havart would explain just what was going on. Charles would pursue peace by 'all good and convenient means', and he begged Henry to attend to what Havart told him (Beaucourt, IV, pp. 456–7). For Havart's lengthy instructions, see Escouchy, *Chronique*, III, pp. 225–39.

Ten

QUEEN CONSORT

During the 1450s, Margaret gradually emerged as a player in domestic politics. Up to this point, apart from her brief intervention in the surrender of Maine, she had remained a 'traditional' queen, tending to her own affairs and being a good lady on the scale that queenship demanded. Two separate but nearly simultaneous events brought about a change in her circumstances. Henry VI's complete mental breakdown in August 1453, from which he did not recover for nearly a year and a half, was the first of these. The second was the birth of Prince Edward two months later. The birth of a son gave Margaret a greater stake in the future of the realm, and she assumed an active role in influencing that future.

For the magnates, Henry's illness brought a heightening of domestic tensions. And while the birth of an heir offered continuity, it also triggered memories of Henry's own lengthy minority. A struggle for dominance – often perceived as a struggle for survival – ensued among the lords, a number of whom were already at odds with one another. By the end of the decade Margaret and the duke of York had become enemies.

The dearth of purely political letters by or to Margaret during this decade requires the inclusion of other documents in which she figures prominently. Some of these have triggered controversy; others have been too readily accepted at face value. To maintain focus on the queen we have excerpted them, retaining only material relevant to a fresh analysis of Margaret's actions.

The first two documents, though very different, provide the earliest 'evidence' we have of Margaret's participation in domestic politics, during Jack Cade's rebellion in 1450. One is a letter written some fifteen years after the events it purports to describe; the other is the preamble to the pardon granted to the rebels. Next is a letter from the duchess of York requesting Margaret's intercession with King Henry on behalf of her husband, who was in political hot water. Several newsletters follow, which trace Margaret's actions from Henry's illness through its aftermath, to the end of York's second protectorate in 1456. A further letter complains of Margaret's enmity, which may – or may not – have been caused by the writer's association with the duke of York. The final two letters, one to and the other by Margaret, though unquestionably political in nature, are undated, which leaves the situations they allude to open to question and places them among the most puzzling and evocative letters in the entire collection.

[99] J. Payne to John Paston, *c.* 1465 (excerpted)
(Gairdner, *PL*, II, pp. 153–6)

Pleasyth it your gode and gracious maistershpp tendyrly to consedir the grete losses and hurts that your por peticioner haeth, and haeth jhad evyr seth the comons of Kent come to the Blakheth and that is at xv yer passed ... And a-none aftyr that hurlyng[1] the Bysshopp Roffe [John Lowe, bishop of Rochester] apechyd me to the Quene, and so I was arestyd by the Quenes commaund[m]ent in-to the Marchalsy, and ther was in right grete durasse and fere of myn lyf, and was thretenyd to have ben honged, drawe, and quarteryd ... but my wyves and j coseyn of myn noune that were yomen of the Croune, they went to the Kyng and gote grase and j chartyr of pardon.

[100] Preamble to the Pardon Granted to Jack Cade and his Rebels, July 1450 (excerpted)
(Maurer, p. 68, n. 4, from C 66/471, m. 13)

Recalling to the reflection and consideration of our [i.e., Henry VI's] mind that among those virtues fitting and proper to the royal person and dignity, none befits him more than clemency ... and considering as well that it is well to show himself such a prince to his subjects as he wishes God to be supreme and high Lord to him, persuaded and moved by these and many other pious considerations, among others by the most humble and persistent supplications, prayers and requests of our most serene and beloved wife and consort the queen ... we have pardoned ...

Are either of these documents accurate depictions of Margaret's activities? Both would have been *credible* in England when they were written, but that is not quite the same as saying they were *true*.

Payn's letter adds weight to the traditionally hostile picture of Margaret as an implacable queen. It is, however, a begging letter of dubious veracity, with a specific aim in mind. John Paston was the executor for the immensely wealthy Sir John Fastolf, who had died in November 1459. In his letter, Payn – claiming

---

1   I.e., the battle of the Bridge, on the night of 5–6 July, when the rebels were defeated and driven out of London.

to have been Fastolf's faithful servant – dwells in convoluted detail upon the 'great losses and hurts' he endured fifteen years before, first at the hands of Cade and his rebels, and then at the queen's hands. He was hoping for 'remuneration', if not a straightforward handout.

A date of 1465 for Payn's letter was inferred by James Gairdner, the letter's editor, who took literally Payn's statement that his troubles had occurred fifteen years in the past, i.e., in 1450. In 1465, Margaret was in exile, and the Yorkist Edward IV was king. Margaret had been making strenuous efforts to raise support for her husband's restoration ever since his deposition. This was common knowledge in England.[2] In a very real sense she remained a significant, though distant, enemy. Payn's inclusion of her in his complaint was an additional and safe way to drum up sympathy.

Identifying Payn is tricky. The likeliest suspect is the John Payn, yeoman and smith of East Peckham, Kent, who was among a group of men indicted in June 1451 for treasons and serious mayhem committed in April during the turmoil that continued after Cade's Rebellion. He and two others were individually pardoned in November, having submitted to the king 'naked to the waist and with ropes about their necks'.[3] East Peckham is close to Rochester, lending credence to the bishop's role in Payn's difficulties. If this is 'our' Payn, it throws a different light upon his story and Margaret's involvement in it. If he was rounded up at the bishop's behest, there is no reason to believe that he was singled out to anyone – much less the queen – as his letter implies. Margaret's involvement in Payn's case only makes sense if his arrest occurred during or immediately after the rebellion, and if she remained behind at Greenwich when King Henry decamped to Kenilworth.[4]

The reliability of Payn's account may be shaky, but what of the preamble to the pardon? It presents a more elaborate version of the simple statement found in the patent rolls: that a general pardon was offered to Cade and a great many other rebels 'at the request of the queen'.[5] This is the familiar trope of queen as

2   Margaret made overtures to King Afonso of Portugal in December 1464 (see below, pp. 263ff), and in early 1465 she pleaded with Louis XI for aid (*CSP, Milan*, p. 116). See also C. Ross, *Edward IV* (1974), pp. 106–7.
3   R. Virgoe, 'Some Ancient Indictments in the King's Bench Referring to Kent, 1450–1452', in *Documents Illustrative of Medieval Kentish Society*, ed. F.R.H. Du Boulay, Kent Archaeological Society Monograph Series 17 (Ashford, 1964), pp. 250–2; *CPR, 1446–52*, p. 497. The most serious charge involved a plot to depose and kill the king, a standard accusation against rebels. This individual seems to be the only J. Payn with an arrest record from the time of Cade's Rebellion.
4   Both Greenwich and Kenilworth were Margaret's possessions. Henry left for Kenilworth before Cade's assault on London, i.e., by the earliest days of July (Griffiths, pp. 613–14; Wolffe, *Henry VI*, pp. 237, 368).
5   *CPR, 1446–52*, p. 338. The pardons were issued on 6–7 July 1450.

intercessor. Margaret had tried to play just such a role in the negotiations with France. *If* she remained in or near London, she would have been the *only* royal presence on the scene whose name could be used to give weight to the official steps being taken to end the rebellion.

For that was the purpose of the pardon. Coming immediately after the rebels were beaten back from London Bridge, it further dampened their ardor by appealing to any and all who might be having second thoughts. It provided a way out. The need to offer pardon *at some point* was a given. Its timing was another matter. The chancellor, Cardinal Kemp, who negotiated with the rebels, was the likeliest person to have made the decision to offer it at that time. The queen's name would have given weight to the pardon, and it is fair to assume that if Kemp used it, he could scarcely have done so without her permission.

The assumption of Margaret's presence near London in 1450 rests solely upon these three documents – the preamble, the patent roll entry and Payn's letter – which purport to establish where she was and what she was doing at the time. An assessment of what she actually did or could have done requires acceptance that she was *there*. The use of her name may support the notion that Margaret did remain near London and was in contact with the chancellor. Further evidence of her interest in the aftermath of the rebellion is provided by the case of John Eve, a Franciscan friar, who received pardon for his part in Cade's Rebellion in May 1451, at the queen's behest.[6] In any event, Margaret's part in issuing the pardons, as represented by the documents, would have been believed by people at that time because it was what they expected of a queen.

[101] **Cecily, Duchess of York to Queen Margaret, [May] 1453**
(Archives of Battle Abbey, 1077–1780, BA 937, fols 2–3, The Huntington Library, San Marino, California)

Besechith with all humblenes and reverence possible youre lowly obeisaunt servaunt and bedewoman, Cecile, du*ches of* York,[7] that where of the plente of your good and benigne grace it pleasid ther unto in your comyng from that blissid, *gracious* and devout pilgremage of our lady of Walsyngham to suffre the comyng of my simple person, replete with such ymmenserable sorowe and hevynesse as y dowt not will of the contynuaunce therof amynuse and abrig*ge my* days as it doth my wordly ioy and confort, unto youre moost worthi and moost high presence, where un to than *you pleased* full benignely to receyve my supplicacon to the same

6   *Foedera*, XI, p. 285.
7   A transcript of this letter was previously published by C. Rawcliffe, 'Richard Duke of York, the King's "obeisant liegeman"', *Historical Research* 60 (1987), pp. 237–8. The manuscript is badly damaged on the right-hand side, leaving words missing or illegible. In our transcript we have indicated words or letters that Rawcliffe supplied by italics.

made for your humble, true man and servaunt, my lord my hus*bond*, whose infinite
sorow, unrest of hert and of worldly comfort, causid of that that he herith him to be
estrangied from *the* grace and benevolent favor of that most cristen, most gracious
and most mercifull prince, the kyng our soverayn l*ord*, whos majeste roiall my said
lord and husbond now and ever, god knoweth, duryng his lif hath be as true, and
as humble, and as obeisant leigeman, and to the performyng of his noble plesur
and commaundement as re*dy, as* wel disposid, and as diligent at his power, and
over that as glad, as joyfull to be there un to commaundid *as any* creatur on lyve,
beyng specified in the said supplicacon. I beseche your highnes and good grace, at
the *mercy* of our Creator now redy to send His grace in to all cristen persons, and
of that blissid Lady to whom ye late *prayed*, in whom habundeth plentously mercy
and grace, bi whos mediacon it plesid our Lord to fullfill your *right* honerable body
of the most precious, most joyfull, and most confortable erthely tresor that myght
come unto this land and to the people therof, the which y beseche His habundant
grace to prospere *in yow*, and at such [time][8] as it plesith Him to bryng in to this
world with all honor, gracious spede, and felicite, *with* also of futhirmore supppli-
cacon of blissid and noble fruite of your said body, for the greete trust and most
confortable su*erty and* wele of this realme and of the kynges true leige people of
the same, to call the good spede of the matiers conteynyd *in this* said supplicacon
in to the gracious and tendir recommendacon of your highnes. Wherunto y shuld
for the same have with*out* slowght or discontenuaunce and with ondelaid deligence
have suyd, ne had be the disease and infirmite that, sethyn *my* said beyng in your
high presence hath growen and growith uppon me, causid not oonly th'encomerous
labor, to me full paynfull and unesy, God knoweth, that than y tokke upon me,
but also the contynuance and addicion of *soche* hevynes that y have taken and
take for the consideracon of the sorowe of my said lord and husbond; and that it
please *your* good grace not to take to ony displesur of strangens that y have not
diligently contynuyd the sute of my said supplicac*on unto* your said highnes, causid
of the said infirmite not hid uppon my wrecchid body. Wherfor y report me to
god, a*nd in* reverence of whom. and of his said grace and mercy to you shewyd, it
please eftsones unto your hygh noble to *be a* tendre and gracious meane un to the
highnes of our said soverayn lord for the favor and the benewillence of his *hand*
to be shewid unto my said lord and husbond, so that thorow the gracious meane
of you, soverayn lady, he *mow* and effectually opteyne to have the same. Wheryn
y beseke your said highnes that my said labor and peyne mow *not be* takyn fryvole
ne infructuose, but the more agreable for my said lord unto your said good grace.
Wher unto, *not with* stondyng my said infirmyte, y shuld not have spared to have
recontynuyd my said sute if y coude or mygh ha*ve done*, that it shuld have plesid
your nobley if that y shuld so have doon the which, as it shall please therunto y

---

8   Although there is no indication in the manuscript that a word has been omitted here, the
     addition of 'time' would make better sense.

shall no*t let*, not sparyng oonly sparyng[9] payn that my body now suffice of any possibilite to bere or suffre, with *Goddes grace*, whom y shall praye to prosper your high estate in honor, joy and felicite.

In the spring of 1453, Margaret made a pilgrimage to the shrine at Our Lady of Walsingham in Norfolk to give thanks for her long-awaited pregnancy. Her offering was a gold tablet, with an angel holding a crucifix garnished with a ruby and nine ornamental pearls. The angel hovered above a large sapphire, and a decorative border containing ten circles of pearls, five sapphires and five spinel rubies surrounded the whole.[10]

As she returned from the shrine Margaret was visited by Cecily, duchess of York, who sought the queen's mediation between her husband and King Henry.[11] The roots of Cecily's intervention can be traced back to the autumn of 1450, when York returned from Ireland unbidden in the aftermath of Cade's Rebellion. Although he did not instigate the rebellion, it was rumored that the rebels intended to depose Henry and replace him with York, while Cade himself had used an alias that called to mind York's lineage and possible claim to the crown. The duke's uninvited return, whatever his intentions, was sufficient to arouse the king's suspicions. Matters were made worse in May 1451, when one of York's councilors, Thomas Young, had the temerity to propose in parliament that the duke be recognized as Henry's heir presumptive until such time as Henry had a son. The king clapped Young into prison and dissolved parliament. Early in 1452, York confronted the king at Dartford in a ham-fisted attempt to force him to charge the duke of Somerset, his rival, with treason.[12] Despite York's protests to the contrary, his action constituted an overt challenge to Henry's authority and ended in the duke's failure and disgrace. Nevertheless, Margaret appears to have remained on good – or at least neutral – terms with York. Her New Year's gifts for 1452 included a substantial gift to his servants, indicating that York had sent her a gift; in the previous year she sent him a personal gift as well.[13] A year later, in the spring of 1453, York still felt his position to be precarious.

Although the queen and duchess had never been close, Cecily regarded

9   This word is repeated here.
10   Myers, 'Jewels', p. 222. The tablet was valued at £29.
11   BL, Egerton Roll 8365. There is a claim for 3s 2d in the Hitchin bailiff's account for Michaelmas 1452 to Michaelmas 1453 for the expenses of York's treasurer staying one night at Hitchin when the duchess of York visited Queen Margaret. Our thanks to Ann Kettle for this reference.
12   Jones, 'Somerset', offers an intriguing analysis of the York–Somerset rivalry.
13   There is no other record of a personal gift from the queen in the extant jewel accounts, although York's servants appear as regular recipients in return for bringing gifts to her. In 1449 her annual gift went to the servants of the duchess (Myers, 'Jewels', pp. 217 and n. 6, 222 and n. 6). Maurer, pp. 85–90, discusses Margaret's gift-giving as a possible signifier of her political neutrality.

Margaret as a promising intermediary; otherwise she would not have ventured to request a meeting. The queen's visit to Walsingham offered a propitious opportunity. Margaret listened sympathetically to the duchess, perhaps because it was the politically sensible thing to do. Cecily had borne her first child at the age of twenty-four after ten years of marriage; by 1453 she had given birth to eleven children, including at least four surviving sons. She was well-placed to offer empathy and encouragement to Margaret, who was twenty-three and facing her first, vitally important pregnancy after eight years of marriage. If Margaret had a son, York could no longer claim to be heir presumptive, which had so angered Henry VI. Whatever the Yorks' private thoughts, Cecily's expressions of pleasure at the prospect amounted to good diplomacy. She claimed that she was under great stress: her husband's anxieties regarding his situation – and doubtless his urgings to approach the queen as go-between – had placed a heavy burden on her. Although he had been summoned to parliament in March, York did not attend, but no one seemed to care. Was this the incentive behind Cecily's visit to Margaret?

Sometime shortly before the feast of Pentecost, which fell on 20 May in 1453, Cecily followed up her supplication with this written petition.[14] She excused herself for not presenting it in person, as protocol required, because her health had deteriorated since their meeting.[15] Cecily reminded Margaret that she had received her first supplication 'full benignly', and then launched into an impassioned defense of York as the king's true, humble and obedient servant. He was suffering serious depression ('infinite sorrow') due to his estrangement from the king, and he was willing, as he had always been, to do anything in his power to be of service. It is impossible not to see York's prompting in a plea that cost the duchess a considerable effort to make.[16]

This demonstrates that the duke and duchess of York believed that Margaret was approachable, that she was not their enemy, which flies in the face of the strong tradition, still adhered to by many historians, that Margaret 'hated' the duke of York almost from the time of her arrival in England. We do not know how Margaret responded to the duchess's appeal. If she did speak to Henry on York's behalf, nothing came of it. Three months later, in August, Henry suffered his breakdown and lapsed into catatonia. For a time, everyone waited: on the

---

14   Cecily's reference to 'the mercy of our Creator *now ready* to send his grace in to all christen persones' implies Pentecost.

15   She refers three times to her 'infirmity', generally signifying a physical condition, which she claims was exacerbated by her continuing anxiety over her husband's situation.

16   Despite Cecily's claim that the toll such stress took was apt to shorten her life, she survived much greater grief, outliving her husband and all of her sons, to die in 1495 at the age of eighty.

impending birth and to see if Henry might recover. On 13 October, Margaret gave birth to a son, Prince Edward of Lancaster, at Westminster Palace, where she remained in seclusion until her churching on 18 November restored her to court life.[17] When she emerged, the political situation had completely changed. Soon after the birth a council had been summoned to deal with the consequences of the king's incapacity. Although initially York may have been excluded, as the premier peer of the realm he had to be consulted in what amounted to a constitutional crisis.[18] Upon arriving in London on 12 November, York took control of the proceedings. On the 23rd, his rival the duke of Somerset was arrested and sent to the Tower.

[102] Newsletter of John Stodeley, 19 January 1454 (excerpted)
(Gairdner, *PL*, II, pp. 295-9)

As touching tythynges, please it you to wite that at the Princes coming to Wyndesore, the Duc of Buk' toke hym in his armes and presented hym to the Kyng in godely wise, besechyng the Kyng to blisse hym; and the Kyng yave no maner answere. Natheless the Duk abode stille with the Prince by the Kyng; and whan he coude no maner answere have, the Queene come in, and toke the Prince in hir armes and presented hym in like forme as the Duke had done, desirying that he shuld blisse it; but alle their labour was in veyne, for they departed thens without any answere or countenaunce saving only that ones he loked on the Prince and caste doune his eyene ayen, without any more.

Item [7], Tresham, Josep, Danyelle, and Trevilian have made a bille to the Lordes, desirying to have a garisone kept at Wyndesore for the saufgarde of the Kyng and of the Prince, and that they may have money for wages of theym and other that shulle kepe the garyson ...

Item [10], the Queene hathe made a bille of five articles, desirying those articles to be graunted; wherof the first is that she desireth to have the hole reule of this land; the second is that she may make [appoint] the Chaunceller, the Tresorere, the Prive Seele, and alle other officers of this land, with shireves and alle other officers that the Kyng shuld make; the third is, that she may yeve alle the bisshopriches of this land, and alle other benefices longyng to the Kynges yift; the iiijth is that she may have suffisant lyvelode assigned hir for the Kyng and the Prince and hir self. But as for the vth article, I kan nat yit knowe what it is ...

---

17   Duchess Cecily was invited to Margaret's churching, along with all the ladies of the land (Lincoln's Inn, Hale MS 12, Item 75). We do not know if she attended. Our thanks to Dunstan Speight, Librarian, for a photograph of the document.
18   *PPC*, VI, p. 163. The wording of York's summons is ambiguous. It implies either that a summons had been sent to him but not been received, or, more plausibly, that a summons had not been sent, but that this regrettable oversight was now being corrected with a 'new' summons.

Thise thinges aforseid ben espied and gadred by my Lord Chaun,[19] John Leventhorpe, Laurence Leventhorpe, Maister Adam, William Medwe, Robert Alman, John Colvyle, Richard of Warderobe, and me, John Stodeley. And as sone as we kun knowe any more in substance we shull send home word. Writen at London, the xix. day of Janyvere.

In January 1454, John Stodeley compiled a newsletter in London recounting recent events and reporting on what he had heard about the principal political figures at that time. By his own admission it is an amalgam of gossip and rumor that he had picked up or heard from some of his acquaintances. How far his information can be trusted is open to question. Not much is known about him. His letter was addressed to someone in the duke of Norfolk's service, probably to Richard Southwell, to whom he may have been related.[20] Two months after Stodeley wrote his newsletter, he and Southwell were named as feoffees of the chief justice, Sir John Fortescue, and of Sir Edmund Hungerford, King Henry's knight of the body.[21] One of Stodeley's informants was John Leventhorpe, and in his will, Leventhorpe left property jointly to Southwell and Stodeley, indicating a possible kinship between the three men.[22] A 'Leventhorpe' was among the bully boys that the duke of Norfolk sent to attack Robert Wingfield during their long-running feud.[23] Of Stodeley's other informants, William Medowe was a king's sergeant-at-arms.[24] The otherwise unidentified 'Richard of the Wardrobe' was well-placed to recount gossip and rumor within the royal household. Master Adam may have been Adam the Surgeon who attended the queen.[25]

England was in an unsettled state, and the future was far from certain. Too many magnates put their own interests ahead of the greater good, and some saw the crisis of King Henry's illness as an opportunity to pursue their feuds and defeat their enemies. The pervasive sense of insecurity found expression within the royal household. Thomas Tresham, William Joseph, Thomas Daniel and John Trevilian banded together to express concern for the king's safety. While it is unlikely that the king or prince were in any immediate danger, they feared for their own future if the duke of York took control of the government.[26] And

19   Gairdner noted this blank space in the manuscript. If Stodeley had started to write 'chaunceller', it would appear to have been a mistake made in haste.
20   For Southwell, see below, pp. 210–11.
21   *CCR, 1454–61*, p. 150.
22   Ibid., pp. 186–7.
23   For Wingfield, see above, pp. 108ff.
24   *CPR, 1446–52*, p. 469; *1452–61*, p. 168. He was still a sergeant at arms in April 1457 (ibid., p. 349).
25   Myers, 'Jewels', p. 225.
26   Thomas Tresham, a royal officer and son of a former speaker of the commons, and William Joseph, a clerk of the signet, were personally disliked and distrusted by York. After the battle

with good reason. When York became protector, he reduced the size of the royal household and their names vanished from the lists of those attending the sick king.[27] They, and others in the household, may have encouraged the queen to intervene in the political scene.

Margaret had traveled to Windsor with the baby prince in December 1453, hoping that King Henry would respond to the sight of his wife and child. First the duke of Buckingham and then Margaret presented the prince to Henry and asked his blessing on the child, but Henry did not react. She then understood the enormity of the situation she faced. With the king incapacitated, only she could represent the dynasty and uphold crown authority over private interests.[28]

Margaret's bid to become regent is known only because it is the tenth item in John Stodeley's rambling newsletter. He reported that she had prepared a 'bill' of five articles: 1) she would become regent for the king; 2) she would appoint all officers of state; 3) she would nominate to all vacant bishoprics; 4) she would require sufficient income to maintain the royal dignity. Stodeley claimed not to know what her fifth article was, and its content has remained a matter of speculation to this day. Although it may have had something to do with the prince, it is more apt to have been a promise to rule with an advisory council if her conditions were met.[29] Margaret was politically inexperienced, and it is unlikely that she could, or would try to, rule alone. English historians have made too much of the 'unprecedented' nature of Margaret's articles.[30] A precedent did exist for a queen regent ruling with a council: in 1253, Eleanor of Provence successfully served as regent for ten months during Henry III's absence on the continent. Queens-regent were not uncommon in Europe. Margaret's grandmother, Yolande of Aragon, and her mother, Isabelle of Lorraine, had acted

of St Albans in 1455, when he needed scapegoats, York blamed Joseph as one of three men who had 'caused' the battle (Armstrong, 'Politics and St Albans', pp. 57–8). Thomas Daniel and John Trevilian were among twenty-nine unpopular members of the royal household whose banishment from court had been demanded in a parliamentary petition of 1451 (*PROME*, XII, pp. 184–5).

27 *PPC*, VI, pp. 222–5.

28 Maurer, pp. 99–101.

29 At the Reading parliament in early 1453, Chancellor Kemp promised to appoint the 'sadde and wyse' council that the commons had requested, and he would be reminded of that promise on 19 March 1454 (*PROME*, XII, p. 256).

30 Storey, *End of Lancaster*, p. 139, calls them 'alien … to all constitutional precedents', but in 1454 there was no precedent. Watts, *Henry VI*, p. 305, n. 193, describes Margaret's proposed powers as 'awesomely wide', but they were the king's powers, which she was attempting to protect. Griffiths, p. 724, says the queen was 'bent on a course of breathtaking novelty'. While Margaret's situation was novel, it was not of her making; it had been brought about by Henry VI's collapse.

as regents for their husbands in Anjou and in Naples.[31] But there was a strong prejudice in England against a regent. Although Henry V had named his brother, the duke of Gloucester, as regent for the baby King Henry VI in 1422, his dying wish was overturned by the English council, and Gloucester became protector of the realm instead.

We do not know if Margaret's bill was formally presented in parliament or how much support for it she expected to receive. Robert Tanfield, her attorney general, was in London in February 1454 for the opening session.[32] Margaret arrived towards the end of the month and received a full civic reception from the mayor and aldermen.[33] The question of who should govern the country remained unresolved until Chancellor Kemp suddenly died on 22 March. Only the chancellor could use the great seal, and without it, government became impossible. A delegation of the lords traveled to Windsor in an unsuccessful attempt to elicit a response from King Henry. When it failed, they named the duke of York protector and defender of the realm on 27 March 1454, an implicitly masculine role in its military connotations.[34] In the final analysis, prejudice and recent precedent won the day, while York's title gave the lords a practical reason to reject Margaret's proposal. She could be regent, but she could not defend the realm. The duke of York could.

[103] Botoner (William Worcester) to John Paston, 8 June 1454 (excerpted) (Gairdner, *PL*, II, pp. 320–1)

Worshypfull Syr, and my gode maister, after dewe recomendacion, wyth alle my trewe servyce precedyng, lyke you wete that as to nouveltees, &c., the Prince shall be create at Wyndesour, uppon Pentecost Sunday, the Chaunceller, the Duc of Bokyngham, and manye othyre Lordys off astate, present wyth the Quene.

As to my Lord Yorke, he abydyth aboute Yorke tille Corpus Crist Feste be passyd and wyth grete worship ys there resseyved.

While parliament still debated the question of governance, the one thing everyone could agree upon was the creation of the infant Prince Edward as Prince of Wales and earl of Chester, with the further proviso that he would become regent for

---

31 The Empress Elizabeth was named to a regency council in 1439; Queen Eleanor of Portugal became regent with her brother-in-law in 1438; Mary of Guelders became regent of Scotland on the death of James II in 1460, and Queen Marie of Aragon was regent for Alfonso V on his frequent absences from the kingdom.
32 Myers, 'Household', p. 192. Earlier, in December, he had met with the king's councilors.
33 CLRO, Journal 5, fol. 150.
34 Maurer, pp. 107–10, for the role of gender in Margaret's failure.

his father when he reached his majority, should this be necessary.[35] A precedent existed. Henry V as Prince of Wales had governed very successfully in his father's name when the latter – Henry IV – became seriously ill.[36] For Margaret, the creation of Edward as Prince of Wales provided public assurance that there would be no challenge to her husband's throne and that her son's rights were recognized by the highest court in the land. York's acquiescence in this may have provided the *quid pro quo* for Margaret to accept him as protector. Ten days after York was formally appointed by patent on 3 April, noting that the prince had not yet been invested, a commission was issued to twenty-two bishops and magnates, including the duke of York, to see that it was done.[37] York was in the north when the ceremony eventually took place at Windsor on 9 June.[38] In the absence of King Henry and the Lord Protector, it was performed by a deputy, probably the duke of Buckingham, who had deputized for the king at the recent meeting of the Knights of the Garter, and it was witnessed by the earl of Salisbury as chancellor. Margaret was present, attended by bishops, lords and courtiers, as the baby prince was crowned with a gold circlet, while a gold ring was slipped over his tiny finger and a gold rod was placed in his small hand.

Margaret remained at Windsor after the investiture and took no further part in national politics. As far as is known, she did not attempt to oppose or undermine York's government. There is some slight evidence that she cooperated with him on occasion. On 5 October 1454, Pope Nicholas V ordered the archbishop of Canterbury, the bishops of Norwich and Hereford, and the archdeacon of Ely to mediate a dispute over tithes involving certain London parishes and their clergy. The queen, the duke of York as protector and the London common council had all written to the pope on what was an important issue. Margaret and the council also sent emissaries to Rome regarding the matter.[39]

[104] Edmund Clere to John Paston, 10 January 1455 (excerpted)
(Gairdner, *PL*, III, pp. 13–14)

Right welbeloved cosyn … Blessed be God, the Kyng is wel amended, and hath ben syn Cristemesday, and on Seint Johes day comaunded his awmener to

---

35 *PROME*, XII, p. 274.
36 Henry VI was never Prince of Wales, although he surely would have received the title had his father lived.
37 *CPR, 1452–61*, pp. 159, 171–2.
38 Whether York's absence was entirely due to a need to suppress rebellion in the north, or whether he wished to avoid the investiture itself and its assertion regarding the succession, is open to speculation.
39 *CPL, 1447–55*, pp. 165–6.

ride to Caunterbury wyth his offryng, and comaunded the secretarie to offre at Seint Edwards.

And on the Monday after noon the Queen came to him, and brought my Lord Prynce with her.[40] And then he askid what the Princes name was, and the Queen told him Edward; and than he hild up his hands and thankid God therof. And he seid he never knew til that tyme, nor wist not what was seid to him, nor wist not where he had be whils he hath be seke til now. And he askid who was godfaders, and the Queen told him, and he was wel apaid.

And she told him that the Cardinal was dede, and he seid he knew never therof til that tyme; and he seid oon of the wisist Lords in this land was dede.

And my Lord of Wynchestr and my Lord of Seint Jones were with him on the morow after Tweltheday, and he speke to hem as well as ever he did; and when thei come out thei wept for joye.

And he seith he is in charitee with all the world, and so he wold all the Lorsds were. And now he seith matyns of Our Lady and evesong, and herith his Masse devoutly ...

Henry VI came to his senses as abruptly as he had left them. Edmund Clere, an esquire in the royal household who served both Henry and Margaret, hastened to send the joyful news to his cousin.[41] Henry could not remember anything that had happened during his illness, and he had no understanding of just how long it had lasted. One of the first things he was told was that it was Christmas; he was sufficiently cognizant to send his almoner, Henry Sever,[42] off to Canterbury with his customary Christmas offering on the twenty-seventh. He may have thought initially that it was Christmas 1453. As his recovery proceeded, the king resumed his routine of daily devotions. For Henry, the only way to understand and accept the experience of his illness was by recourse to his faith.

Because he had been catatonic for so long, the persons who attended him observed him carefully over the next days, fearful that his recovery might not last.[43] They shielded him from stress and any sudden surprises that might set him

40 St John's (the Evangelist's) day fell on 27 December, a Friday in 1454. The Monday after would have been 30 December.
41 Edmund Clere of Ormesby in Norfolk was a king's esquire before Margaret came to England (*CPR, 1441–46*, p. 229). He remained in the royal household until at least 1458 (Gairdner, *PL*, III, p. 126). Gairdner's dating of this letter was off by one day. Clere stated that he wrote it on the 'Thursday after Twelfthday', which in 1455 would have been 10 January. Clere died in 1463 (Richmond, 'Elizabeth Clere', p. 262, n. 35).
42 For whom, see above, pp. 150, 152.
43 The lords designated by the council to attend the king (though not always in personal attendance) were his confessor, the bishop of Winchester; his Tudor half-brothers, the earls of Richmond and Pembroke; Viscount Beaumont, Lord Cromwell, Lord Beauchamp of Powick and Lord St Amand (*PPC*, VI, p. 222).

off again. Margaret's role was key in this. She had kept the court and household functioning, and everyone looked to her for guidance. She proceeded with caution, waiting a full five days to make sure Henry was sufficiently recovered before she introduced him to the fourteen-month-old son whom he had never known. By then, Henry had some inkling of just how long he had been 'absent' – astonishing news in itself – but there were important developments of which he would gradually be informed.

Henry had, of course, known of his wife's pregnancy. He had awarded a lifetime annuity to Richard Tunstall, the esquire who formally notified him of it, while he was attending the parliament at Reading.[44] But he had not been aware at the time of his son's birth. When Henry learned that the prince had been born on St Edward the Confessor's Day – a good omen – and named for the saint, he was delighted and grateful. He observed with wonder and amazement, and perhaps also with regret, that so much had happened while he was sick. His next question involved the child's baptism, the ritual that established his place in the Christian community and, ultimately, his soul's place in heaven. When Margaret told him that Prince Edward's godparents were Cardinal Kemp, the duke of Somerset and the duchess of Buckingham, Henry was again well pleased. He was as yet unaware that Kemp was dead and that Somerset was imprisoned in the Tower. When Margaret carefully broke the news to him that the Cardinal had died, Henry took it calmly, for Kemp was well-advanced in years.

It was a critical piece of news, however, for Kemp's death had precipitated the establishment of York's protectorate. The protectorate itself would not have surprised Henry; there had been one during his minority. But he might not have been pleased to find out that the protector was the duke of York, with whom he had been at odds immediately prior to his illness, the latest time of which he had clear memory.

Henry's confessor William Waynflete, bishop of Winchester, visited him just over a week later, on 7 January. Henry would have expected to see him, and Waynflete could discuss his illness with him, pray with him and help him to come to terms with all that had happened. At some point Henry would have asked about the duke of Somerset. Where was his favorite; why had the duke not come to attend on him? This would have taken some explaining, perhaps by Margaret or perhaps by Waynflete. Rivalry among the lords was nothing new, but Henry found it upsetting that it had become more bitter during his illness. While it is reasonable to conclude that efforts were made to shield Henry from too much disturbing information, there would have been no way to hide it completely. His

44 *PROME*, XII, p. 423.

observation that he was at odds with no one reflected his wish that all the lords might share in such a feeling, though he sadly knew that they did not.

With King Henry's recovery, the duke of York's protectorate came to an end. The duke of Somerset was released from the Tower and restored to favor. This proved to be a prescription for violence as York placed no faith in a proposal to arbitrate their differences. He withdrew from court and together with the Neville earls of Salisbury and Warwick set about raising an army. They confronted the king and his entourage at St Albans on 22 May 1455, while Henry was en route to a meeting of a great council at Leicester. The Yorkists demanded that Henry surrender the duke of Somerset to them for judgment. This was tantamount to usurping the king's authority, and Henry refused. Battle ensued, in which Somerset and the earl of Northumberland, who was the Nevilles' enemy, were killed and the king himself was slightly injured. Following their victory, the Yorkists immediately submitted themselves to the king, pledged their loyalty and conveyed him back to London in suitable style.[45] Despite the façade of normality, the reins of power had changed hands. In the aftermath of battle, Henry could not be regarded as a free agent.

The victors celebrated the weeklong Whitsun festivities, and King Henry remained in London long enough to give royal authority to the duke of York's changes in council personnel. The Yorkists and their affinity took over the offices that had been held by the deceased, or by men loyal to King Henry who had escaped the battle. In June the royal family withdrew to Windsor, and then to Margaret's dower lands at Hertford Castle. York stationed himself in adjacent Ware to keep an eye on Henry. Parliament met in July. The Yorkists' parliamentary absolution from all blame, with the further stipulation that nothing more was to be said about the battle, did nothing to alleviate tension in London. How could it, when Yorkist soldiers patrolled the streets fully armed and ferried weapons up and down the Thames?[46] Unrest simmered throughout the country, culminating in outbreaks of violence in the West,[47] while rumors surfaced that 'some men feared' the king might again be ill.[48] On 17 November 1455, at the beginning of a more sparsely attended second session of parliament and in the king's absence,

---

45   Armstrong, 'Politics and St Albans', still offers the best account of the battle.
46   A contemporary report describes the situation. A proclamation 'in the king's name' forbade the bearing of arms; its effect goes unmentioned. In a postscript the writer asks that his report be destroyed (Gairdner, *PL*, III, pp. 43–5).
47   See above, p. 138, for the Courtenay–Bonville feud.
48   Gairdner, *PL*, III, p. 50. The visits to Henry by three surgeons and the physician, Gilbert Kymer, could have occurred for a number of reasons, proving nothing in particular (see above, pp. 19–20 and nn. 12–13).

the lords appointed York as protector for a second time, after intense lobbying by a commons delegation led by one of the duke's councilors.[49]

Margaret's thoughts regarding these events, though not explicitly known, are not difficult to imagine. If she had earlier felt apprehension over where the lords' antipathies might lead, the Yorkists' resort to force of arms at St Albans, which amounted to treason despite their protests to the contrary, gave her a genuine reason to fear York.[50] St Albans and its aftermath marked a turning point.

[105] John Bocking to Sir John Fastolf, 9 February 1456[51] (excerpted)
(Gairdner, *PL*, III, pp. 74–5)

[On] this day my Lordes York and Warwik comen to the Parlement in a good aray, to the nombre of iij^c (300) men, all jakkid and in brigantiens, and noo lord elles, wherof many men mervailed. It was seid on Saterday my Lord shuld have ben discharged this same day. And this day was seide, but if he hadde come stronge, he shuld have bene distrussid; and no man knoweth or can sey that ony prese may be hadde by whom, for men thinken verily there is no man able to take ony suche enterprinse.

The Kyng, as it was tolde me by a grete man, wolde have hym chief and princepall counceller, and soo to be called hise chef counceller and lieutenant as longe as hit shuld lyke the Kyng; and hise patent to be made in that forme, and not soo large as it is by Parlement. But soome men thinken it wil ner can otherwise bee; and men speke and deyne moche matere of the comyng this day in suche array to Westminster. And the Lordes speken this day in the Parlement of a greet gleymyng sterre that but late hathe be seen diverse tymes, merveilous in apperyng. The resumpsion, men truste, shall forthe, and my Lordes of Yorkes first power of protectorship stande, and elles not, etc. The Quene is a grete and strong labourid woman, for she spareth noo peyne to sue hire thinges to an intent and conclusion to hir power.

York's second protectorate lasted just over three months. Bocking's letter establishes that by February 1456 the duke had gotten wind of the tenuous nature of his position. Rumors abounded. Some men predicted that he would be discharged outright, but one eminent personage told Bocking discreetly (we may imagine the

---

49 The events leading up to York's second protectorate have spawned considerable discussion. Lander, 'Henry VI', took a skeptical – and cynical – view of the whole affair. Others who have weighed in, accepting some of his observations while reaching separate conclusions about what it all meant, are Griffiths, pp. 752–6; Johnson, *Duke Richard*, pp. 168–70; Watts, *Henry VI*, pp. 319–21; Maurer, pp. 119–23.

50 When Margaret learned of St Albans, she took refuge with Prince Edward in the Tower of London. This was a measure of her fear (Watts, *Henry VI*, p. 317, n. 246).

51 This letter was written on the Monday before Shrove Tuesday, 9 February in 1456.

hushed voice imparting his 'privileged knowledge') that York would be retained by the king, perhaps as chief councilor, but without the powers he had held as protector. On the day of Bocking's letter York and the earl of Warwick arrived for the opening of the third session of parliament backed by several hundred armed men. This in itself was alarming, to the point that other lords stayed away; the Yorkists' excuse – perhaps originating with Warwick – that they did so to keep themselves from being arrested only added to the confusion.[52] No one who witnessed their display could imagine how they *could* be arrested or who might have the nerve to try it.[53] Which may have been the point: to demonstrate by a show of force that York and the Nevilles, who had obtained their ascendancy through force, were prepared to use it again if faced by opposition. As luck – or misfortune – would have it, a comet appeared in the night sky. To the medieval mind, these celestial wanderers were harbingers of great events both good and ill; they heralded profound changes. The lords debated what this one 'meant', but its appearance only added to their unease.

In addition to anxieties regarding the second protectorate and York himself – and it seems clear that many had genuine misgivings – there was a further matter of great concern. In the previous sessions of parliament, the commons had pushed for a far-reaching resumption, with York's support. Resumption, particularly when it involved restricting the king's right to grant exemption, threatened the lords' wealth and power. If men associated the passage of an act of resumption with the continuation of York's protectorate, as suggested by Bocking's letter, some lords may have concluded that the duke had betrayed his trust and his own class. It also created a mutual interest between the lords and members of the royal household, who stood to be pricked with the same knife. In early 1456 there was a confluence of concerns and interests regarding the resumption that, at least for some of the participants, intersected with their misgivings regarding York and his protectorate.[54]

Margaret's role in what ensued has remained opaque, thanks to Bocking's letter, if not entirely misunderstood. Although she was deeply involved, this was

52 'Distressed' often meant 'attacked', but in this case it is difficult to see just who might dare to attack York. With talk of his imminent dismissal making the rounds, it is more likely that an official form of action is here intimated, i.e., an arrest.

53 Henry VI never did arrest the duke of York, although he could have done so on assorted charges at any time from 1450 onwards. Handling the highest-ranking lord of the realm was a delicate matter. The trick was to manage him without provoking worse trouble: a balancing act that ultimately failed.

54 'Benet's Chronicle', p. 216, blames the lords' opposition to the resumption for the ending of York's second protectorate, but Watts, *Henry VI*, pp. 332–3, is surely correct in linking this issue to their 'deep-seated concern about both the fact and consequences of York's usurpation of the royal power'.

no single-minded effort to seize power for herself. Instead, it was she who was lobbied, 'labored' to use her influence. Assuming that it was people in the royal household and those at court who did the lobbying, Margaret was being urged to encourage the disaffected lords in parliament, together with any of the commons who had household ties, to hold the line on the resumption and to resist passing the bill until it could be modified, or until King Henry was prepared to come to parliament to veto it or change it in the interests of those whom it affected. Margaret set out to do this to the fullest extent that she could ('to her power'). As queen, she was a natural conduit between the lords and the king, and some of them undoubtedly turned to her for assistance. York had made it obvious on 9 February that he was prepared to meet opposition with armed force. He could not be safely opposed outright. But Margaret could persuade men to rally around the king, to whom loyalty remained strong and whose authority stood above all else. To make use of Henry's authority, however, he had to be brought to Westminster. Henry had come to rely on Margaret, and he listened to her advice. Her concern at this point was to stop the erosion of the crown's power, and she was among those urging him to take action.

Henry came to parliament, and on 25 February 1456 he formally relieved York of office, with the advice and assent of the lords as required by the terms of his appointment. The duke's response was initially passive. He attended the great council meeting at Coventry in October 1456 when King Henry reorganized his council. Henry greeted York courteously – he was not prepared to provoke the duke – but he did not reinstate him in any capacity. Margaret was less discreet. One of the Pastons' correspondents reported that 'my Lord of York ... is departed ageyn in right good conceyt with the King, but not in gret conceyt with the Whene [Queen]'.[55]

[106] Richard Southwell to John Paston, 6 October [1458] (excerpted)
(Gairdner, *PL*, III, p. 4)

I beseche you to remembr that I have aforetyme b(en) accused unto the Kings Highnesse and the Quenes for owyng my pore gode will and service unto my Lord of York and other, &c. Wherof I suppose that Thomas Bagham is remembred that I brought hym oones from my Lady a purs and v marc therin, and to Ser Phelipp Wenteworth an other and a Cs. (100s) therin for their gode will and advise therin to my Lady and all us that were appelled for that cause, notwithstanding the King wrote to my Lord by the meanes of the Duc of Somersette, that we shuld be avoyded from hym, &c., and within this ij yer we wer in like wise laboured ageyns to the Quene, so that she wrote to my Lord to avoyde us, saiying that the King

55 Gairdner, *PL*, III, p. 108.

and she coude nor myght in no wyse be assured of hym and my Lady as long as
we were aboute hym, with muche other thing, as may be sufficiently proved by the
Quenes writing under herr own signett and signe manuell, the whiche I shewd to
my Lord of Caunterbury and other Lordes, &c.[56]

Richard Southwell had been a servant of the duke and duchess of Norfolk,
the lord and lady of his letter, since at least 1448 and probably earlier.[57] He was
named escheator for Norfolk in 1455 under York's second protectorate.[58] John
Mowbray, duke of Norfolk, had been York's strongest supporter in the latter's
bid for power in 1453 and was still closely associated with him in 1455. Southwell's
purpose in writing to Paston was to obtain the latter's aid in gaining the favor
of a third party; he was concerned that royal hostility towards him on account
of his association with the duke of York as Norfolk's servant would stand in his
way. It appears that the duchess of Norfolk and others of Norfolk's affinity had
thought it prudent to influence (or bribe) men close to the king and queen in an
attempt to regain royal favor, possibly in 1456, when York lost the protectorate
and it looked as if he would be permanently estranged from the court. Sir Philip
Wentworth had become the king's carver by 1452, which brought him into daily
contact with Henry VI and probably Margaret as well. In 1453 he received a
wine flagon from the queen.[59] Wentworth was apparently not averse to using his
influence on behalf of whosoever was prepared to pay.[60] Thomas Bagham may be
identified with Thomas Babham, a yeoman of the queen's household from 1445,
who became the yeoman of her robes by 1458.[61] The duke of Somerset, cited as
the king's message-bearer, would not have been Edmund Beaufort, York's old
rival, who was killed at St Albans, but his son Henry.

According to Southwell, Henry VI had warned Norfolk that if he wished to
regain, or maintain, influence at court, it would be wise to stop identifying himself
too closely with York. He also refers to a specific incident by which he and some

---

56   Ibid., pp. 3–4, dated this letter to 1454, but N. Davis, ed., *Paston Letters and Papers of the Fifteenth
     Century*, II, EETS, s.s. 21 (Oxford, 1976), p. 176, has convincingly argued for the later date of
     1458. We note also that in autumn 1454 the king was still catatonic and Edmund Beaufort, duke
     of Somerset, was in prison. The incidents referred to by Southwell predate his letter.

57   *CPR, 1446–52*, p. 236.

58   Castor, *King, Crown and Duchy*, p. 180.

59   Wedgwood, pp. 934–5; Myers, 'Jewels', p. 224. According to Wedgwood, Wentworth was overseas
     during 1457–58. This supports the suggestion that the relevant incidents predate 1458.

60   Besides the payment of 100s from the duchess of Norfolk, Wentworth had received money
     from the duchess of Suffolk in 1453 for helping her recover possession of some disputed manors
     (for which, see below, p. 210 and n. 62).

61   *CPR, 1452–61*, pp. 421, 462. Margaret gave him a silver cup as a marriage gift in 1448–49 (E
     101/410/2).

other men had incensed the queen, though not necessarily in connection with the duke of York. Margaret wrote directly to Norfolk, in her name and Henry's, advising (or ordering) him to get rid of Southwell and the others because she could not trust him as long as they were in his service.

Southwell and his fellows had been 'laboured ageyns to the Quene', but by whom? The answer may lie in a land dispute. Norfolk had long claimed that two manors owned by the duke of Suffolk rightfully belonged to him.[62] In 1453 he had wrested them from Alice, the widowed duchess of Suffolk, by main force. Although she shortly got them back with Wentworth's help, Norfolk named Thomas Bourgchier, archbishop of Canterbury, and his brother Henry, Viscount Bourgchier (who were his wife's brothers), and a John Southwell as his feoffees in these manors. In the summer of 1455, after the Yorkists' victory at St Albans, they presented a petition setting out his claims. At that time the Bourgchiers were well-placed to seek favor from a Yorkist-controlled government: Thomas had followed the earl of Salisbury as chancellor in March 1455, while Henry became treasurer after St Albans. Alice of Suffolk had been one of the queen's closest friends, and although she did not come to court after her husband's disgrace and death in 1450, Margaret would not have looked kindly on any of Norfolk's men who tried to intimidate her. Lawyers representing the crown joined Duchess Alice's attorneys in fighting the petition, and Norfolk, whose claim was weak, lost his case. In 1456, Richard Southwell, presumably acting on Norfolk's orders and in his capacity as escheator, once again seized the manors from Alice. She petitioned for restitution, and they were restored to her after the shake-up in government in the autumn of 1456 that saw the Bourgchier brothers dismissed from office.

Southwell apparently succeeded in re-establishing his credibility at court. Ironically, he was appointed to commissions to enquire into the lands and goods of York's chamberlain, William Oldhall, after the latter was attainted for treason in 1459.[63] He also prospered under the Yorkist kings, receiving grants and commissions throughout the reigns of Edward IV and Richard III long after his patron, the duke of Norfolk, was dead.[64] Duchess Eleanor lived on until 1474.

Although the remaining two letters cannot be dated with certainty, the political nature of their content (despite its vagueness in the second) dares the historian to place them. When we found that we could not agree upon dates, we decided to let our separate arguments stand. As a result, these letters appear outside the

---

62   For the following account of the land dispute, see Castor, *King, Crown and Duchy*, p. 179 and n. 111, citing BL, Egerton Roll 8779 mm. 4, 9, for Alice's payment to Wentworth.

63   *CPR, 1452–61*, pp. 561–2, 604, 606.

64   *CPR, 1461–67*, pp. 33, 45, for the first of these in summer 1461, followed by a great many more straight through to 1483–84 (*CPR, 1476–85*, pp. 397, 490).

chronology of this chapter and in no particular relation to each other. We hope they demonstrate that history is an argumentative process, always subject to challenge.

[107] Richard Neville, Earl of Salisbury, to the Prior of Arbury, 7 March [1454 or 1458?]
(BL, Cotton Vespasian F xiii (i), art. 64)

[Addressed on dorse: To the reverent father in god and my right especiall and tendre frende the priour of Erdebury]

Reverent father in God and my right especial and tendre frende. I recomaunde me to yow, and in my right hertie and feithfull wise thanke yow of al your true and grete diligences and undelaied devoire that ye have many tymes put yow in at my special request and prayer to that that myght serve to theobteignyng of my right fervent desire to knowe and fele the good ladyship of the Quene oure sovereign lady to me hir humble true servaunt, and in especial of your grete labour in that bihalve sith my last speche with yow, as by your lettres brought me by the berer of thies. I conceive at large wherin among othre thing is contenede your desire and exhortacion me nat to varye from that I have promitted, hertofore right largely by yow openned to hire said highnesse, and that I see ye be nat dishonorede of your reportes in that bihalve; wherunto will ye wit that of eny promysse that I have made unto yow at eny tyme for my declaracon unto the said highnesse, and to have and stand in the favoure of hire good grace, for the whiche oon of my moost erthly desires I pray yow as tendrely as I can to contynue therin your good will and devoir for my singular consolacon, I shal at al tymes kepe yow or eny other that labour for me to that entent undishonored and nat to varie fro my said promisse with Godes mercie. And as toward the blessed disposicon of the said good grace ...⁶⁵ unto that that myght serve to rest [peace] and unitee comprised in hire gracioux lettres late directed to my lordes of the counseill, wherof to my grete joy I have herd and God shal I doubt nat be pleased therwith and prospre hire hie estate and the said lordes nat oonly, bot also al thoo whome the matiers of the said blessed lettres touchen owe humbly and lowly to yeve laude and thanke to hire said highnesse therfore, as that I doo in my moost humble wise as soo on my bihalve as hire true servaunt with al myn hert and service, in that that mowe be to hir hie pleasure I pray yow to declare me unto hire said grace.

And where in your said lettres it is expressed that ye have herd language [rumor] of accusacions of right hie estates to bie made by my lord of Yorke, my son of Warwice and me in materes that have nat bee disclosed herebifore, to their grete rebuke and etc., truely it is to my grete mervail by whate coloure reason or grounde eny such language by eny personne erthly myght bie utred or saied, for as for myn own partie as I wol answere to Our Lord I nevere ymagined, thought ne saied eny

65 There is a small hole in the manuscript here.

suche matter or eny thing like thereunto in my dayes. And in like wise I dare well say for my said lord and son as ferre as ever I herd or in eny wise knowe unto their honire, as I doubt nat thai wol at al tymes right largely declaire theim silf. And therfore, therin or in eny othere concernyng my trouth I pray yow alway to aunswere largely for me. And if there bee thing that I may doo fo your wele certifieth me, and ye shal to the performing therof fynde me right hertly disposed as Our Lord knoweth, which have yow ever in His blessed keping. Written at London the vij day of Marche.

      Your good frende Richard
          Erl of Salisbury

This letter from the earl of Salisbury is controversial. Dated only to 7 March, but lacking a year, the matters it touches upon become frustratingly opaque.[66] The letter can be divided into two parts: the first deals with efforts by the prior of Arbury to obtain Margaret's favor for Salisbury; the second, with disturbing rumors the prior had heard involving the earl, his brother-in-law the duke of York, and his son the earl of Warwick. Arbury was a small house of Augustinian canons a little north of Kenilworth and close to Nuneaton Priory, in the heart of the queen's Midlands holdings.[67] When Salisbury wrote to the prior, he did so as a private person: the favor he sought was for him personally. He trusted the prior and considered him a desirable intermediary, whom the queen likewise trusted. The prior had already commended Salisbury to Margaret on previous occasions, most recently following a personal meeting with the earl. Either during that meeting or earlier, Salisbury made a promise or gave an undertaking for the prior to convey to her. But the prior had recently become uneasy; endorsing promises for someone who failed to keep them was a serious matter: a 'false' man was dishonored, and so was anyone who supported his 'falsehood'.[68] In his letter Salisbury declared himself the queen's 'true servant' and insisted that his word was good. He asked the prior to continue to seek her favor.

Salisbury wrote from London, in a year when Margaret communicated with the council. He refers to her letters regarding 'rest and unity', but when and why would they have carried the weight that he ascribes to them? His praise indicates that he saw himself as one of their beneficiaries. We cannot assume that Margaret *wrote* because she was far away. Since the queen had no place on the king's council,

---

66   Widely separated attempts to date it are unsatisfactory. C.L. Kingsford, *English Historical Literature in the Fifteenth Century* (1913), p. 213, dated it to 1455; Hicks, *Warwick* (1998), pp. 155–6, to 1459. Maurer (2003), pp. 216–21, discussed and dismissed both. Pollard, *Warwick* (2007), p. 205, suggested 1457. It is easier to pick holes in an argument than to construct one that is watertight!

67   VCH: *Warwick*, II, pp. 89ff. See above, pp. 24–6, for Nuneaton.

68   As in Gough's involvement in the Camoys ransom; see above, p. 128.

she would not have attended a council meeting, and any communication from her would have been by letter, regardless of where she was.

The rumors reported by the prior explain Salisbury's urgency: he answered immediately, his reply to be carried by the bearer who had brought him the prior's message. In high dudgeon, the earl proclaimed his own innocence and ventured to assert his relatives' as well, though he cautiously added that they would surely speak for themselves.

We have postulated two possible years for this letter. One of them is 1454, when William Woodcock was prior of Arbury.[69] Salisbury attended council meetings on 6, 9 and 13 February and on 12 March.[70] Although he was absent when Margaret's letters arrived, he would have learned of them almost immediately. The queen's circumstances are compatible. King Henry was catatonic; many lords were arming, and Margaret was contending to become regent. In an atmosphere of insecurity, suspicion and rumor would have been common currency. It is significant that Salisbury never mentions the king in *any* connection. He asserts his loyalty to Margaret alone; he does not seek her intercession with the king. Indeed, the council seems to be the focus of authority. Henry's complete absence from the letter is perhaps the strongest argument for 1454.

The council meeting of autumn 1453 provides context. Its explicit purpose was to set 'rest and union' among the lords, preparatory to dealing with the overarching matter of who would govern the country while King Henry was ill. Instead, rivalries escalated. Although Margaret saw her regency as the solution, it complicated matters by presenting an alternative to the duke of York, who by lineage alone was the default *male* choice to head an interim government. Letters from Margaret pledging her commitment to the desirable, though elusive, goal of 'rest and unity' would have been welcome as parliament met in February/March and the lords debated the question. Their recognition in parliament of Prince Edward as Prince of Wales likewise would have reassured the queen. Both were bargaining moves.

In this scenario, Salisbury first sought Margaret's favor simply because she was the queen, whose good ladyship might prove helpful in many different situations. On at least one occasion he invited her to hunt in his park of Ware.[71] In early 1454 his loyalty remained unquestioned: had he not stood with Henry VI against York

---

69 We do not know when Woodcock assumed office. His predecessor, William Cotton, had been appointed in 1439. Woodcock resigned in 1456, when he was succeeded by John Bromley (VCH: *Warwick*, II, p. 91).

70 C 81/1546 mm. 73, 74, 75, 76 and 78, when he signed warrants. A meeting is recorded for 2 March, when the council received a petition. No signatures exist for that date (m. 77).

71 In 1448, if our dating of Margaret's letter to Salisbury's parker is accepted. See above, pp. 164–5.

at Dartford in 1452? But in the early 1450s the Nevilles suffered losses as a result of official actions, and in summer 1453 violence broke out between Salisbury's younger sons and the Percies of Northumberland.[72] Meanwhile, Salisbury's eldest son Warwick was at odds with the duke of Somerset, York's rival. If, as seems likely, the Yorkist alliance came about through a convergence of interests and opportunism, it is equally probable that Salisbury initially tried to play both sides of the game. This meant assuring the queen of his continuing devotion, and a specific promise – perhaps to support the queen's and prince's interests and to oppose any attempt to obstruct them – at a time when word got out that she intended to be made regent, even as Salisbury was raising troops to come to London: an act that itself called for loyal protestations. Woodcock's suspicion that the earl was getting too thick with York would account for his misgivings.[73]

Several questions arise. Did Salisbury initiate or strongly endorse the lords' decision to recognize the infant Edward as Prince of Wales, in keeping with his promise to the queen? Although it is generally believed that Salisbury became chancellor because he was acceptable to York, was his appointment agreeable to Margaret as well? This is worth considering, since traditionally, with rare exception, the chancellor was a bishop. And, since York was eventually *chosen* over Margaret to head the government, did she not at some point have to *agree* to the choice and withdraw her own candidacy? A recalcitrant queen would have been awkward, and it appears that she acquiesced gracefully. Was Salisbury's appointment as a perceived brake on York the condition for her acquiescence?

The second part of Salisbury's letter addresses the prior's report of rumors that he, York and Warwick would be accusing certain high-ranking persons of shameful things previously undisclosed. There are compelling reasons to believe that this has nothing to do with the first part of the letter. Not once is Margaret mentioned. Salisbury evinces no particular need to reassure *her*, nor does he invoke her name again at the letter's end, as he surely would have done if the rumors concerned her. Instead, he closes his letter by asking the prior to speak for him in this or any other matter impinging on his honor and makes the standard offer of reciprocity. The corollary to this is that the persons 'of hie estate' could not have been the king, queen or prince. Slanders against the royal family were treasonable; at the very least, such rumors would have elicited further declarations of loyalty, not just to Margaret, but to King Henry and the prince as well. And would Salisbury have thought Margaret amenable to Woodcock's further

---

72   Hicks, *Warwick*, pp. 76ff, 86–9.
73   Stodeley's newsletter of 19 January gives the impression that York and the Nevilles were acting in concert (Gairdner, *PL*, II, pp. 297–8). Salisbury might equally well have pledged not to support a coup by York.

assurances – or her letters to the council so comforting to him – if she thought he would impugn the king's, the prince's or her own honor?

Who, then, was the target of the accusations? Although the letter indicates persons, plural, *one* person is an excellent candidate in 1454: the chancellor, Cardinal Kemp. Circumstantial evidence favors him. When the duke of York took charge of the council in autumn 1453, he had the duke of Somerset arrested and thrown into the Tower. As chancellor, Kemp had been acting with Somerset to keep the government going after King Henry fell ill, and he may have opposed Somerset's arrest.[74] He also appears to have been reluctant to appoint York to open parliament.[75] Years later, William Worcestre claimed to have evidence of a plot shortly before Kemp's death to remove him from office.[76] Stodeley's January newsletter reported that Kemp had been arming his servants to serve as bodyguards. He clearly went in fear.[77] If the target was Kemp, the charges could have included reasons for removing him as chancellor. Whether the rumors were reliable or not, Salisbury had been implicated, and he wanted the prior to deny his involvement in any and all situations in which the matter arose.

An objection may be made that in 1454, York and the Neville earls were not yet automatically linked in the public's perception. That said, they could still be seen as acting together, as when Stodeley reported their preparations to come to London in force.[78] Prior Woodcock resigned in 1456. If he interceded for Salisbury in 1454, we may wonder: in the aftermath of St Albans and York's second protectorate, with the restoration of royal authority and Margaret's reasserted prominence, did he find himself dishonored?

Another possible date for Salisbury's letter is 1458. By that time the prior of Arbury was John Bromley, who had been prior of Ranton in Staffordshire since 1433 and became prior of Arbury in 1456.[79] Margaret's principal dower lands were in Staffordshire, and she could have become acquainted with him at any time after 1446. Salisbury's statement that the prior had been his advocate to the queen 'many tymes' may have no political connotation. Margaret's correspondence

---

74   The Yorkist-leaning 'Benet's Chronicle', p. 211, described him as Somerset's chief friend at that time.

75   Parliament was prorogued three days from its intended opening, and Kemp raised the question of who should preside at the last possible moment (Johnson, pp. 129–30). The warrant of 13 February that made York the king's lieutenant was signed by Salisbury, among others, but not by Kemp (C 81/1546/76).

76   W. Worcestre, *Itineraries of William Worcestre*, ed. J.H. Harvey (Oxford, 1969), p. 153. Worcester, writing in 1478, implicates the duke of Norfolk in the plot. Norfolk had spoken against Somerset on York's behalf in November 1453.

77   Gairdner, *PL*, II, p. 296, for the bodyguards. See Maurer, pp. 103–4, for Kemp.

78   See above, n. 73.

79   VCH: *Stafford*, III, p. 255; *Warwick*, II, p. 91.

establishes that in the early years her primary concern was to act as 'good lady' to just about everyone. If Salisbury was seeking the favor of an office or land grant for one of his tenants or clients, or even for himself in a local matter, he may have used Bromley, who was known to Margaret, as his intermediary.

A great council was in session in February/March 1458. King Henry had explicitly ordered the council to find a solution to the animosities engendered by the battle of St Albans and its aftermath between York, Salisbury and Warwick on one hand, and the sons of Edmund, duke of Somerset, the earl of Northumberland and Lord Clifford, on the other.[80] Fifteen members of the council were named as arbitrators: their award was to be final and would be announced by the king in a 'loveday' to end the strife that threatened to paralyze government business. Surprisingly, Salisbury was among them.[81] But his standing with King Henry was different from that of York. Henry trusted him; despite Salisbury's presence at St Albans, he had retained him as a councilor after ending York's protectorate in 1456 and confirmed him in the influential and lucrative post of chief steward for the Northern Parts of the duchy of Lancaster.[82] Henry had specifically sent for Salisbury to attend the great council in November 1457 when he tried and failed to reconcile his lords.[83] Salisbury's letter fits into the context of the negotiations leading up to the loveday settlement. He was concerned to retain Margaret's goodwill because he knew that to lose her favor was to lose the king's.

But what had Prior Bromley heard that so alarmed him and caused Salisbury to deny his involvement? The point here, surely, is not that Salisbury was going to make accusations, but that accusations *were being made* in his name, together with those of York and Warwick. The key sentence in Salisbury's letter is that the prior has 'herd language of accusacions of right hie estates to bie made by my lord of Yorke, my son of Warrwice and me in materes that have nat bee disclosed herebifore to their grete rebuke and etc.'. *Someone* was accusing Salisbury, York and Warwick of raising damaging questions that had not been brought into the open before but were now being aired in the context of the arbitration. What were they? That Prince Edward was not King Henry's son? That Henry surrounded himself with incompetent councilors and relied too heavily on the queen while excluding the duke of York, who had a right to a place in council? That Henry had not taken reprisals against the French in the wake of the attack on Sandwich? Any or all of these? We do not know. None of these questions

---

80 *Reg. Whethamstede*, I, pp. 296–7.
81 *CCR, 1454–61*, pp. 281–2, for bonds posted by the arbitrators to the chief justices as a standard pledge to turn up and judge fairly.
82 Somerville, *Duchy of Lancaster*, p. 421.
83 *CPR, 1452–61*, p. 428.

was new, and they would form part of Yorkist propaganda against Margaret after 1458. What was new was that Salisbury, York and Warwick were being accused of raising them. Fearful of the consequences if such untrue accusations reached the queen's ears, Salisbury refuted the suggestion that they could ever have originated with him, or with York or Warwick to the best of his knowledge, but they must answer for themselves.

Bromley was concerned for his own standing with the queen since he had conveyed a promise from Salisbury to Margaret, possibly in 1456 when Salisbury was retained on the king's council. What that promise was we do not know, perhaps that he had put the past behind him and that he was, and would remain, loyal to the crown. Salisbury assured Bromley, and asked him to reassure Margaret, that he would not go back on his word.

In the end Salisbury did well out of the loveday settlement: unlike York and Warwick, he was not required to pay compensation.[84] Although he threw in his lot with the duke of York at the end of 1458, in March he was keeping his options open and needed to retain Margaret's favor.

Salisbury applauded Margaret's 'gracioux lettres late directed to my lordes of the counseill' on the theme of 'rest [peace] and unity'. The suggestion that Margaret was actively promoting the loveday settlement and that her letters to the council were to this end flies in the face of tradition, of course, but she is reported to have influenced the king in its favor. John Whethamstede, the abbot of St Albans, whose account of Henry's judgment reads like a verbatim report, acknowledges Margaret's part in the loveday's inception and success. According to him, the settlement was accomplished 'at the oft repeated request and insistence of the queen, whose heartfelt wish was for us to do this; she has been, and still is, desirous of the said unity, love and accord, and wishes for it, as strongly as she possibly can'.[85]

[108] Queen Margaret to Various, a Circular Letter
(BL, Add. MS 46,846, fol. 33)

By the Quene
Trusty and welbeloved: We wol and charge you that, all excusacions cessing and other occupacions y-left, ye shape yow for to be with us in all haste possible for certeine causes that moven us, which shalbe declared unto yowe at your commyng. Yeven, etc.

---

84 *CPR, 1452–61*, p. 424; *CCR, 1454–61*, p. 369. York was to pay 5,000 marks to the widowed duchess of Somerset and Somerset's heir; Warwick, 1,000 marks to the young Lord Clifford. York and the Nevilles were to contribute £45 a year to the abbey at St Albans for masses to be said for the souls of those who were slain and buried there.
85 *Reg. Whetehamstede*, I, p. 301.

This letter presents us with a conundrum: we simply do not know when Margaret wrote it or what it was about, although a few things can be established. It is a circular letter to various people – we do not know how many. They probably belonged to different social ranks. Letter greetings usually reflected the recipients' status. Had this been a homogeneous group consisting solely of lords (secular or clerical), for example, the greeting would have been rather more elaborate. The letter's admonition to attend the queen in all haste, with no delays or excuses, is a standard summons, but in this case Margaret really did expect the people she had addressed to show up promptly. Whatever she wanted was of considerable importance to her. Although the bearers of messages were routinely expected to convey their import when the sender did not want to write it down, that is not indicated here. Margaret says that her reasons will only be revealed upon the recipients' arrival in her presence, so she intended to tell them herself. This suggests a matter of some political sensitivity. Since the letter says nothing about coming defensibly arrayed or accompanied by armed troops, it rules out an impending military situation. Margaret needed support, but not military action. King Henry's name is not associated with the summons, so it belongs to a time when he was either incapacitated or when Margaret was not in his company but had his agreement to what she was doing.

When might this letter have been written? Possibly at the time of Margaret's quest for a regency, at the end of 1453 or the beginning of 1454 when she was preparing her bill.[86] In these circumstances she may have appealed to men outside the royal circle whom she believed she could call on to support her effort. She needed to keep her intentions quiet until she was ready, hence the deliberate opacity of her letter.

If not to 1453–54, the letter may date to 1456. In May, following King Henry's dismissal of the duke of York as protector, Margaret retired with Prince Edward to her castle at Tutbury in Staffordshire. If, as tradition has it, she had her sights set on assuming direct personal authority at this time, her behavior in leaving London is inexplicable. The king was the only source of legitimate government, anointed by God with spiritual and temporal authority. But Henry had been totally incapacitated for a significant period, and in the autumn of 1455 when he did not attend parliament, it had been rumored that he was again ill. Whatever Henry's actual state of mind between August 1455 and February 1456, he had withdrawn from the political world. Neither Margaret nor anyone else, including the king and the council, knew if his illness would strike again, and precautions had to be taken against that possibility.

86   See above, pp. 200–2.

The country required an alternative source of *royal* authority to confer legitimacy on conciliar rule. The baby Prince of Wales was, after his father, the only surviving member of the direct Lancastrian line; it would be many years before he could be protector in anything but name. There was, however, one other person who had been crowned and anointed by God: the queen. Margaret, as Queen Mother, could act in conjunction with a council in her son's name.[87] If a policy was being considered of vesting royal authority in the Prince of Wales as a surrogate for his father, with Margaret in a political role, it was advisable for her to remove herself and the prince from Westminster while so tendentious a question was being thrashed out. She had learned her lesson during her bid for the regency: the final decision was not hers; it lay with King Henry and the lords in council.

For the scheme to work, widespread acknowledgement and acceptance of the Prince of Wales was vital. Margaret would have to fill the years of Edward's childhood by establishing his status, and her own, while maintaining the king's ultimate authority. Although more acceptable than her regency, it was a novel idea that was bound to meet with resistance; Margaret took positive steps to implement it.

In the summer she moved from Tutbury to Prince Edward's castle at Chester, where the baby prince could be put on display and the local lords and gentry could be royally received.[88] A circular letter would summon men who had affiliations with the duchy of Lancaster and with the prince's lands to attend her. The *English Chronicle* reports that Margaret distributed swan badges shortly before the battle of Blore Heath in 1459.[89] But its chronology is often confused, and the assumption that the swan was a *military* emblem because it is recorded in conjunction with Blore Heath is erroneous. The white swan had been the badge of Humphrey, duke of Gloucester, and by adopting it for the Prince of Wales, Margaret identified her son with Duke Humphrey who had been protector of England during Henry VI's minority.

This explanation of the circular letter fits into the pattern of events that followed. In September 1456 an elaborate pageant was staged at Coventry, shortly before a shakeup in the council and the reassignment of the great offices of state. Margaret played the central role in the pageant as Queen Mother to the

87 This is what happened in January 1457 when King Henry issued letters patent establishing Prince Edward's council, with Margaret's authority embedded in it. See Maurer, pp. 133ff.
88 She was at Chester on 16 August 1456 (see above, p. 62).
89 Marx, *English Chronicle*, p. 78: the queen 'allyed vnto her all the knyghtes and squyers of Chestreshyre forto haue theyre benyuolence, and helde open householde among theym' and she 'made her sone called the prince yeue a lyuery of swannys to alle the gentilmen of the contre, and to many other thorought the lande'.

Lancastrian heir. It gave her public visibility and reinforced her claim to be an actor on the political stage.[90] In January 1457, Margaret was authorized to supervise Prince Edward's council in letters patent issued on the king's authority. To mark her status, she insisted on being escorted from Coventry with the same ceremony as was officially used for the king's departure, which shocked the mayor and city officials. Having realized her mistake, she subsequently restricted her arrivals and departures to more traditionally acceptable behavior.[91]

90   Harris, *Coventry Leet Book*, pp. 287–92; J. Laynesmith, *The Last Medieval Queens* (Oxford, 2004), pp. 140–3; Maurer, pp. 140–1.
91   Harris, *Coventry Leet Book*, pp. 298–9, 300.

Eleven

LANCASTRIAN QUEEN

Hopes of peace and reconciliation raised by the loveday proved superficial and short-lived. Although at first the Yorkists appear to have been treated fairly, the duke of York received no particular favor from King Henry, and the earl of Warwick proved to be a lightning rod for trouble. He remained captain of Calais, and he continued to commit acts of piracy in the Channel, which embarrassed the government. In autumn 1458, while Warwick was in England for a council meeting, some of his men – and perhaps the earl himself – engaged in a 'vulgar brawl' with men of the royal household.[1] Warwick returned to Calais, from where he declared that he would never give up his captaincy.[2] The political situation deteriorated. Matters came to a head in October 1459 in an armed confrontation between the Yorkists and the king outside the town of Ludlow. Faced with a superior royalist force and desertions within their own ranks, the Yorkist leaders fled: the duke of York to Ireland, and the earls of Warwick, Salisbury and March to Calais.[3] A parliament held at Coventry attainted them in November, making further confrontation certain as they plotted their return.[4] From Calais, the earls launched a propaganda campaign to raise public sympathy for their cause. As in the past, they swore that they were loyal to Henry VI and meant *him* no harm; their quarrel was with the malicious persons about him who had wronged *them*. They were coming to rescue the realm. The resulting invasion in June 1460 was a stunning success. Having gained entry to London on the basis of their sworn

1   Flenley, 'Rawlinson B. 355', p. 113; Storey, p. 186.
2   Stevenson, I, pp. 368–9. He would later characterize the incident as an attempt on his life.
3   The earl of March was York's eldest son, Edward.
4   Sixty-six lords attended, a record for the Lancastrian dynasty. A. Curry notes: 'In spite of Yorkist claims ... that the house had been packed, it was not an aggressively partisan assembly ...' (*PROME*, XII, pp. 448, 464–7).

intentions and the threat of violence from their armed followers, Warwick and March continued north with an army to confront the king.

The battle of Northampton (10 July 1460) was devastating for the Lancastrians: among King Henry's supporters the duke of Buckingham, the earl of Shrewsbury, Viscount Beaumont and Thomas Percy, Lord Egremont, were killed; Henry himself was taken prisoner. Although Warwick, Salisbury and March swore fealty to him, few onlookers doubted that power had irrevocably changed hands. The victors could not realistically be expected to submit themselves again to Henry's will. Warwick became the dominant personality. He replaced the government's officers and Henry's household personnel with men loyal to him.[5] The defeat brought Margaret to the forefront of domestic and foreign politics. Warwick's propaganda insinuated that she was an adulteress and her son a bastard, implying that a dynastic change was being contemplated.[6] A Milanese ambassador reported that the duke of York's supporters would 'make a son of the duke of York king, and … pass over [Henry's] son, as they are beginning already to say that he is not the king's son'.[7]

The Yorkists' first order of business was to get their attainders repealed. To do this and to legitimate their coup at Northampton, they summoned parliament to meet on 7 October. Warwick, Salisbury and March again declared themselves Henry's true lords. The duke of York arrived from Ireland three days later, having made a stately progress towards London with the arms of England borne before him as if he were the king.[8] He announced in the parliament chamber that the crown was his by right. *Everyone*, including York's son, the earl of March, was reported to be *shocked* by his action. But were they? Or was their reaction a matter of political expediency? Some men believed York; others did not, but there was also genuine consternation. All those present had sworn oaths of fealty to King Henry on more than one occasion, and oath breaking was not to be taken lightly.[9] York's claim provided a simple remedy: he was king by *lineal* right; hence, all oaths to Henry had been sworn under false pretenses and were therefore invalid. Even so, York's position caused division and anxiety until it was finally agreed that Henry should remain king for life, unless he chose to abdicate, and that York and his sons should succeed him. This absolved the lords from any possible charge of being foresworn. Prince Edward, aged eight and alleged to be a bastard, could be

5   Griffiths, pp. 864–5, for the extent to which new men replaced the old.
6   Maurer, pp. 176–9.
7   *CSP Milan*, p. 27.
8   Griffiths, p. 867, for this and other indications that York had decided to claim the throne.
9   *Reg. Whethamstede*, I, pp. 378–80; *PROME*, XII, pp. 516–17; Maurer, pp. 182–3.

more readily dismissed. On 25 October, under considerable pressure, Henry VI agreed to this settlement, which became known as the Westminster accord.

Margaret was well informed of these developments, and they were entirely unacceptable to her. They represented the culmination of her fears, and her son's disinheritance made her the Yorkists' implacable enemy. Henceforth she became the *de facto* leader of Lancastrian resistance.

After the battle of Northampton, Margaret did not wait to see what the Yorkists would do next.[10] Henry was in their hands, accorded respect as king but effectively a prisoner. Her course was clear: to make sure that she and her son remained at liberty. With a small escort they fled into Wales, where Henry's half-brother Jasper Tudor, earl of Pembroke, had great influence, arriving there by early September.[11] From this temporary haven, Margaret was able to communicate with various Lancastrian supporters. For supporters there were. The parliament that confirmed the Westminster accord was ill attended. It was reported in Norfolk that the bishop of Norwich and the duchess of Suffolk favored the queen and prince, implying that they might pose a threat to the new regime.[12] The earl of Northumberland was assembling an army in the north. Margaret instructed the duke of Somerset and the earl of Devon, in the south and west, to raise men and bring them to Hull to rendezvous with Lords Roos, Clifford, Greystoke, Neville and Latimer, who were providing forces to serve under the duke of Exeter. She also summoned the chief officers of her own estates to do the same.[13] Parliament's preoccupation with York's claim to the throne made it possible to assemble a substantial force in the north of England before anyone in London realized what was happening. It was a 'striking achievement'.[14]

But raising an army was insufficient. The Westminster accord heightened Margaret's need for public support, and it provided an opportunity for propaganda to attack the Yorkists' credibility. The first letter, from Margaret to the corporation

10   'Gregory's Chronicle', p. 209, places her at Coventry; Stevenson, II, ii, p. 773, at Eccleshall. She did not remain anywhere long; it was too dangerous. Warwick wanted her and the prince in custody.

11   The Paston letter of 12 September reports that they were then in Wales with the duke of Exeter and others (Davis, *Paston Letters*, II, p. 216, where the letter is re-dated to 1460).

12   Gairdner, *PL*, III, p. 228. The bishop, Walter Lyhert, had been Margaret's confessor; the duchess had known Margaret from the time her husband negotiated Margaret's marriage and had become a friend.

13   'Gregory's Chronicle', pp. 209–10. Somerset was holding Guisnes Castle, outside of Calais, when Northampton was fought. He was forced to surrender but managed to return to Corfe Castle in England. 'Gregory' put the number of the resulting force at 15,000 men, a figure that is likely to have been inflated.

14   A. Goodman, *The Wars of the Roses* (1981), p. 42, underestimates the time it took. See also the Paston letter of 12 September 1460 (above, n. 11).

of London, is a part of that appeal. Subsequent letters trace her efforts to restore Henry VI to the throne.

[109] Queen Margaret to the Corporation of London [November 1460]
(BL, Add. MS 48,031 A, fol. 38v)

Right trusty and welbeloved wee grete you hertile wele. And where as the late duc of N [York] of extreme malice long hid undir colours imaginyng bi divers and many weyes and menynes the destruccion of my lordis good grace, whoom God of his mercy evur preserve, hathe now late upon an untrewe pretense feyned a tytle to my lordis coronne and roiall estate and preminence contrary to his liegeaunce and divers solempne othes of his owne offre made uncompelled or constraigned and fully prepose tahave deposed him of his regally, ne had bene the sadde, unchaungeable and trewe disposicions of you and other his trewe liegemen, for the whiche your worshipfull disposicions we thank you as hertile as we can. And howbeit that the same untrewe, unsad and unadvised persone of verray pure malice disposed to continue in his cruelnesse to th'uttrest undoing yif he mighte of us and of my lordis sone and oures, the prince, whiche with Goddis mercy he shalnotbe of power ta'perfourme, by the helpe of you and all other my lordes feithefully desposed subgettes hath throwen amoung you as we be certainele enfourmed, divers untrewe and feyned matteres and surmises, and inespeciall that wee and my lordes said sone and ours shulde newly drawe toward you with an unsen power of straungeres disposed to robbe and to dispoile you of your goodes and haveurs. We will that ye knowe for certaine that at suche tyme as we or our saide sone shalbe disposed to se my lord as our dute is, and so bynde us to do, ye nor noon of you shalbe robbed, dispoiled nor wronged by any personne that at that tyme we or our sayde sone shalbe accumpanyed with or any other sent in our or his name, praying you in our most herty and desirous wise that all eorthely thing ye will diligently entende to the surete of my lordis roial personne in the meane tyme. So that thoroughe malice of his saide ennemye hebe no more troubled, vexed ne jeoparded. And so doing we shalbe unto you suche lady as of reason ye shalbe largely content. Yeven undir our signet, etc.

Margaret's first move was to challenge the legitimacy of York's claim (and, by extension, of the resulting accord), insisting that they were the products of long-held malicious intent. It was a credible charge. York's actions cast doubt upon his many assertions – and sworn oaths – that he was the king's true liegeman. It also called into question the Calais earls' oaths and affirmations of loyalty to Henry after they captured him.

Margaret next addressed Yorkist propaganda that she and the prince would lead a host of 'strangers' south to ravish and pillage London. In fact, the 'strangers' alluded to included a large number of men from the south and midlands, but

this did not suit the theme of marauding barbarians from the wild north that
Warwick put out to stoke southern fears of a Lancastrian army. Margaret insisted
that when they did come, it would be to rescue King Henry. She would allow no
harm to be done to London by any person whatsoever. Her letter ends with a plea
to the City to keep the king safe. Henry's death would trigger the Westminster
accord; alive and in Margaret's hands, his authority could be used to undo the
dynastic damage it had caused.

The date of this letter has been a source of confusion. When Mary Anne
Everett Wood first published it in the mid-nineteenth century, she ascribed it to
early 1461, *after* York's death in the battle of Wakefield, because it describes him
as 'late duke'.[15] As a result, historians have assumed that Margaret was sending
reassurances to London because of depredations that had *already* occurred on
her army's march. But the wording of the letter, which refers to York's activities
in the present tense, indicates that he was still alive when it was written, while it
also makes clear that the mission to free Henry was still a matter for the future.
The phrase 'late duke' refers to York's attainder in 1459, which deprived him of
his title and his lands. Hence, this letter was written *before* the end of 1460, while
York was still alive and well.[16] A separate letter 'by' the prince was written at the
same time.[17]

It is likely that these are two of three letters received by the London common
council on 2 December 1460.[18] Thomas Cook, who became mayor in 1462, was an
avid collector of documents, which he added to an archive begun by his father.
John Vale, who was Cook's servant in the early 1460s, copied parts of this archive
into his notebook.[19] We suspect that Margaret's and the prince's letters were
among Cook's 'acquisitions'.

Meanwhile, the Yorkists had not forgotten Margaret. As long as she and Prince

15   M.A.E. (Wood) Green, *Letters of Royal and Illustrious Ladies of Great Britain,* I (1846), pp. 95–7.
     Her modernized transcript was made from BL, Harleian MS 543, fol. 147, which is Stowe's
     copy of various documents in what is now BL, Add. MS 48,031 A. The latter was edited and
     published as *Vale's Book*, with Margaret's letter appearing on p. 142, where the editors accept
     the date of 1461.
16   B.M. Cron, 'Margaret of Anjou and the Lancastrian March on London, 1461', *The Ricardian,*
     XI:47 (December 1999), pp. 593–4.
17   *Vale's Book*, pp. 142–3. The prince's letter applies the phrase 'calling himself duke' to York and
     avoids the confusion of date. His age guarantees that it was written for him. Together these
     letters show the gendering of authority (Maurer, pp. 190–1).
18   CLRO, Journal VI, fol. 279, records them having been received. It does not indicate their
     content, and the letters themselves are unaccounted for. The third letter was from Jasper Tudor,
     earl of Pembroke.
19   *Vale's Book*, p. 73. The archive is no longer extant. For Cook, see above, p. 124 and n. 30; below,
     p. 249.

Edward remained at liberty, they posed a threat to the Westminster accord. Along with the propaganda campaign to discredit both queen and prince, the Yorkists tried to lure Margaret to London on the pretext that King Henry had sent for her. She did not fall for it.[20] In early December, around the time that the London common council received the letters from Margaret and Prince Edward, the Yorkists turned their attention to the Lancastrian army gathering in the north. The duke of York and the earl of Salisbury set out for Yorkshire, seriously underestimating the strength of the force that awaited them. York was killed at the battle of Wakefield on 30 December; Salisbury was captured and later executed. The outcome immediately raised the stakes for both sides.

Margaret was at Lincluden in Scotland, seeking aid from the queen regent, Mary of Guelders, while the battle of Wakefield was being fought. The sudden reversal of fortune apparently tipped the balance in their negotiations. An agreement was reached on 5 January. Its terms involved a proposed marriage between Prince Edward and a sister of James III, Mary's son, and 'help and supply' – probably meaning provisioning – for the Lancastrians.[21] Margaret had to act swiftly; she joined the Lancastrian lords who had gathered at York. There, on 20 January, twelve lords pledged themselves in Margaret's presence to persuade Henry VI to accept the Lincluden articles, provided, of course, that they would first free him from the Yorkists.[22] Two days later, on 22 January, a circular letter went out as a commission of array to raise more troops.

[110] **Instructions for Proclamations from York, 22 January 1461**[23]
(BNF, MS Latin 11892, fol. 187)

By the Prince
Trusty and welbeloved [blank space]. We grete you wel. And wol and straitly charge you that incontinent [immediately] after the sight herof ye provide that proclamacions be made thourghout al my lordes counte of York in alle hast possible after the fourme that foloweth. The Shireve commaundeth in the kynges name, the queenes, and my lord princes: That for asmuch as it is not unknowen to all this land that by false malicious meanes the queene and my lord prince have unrighfully and unnaturally be straunged [estranged] and kept from the kynges presence. And to that entent, And to reliese the kynges goode grace oute of the jeopert [jeopardy] and constreynt that he hath longe soufred, they purpose with Goddes myght to drawe

20   'Gregory's Chronicle', p. 209. This effort may be alluded to in Francesco Coppini's letter, below, pp. 229–30.
21   W.A. Craigie, ed., *The Asloan Manuscript*, I, Scottish Text Society 14 (Edinburgh, 1923), p. 230.
22   BNF, MS Fr. 20488, fol. 23, published and discussed by Hicks, 'Minute of the Lancastrian Council'.
23   We have reversed chronological order for this and the next letter.

thaim towardes him. Therfore, that every man that tendreth and loveth the kynges
welfare, the queenes, and my lord princes be redy in his best araye to awaite uppon
thaim to the same entente. And to be with thaim on [blank space] next commyng,
suche oonly except as by the queenes highnesse have in commaundment to putte
theim in devoirs [tasks, duties] otherwise. And they shalbe right wel seen unto
and rewarded therfore. And these our lettres shalbe your warant. Yeven under our
signet at York the xxij day of Janwer.

Three things about this letter deserve attention. First, it was written in the
prince's name to provide royal authority. But second, as written, it applies only
to Yorkshire. It seems doubtful that the Lancastrians initially planned to mount a
winter campaign. With York dead, however, the advantage provided by Wakefield
had to be converted to a final victory before it was lost. It was necessary to raise
more men as quickly as possible and to begin the march south, which indeed
happened towards the end of the month. With little time in which to act – roughly
a week – it made sense to focus on Yorkshire. But does that mean that similar
letters were not sent elsewhere? From mid-January, the Yorkist government in
London issued a spate of commissions and orders to deal with the impending
Lancastrian threat.[24] Initially broad in scope, their focus subsequently narrowed
both geographically and substantively. Of particular interest is a commission of
26 January involving Norfolk 'and other counties adjacent, if necessary', against
illicit gatherings of 'evildoers' as well as efforts to provide such persons with
victuals, arms and armed men. A further commission of 28 January sought to
discover which Norfolk port was shipping wheat and victuals to persons guilty of
insurrection, while a similar commission was sent to Cambridge on 7 February.[25]
Persons in these counties would have been in communication – probably ongoing
– with the queen's party, and whatever activities transpired in them were likely
to have been in response to her mandate.

The third point to note is that this letter indicates – without identifying – a
rendezvous point at which the Yorkshire contingents would meet the core of the
Lancastrian army. In addition to York itself, Hull was a logical place to meet – it
had served as the gathering place for the Lancastrian lords prior to Wakefield[26]
– and there may have been more than one rendezvous point. This observation,

24   *CPR, 1452–61*, p. 655ff. The first of these, dated 11 January, named a commission to arrest and
      imprison persons 'guilty of unlawful gatherings, congregations, associations and combinations'
      in the counties of Nottingham (named twice, perhaps with Northampton intended the second
      time), Bedford, Buckingham, Hertford, Huntingdon, Cambridge, Warwick, Leicester, Derby,
      Stafford and Lincoln, and to raise 'all lieges … to resist the same as enemies and rebels'.
25   Ibid., pp. 656, 658, 659.
26   'Gregory's Chronicle', pp. 209–10.

together with the evidence regarding food supply, may suggest something else about the Lancastrians' strategy. In winter, food was a problem for a large army on the move. Apart from the political goal of raising as much of the south as possible to support her cause, it would have made good sense for new contingents to join Margaret's army at successive points along its route. A contemporary source suggests that people did join the Lancastrian force along its march, though some modern historical opinion concludes that its numbers were likely to have shrunk overall.[27]

The defeat at Wakefield was also a game-changer for the Yorkists. Just as Margaret needed to act quickly to take advantage of the situation, it meant that Warwick would have to exercise prompt damage control to counter the Lancastrian threat.

The next letter was written by one of the more bizarre characters involved in the conflict. Although it was not addressed to Margaret directly, the first part of it was intended to be communicated to her. The rest consisted of a strenuous effort to divert supporters from her cause.

[111] **Francesco Coppini, Bishop of Terni and Apostolic Legate, to Master Lorenzo de Florencia, a Friar with the Queen, 9 January 1461** (*CSP, Milan*, pp. 37–41)

Owing to manifest causes and dangers, we are writing to you, as we cannot proceed in person to the queen and the lords with her, as you know. First and foremost ... we require you to declare and offer on your own behalf, that should it ever be found that we have excommunicated or cursed anyone assisting her Majesty or being with her, or if we have ever committed or consented to such things, we will gladly be flayed alive or torn asunder, for we excommunicated no one, cursed no one and wronged no one at any time in this kingdom, but we shall be ready to do all these things and more still, if we are called upon to do so for [the queen] and for her wellbeing and obedience. The things we have said and done are contained in our letters ... a copy whereof we sent by your hand to [the queen], and send again enclosed, and what we purpose for the present and the future is contained therein ... and whereas we have heard it said ... that those who were slain at Northampton could not be buried without our leave, this was not our fault, but owing to the opinions of men who considered as excommunicate those who would not yield to our wise and honest counsel ... but resisted the orders of his Holiness ... though they are so immediate that those who do not honor them are not true Christians ... That we love and revere [the queen] as much as any man living she herself knows, and she has seen and experienced that we did not abandon

27   Gairdner, *Three Chronicles*, p. 76; Goodman, *Wars of the Roses*, p. 47.

her when she was in difficulties,[28] and for her cause and wellbeing we are ready to suffer anything in this world.

We have prefixed these remarks because you are a faithful man ... You know what you told me at the time of the parliament, on the queen's behalf, and what [she] wrote to us, although the writer displayed too great passion, and what we communicated about the manner and the conditions of peace, etc. You also knew ... that you should wait a few days, so that we might be able to treat, as that lord of whom you spoke to us, of all the others, always remained well disposed to us as well as to the honour and safety of [the queen] and to peace,[29] as experience afterwards showed, but you could not wait any longer. Subsequently we saw and heard of the scandals which ensued from lack of mediators ... and now things have come to such a pass that acts of vengeance are committed even beyond what was due ... [but] as there is now an opportunity for peace, our office requires that we must desire it to be made, because such is the will of God, and [the king] wishes the same. Accordingly we notify you, as a faithful man trusted by the queen and those lords, that they may have an honourable peace, if they will attend to the wise counsel of the Apostolic legate ... The conditions of peace will be such that they may well be satisfied ... If you come in person, as you may in perfect safety, we do not doubt but that a satisfactory peace will be made.

Tell those lords, and especially the Duke of Somerset, whom we admire for his character and because ... he loves the queen ... as we do ourselves, that if they do not attend to our advice they will bring desolation upon the whole realm and the estate and wellbeing of [the king]. They must not be arrogant because of the trifling victory they won ... because we have seen and know ... that all the people are incensed and in the worst possible humour against those who do not desire peace. There are two reasons for this: firstly, the countless acts of cruelty related of them, whereas these here were not cruel, but received into favour those who wished to come;[30] secondly, because they recognise ... that [the king] and the lords with him and ourself ... are really disposed to an honest and honourable peace ... Therefore, if your influence with them does not suffice, their cause will be in the worst possible case, because the feelings of the people are incredibly incensed against them, and they will see more than two hundred thousand desperate men rise against them, who are constantly assembling, offering to devote their goods and their persons in such an honest and just cause ...

Whatever else they disregard, let them attend to this one thing. Formerly, when we were with those lords, and especially with the Earl of Warwick (for whose sincere intentions towards [the king] and the welfare of the kingdom we chiefly

28 Possibly a self-serving reference to the earlier attempt to lure Margaret to London, alluded to in the next paragraph, in which Coppini apparently served as intermediary.
29 We have no idea who 'that lord' might have been.
30 A reference to the line taken by Warwick's propaganda, wherein Margaret and her 'northerners' were cruel, whereas he and his supporters were not.

came), although we were not then with [the king]... God Almighty was with us. How much more then must they believe Him to be with us now, when we are with [the king] in body and soul, and intent on his glory, welfare and honour ... He is not constrained against his free will, as some perverse persons falsely declare, but enjoys his full liberty, and access to him is open to all. This was not the case formerly, ... for we could neither approach him nor deliver our Apostolic letters to him, as is notorious. Accordingly they are to obey [the king] and to believe us, who are laboring for peace and justice, according to the command of God and the order of the Apostolic See, as well as the express and free wish of [the king], who is grieved by wars, murder and rapine and all the other ills which arise therefrom. Therefore let them be devout ... and obedient, and they shall have an honest peace, which we offer according to the tenor of these presents of [the king's] free will; otherwise we ... fear their ruin and destruction. With the tears of our heart we beg them to try and avoid this, now that they have so honourable a way out ... Therefore, let them receive us in charity as we have received them ... having voluntarily exposed ourselves to so many dangers when we might have gone away and lived in peace outside the kingdom ... If now they despise or neglect the peace offered by the instrumentality of His messenger ... then indeed they will richly deserve the judgment of God ...

After this offer, if they refuse to listen, we shall be discharged in the sight of God and man, and we shall not mind the slanders of those who accuse us ...

[dated 9 January 1461 and signed by the apostolic legate]

Postscript[31] – Messer Lorenzo, tell those lords not to attach so little importance to my letters because they are of a different effect than has been supposed hitherto ... If any are dissatisfied or ill-disposed, tell them ... that it is better to make peace after a victory than after a defeat ... Let them also consider how much they have to do before they have conquered, and with whom they have to do. Tell them in particular that ... the king, from his experience of my Lord of Warwick and his followers, has determined to protect and defend them to the death, because he never had any more loyal. All the people are of the same mind ... Therefore let them pay heed to what we write, as we offer them a peace to their honour and advantage ... [the terms of which] are not such as can be put in writing; if you come you shall see them ... I beg you to see that our letters are read and listened to, as you value your own wellbeing. We command this from the obedience that you owe to those to whom you are bound as legate.

(*Endorsed*) Venerabili viro fratri Laurentio de Florentia Sacre theologie Magistro, ordinis predicatorum dilectissimo nostro, et in ejus absentia Sacre Reginali Majestati et dominis assistentibus.

---

31   This postscript was in Italian (perhaps to ensure its privacy), although the rest of the letter was in Latin.

Francesco Coppini, bishop of Terni, was a man consumed by a vision of himself as a cardinal.[32] In pursuit of this goal, he eagerly embraced any activity that enhanced his standing. Opportunity seemed to knock when Pope Pius II sent him to England in 1459 to drum up support for a crusade against the Turks.[33] Unfortunately, the English were preoccupied, and their response to the pope's proposal was less than enthusiastic. In December, Pius II increased Coppini's authority by making him a legate *de latere*, with a new assignment: to mediate peace between the Yorkists and the king. But reconciling King Henry's government with magnates who had been attainted in parliament was more than Coppini could hope to accomplish. He left England in the spring of 1460 and joined the earl of Warwick in Calais. In June he accompanied the Yorkist earls when they invaded England.

From Warwick's point of view, having a papal legate in their midst enhanced their credibility. Coppini would sing their song: that they were loyal subjects who meant no harm to their anointed king. This repeated insistence – or posturing – allowed them to enter England virtually unimpeded.

On 4 July, as the earls of Warwick and March set out from London to confront the king at Northampton, Coppini sent a lengthy letter to King Henry.[34] It was both exculpatory and threatening. He claimed that the Yorkists had asked him to resolve their conflict with the king. He had already sent copies of their missives to Henry VI along with his own offer to return to England as a peace negotiator.[35] According to Coppini, when he reached Calais he found everyone in a state of great excitement, preparing to leave for England. At the Yorkists' urging he agreed to accompany them to prevent bloodshed. Before leaving Calais, as earnest of their honorable intentions, they addressed a letter to Coppini setting out their conditions for a rapprochement.[36] He was sure that King Henry would approve them if he considered them 'with a tranquil and open mind'. Coppini failed to mention the Yorkists' statement that if they did not get what they wanted, they would resort to force. The remainder of Coppini's letter contained a further threat aimed at King Henry: if bloodshed did occur, he alone would be responsible and

32 Scofield, I, p. 72, describes Coppini as 'possessed [of] a good deal more eloquence than discretion, not to say a good deal more self-conceit than Christian humility'. C. Head, 'Pope Pius II and the Wars of the Roses', *Archivium Historiae Pontificiae* 8 (1970), offers a more recent assessment.

33 The Turks had taken Constantinople, the heart of Orthodox Christianity, in 1453, evoking fear throughout Europe.

34 *CSP, Milan*, pp. 23–7.

35 These letters, if they ever existed, are no longer extant.

36 H. Ellis, *Original Letters Illustrative of English History*, third ser. 1 (1824), pp. 85–8. Scofield, I, pp. 75–6, summarizes its content. Although addressed to Coppini, it was ultimately meant for Henry.

answerable to God. The only way to avoid this dreadful outcome was to listen to 'God's messenger' [i.e., Coppini], and send away all those 'ministers of the devil' who counseled otherwise. Although Coppini allowed that Henry might reject the Yorkists' terms and take up arms, the thrust of his message was that the only way for the king to assure his personal salvation was by capitulation to their demands. Coppini claimed to have sent a copy of this letter to Margaret, and a second copy accompanied his letter to Lorenzo de Florencia.[37] On 4 July, the same day that he wrote to Henry VI, Coppini also wrote to Pope Pius II, presenting an enthusiastically rosy picture of the situation in England and emphasizing the importance of his own role as 'an angel of peace and a mediator'. There was only one small difficulty: King Henry had not succumbed to his blandishments. The king was at Northampton with an army. Nevertheless, Coppini remained hopeful 'for many good things ... for the glory of Your Holiness and the Church ... if continued favor and authority are granted me by the same'.[38] The favor he sought was a cardinal's hat.

After the battle of Northampton, the presence of the papal legate was again useful to Yorkist credibility. Coppini may have been involved in the attempt to lure Margaret to London. By his own account, the queen 'displayed too great passion' and wanted nothing more to do with him.[39] It was widely believed that Coppini had excommunicated the king's supporters prior to the battle, while granting absolution to the Yorkists. His response to the charge in his letter to Lorenzo was a tissue of denial and obfuscation. He had never excommunicated anyone *assisting the queen* (quickly extended to 'anyone in the kingdom'), though he would gladly do so (if he were called upon) for 'her wellbeing and obedience'. The gist of his message was that Margaret should follow Coppini's guidance, as he had her best interests at heart.

The rest of his letter, however, offered harsh advice to Margaret's supporters. It was now time to make peace, and he, the pope's emissary, would offer them conditions, yet to be revealed, for an 'honorable peace'. Should they choose to defy him, they would be 'rebels against the commands of God and the Apostolic See [rather than] true Christians' and would deserve God's judgment. The reader – or

37 Coppini added a marginal note to the second copy: 'This letter was sent by the legate when he decided to cross to England with the Earl of Warwick and other lords who were at Calais, and although it is old, yet the copy is made to set forth the proceedings of the legate and his honesty, as an answer to the calumnies of his adversaries' (*CSP, Milan*, pp. 26–7).
38 Scofield, I, pp. 83–5, summarizes this letter, from Vatican Transcripts, portfolio 62.
39 Above, p. 230. It is unclear just when the effort to get Margaret to London occurred. 'Gregory's Chronicle', p. 209, implies that it took place while parliament met, but its chronology is murky. R. Fabyan, *The New Chronicles of England and France*, ed. H. Ellis (1811), p. 637, written much later, said that it took place after the Westminster accord.

listener – might reasonably conclude that Coppini had once again threatened the Lancastrians with excommunication.

With Margaret still at liberty and royalist opposition growing in the north, Coppini's claim to be the pope's representative itself became an issue. Doubt regarding his legitimacy could undermine the credibility of Warwick's regime, whereas certainty that he represented the voice of papal authority would measurably strengthen Warwick's hand. Around this same time, Warwick wrote to Pius II regarding the legate. His letter amounted to a demand: Coppini must receive advancement to allay all doubts regarding his authority 'if … you value my allegiance [and that of the other Yorkists]'.[40]

Neither Margaret nor her supporters cared what the legate had to say – it simply made them more determined. As the Lancastrian army approached London, Coppini, frightened by his own propaganda, developed cold feet and took ship, fetching up in Holland.

Coppini's letter to Lorenzo de Florencia poses one last intriguing question. In early 1461, perhaps in the aftermath of her victory at the second battle of St Albans, Margaret sent a pair of Dominican friars to France as envoys. One of them was to continue to Rome to lodge a formal complaint with the pope about Coppini.[41] Lorenzo was a Dominican. How many Dominicans would have been in Margaret's entourage? Was he her emissary? Although Coppini addressed Lorenzo as 'a faithful man' and seemed to expect him to accept what he said without question, the last two sentences of his postscript suggest otherwise. They may constitute a warning: that the legate would brook no dissention or insubordination. Do they call Lorenzo's loyalty to Coppini into question? Whom would Margaret choose to represent her on so delicate a mission? Who could speak from experience to the pope regarding Coppini's actions?

Pius II summoned Coppini back to Rome in 1462. There he was questioned at length about his activities in England and was eventually found guilty of having abused his office by performing illicit excommunications of King Henry's supporters at Northampton. The pope annulled these actions as contrary to his own wishes.[42] Coppini was relieved of his bishopric and imprisoned for a time, then packed off in disgrace to spend the rest of his life as a monk. He changed his name to Ignatious and died on 29 September 1464, while trying to get the Church to rehabilitate him.

---

40   *CSP, Milan*, p. 44.

41   For their business with Charles VII, see below, p. 234.

42   Head, 'Pope Pius II', pp. 170–5, argues that Coppini's fall from papal grace had more to do with his machinations in France since returning to the continent than with his deeds in England, to which Pius had made no objections at the time.

[112] Pierre de Brezé to Charles VII of France, 24 February [1461][43]

(T. Basin, *Histoire des regnes de Charles VII et de Louis XI*, IV, ed. J. Quicherat [Paris, 1859], pp. 358–60, from BNF, Gaignières, vol. 304, fol. 15)

Au Roy,

Sire, je vous anvoye Doucereau, ainsy qu'il vous a pleu me escripre. Les causzes pour lesquellez je desiroye aller devers vous sont tellez. La royne, vostre niepce, m'a fait savoir par ledit Doucereau que incontinent alasse devers vous pour vous parler de ceulx quy doivent venir, et luy fere savoir de vos novellez au certain. Et ce qu'elle demande est que vouloir vous avez anvers le roy, vostre neveu, et elle; car selon qu'elle santira vostre vouloir, elle les instruira ce qu'ilz aront à faire. Ausy elle m'a mandé que je mette toutte la paine que je pourray à guaingner le navire du conte de Warvich, et que en touttez fasons que je pourray le grever et fere dommage, que je le face, car, ainsy qu'il luy semble, cela servira beaucoup à son fait et à la matère pourquoy elle antant anvoyer les gens de par de sà; et pour ce j'ay commancé à faire abiller le navire, et me semble que, cy c'est vostre plesir, que ledit Warvich s'an santira; et est nécessité qu'il se face. Ausy je vous vouloye dire les segrettez chozes qu'elle m'a mandé, par quoy eusiez conneu le bon vouloir qu'elle a eu et a anvers vous, qui n'est pas peu de chosze. D'aultre part, je vouloye savoir comme à leur arivée je me doy conduire; car je ne fais point de doupte qu'ilz ne parlent de la causze de leur venue et que d'isy ils ne ranvoyent homme pour fere savoir qu'ilz sont seurement passez et ce qu'ilz aront trouvé à leur aryvée, et sans parler à vous je ne saray que leur dire; et ce n'est pas matère quy ne se doye débatre, car quy bien commance, bien achève. Ausy, syre, je ne sçay sy les fauldra aler querir, et je croy que ouy, car à la vérité ilz n'ont point de navire pour eulz sauver devant celuy de Calays. Tous ces poins vouldroye débatre avecquez vous et d'aultrez, car c'est merveillez des mistères quy se jouent an Flandrez. Pour ce vous plesze me mander ce que'array à fere.

Sire, vous m'escripvez que le tans s'aprouche que me devez mander. Si vous ne le faittez avant que ledit Doucereau soit passé, je ne voy pas que bonnement ce puisse fere, pour ce qu'il sera bessoing que je soye ycy à leur arrivée pour les recuillir ou pour fere partir le navire, s'il est besoing les aler querir, ou à l'avanture avant leur venue me feront savoir quelque aultre chosze que, sy je n'estoye ycy, ce seroit mal fait. D'escripre à la royne, synon par ledit Doucereau, il n'est possible ne raisonnable, car escripre et (si) les lettrez estoient prinszes, il ne fauldroit aultre procès pour la fere mourir; car (si) ceulx quy sont à elle et de son costé savoient son antansion et ce qu'elle a fait, ilz se joindroient avecquez les aultrez pour la faire mourir. Ausy je

---

43 Disagreement over the date of this intriguing letter has been largely overlooked, and its content has received remarkably little analysis. Quicherat's belief that it was written in 1460 was accepted by Beaucourt, VI, pp. 287–8, and P. Bernus, 'Le Rôle politique de Pierre de Brezé au cours des dix dernières années du règne de Charles VII, 1451–1461', *Bibliothèque de l'École de Chartes* 69 (1908), pp. 333–4 and note. Scofield, I, pp. 160–1, attributed it to 1461 without explanation. After considering both dates, we find that we agree with Scofield. Brezé's remark about Flanders conclusively pegs it to 1461. See below, pp. 239–40 and n. 60.

n'ai nul sauf-conduit pour y anvoyer homme, et quant j'en aroye, sy ne vouldroye descouvrir ceste matière que audit Doucereau, et ne chet pas, veu le personnage, mettre la chosze an tant de mains. Et vos suplie. sire, que autres que mestre Estienne ne voye cestez lettrez, ne aussy ce que ledit Doucereau vous monstrera, pour les dangers quy an pourroient ansuir à vostre dite niepce, dont trop sariés desplaisant, et sy vous seroit grant dommage; lequel je prie Nostre Seigneur que jà n'aviegne, et qu'il vous doint très bonne vye et longue.

Escript ce XXIIIIe de février.

Sire, ne soyez anvieux du bien que vostre neveu et nièce vous font dire de moy, car vous savez que je suy ung genty chevalier.

Vostre très humble et très obéissant suget et serviteur, BRESZÉ

To the King

Sire, I am sending Doucereau to you, just as it pleased you to write to me.[44] The reasons I desired to meet you are as follows: The queen, your niece, has informed me through the said Doucereau that I should straightaway meet with you to tell you about those [the envoys] who are coming, and to let her have your news for certain. And what she requests is [to know] your disposition towards the king, your nephew, and her; for she will instruct [her envoys] as to what they must do, in accordance with what she perceives [to be] your feelings.

Also, she has asked me to make every effort to capture the earl of Warwick's fleet, and to hinder and damage it in every way I can. May I do so? For it seems to her that this will greatly serve her cause and the reason why she intends to send people over here; and therefore I have begun to make the fleet ready, and it seems to me that, if it is your pleasure, the said Warwick will know of it; and it is necessary that it be so.

Also, I wanted to tell you the secret matters she has conveyed to me, by which you would have known the good will she has had, and has, towards you, which is not insignificant.

In addition, I wanted to know how I must behave on [her envoys'] arrival; for I do not doubt that they will not mention the [real] reason for their coming, and that they will not send anyone back from here to report that they have crossed safely and what they will have found on their arrival; and, without speaking to you, I do not know what to say to them; and this is a matter which should be discussed, for what begins well, ends well.

Also, Sire, I do not know whether it will be necessary [for me] to go and fetch them, and I think it will be, for in truth they do not have a fleet to protect them, other than the one at Calais. I should like to discuss all these points with you, and other matters [as well], for the mysterious happenings in Flanders are wondrous [indeed]. Therefore, may it please you to inform me of what I am to do.

---

44   We are grateful to Professor Glynnis Cropp for her assistance with the translation of this difficult letter.

Sire, you write to me that the time is approaching when you must issue orders [to me]. If you do not do so before the said Doucereau has gone, I do not see that I can conveniently do this, as I need to be here when [the envoys] arrive to welcome them, or to have the ship set sail if it is necessary to go and fetch them. Or if it chance, before their coming, [that] they [send to] inform me of something [else]; if I were not here, things would go badly.

Writing to the queen, except by way of Doucereau, is neither possible nor reasonable, for if one wrote, and the letters were intercepted, no other procedure would be necessary in order to put her to death. For [if] those who are with her and on her side knew her intention, and what she has done, they would unite with the others to put her to death.

Also, I have no safe-conduct for sending someone [to England], and [even] if I had, I would want to reveal this matter only to the said Doucereau; considering the personage [involved], it is not appropriate to put the matter into so many hands.

And I beseech you, Sire, that no one other than master Etienne [Chevalier] see this letter, nor what the said Doucereau will show you, because of the danger which could ensue for your said niece, which would be very disagreeable, and it would [also] be harmful to you. I pray to Our Lord that this may never happen, and that He may grant you a very good and long life.

Written this 24th February.

Sire, do not be envious of the good things your nephew and niece let be said to you about me, for you know that I am a worthy knight

Your very humble and very obedient subject and servant, Brezé.

Pierre de Brezé, Sieur de la Varenne, had known Margaret since her childhood. He was a near contemporary of Margaret's father, René of Anjou, and began his political career in René's service.[45] René appointed him seneschal of Anjou and captain of the castle at Angers, where Margaret spent her formative years.[46] René's brother, Charles of Maine, introduced Brezé to the French court, where he became a favorite of King Charles VII and a member of his council.[47] He acquired a reputation for being an excellent – and persuasive – speaker.[48] He was the principal French negotiator for Margaret's marriage to Henry VI at Tours in 1444 as part of the truce between England and France.[49]

Brezé was also a fine and fearless soldier. One English chronicler went so

---

45   Bernus, 'Rôle politique', pp. 303–4.
46   *Dictionnaire de biographie française* (Paris, 1933), VII, p. 264.
47   P.S. Lewis, *Later Medieval France* (1968), pp. 125–6.
48   G. Chastellain, *Oeuvres*, 8 vols, ed. Kervyn de Lettenhove (Brussels, 1863–66), III, pp. 380–1; VII, p. 73.
49   Beaucourt, III, pp. 276–7; Vale, *Charles VII*, p. 104.

far as to call him 'the best warrior of all that time'.[50] He played a major role in recovering Maine and Normandy from the English. In 1449 when Charles VII made his triumphal entry into Rouen, Brezé rode with him and was entrusted with the keys of the city.[51] He fought at Formigny in 1450, where the English army was decisively defeated, and Charles created him grand seneschal of Normandy in 1451.[52] In 1457, while commanding a fleet in the Channel searching for English pirates, Brezé sacked the town of Sandwich, the supply port for Calais, and carried away valuable booty and a few wealthy citizens to be ransomed.[53]

As England moved towards civil war, Brezé kept himself (and King Charles VII) well informed of events there. His secretary Maurice Doucereau frequently served as a go-between with the English.[54] Doucereau was in England in the summer of 1460 and was reported to have been with Henry VI at Northampton, where he may have been 'detained' by the Yorkists for a short time.[55] On 31 July, Brezé wrote to Etienne Chevalier, the king's secretary, that he was waiting to hear from Doucereau and others that he had sent to Margaret.[56] Doucereau was probably with Margaret in the north of England in early 1461 after Wakefield. He left England for France before Margaret's victory at the second battle of St Albans on 17 February, carrying letters and messages from her to Brezé.[57] Margaret sought Brezé's help, both practically and theoretically. She was planning to send envoys to Charles VII, but she wanted to know exactly how far Charles was prepared to go to support her bid to re-establish her husband on the throne.[58] She had

---

50 J. Warkworth, *A Chronicle of the First Thirteen Years of the Reign of King Edward IV*, ed. J.O. Halliwell, Camden Society, old ser. 10 (1839), p. 2.
51 Beaucourt, V, pp. 19–24; Vale, *Charles VII*, 202–3, for the entry ceremonies.
52 Beaucourt, V, pp. 31–4; Vale, *Charles VII*, p. 120.
53 Griffiths, p. 815. Beaucourt, VI, pp. 145–6.
54 Bernus, 'Rôle politique', pp. 326, 329–33.
55 At Louis XI's request, Gaston de Foix provided a written account of what he knew of Charles VII's recent dealings with the English. He told a wild tale of Doucereau's capture and subsequent rescue by the duke of Somerset before being sent back to England to tell Margaret that Charles VII favored her cause (P. de Comines, *Mémoires de Philippe de Comines*, ed. M. l'Abbé Lenglet du Fresnoy, II [Paris, 1747], p. 308). Somerset returned to England in September. He recruited reinforcements and led them north to form part of the Lancastrian army (Marx, *English Chronicle*, p. 92; Stevenson, II, ii, pp. 774–5; 'Gregory's Chronicle', pp. 209–10). That he could have arranged Doucereau's release seems improbable, to say the least.
56 Beaucourt, VI, p. 291, n. 5, citing MS Fr. 20428, fol. 17 *bis*.
57 Brezé's letter says nothing about the battle, although Doucereau *could* have taken ship for France immediately afterwards. Would this have allowed Brezé time to send a message to Charles VII and to expect a response *before he wrote this letter*? Given the vagaries of February weather, we think not.
58 On 17 February the Milanese ambassador to Burgundy wrote that the queen of England planned 'to make a league with the king of France', but he dismissed the idea because of the enmity between the two realms (P.M. Kendall and V. Ilardi, *Dispatches with Related Documents*

something to offer in return for French military aid, but it was potentially so dangerous that it sent Brezé into a spin.

Brezé's letter indicates that he had already requested a personal meeting with the king in connection with Margaret's business, but Charles VII instructed him to send Doucereau to court instead. Perhaps Charles wanted a firsthand report of the conditions in England, or he may have intended to use Doucereau as his envoy to Margaret. A further factor should be considered: Charles was then gravely ill, and the pain associated with his illness may have made him testier than usual and unable to reach a decision, thus delaying his response to Brezé's initial request.[59] Charles VII remained cautious about becoming entangled in English politics. He had authorized Brezé to prepare a small fleet, perhaps for the transport of troops, but Margaret wanted him to put to sea at once and harry Warwick's fleet in the southern ports by way of a diversion; it might even entice Warwick to leave London. Brezé was eager to perform this service; he enjoyed war at sea. At the same time, he was reluctant to leave Rouen before the English envoys arrived. If he did not meet them, he would not know what exactly they intended to say to Charles VII, or what the latest news from England might be. Above all, Brezé did not know what Charles wanted him to do – was he to await the envoys' arrival or not? Should he 'fetch them', i.e., meet them somewhere along their route? And what was he to say to them when they arrived? Brezé was a very worried man. He knew better than to make any commitment, however vague, on Charles's behalf without explicit instructions from the king, and he needed instructions fast. Margaret's envoys might arrive at any time. He hoped that Charles would grasp the seriousness of his predicament, and he urged the king to send Doucereau straight back to Rouen with orders and, if necessary, royal authority. From a man renowned for his eloquence, Brezé's letter is a mess. It reads as if he were on the verge of panic. He hastily outlined what was preying on his mind, jumping from one topic to another and omitting a word here and there.

Even in his haste, however, Brezé was careful to reassure the suspicious king that although he was concentrating on Margaret's plight, English affairs were not his only concern or his sole commitment: he was, primarily, a loyal Frenchman who had *all* the king's interests at heart. He looked forward to hearing more about 'the mysterious happenings in Flanders'. The wondrous news was that the

---

of Milanese Ambassadors in France and Burgundy 1450–1483, 3 vols (Athens, OH, 1970–71), II, p. 98). Written on the same day as Second St Albans, the letter demonstrates that talk of a possible alliance was current on the continent.

59   Between 1 October 1460 and 31 March 1461, Charles was unable to sign his name to accounts as he had always done (Vale, *Charles VII*, p. 142). On 3 March the Milanese ambassador wrote that the king had been gravely ill for six days (Kendall and Ilardi, *Dispatches*, II, p. 142). See Vale, *Charles VII*, pp. 174–7, 188–9, for his final illness and death.

Dauphin Louis had fallen out with the duke of Burgundy. The dauphin had fled to Philip of Burgundy's court in 1456, in defiance of his father. Philip had sheltered him and refused Charles VII's requests that Louis be returned to France. By 1461, however, a rift had opened up between them, and Louis was making overtures for a possible reconciliation with his father.[60]

It appears that the help Margaret sought from Charles VII was of a military nature, not just money. Gaston de Foix, recording his recollections of these events for Louis XI, claimed that Margaret sent Doucereau and two Dominican friars to King Charles around this time to request four things of the king: that he loan Margaret 80,000 *écus*, that he send an army against Edward of York by sea, that he revoke all safe conducts and issue no more to the Yorkists, and that he extradite certain Englishmen who had arrived by sea and had been taken prisoner. Charles refused all but the second – the request for military aid – on various grounds. We suggest that the friars were the envoys that Brezé was expecting, and that Doucereau had arrived ahead of them.[61] He may have had some inkling of what Margaret wanted and was willing to offer in return – and passed it on to Brezé to the latter's great fear and dismay – but he could not act as Margaret's official representative. He was, after all, the *French* go-between. England and France were still, technically, at war, and any collaboration between the two was bound to be fraught. An appeal for French support against rebels who were also Englishmen could be construed as a betrayal of England's interests by England's queen. Brezé went so far as to say that if her request became public, she stood in danger of being put to death. In his nervousness Brezé overstated the case; it was not customary to put noblewomen, let alone queens, to death in fifteenth-century England. Nevertheless, Margaret's request would alienate many of Henry's loyal subjects, who were imbued with anti-French sentiments, and the earl of Warwick, a master of propaganda, would exploit it for all it was worth. Margaret was well aware of the risks. She wrote that her envoys' instructions would vary according to what they discovered when they arrived. Only if conditions appeared favorable would they offer a *quid pro quo*.

Brezé was adamant that neither the written nor the verbal communications carried by Doucereau should be entrusted to anyone other than the king's secretary, Etienne Chevalier, for fear of a leak. The risk to Margaret was obvious,

---

60 Beaucourt, VI, pp. 312ff. Brezé's interest was not entirely high-minded; Louis was his enemy. His observation about Flanders, having nothing to do with the rest of the letter, proves the date of 1461. In 1460, there was nothing going on to cause such wonderment.

61 Gaston de Foix said that Margaret sent all three *after* the battle in which she recovered King Henry VI. One of the friars was to continue to Rome to complain about the behavior of the legate Coppini (Comines, *Mémoires*, II, pp. 309–10).

but animosity was strong on both sides of the Channel, and Charles's reputation might suffer if he appeared to be actively supporting his 'enemy', the king of England. Margaret hoped that Brezé would influence the king in her favor.

So what did Margaret have to offer Charles VII that caused Brezé such distress? Her need was desperate. Prince Edward's future and that of the Lancastrian dynasty hung in the balance. Just over a year later she would make a 'secret' offer to King Louis XI, and it would be accepted.[62] It is likely that Margaret made the same offer, or something very similar, to Charles VII: she would mortgage Calais to the French king in return for men and money to help regain Henry's throne. Despite Brezé's warnings, a rumor of what was in the wind did leak out. On 23 March the Milanese ambassador reported: 'We have knowledge here [in Burgundy] that the king [Charles VII] is gathering an army and navy in Gascony, to what purpose no one knows. Most people think he will obtain Calais by means of the queen of England.'[63]

We do not know what sort of reception Margaret's envoys received, only that Charles did not respond favorably to all their requests. It appears that he did assemble an army since it was disbanded by Louis XI after his accession.[64] As to whether Charles was amenable to any kind of larger bargain, perhaps involving Calais, we can only speculate. Gaston de Foix, when asked if Charles VII had ever made an alliance with Henry VI and Margaret, wrote that he knew of none, but that Charles had always said that 'when Henry was restored in his realm and had subjugated his adversaries who impinged on his liberty to make war or peace, then would be the time to talk'.[65]

This was not to be. Although Margaret defeated Warwick's army and retrieved Henry at Second St Albans, the Lancastrians were unable to enter London and consolidate her victory. At the approach of a new Yorkist force led by Edward, earl of March, they retreated to the north.[66] Edward was acclaimed king in London, and he set off in pursuit. King Henry and Margaret were at York on 29 March when the Yorkists defeated the Lancastrians at the battle of Towton. On the following day, they fled across the border into Scotland and exile. On 26 June, the victorious Edward was crowned at Westminster as King Edward IV, the first Yorkist king. Margaret did not give up. Although she surely would have

---

62   See below, pp. 253ff. It was Margaret's misfortune that the sympathetic Charles VII died in July 1461 and was succeeded by the hostile and ruthless Louis XI.
63   Beaucourt, VI, p. 327.
64   Scofield, I, p. 189, citing Mandrot, *Dépêches des ambassadeurs milanais en France*, I, p. 8.
65   Comines, *Mémoires*, II, p. 310.
66   Maurer, pp. 196–200, for a timeline and analysis of the standoff with London.

known that her uncle Charles's health was failing, she set herself to appeal to him once again.

[113] Robert, Lord Hungerford, and Sir Robert Whittingham to Queen Margaret, 30 August 1461[67]
(Gairdner, *PL*, III, pp. 306–7)

A la Reyne D'Engleterre (en) Escote

Madam, please it yowr gode God, we have sith our comyng hider, writen to your Highnes thryes. The last we sent by Bruges, to be sent to you by the first vessell that went into Scotland; the oder ij letters we sent from Depe, the ton by the Carvell in the whiche we came, and the oder in a noder vessell. But ma dam, all was oon thyng in substance, of puttyng you in knolege of the Kyng your uncles deth, whom God assoyll, and howe we sta(n)de arest (*arrestea*) and doo yet; but on Tuysday next we trust and understande, we shall up to the Kyng, your cosyn germayn. His Comyssaries, at the first of our tarrying, toke all our letters and writyngs, and bere theym up to the Kyng, levyng my Lord of Somerset in kepyng atte Castell of Arkes [Arques-la-Bataille, southeast of Dieppe], and my felowe Whityngham and me, for we had sauff conduct, in the town of Depe, where we ar yete. But on Tyysday next we understand, that it pleaseth the said Kyngs Highnes that we shall come to hys presence, and ar charged to bring us up, Monsieur de Cressell, nowe Baillyf of Canse, and Monsieur de la Mot.

Ma dam, ferth (fear) you not, but be of gode comfort, and beware that ye aventure not your person, ne my Lord the Prynce, by the See, till ye have oder word from us, in less than your person cannot be sure there as ye ar, (and) that extreme necessite dryfe you thens; and for God sake the Kyngs Highnes be advysed the same. For as we be enformed, Th'erll of March is into Wales by land, and hath sent his navy thider by see; and, Ma dame, thynketh verily, we shall not soner be delyvered, but that we woll come streght to you, withaut deth take us by the wey, the which we trust he woll not, till we see the Kyng and you peissible ayene in your Reame; the which we besech God soon to see, and to send you that your Highnes desireth.

Writen at Depe the xxx dey of August.

Your true Subgettes and Liege men,

HUNGERFORD

WHITYNGHAM

In late July 1461, Margaret sent Robert, Lord Hungerford (often referred to by his contemporaries as Lord Moleyns, his title for most of his life), and Sir Robert Whittingham as envoys to France. They carried a large number of letters and

---

67   This and the next letter must be considered together. We have reversed their chronological order to make explanation easier.

documents intended for King Charles VII and various other recipients. Henry Beaufort, duke of Somerset, had already been dispatched on a separate mission to the Burgundian court and, specifically, to Charles the Bold, count of Charolais, whom he regarded as a friend. He was also to seek out the Dauphin Louis, who had been living as an exile at the Burgundian court since 1456. Whereas King Charles VII had been cautiously supportive of Henry and Margaret and perhaps bore a genuine affection for his niece, Louis was another matter. It was in Margaret's interest to ensure that he would support whatever agreements she reached with his father.

Somerset probably landed in Dieppe, as did Hungerford and Whittingham a little later. He set out to meet Charolais and had reached Eu (about a day's ride from Dieppe) when he learned that Charles VII had died on 22 July.[68] He now urgently needed to contact Charolais to obtain further information and to decide how best to proceed. He also sent a message back to Dieppe to warn Hungerford and Whittingham that their mission to King Charles must be aborted. He probably instructed the two to meet him in Eu.

Somerset's message reached Charolais, and a messenger from the count was soon posting back to Eu. Louis, now King Louis XI, also learned of Somerset's arrival. Because of his estrangement from his father and the extreme secrecy of Margaret's dealings with Charles VII, Louis believed that he had been kept in the dark as to what was going on. So he immediately sent men to discover Somerset's business and to detain him until he could decide what to do with him. Louis's men encountered Charolais's messenger en route and, after learning from him where to find Somerset, reached Eu in record time on 5 August. There they found Somerset and Hungerford having a meal. Jean de Reilhac, the king's secretary, provided King Louis with a full report of what transpired, as well as an inventory of all the documents carried by the English envoys.[69]

Reilhac warned Somerset that the king had not been advised of his coming and asked his business. Somerset responded that he had come to request aid from the count of Charolais on behalf of the queen of England and also to speak with the dauphin (now the king). In addition, he had a few more things to discuss with Charolais. Reilhac then asked Somerset to show them all the letters, safe conducts and other documents he carried. Somerset cagily replied that he had only one letter addressed to the dauphin, but that he had no safe conduct as he was traveling under the queen's security, and he produced that letter for them to

---

68 Reported by the Milanese ambassador to Burgundy, who only spoke of Somerset (*CSP, Milan*, p. 101).
69 Reilhac, pp. 102–4, for the report; 104–7, for the inventory. We base our account on his report.

see.[70] Reilhac took charge of all of Somerset's letters, and Somerset begged him not to show them to anyone but King Louis and Charolais.

Reilhac next questioned Hungerford, who said that the queen had sent him to the old king (Charles VII) under a French safe conduct, with letters for him and others. He was to ask the king for three things: to send an army to Neufchatel, to provide aid in the form of twenty thousand *écus*, and to agree to a truce between England and France so that the king and queen of England 'might withdraw here' if they could not obtain help elsewhere.[71] The letters and papers carried by Hungerford and Whittingham were likewise confiscated; the entire collection was inventoried, and the envoys were told that the documents would be kept in a safe and secret place. The envoys were then placed under guard and told to stay put.

Charolais's messenger arrived in Eu several hours after Reilhac. He was only allowed to meet with the envoys in the presence of the king's men to exchange verbal messages. This judiciously avoided giving offense to Charolais, a powerful prince, while keeping any written messages from changing hands.

On the next day, 6 August, Margaret's envoys were politely arrested. Somerset was sent to the castle at Arques with some people to keep him company (and to keep an eye on him), while Hungerford and Whittingham and their party were confined in Dieppe. Reilhac told Somerset that he would return to King Louis straightaway to learn his pleasure, and that they would hear from him within a few days.

This letter of 30 August was the fourth in a series of efforts by Hungerford and Whittingham to get word to Margaret about King Charles's death and their own circumstances. We do not know if any of them ever reached her. Their first, probably written as soon as they learned of the king's death, was sent with the ship on which they had arrived. Our letter was intercepted at sea according to Henry Windsor, who copied the original and sent it to John Paston.[72]

---

70   The letter to Louis is the first item on Reilhac's inventory. Among the letters carried by Somerset was one bearing the salutation 'cousin', signed by the queen of England, but with no named addressee and which may have been the security he claimed. He also had three letters addressed to him in English, all apparently unsigned, and a letter to him from the queen of Scotland in Latin.

71   The contents of Hungerford's and Whittingham's bags included two personal letters to King Charles, Henry VI's authorization for Hungerford and two others to treat for peace with him, a power to obtain money from him and from other French lords, a designation of Hungerford as Henry's lieutenant to receive and conduct a French army to England, a power for Margaret to make peace with the Scots, a letter concerning the marriage of Prince Edward to a Scottish princess, a letter from Brezé to Margaret, and letters to him and other lords associated with the French court. These items confirm the intended nature of their mission.

72   Gairdner, *PL*, III, p. 312.

The two envoys, who had a safe conduct issued by Charles VII, were confident that they would shortly be escorted to King Louis. They were to be disappointed. The new king kept them waiting until October, when he summoned them, together with Somerset, to Tours.[73] What happened next is murky. The count of Charolais pleaded with Louis to free Somerset, his friend and cousin. The king eventually granted this request and gave Somerset some money; Somerset then went to Bruges, hoping to meet with Charolais at last.[74] It is not known exactly when Hungerford and Whittingham were set free. All three were at liberty in March 1462, when Hungerford and Somerset were reported to be separately en route to Scotland.[75]

Robert, Lord Hungerford, came from a family distinguished by its long service to the house of Lancaster. His grandfather, Walter, fought in the wars in France under Henry V and was at the battle of Agincourt. He was an executor of Henry V's will and served on the council during Henry VI's minority. Walter was succeeded by his son, Robert, who was one of Margaret's knights of the body when she came to England. This Robert's son, another Robert, became Lord Moleyns in right of his wife in 1444 and was known by this title for most of his life.[76] He suffered for his loyalty to Lancaster. After being captured at the battle of Castillon in 1453, his ransom was set at £6,000. His father managed to raise £2,000 by borrowing and by mortgaging his estates, and shortly before his death in 1459 he paid this amount to obtain his son's release. When the younger Robert returned to England, he mortgaged his wife's dowry to pay off the balance. In June 1460, in anticipation of the earl of Warwick's invasion from Calais, he and Thomas, Lord Scales, held London for King Henry. When the city opened its gates to the Yorkists, they and other Lancastrian supporters fled to the Tower. A force commanded by the earl of Salisbury laid siege, intending to starve them out. The defenders fired on the besiegers, which accomplished nothing beyond antagonizing the city.[77] They held out until Henry VI was defeated at Northampton, when their capitulation was inevitable. Scales and Hungerford were guaranteed

---

73   Scofield, I, p. 209.
74   Chastellain, *Oeuvres*, IV, pp. 68–9; J. de Wavrin, *Anchiennes Croniques d'Engleterre*, 3 vols, ed. L.M.E. Dupont (Paris, 1858–63), II, p. 314 note; Comines, *Mémoires*, II, p. 175.
75   Gairdner, *PL*, IV, p. 35. In this report dated 14–20 March, Hungerford was said to be aboard a carvel out of Dieppe. On 25 March a letter sent from Bruges to the papal legate reported that Somerset was still there (*CSP, Milan*, p. 107). He may have attempted to reach Scotland but turned back to avoid an ambush by Edward IV's men (Wavrin, *Anchiennes Croniques*, II, p. 314 note).
76   GEC, VI, pp. 618–20; *ODNB*, XXVIII, pp. 823–4, for the younger Robert Hungerford.
77   Yorkist-leaning chronicle accounts suggest that the Lancastrians fired randomly on the city, but this would serve no practical purpose and hence makes no sense. See, e.g., Marx, *English Chronicle*, p. 90; 'Benet's Chronicle', p. 226.

their safety if they surrendered.[78] Hungerford's mother obtained a license for him
to go abroad, and he departed for Florence. But he rejoined the Lancastrians in
time to take part in the battle of Towton along with his brother, Sir Arnold, who
was killed there. He went into exile with Henry and Margaret and was attainted
by Edward IV's parliament in November 1461. He was finally captured at Hexham
in May 1464 and executed for treason.

Robert Whittingham had more intimate connections to Margaret. In 1448 he
married Katherine Gatewyne, one of Margaret's ladies, and their daughter was
named for the queen.[79] In 1456 he became receiver general to Edward, Prince of
Wales, and sometime thereafter keeper of Margaret's great wardrobe.[80] He was
knighted by the young Edward after the second battle of St Albans, in February
1461. Edward IV promptly placed a bounty of £100 on Whittingham's head on
6 March.[81] Like Hungerford, he fought at Towton, fled to Scotland with Margaret,
and was attainted by Edward IV's first parliament. In 1463, Whittingham went
into exile at Margaret's court at Koeur.[82] He returned to England with Margaret
and the prince in 1471 and was killed at the battle of Tewkesbury.[83]

[114] Queen Margaret to her 'Cousin' Henry Beaufort, Duke of Somerset,
22 July [1461][84]
(BNF, MS Fr. 20855, fol. 64)

Cousin, nous vous remercions de ce que vous aves exerce tousjours vostre faveur
*de*vers mon seigneur et nous contre noz rebelles, et croies que nous airons tel*lement*
en re(*connaiss*)ance ce que aves fait pour nous, et que, tant vous estes emploie pour
nostre bien, que au derannier congnoistres que aves servy en mon seigneur ung
liberal prince, et en moy une telle dame qui ce acquictera devers vous en telle
maniere que devies estre content.

78 Scales was subsequently murdered while trying to reach the sanctuary of Westminster Abbey.
    Seven persons of lesser rank were executed, including Sir Thomas Brown (see above, p. 125).
79 Myers, 'Household', p. 183, n. 2; *CPR, 1446–52*, p. 165, for a grant to the couple, from February
    1448, of 40 marks p.a. in survivorship. Katherine, who was born in Anjou, received letters of
    denization in March 1449, along with a number of Margaret's other ladies (ibid., p. 240). Their
    daughter married Sir John Verney (Wedgwood, pp. 905–6). In 1472, Verney obtained a reversal
    of Whittingham's attainder, making it possible to retain Margaret's inheritance of Pendley,
    Hertfordshire, the Whittingham family home.
80 *CPR 1452–61*, pp. 323, 429.
81 *CCR, 1461–68*, pp. 55–6.
82 J. Fortescue, *De Laudibus Legum Anglie*, ed. S.B. Chrimes (Cambridge, 1949), p. 145; Kekewich,
    'Lancastrian Court in Exile', pp. 98–9.
83 Wedgwood, pp. 943–4.
84 Calmette and Périnelle, *Louis XI*, p. 293, published a transcript of this letter, which they dated
    to 1463. Some words in the upper right corner of our copy are very faint to nonexistent; our
    borrowings are in italics.

Et oultre, vous prions que adjoustees foy et credence a nostre cousin de Hungerforde et sire Robert Whityngham, chevalier, et quil vous plaise tenir lamain que monseigneur puisse avoir Thomas Wakam, Philippe Malpas, Forster et autres rebelles de mondit seigneur, comme autreffois vous avons rescript; et ceulx qui les detiennent seront recompenses.

Dieu vous ait en sa sainte garde. Escript a Edynbourgh, le xxii jour de juillet.
[signed] Marguerite

Cousin, we thank you that you have always shown favor towards my lord and us against our rebels, and [please] believe that we shall have what you have done for us so much in memory, and how much you have worked for our well-being, that you will know in the end that you have served in my lord a gracious prince, and in me a like lady, who will acquit herself towards you in such manner as will content you [lit. 'as you should be content'].

And further, we ask you to give faith and credence to our cousin of Hungerford and Sir Robert Whittingham; and, if you please, to use your influence that my lord may have [the return of] Thomas Wakam [*sic*, Vaughan], Philip Malpas, [John] Forster, and others of my lord's rebels as we previously have written to you. And those who are holding them will be recompensed.

God have you in His holy keeping. Written at Edinburgh the 22nd day of July
Marguerite

Confusion has surrounded this letter regarding its date and its intended recipient. Written at Edinburgh and bearing only a date of 22 July, it cannot be attributed to 1463, as Calmette and Périnelle believed. Margaret was in the north of England that summer, and in late July she sailed to the Netherlands (Flanders) from Bamburgh.[85] Nor can she have written it in 1462, for she left Scotland for France in April and remained there until October. The only possible date is 1461, when Margaret was in Edinburgh. There is every reason to believe that this was one of the letters carried by Hungerford and Whittingham on their ill-fated mission to France.

But which one was it? To whom was it written? This letter cannot have been written to King Charles VII, as Scofield supposed.[86] He was Margaret's uncle; she would not have addressed him as 'cousin'. Reilhac's inventory lists two letters intended for Charles: one addressed to 'bel oncle de France', and the other to 'tres hault & excellent Prince nostre tres chier et tres ame oncle de France'. Unfortunately, the inventory does not identify the signatory of either one.[87]

85   Scofield, I, pp. 300–1; 'Gregory's Chronicle', p. 220.
86   Scofield, I, p. 188, identified this as one of the letters carried by Hungerford and Whittingham. She assumed that Somerset traveled *with* them, which led her to misidentify its recipient.
87   Reilhac, pp. 105, 106.

Assuming a later date, Calmette and Périnelle thought this letter was intended for Louis XI, who was, indeed, Margaret's cousin. But even if written before his accession, the opening is too abrupt. Somerset told Reilhac that he carried only one letter addressed to Louis, and the inventory lists only one item thus explicitly addressed: 'A tres hault & tres excellent prince nostre tres cher et tres ame cousin le Daulphin.'[88] A letter to Louis would not have the abbreviated opening 'cousin', omitting the niceties required by decorum when his identity was in fact known. Moreover, Margaret thanked the person to whom she wrote for his support of her and of King Henry 'contre noz rebelles'. The dauphin had not supported the Lancastrians, mainly because his father, with whom he was at loggerheads, did. Louis's host, the duke of Burgundy, had sent a contingent of Burgundian soldiers to fight for Edward IV at the battle of Towton, and one of them had carried the dauphin's banner.[89]

A further aspect of the letter's language effectively rules out anyone else in France or Burgundy whom Margaret might have addressed as 'cousin'. It speaks of *service* to Henry VI and promises that such loyalty will be appropriately rewarded in the future. The intended recipient had to be someone who normally owed allegiance to Henry and Margaret, who would also be dependent upon them for reward and whom they *could* reward if their enterprise prospered. Service to one's overlord – or lady – was an honorable activity, and, though politely worded, the letter contains a specific request that could be regarded as further service.

The recipient of this letter was identified long ago, but subsequently overlooked. G. du Fresne de Beaucourt, writing in the late nineteenth century, briefly mentioned a letter from Margaret to the duke of Somerset: this letter.[90] Henry Beaufort, duke of Somerset, was second cousin to Henry VI in the male line. At the age of nineteen he had fought – and been wounded – in the first battle of St Albans, where his father Edmund was killed. Thereafter, he was involved in a grudge feud directed at the duke of York and the Nevilles. After the confrontation at Ludlow in 1459, he attempted to recover Calais from the Yorkists, without success. He was among the Lancastrian commanders at Wakefield, Second St Albans and Towton. In the summer of 1461, after so much effort that led nowhere, it would have been fitting to assure him that, eventually, his labors would prove to have been worthwhile. A year and a half later, with no reward in sight, Somerset's career

---

88   Ibid., pp. 103, 104.
89   P.M. Kendall, *Louis XI, the Universal Spider* (New York, 1970), p. 106.
90   Beaucourt, VI, p. 345, and n. 6. The reference appears in the last paragraph of Beaucourt's biography of Charles VII. He misread the date as 20 July, although the manuscript clearly shows that it was the 22nd. Scofield, I, p. 188 and n. 3, was aware of Beaucourt's reference, but mistook its recipient.

took a strange turn. He surrendered to the Yorkists when the northern castles of Bamburgh and Dunstanburgh were starved into submission in December 1462. King Edward pardoned him and restored his lands and title, probably hoping – if not believing – that he could be turned. This was wishful thinking, for within a year Somerset returned to his old allegiance. He was captured and executed following the battle of Hexham in 1464, along with Robert, Lord Hungerford.

Reilhac's inventory of the letters and documents he confiscated from the three envoys lists two letters that begin simply with the greeting 'cousin' and were signed by Margaret. One was carried by Somerset; the other, by Hungerford. It is most likely that this letter was the one carried by Hungerford, since it names him and Whittingham and functions as a letter of credence, asking the recipient to attend to what they will tell him. Among the documents that Hungerford carried, along with his authorization to receive and conduct a French army to England, was a further authorization, addressed to Somerset, to receive the French army and to use it against the king of England's rebels.[91] This would have been an appropriate matter to discuss with Somerset when they met up. Given that their original mission was to Charles VII, it may be that the details regarding this army and its intended use had not yet been finalized. It was disbanded by Louis XI.

Whatever Hungerford and Whittingham were to convey to Somerset probably had nothing to do with Margaret's second request, which was a follow-up to one already made: Somerset should try to obtain the extradition of three men as rebels against her husband. Two of the three 'wanted' men were Philip Malpas and John Forster, wealthy Londoners who shared a family connection. Malpas was a draper who became a well-known money lender and acquired a reputation for usury.[92] During Cade's Rebellion in 1450, Malpas's house was ransacked, and goods, jewelry and money were stolen.[93] One of his two daughters married Thomas Cook; their daughter – thus Malpas's granddaughter – married John Forster, who was educated as a lawyer. As the eldest son of a wealthy family who stood to acquire more wealth through his wife, his future was secure.[94] Both men were in a position to provide financial support to the earl of Warwick after the battle of Northampton, if not earlier.

---

91 Reilhac, pp. 105, 106. The Milanese ambassador to Burgundy reported on 28 August that 20,000 troops had been mustered and that Somerset was to lead them 'to the camp at Calais' (*CSP, Milan*, p. 101). The number was surely exaggerated, and his report was probably based, at least in part, on hearsay. Upon Charles VII's death, of course, all these documents became irrelevant.

92 *Vale's Book*, pp. 78 and n. 25, 79–80. He appears to have been an equal-opportunity lender, with the duke of York and members of the duke of Suffolk's court circle among his clients.

93 Flenley, 'Bale's Chronicle', p. 133, 'Gough London 10', p. 155.

94 *Vale's Book*, pp. 98, 99–100. Forster's father was a fishmonger and ship owner who served a term as mayor; his mother had the means to support building projects during her widowhood. Malpas's other daughter married Ralph Josselyn, for whom see above, pp. 92–3.

Thomas Vaughan was different: he was an up-and-comer and a turncoat. A Welshman, he received letters of denization at the request of Edmund, duke of Somerset, and Adam Moleyns in March 1443.[95] Within a short time, he had become a king's esquire. Henry VI treated him generously: in 1450 he was appointed master of the ordnance for life; three years later Vaughan received an annuity of 50 marks and, in a separate grant, lands and tenements including 'a messuage called Garlyk'.[96] He was a JP for Middlesex from 1457 to April 1458.[97] In May of that year, he traveled to Calais with Warwick's embassy to treat with Burgundy.[98] And then something happened. It appears that he switched his allegiance to the earl of Warwick. At the Coventry parliament of 1459, he was attainted along with the Yorkists for allegedly engaging in a treasonable conspiracy with Sir William Oldhall in July at 'Garlickhythe'.[99] The attainder cancelled any offices he held. Vaughan was with Warwick's army at Northampton, and he was reinstated soon after as master of the ordnance.[100] On 1 September, he became keeper of the great wardrobe 'during good behavior'.[101] During October and November, Vaughan was granted all the forfeited lands and possessions of Sir Thomas Brown (who had been attainted) jointly in survivorship with Brown's widow, in return for a fine of £1,000.[102]

According to chronicle sources written long after the events they describe, Malpas, Vaughan and others panicked after Margaret's victory at St Albans in February 1461. Fearing retribution when she reached London, they fled by ship to seek sanctuary in Burgundian domains or possibly in Ireland. Unfortunately for the fugitives, they were captured by a French ship and held for ransom.[103]

Soon after his acclamation, Edward IV sent a request to his 'cousin' George

95   *PPC*, V, p. 256.
96   *CPR, 1441–46*, pp. 419–36; *1446–52*, p. 332; *1452–61*, pp. 29, 83 and 359. 'Garlyk' had been granted to him jointly with Jasper Tudor, earl of Pembroke, in 1456.
97   Ibid., p. 671.
98   *Foedera*, XI, pp. 410–11.
99   *PROME*, XII, p. 461. *CPR 1452–61*, pp. 572, 597. Griffiths, p. 847, n. 274, suggests that their crime had been to send word of the great council meeting in June to Warwick, then in Calais. Maurer, pp. 164–5, is less sure about what happened at that council.
100 Commissions of 14 and 17 August 1460 refer to him as master of the ordnance (*CPR, 1452–61*, pp. 599, 612).
101 Ibid., p. 646.
102 Ibid., pp. 629, 631. The intention of the grant was eventually to divide these lands among the Browns' seven sons. According to the *ODNB*, Vaughan married the widow.
103 A.H. Thomas and I.D. Thornley, eds, *The Great Chronicle of London* (1938), p. 195; Kingsford, *Chronicles of London*, p. 174; Fabyan, *New Chronicles*, p. 638, say that the ransom for Malpas – which he eventually paid – was set at £4,000. Although only Malpas and Vaughan are named, it is likely that Forster accompanied them; otherwise it is difficult to explain how he came to be held along with them.

Neville, bishop of Exeter and now chancellor, reporting – and deploring – the capture of Philip Malpas, Thomas Vaughan and others 'by foreign enemies [as] they were escaping from England with great riches'. There were rumors that other Londoners 'planned to send out more goods to ransom them'. Edward emphasized that this must not be permitted. The mayor and aldermen must 'proclaim that no one is to send any sum out of the country … upon pain of death'. The chancellor was ordered to find out what goods the missing gentlemen had taken with them 'and to whom they belonged'.[104] Edward's concern was financial.

Both the Yorkists and the Lancastrians were desperate for money. The Lancastrians were penniless, and the Yorkists had resorted to loans from the moment they invaded; one of the first things Edward IV did as king was to hit up the London merchants for more money.[105] Wealthy Londoners were not particularly eager to see their money drained away by either side. The wealth Malpas and Forster conveyed out of the country was likely to have been their own and perhaps some other merchants' private capital, with possibly a few crown valuables thrown in by Vaughan, who had access to the Tower and the great wardrobe.[106] Seen in this light, their flight takes on a different color. Although they may have feared for their lives, they also intended to safeguard their wealth until things settled down. King Edward's demand to know what wealth they had taken with them and whose it was could serve as a lever to extort more money from the offenders, since sending bullion or goods out of the country without license was illegal. Recovering the money itself would be a bonus. The bottom line, though, was that no more money was to leave the country, for any reason.

Margaret's concern was probably also monetary. If she were able to lay hands on these men, she could convict them as rebels and seize their money, which she desperately needed. Indeed, this was exactly how she characterized them – as aiders and abettors of the earl of Warwick and Edward, earl of March 'in all their treasons' – when she first tried to obtain their extradition from Charles VII. He denied her request, saying that the Englishmen would be kept under guard but could not be released without their captors' consent.[107] Charles VII was perfectly capable of bending facts to suit his purposes, but in this case he may have been telling the truth: the fugitives were not in his possession. Having failed to obtain satisfaction from Charles VII, Margaret then handed the mission off to Somerset to see what he could do. Her promise in this letter to recompense whoever was

---

104 *Vale's Book*, p. 160, whose editors identify the letter's recipient.
105 Ross, *Edward IV*, p. 35.
106 According to Scofield, I, p. 99, n. 1, Vaughan held the office of keeper of the wardrobe for only 169 days, which would put his loss of it around the time that he absconded.
107 According to Gaston de Foix's report (Comines, *Mémoires*, II, pp. 309, 310).

holding them suggests a more casual approach than a formal ransom procedure: hand them over, and we'll make it worth your while.

Margaret's efforts failed. Edward IV's embassy to Louis XI succeeded in October 1461. Malpas and Forster seem to have paid for their own release; Edward provided the money for Vaughan.[108] All three prospered under him. Malpas returned to money lending.[109] Forster was Queen Elizabeth Woodville's receiver general from 1464.[110] Vaughan later became chamberlain to King Edward's eldest son.[111]

108 Scofield, I, p. 210 and n. 3. On 31 March 1462, Louis XI issued a safe conduct to Vaughan as Edward IV's ambassador (Calmette and Périnelle, *Louis XI*, pp. 279–80). Had Vaughan helped Edward to recover some of the 'lost treasure', with his leniency and favor the result?
109 *CPR, 1461–67*, pp. 381, 410.
110 Myers, 'Household', p. 257.
111 Scofield, II, p. 6.

Twelve

QUEEN BEYOND THE SEA

When Margaret's embassies all failed, she became an ambassador herself and then an exile. After a year in Scotland following the Lancastrian defeat at the battle of Towton, she and Prince Edward sailed from Kirkcudbright in April 1462. Margaret's eventual purpose was to bargain with Louis XI for aid, but she landed first in Brittany, where she was well received by Duke Francis II, and then went on to meet her father and Pierre de Brezé at Angers in May. After these preliminaries, which may have offered her encouragement and support, she met with King Louis at Chinon in June.

Margaret came as a suppliant; she needed military aid in the form of men and money to continue the fight for the throne. But she also had a bargaining counter that Louis coveted: Calais, whose recovery had been desired by the kings of France ever since its conquest by King Edward III in 1347. Following Charles VII's recovery of Normandy in 1449–50 and of Gascony in 1453, it was the last piece of former French possessions still in England's hands. But Calais and its outpost towers were surrounded by Burgundian, not French, territory, so access for a French attack required Burgundian cooperation, which had not been forthcoming. Margaret's offer of Calais to King Louis was a desperate gamble, for it was of even more importance to the English than it was to the French. Edward III had granted Calais a monopoly as the wool staple, through which all exports of that precious commodity must pass, paying customs duty to the staplers and to the crown. Psychologically, its importance to the English was incalculable, for it was their last foothold, however tenuous, on French soil.

[115] **Queen Margaret to Louis XI of France, 24 June 1462 at Chinon**
(Wavrin, *Anchiennes Croniques*, III, pp. 176–7, from *Trésor des Chartes*, J 648, n° 2)

Nos Margareta, regina Anglie, fatemur nos recepisse ab illustrissimo et serenissimo principe cognato nostro germano Francie Ludovico viginti milia libras turonensis monete nunc currentis in Francia, ad quorum viginti milium librarum turonensium solucionem, virtute commisisionis et potestatis nobis date a serenissmo principe domino meo rege Anglie, obligamus dicto cognato nostro, per expressum, villam et castrum Calesie sub forma que sequitur, videlicet: Quod quam cito dictus Dominus meus rex Anglie recuperaverit antedictam villam et castrum Calesie, vel aliquis de suis pro eo et in ejus nomine ea recuperaverit, Dominus meus antedictus constituet ibi predilectum fratrem nostrum Jasperem, comitem Pembrochie, vel dilectum consanguineum nostrum Johannem de Foix, comitem de Hendale, in capitaneum, qui jurabit et promittet reddere, tradere et deliberare antedicta villam et castrum Calesie in manus illustrissimi principis cognati nostri Francie antedicti, vel in manus suorum commissariorum infra annum ex tunc venturum, vel alias reddere et restituere eidem consanguineo nostro Francie antedicto predictam summam viginti milium librarum infra annum predictum. Ita tamen quod si dicta summa viginti milium librarum non fuerit predicto cognato nostro Francie infra annum, ut premittitur, soluta, obligamus nos per presentes, et in vim prefate nostre commissionis facere tradi et deliberari predicto cognato nostro villam et castrum Calesie antedicta: cum hoc quod idem cognatus noster solvat domino nostro regi Anglie antedicto quadraginta milia scutorum ultra viginti milia libras prenominatas. Ac eciam promittimus per presentes quod dominus meus rex Anglie antedictus obligabit seipsum ad omnia premissa ut premittitur observanda, et super hiis deliberare faciemus litteras convenientes in manus comitis de Maulevrier, vel alicujus alterius persone, ad complacenciam dicti cognati nostri, apud Dominum meun antedictum pro ea re transmittende. In cujus rei testimonium signetum meum presentibus manu nostra propria subscriptis apposuimus.

Datum apud Caynonem, xxiiij^a die mensis Junii, anno Domini millesimo cccc^mo lxii° et regni Domini mei antedicti quadragesimo.

MARGUERITE. *Manfeld*

Sceau en cire rouge sur simple queue.[1]

We, Margaret, queen of England, state that we have received from the most illustrious and serene prince, our cousin Louis of France, twenty thousand pounds *tournois*, money now current in France, for the payment of which twenty thousand pounds, by virtue of the commission and power given us by the serene prince, my lord the king of England, we expressly pledge to our said cousin the town and castle of Calais, in the following form. That is to say:

That as soon as my said lord the king of England shall have recovered the aforesaid town and castle of Calais, or anyone of his people recovers it for him and in his name, my aforesaid lord will there constitute our dear brother Jasper, earl of Pembroke, or our dear cousin Jean de Foix, earl of Kendal, in the captaincy, who will then swear and promise to hand over, surrender and deliver the said town and castle of Calais into the hands of the illustrious prince, our aforesaid cousin of

1   The editor, L.M.E. Dupont, made this note.

France, or into the hands of his commissioners, within a year, or otherwise return and restore to the same our cousin of France the aforesaid sum of twenty thousand pounds within the aforesaid year.

Provided, however, that if the said sum of twenty thousand pounds shall not have been paid to our cousin of France within the year as previously stated, we bind us, by this present writing and in the strength of our aforesaid commission, to cause the aforesaid town and castle of Calais to be handed over and delivered to our aforesaid cousin, with the proviso that our same cousin pay my aforesaid lord the king of England forty thousand *écus* in addition to the twenty thousand pounds previously named. And we also promise by this present writing that my aforesaid lord the king of England will bind himself to observe all the premises as stated. And over and above these things we will cause suitable letters to be delivered into the hands of the count of Maulevrier or any other person at the pleasure of our said cousin, to convey these matters to my aforesaid lord. In testimony of which we affix our seal to the present writing, signed with our own hand.

Dated at Chinon the 24th day of June 1462, and in the 40th year of the reign of my aforesaid lord.

Marguerite. *Manfeld*

A red wax seal at the foot of the document

This agreement seemed to offer the military aid that Margaret needed, while her pledge of Calais contained a condition that made it possible for the English to retain possession. It was a high-risk move, but Margaret did not intend to fail.

Her pledge of Calais was never a simple trade-off, as it was later seen and often portrayed. Instead, she offered it to King Louis as collateral for the repayment of his loan to the king of England. She did not sell it outright. In 1462 it was not hers to sell: Richard Neville, earl of Warwick, held Calais for Edward IV. Margaret's terms were complicated: when Calais was recovered, it would be placed in the hands of a trustworthy lieutenant who would become captain of Calais and hold it for one year, allowing time for Henry VI to repay the loan. If it was not repaid, the captain would surrender the town to Louis XI. If Louis gained possession of Calais in this manner, he was to pay Henry an additional 40,000 crowns.[2] She named Henry's half-brother Jasper Tudor, earl of Pembroke, and Jean de Foix, earl of Kendal, as potential captains of Calais who would honor her undertaking.[3] Margaret was acting in Henry VI's name and with his full authority, and she undertook to have letters setting out the agreement's terms

2   The *écu* was the standard French gold coin; it was worth 30 *sous* or 7.5 *deniers tournais*. So the total price put on Calais was 80,000 *livres tournois*, or approximately £10,500.

3   Jean de Foix was a southern French magnate who had remained loyal to the king of England even after Charles VII recovered Gascony.

carried to him in Scotland, either by the Comte de Maulevrier or by any other envoy Louis XI chose to name.

Margaret's use of the term 'cousin' was not just a formality; she and Louis were first cousins. His mother, Queen Marie, was the sister of Margaret's father, René of Anjou. It should also be noted that in addressing Louis, Margaret did not use her full, traditional title of Queen of England and France and Lady of Ireland. She also fudged his title by not referring to him as king of France. So that formal impasse was preserved.

After signing the agreement on 24 June, the royal party left Chinon for Tours, where on 28 June a treaty of alliance between France and England was publicly announced. Under its terms, a truce between Henry VI and Louis XI would begin immediately and last for one hundred years. Neither sovereign would ally himself with any rebellious subjects of the other. Louis would not grant safe conducts to adherents of Edward IV; he would publicly espouse the Lancastrian cause and forbid French subjects to trade with England while Edward IV remained king. Until Henry VI recovered the throne, no English subjects would visit or trade with Gascony without permission from Louis. The other signatories to this extraordinary document – which Louis XI, at least, signed tongue in cheek – were the loyal Lancastrian exiles gathered around Margaret: the earls of Pembroke and Kendal, Lords Hungerford and Roos, John Morton, and Sir Edmund Mountfort. Optimistically, they further undertook that the treaty would be signed by Henry VI and ratified by the English parliament before Christmas 1462.[4]

News of Margaret's negotiations with Louis XI reached England soon after she signed the Treaty of Tours. Fears and rumors regarding her intentions prompted a Paston correspondent to write that 'the Qwen and Prince ben in Fraunce and ha mad moche weyes and gret peple to com to Scotland and ther trust to have socour, and thens to com in to Inglond; what schall falle I can not sey'.[5] The terms of the treaty appear to have reached Edward IV in garbled form, for by September he expected that Louis XI would attempt to blockade Calais. Another Paston correspondent heard that forty ships had been arrested in the Thames in order to convey men to Calais 'in all haste', for fear that the French king would lay siege to it. He had also been secretly informed that 'there were CC in Caleyse sworn contrary to the Kyngs well [weal], and for defaute of there wages; and that Qwen Marget was redy at Boleyn [Boulogne] with myche sylver to paye the soudyers, in cas they wold geve here enttresse. Many men be gretly

4   Scofield, I, pp. 252–3.
5   Gairdner, *PL*, IV, p. 51.

aferd ...'[6] The English garrison at Calais was perennially disaffected since their wages were always in arrears, so the prospect that some would defect to Margaret if she paid them was all too real. The earl of Warwick as captain of Calais was not on hand to control the situation; he was in England, preparing to repulse the threat of a Lancastrian invasion from the north.

Margaret left Tours for Rouen, where, on Louis XI's orders, she was received with the same ceremony as that accorded the queen of France.[7] Did any of the civic dignitaries remember that just over fifteen years earlier they had welcomed her into the city as England's queen, and theirs? Margaret remained in Rouen for a month, until 12 August, when Louis, accompanied by Pierre de Brezé, made his state entry.[8] By 1 September 1462 she was at Harfleur where she waited to embark, while Brezé remained in Rouen making final preparations for the Lancastrian invasion.

[116] Queen Margaret to Pierre de Brezé, 1 September [1462]
(P. Bernus, 'Louis XI et Pierre de Brezé, 1440–1465', *Revue de l'Anjou*, n.s., vols 62–3 (1911), p. 369; from Arch. de Maine-et-Loire. E. 1828)

Tres cher et tres amé cousin, nous recommandons à vous de tres bon cuer. J'ai receu les lettre [*sic*] que m'avez escriptes et en escrips à Pierre Bendin à vostre entencion, ainsi que ai montré à vostre secretaire. Maiz quant est des II^c escuz miz à une part, en verite, mon cousin, je n'en sçai riens et riens n'en ai eu. Maiz des VIII^c, au plaisir de Dieu j'ai esperance de m'en descharger et vous aussi, car c'est mon fait et plus faire pour vous s'il met possible, en quoi me povez bien aider, comme vostre homme vous dira, tant devers le Roy que ailleurs où vous semblera estre necessaire. Aussi Eduard, mon filz, vostre cousin, se recommande à vous et voluntiers vous verroit. Tres cher et tres amé cousin, le benoict filz de Dieu vous doint bonne vie et longue et grace d'accomplir voz gracieux desirs. Escript à Harrefleu, le premier jour de septembre.

MARGUERIT

Very dear and well-beloved cousin, we heartily commend ourselves to you. I have received the letter(s) that you wrote to me, and [a copy of] one written to Pierre Bendin concerning your intention, which also was shown [to me] by your secretary. But as regards the 200 *écus* sent separately, in truth, my cousin, I know nothing about them and did not receive them at all. But as for the 800 *écus*, I hope to discharge myself of them and you also, God willing, for it is indeed my faith to

6   Ibid., p. 57. This letter led many early historians to believe that Margaret sailed from Boulogne rather than from Harfleur. Boulogne was in Burgundian territory, where her enterprise was unwelcome.
7   Scofield, I, pp. 251–2, 253.
8   Comines, *Mémoires*, II, p. 373.

do more for you if it be possible, as you are able to succor me well, as your servant [lit. 'man'] will tell you, in relation to the king [Louis] as elsewhere, where it will seem to you to be necessary. In addition, my son Edward, your cousin, commends himself to you and would see you with pleasure. Very dear and well-beloved cousin, may the blessed Son of God give you a long and prosperous life and the grace to accomplish your gracious desires. Written at Harfleur, the first day of September.

Marguerit[e]

As part of Margaret's deal with Louis XI, Pierre de Brezé was to raise an army to return to Scotland with her. Beginning in July, the king provided Brezé with money amounting to 1,500 *livres tournois* to support the expedition.[9] On 16 August he issued orders to impress ships and mariners, and by the end of the month Brezé was assembling ships and men.[10] It appears from this letter that he had sent money of his own to Margaret for her private expenses, and some of it had gone missing. Nevertheless, she promised to repay the amount that she had received as soon as possible. She also undertook to do whatever she could to show her gratitude. Brezé was not Henry VI's subject, so what that might be would depend on future circumstances. She might put in a good word for him with King Louis, or perhaps King Henry would choose to reward him in some way. Whatever the future held, she assured him that he could count on her good ladyship. A greeting from Prince Edward was also a mark of favor, as was the honorary addressing of Brezé as 'cousin'.

The warlike actions of Edward IV in England and especially the presence in the Channel of an English fleet that raided along the French coast gave Louis pause. Always parsimonious, he became less willing to support the Lancastrian cause, leaving Brezé to pick up part of the tab for the expedition.[11] The wind too was contrary, and only on 9 October was Margaret finally able to sail with 800 men commanded by Pierre de Brezé.[12] Their ill-fated expedition first went to

9   P. Bernus, 'Louis XI', p. 267, citing BNF, p. orig. 509, dossier Brezé, no. 48; and BNF, MS Fr. 32511 (cab. de titres), fol. 227. The payment came in two installments, as part of the 4,000 *l.t.* that had been agreed upon.

10   Comines, *Mémoires*, II, p. 373.

11   Chastellain, *Oeuvres*, IV, pp. 230–1, claimed that Brezé told him that he had personally contributed 50,000 *écus* towards its cost. This would have been an enormous sum, more than Brezé was likely to be able to lay hands on. We suspect that Chastellain, who was a great admirer of Brezé, either exaggerated or mistakenly wrote *cinquante* for *cinq*. Five thousand *écus* would be a more reasonable figure. Calmette and Périnelle, *Louis XI*, p. 30, say that Louis XI provided an additional 1,000 *écus*, citing D. Morice, *Preuves*, III, col. 66.

12   A letter of 7 October from Bertrand de Beauvau to Louis XI reported that the wind was then favorable and that Brezé hoped to depart with his fleet on the coming Saturday, which would have been the 9th (Bernus, 'Louis XI', p. 370). See Chastellain, *Oeuvres*, IV, p. 230, for the 800 men.

Scotland to pick up King Henry, and then to Northumberland, where they landed near Bamburgh on 25 October.[13] Although Margaret's supporters were able to re-establish themselves in the castles of Bamburgh, Alnwick and Dunstanburgh, their success was short-lived. At the approach of Warwick's army, Margaret, King Henry, Brezé and a remnant of their force put to sea again on 13 November and almost drowned in a storm. Their ship sank, and they ignominiously reached safety at Berwick in an open boat.[14]

Following this failure, Margaret sailed from Scotland to the Burgundian county of Flanders in July 1463, accompanied by Prince Edward, Pierre de Brezé and a small entourage.[15] Margaret met briefly with Philip, duke of Burgundy, at St Pol on 31 August. Philip's son, the count of Charolais, continued to profess his affection for Margaret and Henry and welcomed her royally. She left Bruges early in September and traveled to the castle of Koeur in her father's duchy of Bar, where she established a small court in exile.[16] From Koeur she launched periodic appeals for help to anyone she thought might conceivably provide her with support or active assistance to restore Henry VI.

The next two letters comprise instructions to ambassadors in furtherance of the Lancastrian cause. At the beginning of 1464, Louis XI, who was still playing off the Lancastrians against the Yorkists, sent his most experienced diplomat on a mission to King Henry.[17] Henry in turn employed Louis's envoy to carry instructions back to Margaret and to others whom he still hoped would support him.

[117] **Instructions from Henry VI to Guillaume Cousinot [22 February 1464]**[18]
(Wavrin, *Anchiennes Croniques*, III, pp. 178–81, from BNF, MS fonds Baluze, n° 9037[7], fol. 184)

Oultre mes instructions. Pour ce que la royne d'Angleterre avoit escript plusieurs lettres au roy Henry et à ceulx de son conseil, les uns par ung nommé Jehan Bron, et les autres par ung nommé Willem Bacquier, qui fut au duc de Xestre, lesquelles lettres contenoient, entre autres choses, qu'elle avoit eu de bonnes nouvelles du duc de Bretaigne et de monseigneur de Charolois, et qu'ilz estoient tout ung ensemble, et tous fermez et joings pour secourir le roy Henry en tout ce qu'il leur seroit

---

13 'Gregory's Chronicle', p. 218.
14 Scofield, I, pp. 262–3; Wolffe, *Henry VI*, p. 334.
15 Stevenson, II, ii, p. 781, which misdates her journey to April. See Scofield, I, p. 301 and n. 3.
16 Ibid., pp. 301–4; Chastellain, *Oeuvres*, IV, pp. 298–9, 310–11, 332. Kekewich, 'Lancastrian Court in Exile', pp. 95–110.
17 He probably did this to keep Edward IV off balance.
18 These extracts from Cousinot's undated memorandum, as recounted to Warvin, were published by Dupont and dated to 1462. Scofield, I, p. 316, n. 1, established that the correct date is 22 February 1464.

possible; et avec ce, estoit venu devers le dit roy Henry ung nommé Preston, qui demeure avec mon dit seigneur de Charollois, lequel lui avoit apporté lettres du dit mon dit seigneur de Charolois, bien gracieuses et confortatives, avec creance de bouche pour lui donner toute l'esperance qu'il estoit possible tant de secours et aide que de bon vouloir qu'il avoit à luy; et qu'il tendroit tousjours son parti sans varier. Et aussi il estoit venu ung navire de Bretaigne à Quicombri, en Escosse, duquel les Bretons qui estoient dedens, en disoient autant touchant Bretaigne, et qu'ilz avoient charge, de par le duc, de bailler au dit roy Henri tout ce qu'il leur demanderoient de leur marchandise, il fut advisé par le dit roy Henri et ceulx de son conseil que, apres ce que j'aurois esté devers le roy, je m'en iroye devers la dite royne d'Angleterre pour ces matieres, et lui declaireroie l'estat d'Angleterre et ce que monseigneur de Sombresset avoit rapporté; c'est assavoir qu'il avoit le serment et scellé de XVII hommes de Galles des plus grans qui feussent ou pays, lesquelx il nomma au roy Henri, et pareillement luy nomma plusieurs autres qui sont devers le West et devers le Su, qui semblablement estoient tous joings et fermez ensemble pour icellui roy Henry. Et, à ceste cause, avoye charge de dire à la dite reyne d'Angleterre que, en entretenant les choses qui estoient entre elle et les dits duc de Bretaigne et monseigneur de Charrollois, elle voulsist tendre à troys fins cy apres declairees.

Le premiere, qu'l y eust bonne amour et bonne aliance entre les dits duc de Bretaigne et monseigneur de Charollois; et que par vertu du povoir que la dite royne d'Angleterre avoit elle y comprensist le dit roy Henry, se jà ne l'avoit fait, en telle forme et maniere comme elle adviseroit à faire pour le mieulx, et qu'elle en baillast telles seurtez comme les autres voudroient avoir; et le dit roy Henry les ratiffieroit.

La seconde fin à quoy la dite royne d'Angleterre devoit tendre, estoit que icelle dame trouvast fasson, par le moien du roy de Secille et des dits duc de Bretaigne et monseigneur de Charollois, que tous les seigneurs de France voulsissent supplier au roy qu'il ne prensist aucunes treves ne appoinctement avec le roy Edouart.

La tierce fin estoit que la dite dame trouvast moien avec mon dit seigneur de Charolloys qu'il envoiast aucun secours à Bambourg d'artillerie ou de vitailles, et que le roy de Secille y envoiast des canonniers et des culuvrynes, et avec ce que icelle dame trouvast quelque fasson pour avoir ung peu d'argent pour entretenir ceulx qui estoient au dit de Bambourg et es [sic, en] autres places.

Et, d'autre part, que la dite dame envoiast devers le duc de Bretaigne, et que moy mesmes y vousisse aller pour ceste cause: c'est assavoir pour trouver maniere qu'il envoiast en Galles mons[ieur] de Pennebrok, avec quelque armee, et ne fust elle ores que de mille ou v^c hommes, et que en faisant ces choses et donnant à faire au roy Edouart par les deux boutz du royaume, avec les faveurs que le dit roy Henri avoit dedans le dit royaume, le dit roy Henry ne faisoit point de doubte que le peuple ne se levast de tous costez et qu'il ne le remist sus ainsi qu'il estoit auparavant; et avoit ferme esperance le dit roy Henry, veu ainsi que lui avoit esté mandé auparavant, que le dit duc de Bretaigne feroit pour luy ce que dessus est dit, et toutes choses qui luy seroient possibles, et en ce ne mectoit aucune difficuté.

My further instructions: In that the queen of England has sent several letters to King Henry and to his council, some by one called Jehan Bron [John Brown?], and others by one called William Bacquier [Baker?], who was with the duke of Exeter; these letters reported, among other things, that she had received good news from the duke of Brittany and my lord [the count] of Charolais, and that they were as one, and entirely united and committed to aiding King Henry in every way that may be possible. And with these, there has come to the said King Henry one named Preston, who resides at [the court] of my said lord of Charolais, who brought very gracious and comforting letters from [him], with oral authority for [Preston] to give all the assurances possible of help and aid commensurate with the good will that [Charolais] has towards [Henry VI], and that he would always be faithful to [Henry's] party without alteration.

And, in addition, there came a ship of Brittany to Kirkcudbright in Scotland; the Bretons manning it spoke at great length about Brittany, and that they had orders from the duke to deliver to the said King Henry whatever he asked for of their goods. I was advised by the said King Henry and those of his council that, after I have been to [Louis XI], I should go to the said queen of England regarding these matters and describe the state of England to her, and what my lord of Somerset had reported: namely, that he had the oath and seals of seventeen men of Wales, the greatest who live in that country, whom he named to King Henry; and, similarly, he named to him several others, who live in the West and in the South, who likewise were all united and steadfast in support of the aforesaid King Henry

And for this reason, I was charged to tell the said queen of England that, in maintaining relations between her and the said duke of Brittany and my lord of Charolais, she should pursue three aims, set out below:

The first: since there exists good love and good accord between the said duke of Brittany and my lord of Charolais, and that by virtue of the powers that the said queen of England has,[19] she should include the said King Henry therein [i.e., in their alliance], if she has not done it already, in such form and manner as she considers to be for the best, and that she should deliver such sureties as the others wish to have, and the said King Henry will confirm them.

The second aim that the said queen of England ought to pursue is that [she] should find a way, by means of the king of Sicily and of the said duke of Brittany and my lord of Charolais, that all the lords of France should beseech the king [of France] not to undertake any truces or arrangement of terms with King Edward.

The third thing is that the said lady should find the means [to persuade] my said lord of Charolais to send some help to Bamburgh of artillery and food, and that the king of Sicily should send cannoneers and culverins, and also that [she] find some way to obtain a little money to maintain those who are in the said Bamburgh and other places.

19 'Power' being the 'full powers', i.e., authorization, vested in Margaret by King Henry. She was acting in the king's name.

And, moreover, that the said lady should send to the duke of Brittany, and that I myself should be willing to go there [to him] for this cause: namely, in order to find a way for him to send my lord of Pembroke into Wales with an armed force. It need be no more than 1,000 or 500 men. And in doing these things, and by attacking King Edward from both ends of the realm with the backing that the said King Henry has within the said realm, the said King Henry cannot doubt but that the people will rise on all sides and that they will put him back [on the throne] as before. And the said King Henry has the steadfast hope, in view of what has been made known to him before, that the said duke of Brittany will do for him what is recounted above, and everything that he possibly can; and to this [i.e., sending Pembroke] he would not raise any objection.

Guillaume Cousinot was a lifelong servant of the French crown. Margaret had first met him in 1445 when, as King Charles VII's envoy, he opened negotiations for the ceding of Maine.[20] Cousinot's memorandum begins with an account of Margaret's letters to Henry VI, telling him of her favorable reception by Charolais and his promises of future support. She had also made contact with Duke Francis of Brittany, who had welcomed her in 1462. She was able to report that he was still sympathetic to her cause, but she made no mention of the duke of Burgundy, who had been polite but noncommittal at their meeting.[21]

The instructions issued to Cousinot in February 1464 were, of course, in King Henry's name. The extent to which they were solely the product of his own thinking is another matter. In December 1463, Henry, duke of Somerset, had abandoned his short-lived reconciliation with Edward IV and joined Henry VI at Bamburgh, bringing news from Wales. It may be that Somerset and others present with the king counseled Henry on the best way to employ Cousinot as an agent on their behalf. Somerset believed that all was not lost: there was still goodwill towards Henry in parts of England and Wales, and every chance that his throne could be recovered with help from abroad. This was the purport of Margaret's letters, too. Her efforts to obtain assistance had so far been successful: Charolais wrote personally to Henry VI, and the duke of Brittany sent provisions in a Breton ship to the impoverished Lancastrians at Bamburgh.

These hopes inspired Henry to make demands of Margaret that she was unlikely to accomplish. She was to persuade her father, René of Anjou, the count of Charolais and the duke of Brittany to convince other French lords to pressure King Louis not to make any pact with Edward IV. Unfortunately, it was already too late for that. In October 1463 at Hesdin, under the auspices of the duke of

20   See above, pp. 174, 176.
21   For her meetings with Burgundy and Charolais, see above, p. 259.

Burgundy, Louis had agreed to a one-year truce with Edward. One of its clauses stipulated that Louis would give no help to Henry, Margaret or their supporters. Nevertheless, Louis always kept his options open, and he had just sent Cousinot to reassure King Henry that he was not entirely forsaken.

While Margaret might obtain further informal promises of support, negotiating a formal alliance between King Henry, Charolais and Brittany would be far more difficult, if not impossible. Henry seems to have thought that she might already have done this since she had his authority to do it. But the duke of Brittany, although fiercely protective of his duchy's independent status, was still a vassal of the king of France. The count of Charolais was Burgundy's heir, but how far he could treat with a foreign power independently of his father, who was also King Louis's vassal, was problematic. In the end, no alliances eventuated, and further aid from Brittany was not forthcoming. Margaret was only successful in persuading Charolais and her father to contribute supplies and money, although René was already supporting her court at Koeur and could not offer her much more.[22]

The year 1464, which began on this optimistic note, went badly. Lancastrian forces were defeated at the battles of Hedgely Moor in April and Hexham in May. The duke of Somerset was captured at Hexham and executed. Henry VI, who had taken refuge at Bywell Castle, was forced to flee. In June, Bamburgh Castle fell to the Yorkists, and by July all Lancastrian strongholds in the north had surrendered to Edward IV. There could be no further hope of a Lancastrian recovery in that quarter. By December, the small band of exiles at Koeur was nearly destitute. Sir John Fortescue, Henry VI's chancellor in exile, wrote that 'we bethe alle in grete poverte, but yet the quene susteynethe us in mete and drinke'.[23] Towards the end of 1464 word reached Koeur that John Butler, earl of Ormond, and Roger Tonge, clerk of the king's council, were at the Portuguese court of King Afonso V. Margaret sent instructions to Ormond in her increasingly desperate, but never despairing, search for allies.

[118] Instructions from Queen Margaret to the Earl of Ormond, 13 December [1464]
(Fortescue, *Works*, pp. 25–8)

Here folowithe an instruccione made by the Quene of Englande unto the erle of Ormonde and to maister Roger Tonge, clerke of the kynges counseille of Englande, for

22 René gave her an allowance of 6,000 crowns (Lecoy, *Le Roi René*, I, pp. 344–5).
23 J. Fortescue, *The Works of Sir John Fortescue*, ed. T. (Fortescue), Lord Clermont (1869), p. 24. A portion of these instructions is also published in Fortescue, *De Laudibus Legum Angliae*, p. 145.

the expedicione of soche materes as the Quene desirethe to be spedde at this tyme for the
kynge her husband withe the kynge of Partyngal here most dere cosyne,

First, that they thanke the kyng, here saide cousyne, of the favoure and gode
wille whiche he hathe alway borne and shewyd to the kynge here husbande; and
namely in this now, his grete trouble and hers. And in specialle, of the grete favoure
whiche he shewyde unto William Josep[h], squier for the kynges body, in his late
beynge with hym by here commaundement for the kynges materes, and pray hym
of like contynuaunce.

Item, that they lete here saide cousyne clerely understonde that (iblessed be
Almyghty God) the kynge here husband is in gode hele, out of the handes of
his rebelles, and in sewerte [surety] of his persone, as here highnesse hadde late
writynge frome him, ensealed withe his signet and signyde with his owne hand,
whiche is ounedoutedly knawene to here selfe and to alle here counseille.

Item, the queen wille that the saide erle and clerke saye unto the saide kynge
here cousyne howe that the kynge here husbande and also here selfe have a fulle,
singuler, and ferme truste uppone the gode wille, frenshipe and ayde of hym in
this theire grettest and extreme necessite; considerynge not onely the nyghnesse
of theire blode, and that they, bothe kynges, buthe descended of the house of
Lancastre, whiche alway hathe bene rennomyde of singuler kyndenesse, faythe and
stabilnesse, but also the longe contynewyd amytee, peace, and gode wille, whiche
have be betwene the same kynges and theire reaumes. And most the queen hathe
in here mynde of how grete noblesse, wysdome, and pruesse here saide cousyn of
Portingale is nowe namyd and knowene through oute the worlde, and therfore
amonge other causes chosyn and made by the saide kynge here husband, while he
was in prosperite, and by the hole chapiter of the ordre of the Garter, a knyghte of
the same ordre, by whiche consideracione she hathe noo litelle truste of the ayde
of the saide kynge here cousyne; but most by consideracion that he is a Christian
kynge, and the wronge whiche nowe is done to the kynge here husband by his oune
subgettes and liegemen is an injurie and dishonoure to alle kynges, and mater of
boldenesse to alle subjectes for to rebelle ayen theire sovereyne lordes, to the perille
and unsiwerte of alle princesse, yf it be not ponysshed. And as a wronge done to a
man of the Chirche whanne it sownythe [pertains] to the dishonoure or perille of
the remenant of the Chirche is, and so aughte be, takyne as a thynge harmefulle
to alle the Chirche, and in like wyse done knyghtes whanne any thynge is done to
the dishonoure of knyghtehode, and wymmen, whane any thynge is done to the
dishonoure of wymmenhode, moche more aughte every kynge make hym selfe
partie whanne any thynge is done to the dishonoure or perille of the religione and
estate of kynges.

Item, that they lete here saide cousyn understande howe that the more partye
of the people of England, and namely the best disposede men of the same, kepyne
trewely and fermely theire faithe and love to the kynge here husband, and fayne
wolde shewe ham selfe soche, but they dar not do so as well for fere of tyrannie and
mordre whiche shuld be done uppon ham as by cause they have no grete lorde to

be theire capitayne that wille and darre shewe hym selfe soche and kepe the fylde, while the kynges welle disposede people myghte be assemblede and come unto hym. Wherfore it shalle nede that the quene gate some notable and manly prince, or other capitayne, accompanyed with iij m [3,000] menne at the lest welle garnysshed with habilymentes of werre, whiche myghte take and kepe a fylde in soche parties of England as the quene's counseille knowithe beste disposede to this case, into the tyme the people myghte by boldnesse of ham shewe ham selfe and come unto ham. Whiche and hit were done they shulde be in myght sufficiant; namely, yf thanne the kynge were withe ham in persone, for by comfort of his presance they shulde sone be grete in nombre, and his rebelles sore ferde to come agayne hym. And soche as shulde be broughte thereto by his rebelles wolde thanne be fayne to come ynne to him, and have his grace, levynge the same rebelles partie or turnynge uppone ham, as is most like. And as the quene is faythfully informede, the most partie of the comyne that buthe nowe ladde by the world fayne do. Wherfor yf the kynge, here saide cousyn, myghte be entretede to helpe the kynge here husband in this case with a capitayne and the nombre of iij m^e men, here counseille seethe clerly that the kynge here husband shuld thereby be surely broughte into his reaume and sette in reste in the same, and that thenne by that meane the kynge of Portingale myght have at his necessite at his oune wille the hole myghte of England to resiste and chastise his ennemyes, and to defende and helpe his frendes, and so in alle his nedes have the hole myghte of bothe reaumes.

Item, the Chaunceller of England and other persones, whiche buthe nowe in thise parties have sufficiaunt auctorite and power under the kynges grete seal to bynde the reaume of England, and alle other of the kynges possessions and lordshippes, for the repayment of alle suche costes and expenses as shalle be done for the kynges cause in this case. And wolle be alwey redy to make the sureties thereof, whenne so ever hit shalle be thoughte unto the queene necessarie that they so do.

Item, yf the saide erle and clerke fynde the kynge of Portingale lovynge and tender to the kynges partie, and of gode hele to helpe hym in his quarelle, thanne they mowe desire the same kynge to write to the Emperoure and to the Emperesse his suster, whiche also is discended of the house of Lancastre, to shewe theire favoures and gode wille to the saide quarelle, and to helpe in that they maye, that the Pope and the collage of Cardinales do the same. And in like fourme that the same kynge of Portingale write to my lord Charles, whiche also is discended of the same house, commendynge hym of his perseverant kyndnesse whiche, after the nature of that house, he shewithe to the kynge his cousyne of Englande in his grete trouble, and praye hym of contynuaunce, letyng hym wete that he wolle do the same.

Item, sithen the kynge of Spayne hathe weddede another suster to the kynge of Portingale, he maye the better be entretede that he allie hym not with the kynges rebelles, but be welle willede to the kynges partie, and that we mowe have free passage throughe his reaume. And yf he wolde take oure partie, we myghte thanne be myghty ynowe bothe by see and by lande, and he therby have with us a perpetualle peace, and thanne have all oure myghte ayene his ennemyes, whiche shulde be the grettest gode that of many yeres hathe comyne to his reaume; and, namely, for the merchandises and shippes of the same. And these ij kynges myght peradventure cause us, and theyme selfe by the means of us, to make and have a perpetualle peace with the reaume of Fraunce.

Item, the kynge of Portingale may sone fynde the meanes howe alle soche cardinales of his reaume and of Spayne, as buthe in the courte, mowe be made frendely to oure partie.

                                    Margaret R

(*Dorso:*) To my cousyn the Erle of Ormonde

John Butler was the second son of the earl of Ormond. His elder brother James inherited the title when their father died in 1452, although he was better known during his lifetime as the earl of Wiltshire, a title bestowed on him by Henry VI in 1449. James and John fought at Towton, and John fled to Scotland with Henry and Margaret.[24] Edward IV executed Wiltshire after the battle, whereupon John claimed the title of earl of Ormond and continued Wiltshire's strong support of the Lancastrian cause. Both brothers were attainted by Edward IV.[25] In 1462, John crossed to Ireland, where the Butler family's estates lay, perhaps to raise a force in King Henry's name. There he clashed with the earl of Desmond and was defeated. In the following year Desmond laid waste to all the Butler lands.[26] Ormond left Ireland for Portugal. His choice of destination is obscure. It may be that he reported on the situation in Ireland to Henry VI and was instructed to proceed to Portugal in the company of Roger Tonge.

Tonge, who also went by the name of Roger Spicer, had an equally mysterious checkered career. As clerk to the common council of London, he was sent to Rome in 1452 with Master John Aleyn, a lawyer, to plead the City's case in an ecclesiastical dispute. The two fell into the hands of the bishop of Cologne, and the intervention of Pope Nicholas was required to secure their freedom. Tonge was back in London by 1455, again serving the common council as clerk.[27] He was dismissed in August 1461 as a Lancastrian partisan.[28] Nevertheless, Tonge appears to have accepted Edward's regime initially, for in December 1461 he received a royal pardon.[29] How he came to join King Henry in exile as clerk of the king's council is not known.

---

24 Gairdner, *Three Chronicles*, p. 161, which erroneously records that John was killed at Towton; Gairdner, *PL*, III, p. 307.
25 *PROME*, XIII, p. 50.
26 A.J. Otway-Ruthven, *A History of Medieval Ireland* (1968), pp. 389–90.
27 Sharpe, *Cal. of Letter-Books: Letter Book K*, pp. 350, 373.
28 Ibid., p. 382.
29 *CPR, 1461–67*, p. 62.

Their presence in Portugal may have been brought to Margaret's attention by one of her servants, William Joseph. Sometime in 1464 (the exact date is unknown), she had sent him to Portugal on a goodwill mission, and he was well received. Joseph had been in the royal household from before 1453, when he was described as a 'king's sergeant'.[30] He incurred the enmity of the duke of York in early 1454 by petitioning the lords in parliament to establish a garrison at Windsor to guard the incapacitated Henry VI and the baby Prince of Wales at a time when York was jockeying for power.[31] The duke was shortly named protector of England, and he did not appreciate the suggestion that King Henry or the prince might be in danger. York had his revenge in 1455: following his victory at the battle of St Albans, he named Joseph as one of the culprits responsible for the encounter.[32] Joseph was indicted in parliament, but his proscription did not last long; in 1456 after York's second protectorate ended, he was named as a royal searcher of ships in the port of Bristol.[33] Joseph fought at the battle of Towton and was attainted by Edward IV.[34] He next appears at Margaret's court at Koeur before she sent him to Portugal.

Informed of the cordial reception Ormond had received in Portugal, Sir John Fortescue, former chief justice of the King's Bench and Henry VI's 'chancellor of England' in exile, was eager to take advantage of his position. He composed a series of instructions for Ormond and Tonge in Margaret's name. An appeal to King Afonso V to aid the Lancastrians would have seemed reasonable and it may help us to explain Ormond's presence. Afonso and Henry VI were both great-grandsons of John of Gaunt.[35] A formal alliance and trading agreements between England and Portugal dated back to 1439. Henry VI had made Afonso a Knight of the Garter in 1447, and relations between the two countries had generally been friendly.[36]

Margaret's approach to diplomatic contacts was always dynastic. She appealed to Afonso to approach other members of the Lancastrian 'family' to solicit their aid. King Enrique IV of Castile ('the Impotent') was also a great-grandson

30 *CPR, 1452–61*, p. 93. Otway-Ruthven, *King's Secretary*, pp. 138, 158, identifies him as a clerk of the signet from 1448 to 1452, but he is not so designated in the rolls. *Reg. Whethamstede*, I, p. 184, describes him as 'armiger et collateralis domii regis' in 1455.

31 Gairdner, *PL*, II, pp. 296–7.

32 *PROME*, XII, pp. 338–43. The others were the duke of Somerset, York's rival, and Thomas Thorp, a baron of the exchequer who had been composing bills against York in early 1454, at the same time as Joseph's petition.

33 *CFR, 1452–61*, p. 173.

34 *PROME*, XIII, pp. 50–1.

35 John of Gaunt's daughter Philippa, by his first wife, Blanche of Lancaster, married King John I of Portugal.

36 J. Ferguson, *English Diplomacy, 1422–1461* (1972), p. 54.

of John of Gaunt.[37] Margaret appears to have known that the Castilian king was negotiating with Edward IV in 1464, and she hoped Afonso would use his influence to make Enrique change sides. Afonso's sisters, Joan and Eleanor, were married to Enrique and to Frederick III, the Holy Roman Emperor, respectively, and Margaret urged Afonso to approach the emperor through his sister. The count of Charolais, as the son of the Portuguese Isabelle, duchess of Burgundy, was yet another great-grandson of John of Gaunt.[38]

Margaret was at pains to point out to Afonso that Henry VI was a free agent; he was not a captive in the hands of his 'rebels' and so was able to negotiate on equal terms with other rulers.[39] These in turn should recognize that his plight might be theirs: all rulers owed a duty to their calling and their knighthood to help each other defend their thrones against rebellious subjects. Margaret also alluded to the disrespect, amounting to insult, that 'rebels' showed towards Holy Church and 'womanhood'. Did she have herself, as a queen, in mind?

Her signature, 'Margaret R', is unusual. 'Marguerite' appears in her other signed correspondence still extant, whether in French, English or Latin. In the instructions to Ormond, although she was in exile in Koeur, she may have sought to emphasize her title and legitimate authority as England's queen and representative of the English crown until Prince Edward came of age. Although she was prepared to act independently of Henry VI, Margaret was careful to include his name, and she constantly associated Prince Edward's name with his father's. Fortescue, as Henry's chancellor, had power under the great seal to guarantee eventual repayment of the costs incurred in sending military aid to England, but only 'whenne so ever hit shalle be thoughte unto the queene necessarie that they so do'.

Margaret's (and Fortescue's) ignorance of foreign affairs outside their immediate milieu is demonstrated by the timing of this letter. Not only were they unsure of Afonso's name, but they also did not know that military aid from Portugal was virtually out of the question. Afonso and Enrique had been campaigning against the Islamic regime in North Africa since 1458. In November 1463, Afonso led an ultimately unsuccessful expedition in an attempt to recover Tangier. The two kings met in Gibraltar in 1464 before Afonso returned to Portugal at Easter.[40] It was probably shortly afterwards that William Joseph visited him. Afonso had no

---

37   John of Gaunt's daughter Katherine, by his second wife, Constanza of Castile, married King Enrique III of Castile.

38   Isabelle was also a daughter of Philippa and King John I of Portugal.

39   How much was widely known of the earlier English events of 1464 is uncertain. Margaret's claims regarding Henry's status put a very good face on things. Although Henry had eluded capture at Hexham, he remained a fugitive.

40   H.V. Livermore, *A New History of Portugal*, 2nd edn (Cambridge, 1976), p. 120.

'notable and manly prince, or other capitayne' to offer; unlike the king of England, he led his troops in person. After fielding large armies over a period of years, it is doubtful he had either 3,000 men or the money to equip them.

Did either Margaret or Fortescue believe what they wrote, or was it all 'diplomatic speak' in a desperate, but unrealistic, attempt to enlist Portuguese aid? Margaret may have hoped that sympathy expressed by another king, even without support, would further her cause. For even she cannot have believed that peace between Spain, Portugal and France could be achieved by English intervention. Margaret and the eleven-year-old Prince Edward also sent personal letters to Afonso. In the event, Afonso was not obliged to respond to Margaret's importunities. Her optimistic appeals never reached Portugal; instead, they ended up in the French archives, almost certainly intercepted by King Louis XI's spies.[41]

A year later, in 1465, Henry VI was captured in Lancashire and imprisoned in the Tower of London. All Margaret's efforts to recover the throne for her husband and her son appeared to have been in vain. Several years would pass before she could summon hope again.

Renewed opportunity came through a breach between Edward IV and the earl of Warwick. Growing disagreement over policy, coupled with Warwick's resentment at what he perceived as personal affronts, led to confrontation in the summer of 1469.[42] Using genuine popular discontent as both cover and opportunity, the earl staged a coup. For a time, Warwick held Edward prisoner while he took charge of the government. But this arrangement proved unsustainable: the king walked away from captivity and reasserted his power. This reversal brought no resolution. If Warwick was not strong enough to overrule the king, neither was Edward strong enough to eliminate the earl. After a brief rapprochement, rebellion broke out again in spring 1470, this time instigated by Warwick and his son-in-law, Edward's brother the duke of Clarence, to depose the king. When their effort failed, the conspirators' only option was to flee. In early April, Warwick and Clarence took ship from England. Calais denied them entry, so Warwick turned to piracy, building a fleet out of captures and Yorkist defectors, and put out feelers to Louis XI for aid. On 1 May, while Warwick's ships were holed up

---

41 Griffiths, p. 894, n. 24. Margaret's letter appears to be no longer extant. The prince's brief holograph letter to Ormond, a more formal one in Latin in his name to King Afonso and Fortescue's letter to Ormond are all published in Fortescue, *Works*, pp. 22–8, along with these instructions.

42 Hicks, *Warwick*, p. 270, identifies three points of contention: King Edward's preference for Burgundy over France and the subsequent failure of his foreign policy, the loss of Neville dominance within the Yorkist government, and Edward's persistent refusal to allow his younger brother George, duke of Clarence, to marry Warwick's eldest daughter Isabel, which thwarted the earl's dynastic hopes. Ibid. pp. 274ff, gives a detailed account of events.

at the mouth of the Seine waiting for Louis's response, Margaret wrote to the German towns of the Hanseatic League.

[119] **Queen Margaret and Prince Edward to the Hanse in Lübeck, 1 May 1470** (*Hanserecesse*, Abth. 2 [1431–1476], Bd. 6, ed. G. von der Ropp (Leizig, 1890), pp. 277–8; from G. Willebrandt, *Hans. Chron.* 2 S. 105)

Prudentissimis et discretis viris, rectoribus et ambaxiatoribus communium civitatum de hansa Teutonica, pro nunc in civitate Lubicensi congregatis, seu eorum commissis et deputatis, amicis nostris sincere dilectis.

Prudentes et magnifici viri, amici nostri ab olim sincere dilecti, salutem et pacis et caritatis amplexus. Norunt vestre per experientiam prudentie, et ut speramus, oculotenus recordantur, qualiter sub temporibus piissimi et nobilissimi domini mei metuendissimi Henrici, dei gratia Anglie regis sexti, per spacium fere quadraginta annorum comitates vestre magnifice suis libertatibus et privilegiis inconcusse, pacifice, quiete absque disturbio seu perturbatione, prout bene merebantur, gavise sunt, prout et impresentiarum gauderent, si staret quietum regnum ipsius. Sed postquam tirannus ille, comes Marchie, comes quocunque Warrewici, cum eorum complicibus, execrabili regnandi cupidine ducti, regium sibi jus aufferre conati sunt, ipsum dominum meum inauditis afflictionibus et injuriis persequentes, optimates regni crudeli neci et potentes spoliacioni et destructioni exponentes, non eis suffecit atrox dicta injuria, nisi etiam in vos et vestri similes, amicos et benevolos ipsius regni, sua seviret impietas et insaciabilis avaricia et cupiditatis vorago, nullis unquam temporibus absque divine providentie frenis cum provisione discreta finem acceptura, prout et adhuc deseviunt in presenti. Quoniam igitur, ut ait sapiens, maliciis hominum obviandum est, et ea, que perperam pravorum ingenio perpetrata sunt, bonorum virorum piorumque studiis, labore et sudoribus, reformari debent in melius, nos, quibus major atrociorque est per prefatos illata injuria, quorum nexus infideles divina dissolvit clementia, amicicias vestras, nobis sub vinculis pacis et dilectionis carissimas, licet minores passas injurias atque damna, rogamus et sinceris affectibus, quantum carius possumus, exhortamur, sub titulis passionis domini nostri Jesu Christi, quatinus ad repulsam injuriarum et malefactorum predictorum nobis vobisque per prefatos tirannos communiter illatorum, attentis animis et viribus una nobiscum studeatis insistere, quod utique levius fiet, et ad finem poterit citius optatum perduci, si vestre discretionis auxilia nostris decreverint consiliis adherere. Scimus enim, vos potentia, diviciis, armis et aptis fulcitos navigiis ceterisque ad bella necessariis. Novimus etiam, nos intra regnum ipsum potentes et fortes, dum affuerit oportunitas, amicos habere propicios, prout et rationis et nature jura suadent, ut dominus meus restituatur, indies prestolantes, ut tirannidis prefate vincla solvantur. Modum quoque, per quem id commodius, utilius et sine perditione hominum aut dissipacione bonorum, salva pace vestra fieri poterit, subtilius leviusque practicare possumus. Que duo si jungantur ad invicem, sub firmis vinculis caritatis, unita eorum virtus in Christo facillime poterit antedicte tirannidis laqueos versutos, divina jam favente clementia dissolutos, disrumpere, juxta nostri sententiam salvatoris: omne regnum in se divisum desolabitur, et: si sathanas in se divisus est, quomodo stabit regnum ipsius? Cum fortis armatus custodit, sed si fortior super-venerit, universa arma ejus, in quibus confidebat, auferet. Aggrediamur igitur nos quos una communis tangit injuria, debite reparationis iter, et capitum nostrorum sensus et advisamenta simul jungamus, et ut id levius et absque periculorum et casuum formidine fieri possit, et citius practicari et sub minori expensa, cum jam apud Bruggas habeatis aldermannum et clericum societatis vestre venerabilis, et nonnullos consiliarios vestros, ubi etiam nos ex nunc habemus consiliarios nostros, in quibus plene confidimus, optamus pro nunc et desideramus, quatinus prelibatis consiliariis et officiariis vestris, atque aliis talibus, quos ad hoc videritis expedire, dare dignemini plenam et firmam potestatem nomine vestro communi tractandi, appunctuandi et concludendi seu alias expediendi, prout melius et aptius vobis visum fuerit expedire, super singulis predictis et eis concernentibus, prout et nos, si ad hoc discreveritis intendere, plenissime pro parte nostra faciemus: advisantes vos, quod si in premissis vestrum efficaciter senserimus auxilium et juvamen, non solum vestras antiquas libertates et jura manutenebimus et in pristino statu restituemus, verum etiam superaddemus quecunque gratuita rationabiliter duxeritis adhibenda. De his vero, que super his decreveritis fore fienda, et intentione vestra, per ipsum aldermannum vestrum et consiliarios vestros apud Bruggas existentes, nos et consiliarios nostros ibidem certiorare curetis, quantocius commode potueritis, et pro causa prudentes et magnifici viri, amici nostri sincere dilecti, venerabilem et magnificam societatem vestram, nobis carissimam, conservare dignetur in prosperis nostri clementia redemptoris feliciter et longeve. Scriptum in villa sancti Michaelis ducatus Barensis, prima die Maji, anno domini 1470.

Marguerite, regina Anglie
Edwardus, princeps Wallie, heres Anglie
De la Berre

To the wise and prudent men, masters and ambassadors of the associated cities of the Teutonic Hanse, presently gathered together in the city of Lübeck, or their agents and deputies, our well-beloved friends.

Wise and noble men, our well-beloved friends from times past, greetings and embraces of peace and charity. Your learned authorities knew by experience and, as we trust, they remember seeing, how in the time [lit. times] of my most pious and noble lord, the most dread Henry VI, by the grace of God king of England, for the space of nearly forty years your noble companies enjoyed their liberties and privileges unchanged, peacefully [and] quietly without disturbance or interference, as they well deserved, [and] as they would enjoy [them] at present if his realm remained at peace. But when that usurper the earl of March [and] the so-called earl of Warwick with their accomplices, moved by accursed avarice to [have the] rule, presumed to take the royal right for themselves, pursuing my lord with unheard of torments and injuries, exposing the nobles of the realm to cruel death and influential men to plunder and destruction, the said heinous injustice did not suffice them. But, in addition, their impiety raged against you and those like you, friends and well-wishers of the realm, just as [their] insatiable rapacity and bottomless greed, which will never end at any time without the restraint of Divine Providence [i.e., in heaven] and prudent foresight [i.e., on earth], still rage now.

Therefore because, as the wise man says, one must oppose the wicked vices of men, and those things that were falsely accomplished by the contrivance of corrupt men must be changed for the better by the zeal, toil and sweat of good and pious men, we, to whom greater and more heinous injustice was done by the aforesaid, whose treacherous bonds divine mercy is dissolving, ask for your friendship, which is precious to us, within the bonds of peace and love although [you] suffered lesser injuries and damages. And with sincere affection, as dearly as we are able, we exhort [you] in the name of the passion of our Lord Jesus Christ, that together with us you strive to apply attentive minds and physical strength to remove the injuries and aforesaid evil deeds brought jointly upon us and you by the aforesaid tyrants. But assuredly it will be done more easily and will bring about the desired goal more swiftly, if the auxiliary troops at your disposal resolve to adhere to our counsels.

We know, indeed, that you are supported by the political power, wealth, arms and suitable ships and other things necessary for war. And we have also learned that we have strong and powerful friends within the realm itself [who are] favorably inclined to restore my lord, while there is opportunity, just as the laws of both reason and nature advise, [and] who daily stand ready to unbind the chains of the aforesaid tyranny. Likewise, we can more precisely and easily contrive the means by which, without the violation of your peace, it can be accomplished more conveniently [and] effectively, without the loss of men or the squandering of resources. And if the two [i.e., the Lancastrians and the Hanse] are reciprocally joined in firm bonds of love, their strength, united in Christ, will very easily shatter the cunning snares of the aforesaid tyranny, [whose] dissolution divine mercy already favors, according to the word of our Saviour: Every kingdom divided within itself will be forsaken, and if Satan is divided within himself, how will his kingdom stand?[43]

When a soldier is strong, he offers protection, but if a more powerful one arrives, he will overcome all the weapons on which the first relied. Therefore, let us set out, we whom a single common injustice touches, [to whom] a way of restoration is owed, and at the same time let us bring together the judgment and the advice of our leaders. And so that it may be done more easily, without the fear of risk and accident, and be contrived more quickly and for less expense, since you already have an alderman and a priest of your venerable society, as well as several of your counselors, in Bruges, where we likewise have our counselors, in whom we have full confidence, we desire and request for now that you deem fit to give your aforesaid

43   Margaret is quoting the New Testament here: 'If a house be divided against itself, that house cannot stand' (Mark 3:25). In the next passage she equates Satan with the alliance of Edward and Warwick that allowed the Yorkists to seize the throne in the first place.

counselors and officials, as well as to other such [persons], whom you may consider to be useful for this [purpose], full and durable power in your joint name to treat, to agree and to conclude or otherwise make arrangements, as will seem to you better and more apt to be expedient, with regard to each of the aforesaid things and concerning them.

Just as we too, on our part, will fully do [the same] if you decide to exert yourselves for this purpose: advising you that if in the foregoing we experience your help and assistance to good effect, not only will we restore and maintain your original ancient liberties and rights, but also we will agree to [lit. 'add'] any additional rewards that you may reasonably request of us. And, through your alderman himself and your counselors who are in Bruges, may you undertake to inform us and our counselors there of these things and your intention, and, in addition, what you decide to do, as soon as you conveniently can; and therefore, excellent and prudent men, our well-beloved friends, may the mercy of the Redeemer deign to preserve your venerable and noble society, so dear to us, in prosperity, happily and far into the future. Written in the town of St Michaels in the duchy of Bar, the first day of May 1470.

> Marguerite, queen of England
> Edward, prince of Wales, heir of England

When Margaret wrote this letter in her name and her son's, it seemed that the Lancastrians' prospects had changed drastically. After years of struggle and repeated disappointment, Providence was finally weighing in on her side. How well-informed was Margaret of the breach between Edward IV and the earl of Warwick? Dissemination of news lagged behind events and was often incomplete, if not downright misleading. Milanese ambassadors at the French court asserted that war was raging in England between them. On 3 April 1470, a Milanese letter stated that Warwick had defeated the king in a great battle and that Edward had been killed. Louis XI – and others, of course – would soon have learned that this was not the case. By mid-May, the Milanese were reporting that Warwick was in France and King Louis was encouraging him to return to England. The ambassadors' informants believed – or hoped? – he would defect to Lancaster and take Prince Edward back to England with him.[44] Similar rumors had existed before and had proved false. It seems likely that Margaret was eager to use any discord between Edward IV and the powerful earl to Lancastrian advantage. This does not mean, however, that she would have automatically – or eagerly – regarded Warwick as a potential ally.

Margaret's letter blamed Edward and Warwick equally for her husband's deposition. She hated both of them and was gratified that Providence had seen fit to dissolve their pernicious partnership. If anything, she seems more

---

44 *CSP, Milan*, pp. 134–6.

contemptuous of Warwick. This is understandable, as he had authored the Yorkist propaganda campaign that claimed, among other things, that her son was a bastard. At the same time, her contempt would have pleased the Hanse merchants who received her letter; they felt no love for Warwick, having been too often victims of his piracy. It required no exceptional insight to expect him to appeal to Louis XI for aid; the earl had always favored the king of France over the duke of Burgundy, and Louis reciprocated. He preferred Warwick to Edward IV. Nor did Margret need a crystal ball to anticipate that Louis would try to use Warwick for his own purposes, which might or might not serve Lancastrian ends; by this time, she could have harbored no illusions regarding Louis's commitment to her cause.

Her appeal to the Hanse was therefore an effort to take control of the situation and its possibilities on her own terms. She wanted the support of men who could provide the means of war independently of Louis – and of Warwick. Hence her desire to deal with them directly, through her own councilors, and for her own commanders to be in charge of any military force they provided. Beyond the outline of her appeal itself, Margaret was very cagey about what she committed to writing. The reference to the two soldiers, the second of whom was able to strip the first of his weapons, *might* allude to the possibility of suborning Warwick, who was widely perceived as the instrument by which Edward had gained his throne. Rather more likely, her request to conduct negotiations – and later planning sessions – in Bruges to avoid 'risk and accident' would have been designed to keep knowledge of her activities *away* from both Louis and Warwick.

Margaret's perspective emerges more clearly if we consider the interests and grievances of the persons to whom she appealed. The merchants of the Hanse were presently in a state of war with England. The long relationship between the Hanseatic League and England had not always gone smoothly. From 1437, Hanse merchants had enjoyed special privileges in England established by treaty, a fact Margaret noted in her letter. These privileges were supposed to be reciprocal. But over time, fueled by the belief that they were not reciprocated, anti-Hanse feelings arose in England. During the summer of 1458, ships of the Hanse became a target for piracy committed by the earl of Warwick as captain of Calais, which had embarrassed Henry VI.[45] Edward IV threatened to suspend their merchants' privileges or to levy a poll-tax upon them, forcing the cities of the Hanseatic League to offer greater privileges to English merchants in their territory, though resentments lingered. Their relations took a dramatic turn for the worse in 1468, when four English ships were seized by Danish pirates. The king's council, with Warwick as its most prominent member, convinced Edward IV

45   Hicks, *Warwick*, p. 147.

that the Hanse had been complicit and should be punished. Hanse merchants in England were imprisoned, their property seized, and they were charged £20,000 as compensation. This was undoubtedly the suffering to which Margaret referred. Although the merchants were later released, the damage had been done. The Hanse wanted reparations, and when these were not forthcoming, war at sea effectively ensued and ushered in a period in which trade between England and the trade-dependent Hanseatic League was at its lowest ebb of the fifteenth century.[46] What Margaret offered, then, was a return to the better, remembered days of yore, with the promise of more expanded privileges as sweetening and a chance for heady vengeance by the by.[47] With Hanse support she would neither need nor want Warwick. On the first of May, in far off Koeur, it may have seemed enough.

Nothing substantial resulted from Margaret's attempt to negotiate with the Hanse merchants, but in June 1470 rumors and speculation surrounding the earl of Warwick's breach with Edward IV solidified. Warwick was prepared, on certain conditions, to restore Henry VI and the Lancastrian dynasty. With no other support on the horizon, Margaret again approached Louis XI's bargaining table.

[120] Sforza de Bettini of Florence, Milanese Ambassador at the French Court, to Galeazzo Maria Sforza, Duke of Milan, 29 June 1470 from Amboise (excerpted)

(*CSP, Milan*, pp. 139–40)

The Queen of England, wife of King Henry, and the prince, her son, arrived in this place on the 25th instant, and were received in a very friendly and honourable manner by his Majesty the king and the queen. His Majesty has spent and still spends every day in long discussions with that queen to induce her to make the alliance with Warwick and to let the prince, her son, go with the earl to the enterprise of England. Up to the present the queen has shown herself very hard and difficult, and although his Majesty offers her many assurances, it seems that on no account whatever will she agree to send her son with Warwick, as she mistrusts him.

---

46 T.R. Lloyd, 'A Reconsideration of Two Anglo-Hanseatic Treaties of the Fifteenth Century', *EHR* 102 (1987), pp. 924–5; Ross, *Edward IV*, pp. 365–6. The decision to retaliate against the Hanse became known as the 'verdict of the council'. Although, officially, enmity was directed towards Edward IV, Warwick would also have been held responsible for his role on the council.

47 In late June 1470, the English fleet had to deal with a renewed Hanseatic threat, and in August the League broke off all relations with England. Though indicative of hostility between England and the Hanse, any effect of Margaret's appeal on these events is opaque. After 1471, when Edward recovered the throne, he realized that bad relations with the Hanse were bad for England (and for him) and made his peace with them – on generous terms.

[121] Sforza de Bettini of Florence, Milanese Ambassador at the French Court, to Galeazzo Maria Sforza, Duke of Milan, 24 July 1470 from Angers
(*CSP, Milan*, p. 141)

The Queen of England and the Prince of Wales, her son, arrived here the day before yesterday, and on the same day the Earl of Warwick also arrived. The same evening the king presented him to the queen. With great reverence Warwick went on his knees and asked her pardon for the injuries and wrongs done to her in the past. She graciously forgave him and he afterwards did homage and fealty there, swearing to be a faithful and loyal subject of the king, queen, and prince as his liege lords unto death. They have not yet spoken of the marriage alliance, though it is considered as good as accomplished, and it is argued that they are only waiting for the arrival of King René, who may come any day, to announce it.

Louis XI met the earl of Warwick in Amboise on 8 June, after significant dickering and lengthy consideration of his own options and the likely benefits for France.[48] By that time, he had probably already consulted with one or more of Margaret's representatives, perhaps with Sir John Fortescue. On 2 June, even before the meeting, the Milanese reported that the arrangement for a marriage between Warwick's daughter and Prince Edward of Lancaster was 'considered certain'. Ten days later, Margaret and Prince Edward were expected at court, and Warwick left Amboise because he did not wish to be there when Margaret arrived, expecting that King Louis would 'shape matters a little with her and induce her to agree to an alliance between the prince, her son, and his daughter and to put aside all past injuries and enmities'.[49] While the Lancastrians would have discussed and calculated what they stood to gain by using Warwick to promote their ends, just as he surely would have considered how using *them* could benefit him, there is no reason to believe that Margaret was eager for a reconciliation and alliance. Nor is it credible that Fortescue, despite being Henry VI's chancellor, would have had *carte blanche* to arrange such sensitive matters as he saw fit or to commit to anything that Margaret did not support.

Margaret did not arrive at Amboise until 25 June, and she then proved 'difficult'. She did not trust Warwick at all; she was most reluctant to ally with him, and under no circumstances would she allow her son to sail with him to England. Louis XI and her father's councilors set about lobbying her to accept the proposed alliance. On 22 July, Margaret finally received Warwick at Angers, where the earl

48 Initially, Louis was annoyed by the earl's presence and importunities. He wanted nothing more than to be quit of the fugitives and for them to go back to England to cause trouble, preferably with the Lancastrians in tow (*CSP, Milan*, p. 136; J. Vaesen and E. Charavay, eds, *Lettres de Louis XI, roi de France*, IV [Paris, 1890], pp. 110–14).
49 *CSP, Milan*, pp. 138–9.

went on his knees before her to beg pardon, which she grudgingly granted. He pledged undying fealty to the house of Lancaster and swore to atone for his past sins by recovering the throne for Henry VI.[50] When this was accomplished, Prince Edward would rule as regent for his father, but Margaret cannot have doubted that the guiding hand would be Warwick's. It had taken almost a month of extreme pressure and a move of the French court from Amboise to Angers, her father's capital and her childhood home, before she finally bowed to the inevitable and accepted the reconciliation and the marriage. Despite her misgivings, Margaret believed, as did many others, that Warwick had placed Edward IV on the throne of England. What Warwick had done once, he could do again.

Margaret's hatred of Warwick, her distaste for a marriage between her son and the earl's daughter and her fears for the prince's safety if he were entrusted to Warwick's care were personal. But she also had diplomatic and strategic reasons to hesitate. Warwick had been preying on foreign shipping since he left England, especially Burgundian and Breton ships. Duke Philip of Burgundy had died in 1467, and the count of Charolais was now Duke Charles the Bold of Burgundy and married to Edward IV's sister. He detested Warwick, and he threatened war with Louis XI unless the French king expelled the earl and his ships from French ports. Although he had no love for King Edward either, he was prepared to go to Edward's aid against Warwick.[51] Allying with the earl would thus deny Margaret any hope of Burgundian support. The same was true of the duke of Brittany, with whom Jasper Tudor had established a rapport. Margaret had received little tangible aid from either duke, but she may have hoped that with a commitment from the Hanse – and her councilors were even then in Bruges (Burgundian territory) negotiating with Hanse representatives – they would consider siding with Lancaster. One of Margaret's explicit arguments against an alliance with Warwick, made at some point during her negotiations with Louis XI, was that she had 'certain parties and friends' who could be lost by such a move, and that their loss might prove more hurtful than any advantage to be gained through cooperation with him.[52] While these 'friends' would have included hardcore Lancastrians, it is likely that they also included potential allies such as Burgundy, Brittany and the Hanse. The loss of their support and the possibility of their active opposition had to be weighed against the value of an alliance with Warwick. In the end, the 'Warwick legend' won.

On 25 July, the marriage of Prince Edward and Anne Neville was agreed upon, and on the 30th Warwick, Louis and Margaret swore formal oaths in the cathedral

50   Ibid., p. 141.
51   Hicks, *Warwick*, pp. 289, 290–1.
52   *Vale's Book*, p. 216.

of Angers to uphold the terms of the agreement they had forged. Warwick sailed for England on 9 September.[53] Although his daughter's marriage had not yet been celebrated as he had initially wished, he was given no choice. All would depend upon the success of his enterprise. On another critical point Margaret also held firm: Prince Edward did not accompany him. Instead, Jasper Tudor went along to provide a trustworthy report of events. At first, victory proved easy. Edward IV fled to Burgundy with a few followers, and Henry VI was restored to his throne. Word came back to France of Warwick's success. The agreed-upon marriage took place around 17 December in Amboise.[54] It only remained for Margaret and her son to return to England to complete and consolidate the Lancastrian triumph.

At that point, Margaret's hopes turned sour. By agreeing to conditions that Louis XI had imposed in brokering her rapprochement with Warwick, she had become both the king's pensioner and his prisoner. He would not permit her to leave France until Warwick fulfilled the second part of the bargain: the earl had undertaken that he, and therefore England, would declare war on Louis's arch-enemy, Duke Charles of Burgundy, as soon as he established his hold in England. The early months of 1471 found Margaret and Prince Edward at Honfleur, anxiously awaiting the news that would end their ten-year exile and allow them to return to England. It was to be the culmination of Margaret's hopes and schemes, but one for which she paid a high price.

[122] Receipt from Queen Margaret to Jean Raguier, Receiver General of
Normandy, 26 February [1471]
(BNF, MS Fr. 20378, fol. 16)[55]

Nous Marguerite Royne d'Angleterre confessons avoir recue de Jehan Raguier controleur duroy et receiveur general deses fin[ances] en Norm[andie] 2,500 livres anous ordonne pour nostre Estat et entretenans en ce Royaume durant les mois de Janvier derrain et ce present mois de fevrier qui est au feur de 800 livres pour nostre despense et 400 livres pour nostre argentrerie par chacun des mois de Janvier fevrier et mars. 26 fevrier 1470.

Marguerite

DelaBarre

53   *CSP, Milan*, pp. 141–2; Vaesen and Charavay, *Lettres*, pp. 130–1; *Vale's Book*, pp. 215–18.
54   Calmette and Périnelle, *Louis XI*, pp. 133, 319–20, opted for the 13th. More recently, M. Barnfield and A. Carson, 'The Marriage of the Lancastrian Prince of Wales and Lady Anne Neville', *The Ricardian Bulletin* (December 2017), pp. 57–8, have argued that the 17th is the preferred date.
55   A copy of this document showing Margaret's seal is published in C. de Mérindol, *Le Roi René et la seconde maison d'Anjou* (Paris, 1987), plate LXX. Three other quittances appear to belong to this same time frame: BNF, MS Fr. 20384, pièces 43–6, r–v, dated 26 February and 10 and 20 March.

We Margaret, Queen of England, acknowledge receipt from Jehan Raguier, the king's comptroller and receiver general of Normandy, of the sum of 2,500 *livres tournois* granted to us for our estate and maintenance in this kingdom, during the past month of January and the present month of February, a payment of 800 *livres* for our living expenses and 400 *livres* for our silver plate for each of the months January, February and March. [dated] 26 February 1470.

Marguerite

De la Barre

Although this receipt is clearly dated 1470, by modern reckoning the date is February 1471. In fifteenth-century France a new year was deemed to begin either at Easter or, more usually, on 25 March, the Day of the Annunciation of the Virgin. Margaret's year of 1470 would not end until a month after the receipt was written.

Jean Raguier came from a family with a long tradition of service to the French king. A Hémon Raguier had come to France in the entourage of King Charles VII's mother, Isabeau of Bavaria, and initially served as her treasurer before moving up the ladder to become the king's treasurer for war and controller of finances. Hémon's son Antoine followed him in these posts. When Antoine died in 1468, his eldest son Jean succeeded him as treasurer of war and also became receiver general for Normandy. Jean Raguier held these posts until the end of 1480.[56] In his capacity as receiver general, he was responsible for providing Margaret with her pension from Louis XI while she remained in France.

The identity of de la Barre, who served as scribe, is more speculative, but he may have been William de la Barre, a former canon of Lincoln cathedral, who was in the service of Thomas Bird, bishop of St Asaph, Margaret's senior cleric at her court at Koeur.[57]

Either de la Barre's or Raguier's accounting was faulty, since 800 *livres tournois* for Margaret's living expenses, plus 400 *livres tournois* for silver plate, amounts to 2,400 *livres* for two months; what happened to the balance of 100 *livres*? Louis XI was never overly generous, but in 1470–71 Margaret was his guest, and her status as queen of England, which Louis recognized, had to be maintained by setting a good table.[58]

Warwick met his obligation to declare war on Burgundy, but bad weather further delayed Margaret's departure until April, just after Edward IV returned

---

56 Stevenson, II, i, p. 15, n. 2; B. Guenée, *Between Church and State* (Chicago, IL, 1991), p. 350; Vaesen and Charavay, *Lettres*, pp. 244–5, n. 1.

57 Kekewich, 'Lancastrian Court in Exile', p. 99.

58 Calmette and Périnelle, *Louis XI*, p. 125, n. 4, for previous payments made to support Queen Margaret, the countess of Warwick and their children.

from Burgundy. Margaret and Prince Edward landed at Weymouth on the evening of 14 April; on the same day Edward IV defeated and killed Warwick at the battle of Barnet.

Margaret and her small party met the duke of Somerset and the earl of Devon at Cerne Abbey and received the devasting news of Wawick's defeat.[59] They decided to move west, hoping to link up with Jasper Tudor's forces in Wales. When they reached Gloucester, the town refused to open its gates. The Lancastrian army camped at Tewkesbury, still hoping to cross the River Severn, and Edward IV caught up with them there. On 4 May, Margaret's last battle was fought. The Lancastrian forces were decimated; Prince Edward of Lancaster was killed, and Margaret was captured immediately after the battle. The victorious Edward carried her back to London in triumph. On the night of her arrival, Henry VI died in the Tower of London.

Margaret remained Edward IV's prisoner until Louis XI 'ransomed' her in 1475. In 1476 she returned to France after renouncing all her claims in England. Louis insisted that she also renounce any claims she had to her father's patrimonies in France. She arrived in Rouen under English escort and was handed over to its captain and to Jean Raguier as receiver general of Normandy.[60] Margaret spent the last years of her life in obscurity at René's manor of Reculée until her death in 1482 at the age of fifty-two. Upon her father's death in 1480, she became King Louis's pensioner. Impoverished at the end, she petitioned him in her will to pay her debts for her soul's sake and his. At her own request Margaret was buried beside her parents in the cathedral of St Maurice in Angers, the home of her childhood.[61]

59   This Somerset was Edmund Beaufort, a younger brother of Henry, who was executed in 1464 after the battle of Hexham. Because of his brother's attainder, his title was not recognized by the Yorkists.
60   Lecoy, *Le roi René*, I, p. 415.
61   Ibid., II, pp. 395–7.

BIBLIOGRAPHY

Place of publication is London except as noted.

Unprinted Primary Sources

Cambridge
    Corpus Christi, Cambridge, MS 170
London
    British Library:
        Additional MSS 23,938; 46,846, 48031
        Cotton Vespasian F xiii (i)
        Egerton Roll 8365
    Corporation of London Record Office:
        Journals V, VI
    Inner Temple Library:
        Petyt MS 538.47
    Lincoln's Inn Library:
        Hale MS 12 Item 75
    The National Archives:
        Chancery (C):
            C 66/471 (patent rolls)
            C 81/1546 (warrants for the great seal)
        Exchequer (E):
            E 28/81 (treasury of receipt, council and privy seal)
            E 101/409, 410 (king's remembrancer, various)
        King's Bench (KB):
            KB 9/259, 260 (ancient indictments)
            KB 27/766 (plea solls)
        Special Collections (SC):
            SC 1/44 (ancient correspondence)

Oxford
  Jesus College MS 124
Paris
  Bibliothèque nationale de France:
  MSS Français 20378, 20488, 20855, 4054
  MS Latin 11892
San Marino, California
  The Huntington Library:
  Archives of Battle Abbey, 1077–1780, BA 937

Printed Primary Sources

Basin, T. *Histoire des règnes de Charles VII et de Louis XI*, IV, ed. J. Quicherat (Paris, 1859)

Bateson, M., ed. *George Ashby's Poems*, EETS, e.s. 76 (1899)

Blacman, J. *Henry the Sixth: A Reprint of John Blacman's Memoir*, ed. M.R. James (Cambridge, 1919)

Calendar of the Close Rolls

Calendar of Entries in the Papal Registers … Papal Letters, VIII, X–XII, ed. W.H. Bliss and J.A. Twemlow (1909–33)

Calendar of the Fine Rolls

Calendar of the Patent Rolls

Calendar of the Plea and Memoranda Rolls, V and VI, ed. P.E. Jones (Cambridge, 1954–61)

Calendar of State Papers … Milan, I, ed. A.B. Hinds (1912)

Calendar of State Papers … Venice, ed. R. Brown (1864)

Campbell, W., ed. *Materials for a History of the Reign of Henry VII*, 2 vols (1873–77)

Carew, R. *The Survey of Cornwall by Richard Carew*, ed. J. Chynoweth, N. Orme and A. Walsham, Devon and Cornwall Record Society, new ser. 47 (Exeter, 2004)

Chandler, J., ed. *John Leland's Itinerary: Travels in Tudor England* (Stroud, 1993)

Chastellain, G. *Oeuvres*, 8 vols, ed. Kervyn de Lettenhove (Brussels, 1863–66)

Christine de Pisan. *The Treasure of the City of Ladies*, tr. with intro. S. Lawson (New York, 1985)

Comines, P. de. *Mémoires de Philippe de Comines*, II, ed. M. l'Abbé Lenglet du Fresnoy (Paris, 1747)

Craigie, W.A., ed. *The Asloan Manuscript: A Miscellany in Prose and Verse*, I, Scottish Text Society 14 (Edinburgh, 1923)

Davis, N., ed. *Paston Letters and Papers of the Fifteenth Century*, 2 vols, EETS, s.s. 20, 21 (Oxford, 1971–76)

Edward, Second Duke of York. *The Master of Game* [1406–13], ed. W.A. and F. Baillie-Grohman (1909)

Ellis, H., ed. *Original Letters Illustrative of English History*, third ser. 1 (1824)

English Historical Documents, IV, *1327–1485*, ed. A.R. Myers (1969)

Escouchy, M. d'. *Chronique de Mathieu d'Escouchy*, 3 vols, ed. G. du Fresne de Beaucourt (Paris, 1863–64)

Fabyan, R. *The New Chronicles of England and France, in two parts*, ed. H. Ellis (1811)

Flenley, R., ed. *Six Town Chronicles of England* (Oxford, 1911)

Fortescue, Sir J. *De Laudibus Legum Angliae*, ed. S.B. Chrimes (Cambridge, 1949)

———— *The Works of Sir John Fortescue, Knight, Chief Justice of England and Lord Chancellor to King Henry the Sixth*, ed. T. (Fortescue), Lord Clermont (1869)

Gairdner, J., ed. *Historical Collections of a Citizen of London in the Fifteenth Century*, Camden Society, new ser. 17 (1876)

———— *The Paston Letters*, 6 vols (1904)

———— *Three Fifteenth-Century Chronicles*, Camden Society, new ser. 28 (1880)

Gascoigne, T. *Loci e Libro Veritatum*, ed. J.E.T. Rogers (Oxford, 1881)

Gibbons, A. *Early Lincoln Wills* (Lincoln, 1888)

Green, M.A.E. (Wood), ed. *Letters of Royal and Illustrious Ladies of Great Britain*, I (1846)

Hands, R., ed. *English Hawking and Hunting in the Boke of St. Albans* (1975)

Hanserecesse, Abth. 2 (1431–1476), Bd. 6, ed. G. von der Ropp (Leipzig, 1890)

Harris, M.D., ed. *The Coventry Leet Book*, EETS, o.s. 134, 135, 138, 146 in one vol. (1907–13)

Harriss, G.L. and M.A., eds. 'John Benet's Chronicle for the Years 1400 to 1462', *Camden Miscellany* 24 (1972), pp. 151–233

Historical Manuscripts Commission: *Eighth Report*, Appendix (1881)

Kekewich, M.L., *et al.*, eds. *The Politics of Fifteenth-Century England: John Vale's Book* (Stroud, 1995)

Kendall, P.M., and V. Ilardi, eds. *Dispatches with Related Documents of Milanese Ambassadors in France and Burgundy, 1450–1483*, 3 vols (Athens, OH, 1970–71)

Kingsford, C.L., ed. *Chronicles of London* (Oxford, 1905)

Marx, W., ed. *An English Chronicle 1377–1461* (Woodbridge, 2003)

Maxwell-Lyte, H.C., and M.C.B. Dawes, eds. *The Register of Thomas Bekynton, Bishop of Bath and Wells, 1443–1465*, 2 vols, Somerset Record Society 49 and 50 (1934–35)

Monro, C., ed. *Letters of Queen Margaret of Anjou and Bishop Bekington and Others*, Camden Society, old ser. 86 (1863)

Myers, A.R., ed. 'The Household of Queen Elizabeth Woodville', in idem, *Crown,*

Household and Parliament in Fifteenth Century England, ed. C.H. Clough (1985), pp. 251–318

——— 'The Household of Queen Margaret of Anjou, 1452–3', in *Crown, Household and Parliament*, pp. 135–209

——— 'The Jewels of Queen Margaret of Anjou', in *Crown, Household and Parliament*, pp. 211–29

Nichols, J., ed. *A Collection of all the Wills ... of the Kings and Queens of England* (1780, repr. Union, NJ, 1999)

Nichols, J.G., ed. *Chronicle of the Grey Friars of London*, Camden Society, old ser. 53 (1852)

Nicolas, N.H., ed. *Proceedings and Ordinances of the Privy Council of England*, VI, *22 Henry VI 1443 to 39 Henry VI 1461* (1837)

——— *Testamenta Vetusta*, 2 vols (1826)

The Parliament Rolls of Medieval England, 1275–1504, ed. C. Given-Wilson, *et al.* (Leicester, 2005)

Reilhac, A.A.M.J. *Jean de Reilhac, secrétaire ... des rois Charles VII, Louis XI et Charles VIII* (Paris, 1886)

Riley, H.T., ed. *Registrum Abbatiae Johannis Whethamstede*, 2 vols, Rolls Series (1872–73)

Rotuli Parliamentorum, V, *1439–1468* (1832)

Rymer, T., ed. *Fœdera, conventiones, literæ, et ... acta publica, inter reges Angliæ ...*, X–XII (1704–35)

Searle, W.G., ed. *The Chronicle of John Stone, Monk of Christ Church, 1415–1471*, Cambridge Antiquarian Society 34 (1902)

Sharpe, R.R., ed. *Calendar of Letter-Books ... of the City of London: Letter-Book G* (1905), *Letter-Book K* (1911)

Stevenson, J., ed. *Letters and Papers Illustrative of the Wars of the English in France during the Reign of Henry VI*, 2 vols in 3, Rolls Series (1861–64)

Thomas, A.H., and I.D. Thornley, eds. *The Great Chronicle of London* (1938)

Ullman, W., ed. *Liber Regie Capelle*, Henry Bradshaw Society 92 (1961)

Vaesen, J., and E. Charavay, eds. *Lettres de Louis XI, roi de France*, IV (Paris, 1890)

Virgoe, R. 'Some Ancient Indictments in the King's Bench referring to Kent, 1450–1452', in *Documents Illustrative of Medieval Kentish Society*, ed. F.R.H. Du Boulay, Kent Archaeological Society Monograph Series 17 (Ashford, 1964)

Warkworth, J. *A Chronicle of the First Thirteen Years of the Reign of King Edward IV*, ed. J.O. Halliwell, Camden Society, old ser. 10 (1839)

Wavrin, J. de. *Anchiennes Croniques d'Engleterre*, 3 vols, ed. L.M.E. Dupont (Paris, 1858–63)

Worcestre, W. *Itineraries of William Worcestre*, ed. J.H. Harvey (Oxford, 1969)

Secondary Sources

Acheson, E. *A Gentry Community: Leicestershire in the Fifteenth Century, c. 1422–c. 1485* (Cambridge, 1992)

The Anglo-Norman Dictionary, AND² Online edition, http://www.anglo-norman.net

Armstrong, C.A.J. 'Politics and the Battle of St Albans, 1455', *Bulletin of the Institute of Historical Research* 33 (1960), pp. 1–72

Ayton, A. *Knights and Warhorses: Military Service and the English Aristocracy under Edward III* (2nd edn, Woodbridge, 1999)

Bagley, J.J. *Margaret of Anjou, Queen of England* (1948)

Barnfield, M., and A. Carson. 'The Marriage of the Lancastrian Prince of Wales and Lady Anne Neville', *The Ricardian Bulletin* (December 2017), pp. 53–8

Barron, C. *London in the Later Middle Ages: Government and People 1200–1500* (Oxford, 2004)

Bassett, M. 'Newgate Prison in the Middle Ages', *Speculum* 18 (1943), pp. 233–46

Beaucourt, G. du Fresne de. *Histoire de Charles VII*, 6 vols (Paris, 1881–91)

Bernus, P. 'Louis XI et Pierre de Brezé, 1440–1465', *Revue de l'Anjou*, n.s., vols 62–3 (1911), pp. 241–89, 355–71

——— 'Le Rôle politique de Pierre de Brezé au cours des dix dernières années du règne de Charles VII, 1451–1461', *Bibliothèque de l'École de Chartes* 69 (1908), pp. 303–47

Calmette, J., and G. Périnelle. *Louis XI et l'Angleterre, 1461–1483* (Paris, 1930)

Carpenter, C. *Locality and Polity: A Study of Warwickshire Landed Society, 1401–1499* (Cambridge, 1992)

Castor, H. *The King, the Crown, and the Duchy of Lancaster: Public Authority and Private Power, 1399–1461* (Oxford, 2000)

Catto, J. 'Masters, Patrons and the Careers of Graduates in Fifteenth-Century England', in *Concepts and Patterns of Service in the Later Middle Ages*, ed. A. Curry and E. Matthew (Woodbridge, 2000), pp. 52–63

Cherry, M. 'The Struggle for Power in Mid-Fifteenth-Century Devonshire', in *Patronage, the Crown and the Provinces in Later Medieval England*, ed. R.A. Griffiths (Gloucester, 1981), pp. 123–44

Cokayne, G.E. *The Complete Peerage of England, Scotland, Ireland, Great Britain and the United Kingdom …*, 12 vols in 13, ed. V. Gibbs, *et al.* (1910–59)

Cron, B.M. 'Margaret of Anjou and the Lancastrian March on London, 1461', *The Ricardian*, XI:147 (December 1999), pp. 590–615

Dictionnaire de biographie française (Paris, 1933)

Doyle, A. 'English Books In and Out of Court from Edward III to Henry VII', in *English Court Culture in the Later Middle Ages*, ed. V.J. Scattergood and J.W. Sherborne (1983), pp. 163–81

Drake, F. *Eboracum, or the History and Antiquities of the City of York* (1736)

Dronzek, A. 'Gender Roles and the Marriage Market in Fifteenth-Century England: Ideals and Practices', in *Love, Marriage, and Family Ties in the Later Middle Ages*, ed. I. Davis, M. Müller and S.R. Jones (Turnhout, 2003)

Dunn, D. 'Margaret of Anjou, Queen Consort of Henry VI: A Reassessment of Her Role, 1445–53', in *Crown, Government and People in the Fifteenth Century*, ed. R.E. Archer (New York, 1995), pp. 107–43

Emden, A.B. *A Biographical Register of the University of Oxford to A.D. 1500*, 3 vols (Oxford, 1957–59)

Fenster, T., and D.L. Smail. *Fama: The Politics of Talk and Reputation in Medieval Europe* (2003)

Ferguson, J. *English Diplomacy, 1422–1461* (Oxford, 1972)

Finucane, R.C. *Miracles and Pilgrims: Popular Beliefs in Medieval England* (New York, 1995)

Given-Wilson, C. *The Royal Household and the King's Affinity: Service, Politics and Finance in England 1360–1413* (1986)

Goodman, A. *The Wars of the Roses: Military Activity and English Society 1452–97* (1981)

Green, R.F. *Poets and Princepleasers: Literature and the English Court in the Late Middle Ages* (Toronto, 1980)

Griffiths, R.A. 'The King's Council and the First Protectorate of the Duke of York, 1453–54', in idem, *King and Country: England and Wales in the Fifteenth Century* (1991), pp. 305–20

——— *The Reign of King Henry VI: The Exercise of Royal Authority, 1422–1461* (1981)

Guenée, B. *Between Church and State: The Lives of Four French Prelates in the Late Middle Ages* (Chicago, IL, 1991)

Hammond, P.W. *Food and Feast in Medieval England* (Stroud, 1993)

Harriss, G.L. *Cardinal Beaufort: A Study of the Lancastrian Ascendancy and Decline* (Oxford, 1988)

——— 'Marmaduke Lumley and the Exchequer Crisis of 1446–9', in *Aspects of Late Medieval Government and Society: Essays Presented to J.R. Lander*, ed. J.G. Rowe (Toronto, 1986), pp. 143–78

Harvey, I.M.W. 'Poaching and Sedition in Fifteenth-Century England', in *Lordship and Learning: Studies in Memory of Trevor Aston*, ed. R. Evans (Woodbridge, 2004), pp. 169–82

Harvey, M.M. *England, Rome and the Papacy, 1417–1464: The Study of a Relationship* (Manchester, 1993)

Head, C. 'Pope Pius II and the Wars of the Roses', *Archivium Historiae Pontificiae* 8 (1970), pp. 139–78

Hicks, M. *Bastard Feudalism* (1995)

——— 'A Minute of the Lancastrian Council at York, 20 January 1461', *Northern History* 35 (1999), pp. 214–21

——— *Warwick the Kingmaker* (Oxford, 1998)

Hookham, M.A. *The Life and Times of Margaret of Anjou, Queen of England and France*, 2 vols (1872)

Horrox, R. *Fifteenth-Century Attitudes: Perceptions of Society in Late Medieval England* (Cambridge, 1994)

——— 'Personalities and Politics', in *The Wars of the Roses*, ed. A.J. Pollard (New York, 1995), pp. 89–109

Huneycutt, L.L. 'Intercession and the High Medieval Queen: The Esther Topos', in *Power of the Weak*, ed. J. Carpenter and S.-B. MacLean (Chicago, IL, 1995), pp. 126–46

Hyland, A. *The Horse in the Middle Ages* (Stroud, 1999)

James, M.K. *Studies in the Medieval Wine Trade*, ed. E.M. Veale, intro. by E.M. Carus-Wilson (Oxford, 1971)

Johnson, P.A. *Duke Richard of York 1411–1460* (Oxford, 1988)

Jones, M.K. 'John Beaufort, Duke of Somerset and the French Expedition of 1443', in *Patronage, the Crown and the Provinces in Late Medieval England*, ed. R.A. Griffiths (Gloucester, 1981), pp. 79–102

——— 'Somerset, York and the Wars of the Roses', *EHR* 104 (1989), pp. 285–307

Keen, M. *Chivalry* (1984)

———, and M.J. Daniel. 'English Diplomacy and the Sack of Fourgères in 1449', *History* 59, no. 197 (October 1974), pp. 375–91

Kekewich, M.L. 'The Lancastrian Court in Exile', in *The Lancastrian Court*, ed. J. Stratford, Harlaxton Medieval Studies, new ser. 13 (Donington, 2003), pp. 95–110

Kendall, P.M. *Louis XI, the Universal Spider* (New York, 1970)

Kingsford, C.L. *English Historical Literature in the Fifteenth Century* (Oxford, 1913)

Knowles, D., and R.N. Hadcock. *Medieval Religious Houses, England and Wales* (1971)

Lander, J.R. 'Henry VI and the Duke of York's Second Protectorate', in idem, *Crown and Nobility 1450–1509* (1976), pp. 74–93

Lasdun, S. *The English Park: Royal, Private and Public* (1991)

Laynesmith, J. *The Last Medieval Queens: English Queenship 1445–1503* (Oxford, 2004)

Lecoy de la Marche, A. *Le roi René: sa vie, son administration ...*, 2 vols (Paris, 1875)

Le Neve, J. *Fasti Ecclesiae Anglicanae, 1300–1541*, 12 vols, ed. J.M. Horn, *et al.* (1962–67)

Lewis, P.S. *Later Medieval France* (1968)

—————— 'Sir John Fastolf's Lawsuit over Titchwell', *Historical Journal* 1 (1958), pp. 1–20

Livermore, H.V. *A New History of Portugal*, 2nd edn (Cambridge, 1976)

Lloyd, T.R. 'A Reconsideration of Two Anglo-Hanseatic Treaties of the Fifteenth Century', *EHR* 102 (1987), pp. 916–33

Lovatt, R. 'A Collector of Apocryphal Anecdotes: John Blacman Revisited', in *Property and Politics: Essays in Later Medieval English History*, ed. A.J. Pollard (New York, 1984), pp. 172–97

Maddicott, J.R. 'The English Peasantry and the Demands of the Crown 1294–1341', *Past and Present*, Supplement I (1975)

Mander, C.H.W. *A Descriptive and Historical Account of the Guild of Cordwainers of the City of London* (1931)

Martin, C.T. *The Record Interpreter*, 2nd edn (1910)

Maurer, H.E. *Margaret of Anjou: Queenship and Power in Late Medieval England* (Woodbridge, 2003)

Mérindol, C. de. *Le roi René et la seconde maison d'Anjou* (Paris, 1987)

Meyer-Lee, R.J. 'Laureates and Beggars in Fifteenth-Century English Poetry: The Case of George Ashby', *Speculum* 79 (2004), pp. 688–726

Mileson, S.A. 'The Importance of Parks in Fifteenth-Century Society', in *The Fifteenth Century V: Of Mice and Men: Image, Belief and Regulation in Late Medieval England*, ed. L. Clark (Woodbridge, 2005), pp. 19–37

Morgan, D.A.L. 'The King's Affinity in the Polity of Yorkist England', *Transactions of the Royal Historical Society* 23 (1973), pp. 1–25

Otway-Ruthven, A.J. *A History of Medieval Ireland* (1968)

—————— *The King's Secretary and the Signet Office in the XV Century* (Cambridge, 1939)

Oxford Dictionary of National Biography (2001–04)

Parsons, J.C. 'Queen's Intercession in Thirteenth-Century England', in *Power of the Weak*, ed. J. Carpenter and S.-B. MacLean (Chicago, IL, 1995), pp. 147–77

Payling, S. 'Identifiable Motives for Election to Parliament in the Reign of Henry VI: The Operation of Public and Private Factors', in *The Fifteenth Century VI: Identity and Insurgency in the Late Middle Ages*, ed. L. Clark (Woodbridge, 2006), pp. 89–105

Piponnier, F. *Costume et vie sociale; la cour d'Anjou XIVe–XVe siècle* (Paris, 1970)

Pollard, A.J. *John Talbot and the War in France 1427–1453* (1983)

―――― *Warwick the Kingmaker* (2007)

Ramsay, J.H. *Lancaster and York*, 2 vols (Oxford, 1892)

Rawcliffe, C. *Leprosy in Medieval England* (Woodbridge, 2006)

―――― 'Richard Duke of York, the King's "obeisant liegeman": A New Source for the Protectorates of 1454 and 1455', *Historical Research* 60 (1987), pp. 232–9

―――― 'Women, Childbirth and Religion', in *Women and Religion in Medieval England*, ed. D. Wood (Oxford, 2003), pp. 91–117

Reddaway, T.F. *The Early History of the Goldsmiths' Company, 1327–1509* (1975)

Richmond, C. 'Elizabeth Clere: Friend of the Pastons', in *Medieval Women: Texts and Contexts in Late Medieval Britain*, ed. J. Wogan-Browne, *et al.* (Turnhout, 2000), pp. 251–73

―――― *The Paston Family in the Fifteenth Century: Endings* (Manchester and New York, 2000)

―――― *The Paston Family in the Fifteenth Century: The First Phase* (Cambridge, 2002)

Robson, M. *The Franciscans in the Middle Ages* (Woodbridge, 2006)

Roskell, J.S. *Parliament and Politics in Late Medieval England*, 3 vols (1981)

―――― , L. Clark and C. Rawcliffe, *The House of Commons 1386–1421*, 4 vols (Stroud, 1993)

Ross, C. *Edward IV* (1974)

Rowney, I. 'Government and Patronage in the Fifteenth Century: Staffordshire, 1439–59', *Midland History* 8 (1983), pp. 49–69

Scofield, C.L. *The Life and Reign of Edward IV*, 2 vols (1923)

Smith, D.M., ed. *The Heads of Religious Houses: England and Wales*, III, *1377–1540* (Cambridge, 2008)

'The Soldier in Later Medieval England Online Database', http://dev.www.medievalsoldier.org

Somerville, R. *History of the Duchy of Lancaster* (1953)

Spencer, M. *Thomas Basin (1412–1490): The History of Charles VII and Louis XI* (Nieuwkoop, 1997)

Storey, R.L. *The End of the House of Lancaster* (New York, 1967)

Strickland, A. *Lives of the Queens of England*, II (1885)

Strohm, P. *Hochon's Arrow: The Social Imagination of Fourteenth-Century Texts* (Princeton, NJ, 1992)

Talbot, C.H., and E.A. Hammond. *The Medical Practitioners in Medieval England: A Biographical Register* (1965)

Touchard, H. *Le commerce maritime Breton a la fin du moyen age* (Paris, 1967)

Tout, T.F. *Chapters in the Administrative History of Mediaeval England*, V (Manchester, 1930)

Vale, M.G.A. *Charles VII* (Berkeley, CA, 1974)
———— *English Gascony, 1399–1453* (1970)
Victoria History of the Counties of England
Virgoe, R. 'The Death of William de la Pole, Duke of Suffolk', in *East Anglian Society and the Political Community of Late Medieval England: Selected Papers of Roger Virgoe*, ed. C. Barron, C. Rawcliffe and J.T. Rosenthal (Norwich, 1997), pp. 247–57
———— 'A Norfolk Taxation List of 1451', in *East Anglian Society*, pp. 65–77
———— 'Three Suffolk Parliamentary Elections', in *East Anglian Society*, pp. 53–64
Watts, J. *Henry VI and the Politics of Kingship* (Cambridge, 1996)
Wedgwood, J.C. *History of Parliament: Biographies of the Members of the Commons House, 1439–1509* (1936)
Wolffe, B.P. *Henry VI* (1981)

Unpublished Theses

James, L.E. 'The Career and Political Influence of William de la Pole, First Duke of Suffolk, 1437–50', B.Litt. thesis (Oxford, 1979)
Marshall, A.E. 'The Role of English War Captains in England and Normandy, 1436–61', MA thesis (University of Wales, 1974)

INDEX

efforts to rescue 224–6, 227–9, 241
follows up actions by 13, 14, 24, 36–7,
 39 and n.93, 53, 55, 57, 69, 70,
 90–1, 119, 125, 126, 129–30, 132,
 149, 209–10
Koeur, court at 142, 156, 246, 259, 263,
 279
letters, assessments of 2–3
and London 47, 75, 91, 173, 203, 226, 241
 letters to 48, 74, 90, 225, 226
and Louis XI 164, 194 n.2, 243, 248, 258,
 261, 274, 275, 276–8, 279, 280
 and Calais 241, 253, 254–6, 257
 treaty of Tours 256
and loveday 218
marriage of 61, 115–16, 173, 191, 237
as mediator/intercessor 33, 131, 133, 176,
 177, 178, 187, 193, 195, 196, 197–8, 209
and papacy 33, 38–9, 153–7, 203, 240 n.61
and parents 68, 117–18, 156, 263, 280
and peace negotiations 173, 175, 179–81
 and n.20, 182, 183, 185, 191
 cession of Maine 174, 175, 176, 177,
 178, 187
and Portugal 267–9
and Prince Edward 152, 192, 203, 220–1,
 224, 241, 277, 278
and regency 199, 201–2, 214, 215, 219
and royal authority 201, 211, 220–1 and
 n.87, 221, 227, 268
 granted explicitly 244 n.71, 254–6,
 261–3
and Salisbury 165, 215
visits Walsingham 8–9, 145, 197
and Warwick 223, 236, 239, 241, 251, 271,
 272 n.43, 273–4
 reconciles with 271, 272 n.43, 275–8
and York 61, 104, 197, 198, 203, 207, 209,
 215
 end of second protectorate 207,
 208–9
 enmity towards 96, 192, 224, 225
 gifts to 134 nn.80 and 81, 197
 mediation sought by 192, 196, 197–8
Margaret of York 87, 277
Marie of Anjou, queen of Charles VII 256
Marshalsea court 91–2
Marshalsea prison 193
Marwarth, Alice 149

Mary of Guelders, queen of Scotland 40,
 202 n.31, 227, 244 n.70
Maulevrier, comte de 255, 256
Medowe, William 200
Merston, John 62–3
 brother of, Richard 63 n.25
 wife of, Rose 63
Middlesex 46, 90, 100–1
Middleton, John 50
Molaner, Antony 71, 72, 73–4
Moleyns, Adam, bishop of Chichester
 (d. 1450) 54, 184, 185–6, 250
Moleyns, Robert Hungerford, Lord. *See*
 Hungerford
Montgomery, Sir John 63–4, 163, 165, 189
 son of, John 163–4
 son of, Sir Thomas 163, 164
 wife of. *See* Boteler, Elizabeth
Morton, John, bishop of St David's 40, 256
Mountfort, Sir Edmund 27, 256
Mowbray, John, duke of Norfolk (d. 1432)
 108
Mowbray, John, duke of Norfolk (d. 1461)
 166 n.38, 200, 210–11, 216 n.76
 association with York 66, 67, 210
 feud with Sharnborne 66–7
 feud with the Wingfields 108–10
 rivalry with Suffolk 66, 108–9, 211
 wife of, Eleanor Bourgchier 210, 211
Mowsherst, Thomas 147–8
Mundford, Osbert 136

Nanseglos, William 85, 95
networking 15, 41, 45, 116, 132, 140
Neville, Cecily, duchess of York 192, 197–8,
 199 n.17
 letter from 195–7
Neville, George, bishop of Exeter,
 archbishop of York, chancellor
 (d. 1476) 31 and n.63, 38–9, 250–1
Neville, John Lord (d. 1461) 224
Neville, Sir John, Lord Montagu (d. 1471)
 96, 114
Neville, Richard, earl of Salisbury,
 chancellor (d. 1460) 26, 31 n.61, 113,
 129, 218, 227, 245. *See also* Yorkists
 allies with York 38, 164, 206, 215
 as chancellor 23 n.24, 38, 56, 203, 215
 letter from 212